DANCE IN ITS TIME

WALTER SORELL, professor emeritus at Columbia University and Barnard College, has also taught at Hunter College and the New School for Social Research. He has reviewed dance and theater for many magazines and newspapers and has seven book translations to his credit, among them Mary Wigman's *The Language of the Dance*. Four of his plays have been produced. *Dance in Its Time* is his fourteenth book. In the past decade, Walter Sorell has also exhibited his paintings in this country and in Europe.

Endpapers: Alvin Ailey's REVELATIONS
(Photo Costas. Courtesy the photographer)

DANCE IN ITS TIME

WALTER SORELL

ANCHOR PRESS/DOUBLEDAY
GARDEN CITY, NEW YORK
1981

Other Books by Walter Sorell

The Dance Through the Ages
The Story of the Human Hand
The Dance Has Many Faces (editor-author)
Hanya Holm: The Biography of an Artist
The Duality of Vision
The Dancer's Image: Points and Counterpoints
Facets of Comedy
The Swiss: A Cultural Panorama of Switzerland
Hermann Hesse: The Man Who Sought and Found Himself
The Mary Wigman Book
Three Women
The Other Face: The Mask in the Arts
Everyman Today: A Modern Morality Play

TRANSLATIONS:

Arch of Triumph by Erich Maria Remarque
Goethe's World, A New Direction Anthology
The Steppenwolf by Hermann Hesse
The Language of Dance by Mary Wigman
Prague by Johannes Urzidil
Woyzeck by Georg Büchner

This is the first publication of *Dance in Its Time.*
Anchor Press Edition: 1981

Quotation from "Byzantium" from Collected Poems *of William Butler Yeats. Copyright 1933 by Macmillan Publishing Co., Inc., renewed 1961 by Bertha Georgie Yeats.*

Library of Congress Cataloging in Publication Data Sorell, Walter, 1905– Dance in its time. Includes index. 1. Dancing—History. 2. Dancing—Social aspects. I. Title. GV1617.S67 793.3 ISBN: 0-385-13418-5. Library of Congress Catalog Card Number 80–913 Copyright © 1981 by Walter Sorell All Rights Reserved Printed in the United States of America First Edition

DESIGNED BY BEVERLEY VAWTER GALLEGOS

*For
Gertrude Maria,
friend and wife*

ACKNOWLEDGMENTS

This book could not have been written had I not seen, loved, and reviewed presentations of ballets and modern dance works in this country and in Europe for a lifetime, or had I not had the opportunity of teaching dance and theater history as well as dance criticism and appreciation at Columbia University and Barnard College for a few decades. I am grateful to my many students who have willingly or reluctantly submitted to the amount of cross-references with which I overwhelmed them week after week, and who followed me on unceasing journeys through the centuries. If they have not learned from our many detours into all fields of human creativity, I have—and my notes over the years have helped me in writing this book. My thanks must also go to my colleagues and co-workers, in particular to Jeanette Roosevelt at Barnard College; and to the many dancers and choreographers who, with their lovable idiosyncrasies, have enriched my life.

Also, this book would not have been written had not my editor, Angela Cox, prodded me into writing it and found words of encouragement and judicious counsel when the material threatened to run away with me. Furthermore, I feel greatly obliged to Elizabeth Frost Knappman, Senior Editor at Doubleday, for her invaluable help in giving this book its final shape. Also, I wish to thank Elaine Chubb for her advice and painstaking perusal of the manuscript. Over the years I have received much appreciated help from the curator of the New York Public Library Dance Collection, Performing Arts Research Center at Lincoln Center, Genevieve Oswald, and her staff. I am indebted to some of my closest friends who, through all these years, remained convinced that this book should be written and to those who were helpful in collecting the pictorial material; the Austrian, German, Italian, and Swedish services of the respective cultural institutes; but above all to Jacqueline Schuller and Elda Aasen of the French cultural services as well as to Dr. Ludwig Kohler of the Zürcher Zentralbibliothek, Zürich, and Alain Bernard, Bern.

Last but certainly not least, I have to thank my wife, who, with apprehensive patience, watched over me from the book's initial conception to the last word in its final chapter.

CONTENTS

ON THE POINT OF DEPARTURE

Dance in Its Time is the story of the dance in the context of its environment. Books have been written on the history of the dance, chronologically telling the story of its development, enumerating and evaluating dancers and choreographers whose contributions were of significance for their own era and all time. Books have dealt with certain dance forms or focused on the life of a single personality; they have revealed highlights of a nation's or a dance company's accomplishments; they have elucidated technical issues. They have all enlarged our knowledge, and we have to be grateful for it.

But, to understand the essence of the dance, we ought to know both the simultaneous creations in other fields of artistic activity and the totality of human experience of the era. "The ideal history of art should embrace all arts," Curt Sachs said in *The Commonwealth of Art*. I desire to re-create the sociocultural image of progressing time with which mankind's ingenuity and creative spirit must unfold. In this play of historic and human forces I wish to cast the dance as the leading character.

It has always puzzled me that none of the serious cultural histories mention the dance as an art form, let alone discuss it. Yet can one really devote many pages to Louis XIV and his era without acknowledging the ballet? After all, Louis took his epithet of "Sun King" from the *Ballet de la Nuit*, in which he appeared in the role of the Sun. Or can we examine the literary activities of the French writer Théophile Gautier without including his ballet criticism and creative participation in the shaping of the Romantic ballet? And was it not Diaghilev and his Ballets Russes that gave a stagnant artistic scene in Paris new impulses, with far-reaching repercussions everywhere?

In writing, one's personal backward vision is as important as the understanding of one's own time. In the 1760s the archaeologist Johann Joachim Winckelmann renewed interest in antiquity. Yet it was a Baroque viewpoint, with which we had to live for a long time. Today's scholars have demonstrated that while Swiss historian Jacob Burckhardt's viewpoint of the Renaissance, which he put forward in 1860, was of a unique and self-generating era, the Renaissance in fact had its roots and beginnings in the Middle Ages. Historians are the products of their own society and view the artistic and cultural achievements of the past under the influence of their own sociocultural and aesthetic currents, even if they advance new ideas. If it is true that a critique often says more about the critic than the work that is criticized, it is also true that any historical account reveals more about the historian and his or her time than the historical period described. Not all of us experience the same reality in the very same way. All the more, therefore, should we admit that the past reconstructed is a very personal account for which we must take full responsibility.

I can see the history of the arts only as a reality evoked and held together by the many dreams of the creative will of human beings. In reliving the past in the present, the role in which the teller of the tale intends to cast himself will be decisive. Does he see himself sitting in libraries perusing innumerable pages of dusty folios? Or does he visualize himself as a strange wanderer through strange lands playing guide to his many selves while discovering the wonders of a distant world coming alive? I prefer to see myself as that wanderer searching to find and to point to a life that once was and to the ways in which it expressed itself: a life which, in the constancy of its many metamorphoses, has given way to ever new manifestations of the glory that is humankind.

THE LONG AWAKENING

A rare fresco from the days of Minnesinger Neidhart, found in the Zürich house "Zum Loch," is an early pictorialization of the "Reigen." (After the original in the Landesmuseum in Zürich. Courtesy Landesmuseum Zürich)

A DECISIVE CHANGE TOOK PLACE IN EUROPE IN THE TWELFTH CENTURY. IT was as if an austere world, limited in its outlook, suddenly enlarged its windows, permitting a view into a landscape of new dimensions. The Romanesque architecture of the eleventh century, with its thick walls and small windows between massive pillars and rounded arches, gave way to the early Gothic style, with its more delicately curved arches turning heavenward and its large window spaces glowing with biblical stories in colors of stained glass.

This change was far more momentous than any date we may decide on as the end of the medieval era and the beginning of the Renaissance—such as 1445, when printing from movable type was begun in the West; or the year 1453, when the Turks conquered Constantinople; or the time about 1440 when the dancing master Guglielmo Ebreo circulated his manual on the basic rules of the dance. However confused and confusing the Gothic centuries were, they witnessed the birth of the modern world.

Although there was never total darkness in those centuries we call the Dark Ages, the people—with the exception of a few learned men and women—were living in a state of abysmal ignorance, with fears that multiplied the dangers threatening them physically and spiritually. They were a fertile ground for the most elaborate and most vicious superstitions. And yet it was an age of faith in which fanatic believers tried to Christianize those people whom they called pagans because their minds were still under the spell of the elemental spirits of nature.

An era dominated by the ravages of violence followed the decay of the Roman Empire. It is a miracle that much of Europe survived the pressures from north, east, and south: from lands that Roman civilization had not yet reached or from where—due to its fatal policy of overextension—it had to withdraw, as well as from the militant power of the Moslem world moving along North Africa into Spain. But in spite of the far-reaching changes then taking place in all parts of Europe, the structure of society was nowhere totally destroyed. It found new forms in accordance with the peoples' historical past.

In the early centuries of the medieval era two different worlds faced each other. The Germanic and Frankish kingdoms were then struggling for the bare necessities of existence. Culture in these lands was on a lower level and as different as their local customs and traditional beliefs. In contrast to these northern regions, Byzantium flourished in the East, the medieval counterpart of the Roman Empire. The mingling of Hellenism and Orientalism enabled Byzantium to unfold a rare spiritual splendor and visual marvels. It is difficult to say when Byzantine art came into being, since in its incipient stages it can only be seen as *early Christian*. Dance was a part of it, and dancing often accompanied services in the Eastern churches, continuing an early Christian tradition. But even though the contrast between North and East was extensive, there were no barriers between these two worlds, and trade remained the most obvious link between them and one from which both profited in their own ways.

What we are saying here about medieval Europe does not altogether apply to Italy and France. Roman civilization was so thoroughly grounded in Italy that it withstood all onslaughts of barbarism as well as all attempts to be incorporated in the Eastern Empire. From time to time the urban life of Italy was weakened, its institutions shaken, save the Church of Rome, which, despite schism and corruption, remained a spiritual stronghold. Italy had often been a coveted prey of the warring nature of the times, but feudalism, though planted in Italy too, never took deep roots there. The country profited spiritually from its Roman heritage and economically from its geographical position as the necessary link between primitive North and sophisticated East. Despite recurring turbulence, most of the cities flourished and were laying the foundation of their future importance.

The Venetians were particularly shrewd and merciless traders, but Florence, Siena, Milan, Pisa, and Genoa were also vital centers of commerce. When the warlords all over Europe grew in power, knighthood became ever more complex and, along with the wars, more costly. Larger funds were needed. Very soon the Italian merchants turned into financiers, and again Italy was the treasure-house for the world. The Italian moneylenders became legendary, and the roots of capitalism can be found then and there. Its concomitants, luxury and leisure, were advantageous for the arts; and, with the cultural assets present in Italy, this region was destined to become the place of human rebirth.

The Italians showed scarcely any inclination toward the Gothic vision. They were far more oriented toward the East: Byzantine influence occurred everywhere, but particularly in Siena, until the twelfth and thirteenth centuries. Moreover, the Italians felt on safe ground absorbing and continuing Roman architecture and their Roman past. Plautus, Terence, Lucian, Vergil, Seneca, the *Natural History* of the elder Pliny, or the *Letters* of the younger one were read not only in the monasteries but also in secular circles. When, on the threshold of the fourteenth century, a decisive breakthrough occurred in Italian painting with the astounding fresco work of Cimabue and Giotto, their early links were to painters who emerged from the Roman school of mosaicists.

Even mimes did not disappear with the Roman Empire. Yet the great art form that the dancing pantomimes had developed in Rome over the centuries, with all its subtlety in movement and expression, deteriorated into a skillful, mostly fun-provoking means of entertainment. Either as solo performers at fairs and village festivities, or as little bands, these mimes appeared in the Byzantine Empire, where shows in the Roman style survived for some time. The art of the mime had always been highly regarded and, on a loftier level, was used in Church spectacles and found its way into some interludes during banquets. Small wonder, then, that it should finally have been absorbed by the *commedia dell'arte* as one of its salient features.

Throughout the Middle Ages, the mimes kept alive a tradition of entertainment, although tailored to the taste of their audiences and their own skill. They also learned to juggle and to play an instrument, and soon the terms for these entertainers became as interchangeable as their way of entertaining. The mime could be a *joculator,* a lower type of entertainer, also known as *Spielmann* in Germany. Mimes were found in England, too, where they sang to instrumental music and were seen in acrobatic dances. In Provençal they were called *joglars* and turned up as important members of the train of the *troubadours,* those famed medieval entertainers who hailed from Provence. Like their German counterparts, the *minnesingers,* the troubadours were aristocrats who composed and traveled about, according to their means, in high or lesser style from castle to castle. These troubadours formed whole companies with *jongleurs* and minstrels, who were the instrumentalists. Some of the troubadours were in great demand, unable to accept all engagements. In some cases they would then delegate their minstrels and jugglers to perform their works. Considering the cost of the grand style and the dangers on the road, the expenses of keeping such a medieval touring company together were often so high that troubadours would find themselves stranded without means. To recoup their losses, they sometimes had to join the Crusaders.

These major and minor medieval entertainers could never have come into existence without the tradition of the joculators, behind whom we can discover the Roman mimes. The troubadours—there were more than four hundred in the twelfth and thirteenth centuries—were a vital force in the cultural life of the twelfth century, and we cannot gloss over the phenomenon of their existence. Their social influence was of unprecedented significance, going far beyond the power of any popular poets who simultaneously had to do justice to the role of entertainer.* We mostly associate their lyrical output with love songs, with which they doubtless set the scene for the age of

---

* Songs written by troubadours about eight hundred years ago are still sung by Catalan peasants today.

chivalry. But even the minnesingers, who took their names from the word *minne,* meaning "love," and who trailed the vogue of the troubadours by about a century, did not restrict their lyricism to romantic love. They also sang about war and many political issues of local interest. After a while they shifted their subject matter from the lady of the court to the wench of the village, and, in homage to the country idyll, many of their songs were written for dancing and in the spirit of the *pastourelle.*

What the minnesingers and troubadours had in common was their intent to define the social ideals of courtly love. The troubadours had an even stronger profile than their German counterparts as far as their freedom of speech and their outspoken liberal attitude were concerned. Most of the time they sided with the Albigensians—and the downfall of this heretical party was to doom their own destiny. Since the troubadours were well traveled, people trusted their judgment and taste. They became the masters of etiquette, thus preparing the setting for the *ballet de cour,* the court dance.

FRANCE was the home of the troubadours, and it was France in which feudalism was most deeply rooted. Here the strength and grandeur of the Gothic style flowered, at times flamboyantly, with the architectural elan of the column ribs rising from floor to vault. Its triumph of verticality became more decorative in England; its German equivalent had a polyphonic quality reminiscent of a Bach oratorio. Thus the Gothic strove not only toward realism but also toward the representation of a harmonious universe, the symmetry in all proportions that was finally perfected by Renaissance culture. If the Gothic aimed at such order, it was an order centered on God. The Renaissance sought another kind of order, one that centered on humanity. If nature was for the medieval mind the measure of all things, it was God's nature. The Renaissance mind, however, neither wished to depreciate the glory of God nor tried to belittle the stature of mankind.

Being duly impressed by the legendary greatness of Italy during the Renaissance, we may easily fail to give the importance of medieval France its due. Besides noting the impact the troubadours exerted on twelfth-century France, we must take notice of the tremendous progress that intellectual development and higher learning made in various cities, in Chartres and Poitiers, in the abbeys of Fleury-sur-Loire and Cluny, somewhat later in Montpellier, Toulouse, and Orléans. But particularly the school of Paris, which was granted privileges under the Capetian kings, developed one of the most important universities of the time. Peter Abelard taught there and was then followed by such men as Albertus Magnus, Bonaventura, and Thomas Aquinas, that great philosopher, who tried to reconcile Aristotle and Christianity, and the English philosopher Roger Bacon, who lectured on Platonism while being fascinated by astrology and alchemy (which was quite indicative of the age).

In trying to understand the many societal aspects that drastically changed in the twelfth century and gave the entire period a pre-Renaissance flavor, let us look at the manner in which people dressed. Clothing has always reflected the character of a period and mirrored the form and manner of dancing.

Until the twelfth century there was an almost ascetic uniformity; for men, the short-sleeved tunics of imperial Rome were predominant throughout. Sometimes two were worn at once, made of undyed woolen cloth. Loose or cross-gartered trousers and a wide cloak made up the outfit. Such simple clothes remained the costume of lower-class men for quite some time to come. Women covered themselves with a long and shapeless dress that fell loosely over an underbodice with tight-fitting sleeves.

It is the saddest praise we can extend to humankind that a great deal of its progress has always been made as a consequence of warfare. When the first Crusaders came back from the bloodiest battles fought in the name of the Prince of Peace they brought with them knowledge of another kind of life, a more meditative, sensuous, and luxurious one with a touch of poetry to it. Thus the feudal lords returning from the Orient introduced silk and damask, and with them new aesthetic notions. Close-fitting hose replaced the men's trousers, gowns became embroidered and bejeweled, decorated belts were worn, and from them hung a pouch, sword, and dagger. It was a new world, fur-trimmed and colorful; garments were now made to fit and reveal the contours of the body; the women's long gowns discovered the beauty of the décolletage; gloves, formerly a status symbol for kings and bishops, became universal among the rich. It was in Paris that the notion of fashion first began to be recognized; and ever since, Paris led the world in it.

If the drab, simple garments remained the dress of those who lived at the edge of existence and in total bondage to a few, their mental outlook also changed little over the centuries. The darkness in which their minds dwelt may gradually have become a shade less dark. They could not help seeing the light that was shining without including them. But this sensation stopped on the threshold of any deeper awareness. They accepted their lot as something God-given and administered by their lords and the clergy. They remained pawns in the political and social evolution of these centuries. Everything was thoroughly organized in the hierarchy of the medieval world. But whatever was, seemed to the people ordained by God. Each lord had vassals, and each vassal, in turn, was lord over other vassals.

Soon, however, certain classes began to crystallize: on the one hand, the peasants and a strong middle class with its active merchants and artisans in the cities; on the other, the various layers of the nobility. The Church stood above all of them as *the* extraterritorial and otherworldly power. The growing wealth of the commoners in the cities was as important to the feudal lords as to the Church. The extraordinary ways of that nascent world and its functioning were based on the notion that the structure of society demanded distinct orders or classes. The words *estate* and *order* were the pillars on which medieval society rested. There was a variety of monastic orders, as there was of orders of chivalry. All lived in their own world. The lower classes had their joys, games, and folk dances just as the upper classes enjoyed their tournaments, hunting parties, and social dances. Of course, this did not mean that class distinction was solidly demarcated, that a knight would not watch or participate in a Maypole dance or that members of the middle class and peasants could not—however separated from the lords—observe a tournament.

As late as in the fifteenth century of Renaissance highlights, few would have doubted the sacred character of this social division. We may trust the word of Georges Chastellain (1415?–75), the chronicler of the dukes of Burgundy and Burgundian court poet, who was also often used on secret and diplomatic missions. His poems are of minor consequence, but the five volumes of his chronicles depict the times and the way people then thought and acted. His position permitted him to criticize his aristocratic patrons, but he remained their panegyrist and neglected to notice the growing self-consciousness of the middle class out of whose midst the towering achievements of the Renaissance artists emerged.

In Chastellain's eyes, the world was well arranged the way it was. God created the peasants, he said, to till the ground, and the merchants to provide through trading the necessary commodities for life; the clergymen were created as intermediaries between God and the human soul; the nobles, to cultivate virtue and the beauties of life, to maintain justice and order and bring to the whole world a pattern of mankind's finest accomplishments; the nobility is charged with the highest tasks: above all, to defend the Church so that faith may be protected and grow. All the good qualities—veracity, courage, nobility—were the characteristics of the upper classes. However one-sided Chastellain's point of view may appear to us, it was the most self-evident thing in most people's minds.

This also explains why there never could be an exact line of demarcation between the Middle Ages and the Renaissance. Not only did the Gothic sense of splendor and its intellectual drive anticipate some of the things to come, but also the people in the fifteenth century were dominated and motivated by medieval thoughts and prejudices, by a wistful look backward. We only have to juxtapose a few examples in order to see how fluid the frontiers were between the Middle Ages and the Renaissance.

Already by the twelfth century scholasticism began to liberate itself from the tutelage of the Church, and an avid desire for learning brought about the establishment of universities. At that time, Bishop Honorius of Autun considered ignorance a greater enemy of man than the devil—truly a

Renaissance thought: "Man's exile is ignorance; his home is knowledge." Yet the greatest Renaissance surgeon, a man of science like Ambroise Paré (1510?–90), used to say when congratulated on having saved a man's life, "I treated him, God cured him!" The most signal characteristic of the Renaissance genius is the belief in the individual and his unlimited potential. One cannot imagine a stronger and more brilliant personality of the twelfth century than Peter Abelard (1079–1142), a man with a mighty mind, a Renaissance type of personality, whose contributions to philosophy, ethics, and logic were vital at the time; a man of daring who wedded passion to love. What a personality in an age whose spirit of collectivism was inclined to suppress personalities!

There are many examples showing the strong impact of medieval mentality with which some of the finest Renaissance artists still wrestled. These were struggles within the artist's psyche. In this context, the example of Fra Angelico adds a technical aspect to those inner conflicts. How this child of the cinquecento struggled between the new school of painting and the past! About 1440—the date with which we associate the first antecedents of the ballet de cour—Fra Angelico painted in his Florentine monastery of San Marco some of his most inspired works, sacred scenes in each monk's cell. Fra Angelico's dilemma was that he could not reconcile his faith and art (with which he expressed his faith) with the new style of perspective. Fra Angelico mistrusted the onset of humanism. He was under the spell of his teacher Giovanni Dominici, who in his writings and teachings defended the traditional spirituality against the new spirit. Fra Angelico believed in the past against the better knowledge of the painter in him. All he wanted was to paint the sacred story in its simplicity and beauty. He was a man of the Renaissance and yet, if we can trust Giorgio Vasari's report on him, he "never reworked any of his paintings . . . because he believed that this was the will of God. . . . He never took up his brush without first saying a prayer."

Fra Angelico was not alone in his dilemma. There were other great Renaissance artists who show the intensity with which medievalism had a hold on their minds. Albrecht Dürer (1471–1528) remained immersed in the medieval world, dreading doomsday with weird visions of the apocalyptic drama. Or let us recall that other northern giant, Matthias Grünewald, who created his works between 1500 and 1530 and whose "Isenheim Altarpiece," now in Colmar, belongs with the masterpieces of all time. There could have been no one more medieval than he. For him art was not a search for the laws of beauty and perfection—one of the decisive tenets of the Renaissance artist—but an expressive need to serve God and his community by painting a sermon in pictures, proclaiming the sacred truths as taught by Bible and Church.

Yet there are always people with an acute sense of the present and a heightened vision of the future. Filippo Brunelleschi (1377–1446) was the master designer who used classical architecture freely and created new modes of harmony and beauty. It was he who first recognized and revived Roman grandeur and gave the Renaissance its new image. While we also know Brunelleschi from several pageants he designed for Lorenzo de' Medici, the greatest achievement of this destroyer of the Gothic was his discovery of perspective. We may consider painting as a craftsman's trade until Brunelleschi based it on mathematical principles and raised it to the realm of the liberal arts. He taught those coming after him how to supplement linear perspective with colors and to focus the composition from several points of view in order to allow the observer to see the painting from whatever position is desired without losing the benefit of depth.

Choreography is deeply indebted to Brunelleschi's innovations. Without his introduction of geometric forms, of distance and depth, no balletic stage image could have taken shape. Yet not until almost two centuries later did the first choreographer, Balthasar de Beaujoyeulx, refer to a geometric pattern while trying to explain what he was doing. In fact, before this event in 1581 we do not encounter any dance presentation based on a choreographic concept and with overall dance patterns going beyond the accepted court dances and their variations. In this visual-minded era, dancing was considered only a part of banquets and court entertainments, or, at best, of social dialogues. Its potential for artistic expression was never contemplated. Similarly, the theater was frozen in poeticizing artificialities before, through several detours, it finally rose to undreamed-of heights in the late sixteenth century.

Beaujoyeulx profited from the experience of many generations. In his days the concept of perspective was an accepted fact and on everyone's mind. What the invention of perspective meant to painting, the application of geometry meant to the dance: the discovery of space and a new approach toward memorized steps based on rules.

A VERY strange breed developed in the Middle Ages. People learned to experience any event, big or small, with far greater intensity than ever before or afterward. They went through an agitated life with their emotions easily whipped up. Preachers would deliver sermons for many hours or days. Late in the fifteenth century, Savonarola's voice still condemned people's vanities. Funerals, solemn processions, or gay pageants called forth a hysteria of tears or hilarity. And with what cruel compassion could people feast on executions, the burning of witches, the tortures inflicted on criminals or on men condemned for treason! The extreme excitability of the medieval soul was carried into the Renaissance. We have Shakespearean proof of it in the cruel feuds between families, the warped notion of honor, and the spirit of revenge. It is the medieval excitability on all levels of life that explains the many outbreaks of danceomania which not only occurred during the years of the plague, but are recorded on many other occasions.

With fear as an overriding factor, society's attachment to a prince was emotionally conditioned and in most cases charged with a feeling of total fidelity. Class hatred did not exist; the first gentle traces of it can be found in the sixteenth century with the peasantry in revolt. Medieval men and women sunned themselves in the splendor and valor of nobility, dazzled and seduced by its gesture of grandeur. Their need to "belong" was both an expression of a mental vacuum and a question embracing the totality of their existence, in which the chronic insecurity of the time played a great part. It was the age of monasteries and fortresses. The castle was a center and stronghold, controlling the territory around it. The feeling of security derived from living in a castle became such a strong concept that Italian noblemen, who mostly were men of means, would build themselves towers in the city and castles outside. The halls of these towers and castles were the hub of everyday living and of events such as banquets and festivities, and these halls were the natural stages of the ballet de cour in the Renaissance. The continual danger made people build walls around their cities. Thus towns were a series of concentric rings, each marking a stage of growth. (Later, these walls were torn down and replaced by broad boulevards.)

The feeling of being pent up and encircled was one of the most characteristic manifestations of medieval days. Add to it the undercurrent of fear of hell and damnation, constantly nurtured by the clergy. There was the looming specter of the end of the world, or the vision of God's punishment through the Black Death. These sensations obviously created the need to break out of one's mental fortress—and this is precisely where dance played its role. The much maligned body liberated the psyche while moving and dancing. For example, St. Francis of Assisi appeared with his ragged brethren in front of Pope Innocent III to petition for the foundation of an order in 1209. When permission was granted, St. Francis and his eleven followers could not contain their joy and danced in front of His Holiness.

We do not know how or what they danced, since the three painters who enthusiastically recorded life and legend of St. Francis—the Florentines Cimabue and Giotto and the Sienese Sassetta—omitted this scene. Pope Innocent III, who had the reputation of a stern dogmatist scorning plays and dance, may have first frowned at such a physical manifestation of exuberance. But for all we know, this shrewd politician may have been disarmed by the innocent joy of these men who had renounced all earthly possessions. This scene is reminiscent of King David's rotary dance before the Lord, when his heart and feet leaped with joy. The future Franciscans may also have skipped or leaped, but more likely they may have fallen—quite unawares—into a choral dance, the *carole* or *Reigen,* that ring-shaped form of earlier times still very much in use during the Middle Ages.

Ambrogio Lorenzetti (1290?–?1348): one of the earliest pictures of the "Reigen" (ring dance), a detail from his wall fresco in the Palazzo Pubblico in Siena, known as "The Effects of Good Government." (Courtesy Alinari/Editorial Photocolor Archives)

Dance was so strongly associated with the carole at the time that any painter who wanted to depict dance did so in this form. Fra Angelico also envisioned dancing choruses in his "Last Judgment," showing a chorus of angels gliding along the spheres of the saints, and pairs of angels and blessed figures dancing through a flowery field upward to heaven. Fra Angelico believed in a Dantesque manner that dancing, in particular the carole, was the principal pastime in heaven, a *ballo dei angeli*. This was the notion the early Christians had of angels: singing and dancing while encircling the throne of God. But is not this image a deeply rooted human need? The Talmud describes dancing as the principal function of the angels; the Tibetan Buddhist iconography depicts the cosmic wheel of life. Is not the cosmic experience *the* eternal round of creating, preserving, and destroying, and does not rebirth follow birth, maturity, and death in this cosmic wheel of being? In such sacral dance lies hidden the revelation of the secret for mankind's being. Also, tao of heaven is symbolized dance for Confucius.

Even a century before Fra Angelico painted his "Last Judgment" we find a fresco, called "The Effects of Good Government," on a wall in the Palazzo Pubblico in Siena, a city that enjoyed great prosperity and security. About 1340 Ambrogio Lorenzetti recorded the active and happy life in Siena, with merchants busying themselves, men building a roof, a hunting party on its way out of the city, peasants tilling their fields. In the left-hand corner of the painting are nine aristocratic ladies dancing a carole and a tenth with a tambourine leading the singing.

This is one of the many proofs of how popular the dance must have been; it simply belonged to the good life of a well-governed community. But if we look for proof, the popularity of dancing can best be judged by the huge literature of its condemnation. Many preachers would claim that dancing resulted in "uncleane kyssinges, clippynges and other unhonest handelynges." And there was not one friar or itinerant preacher who would not have depicted dancers as being struck by lightning, consumed by heavenly fire, or cursed to dance until they fell dead.

Devil and Death, Fools and Flagellants

THE DEVIL HAS THE BEST LINES IN EVERY MORALITY PLAY, AND THE CLERGY could not help thinking that it was Satan who made the people fall back on their ritualistic dances, which, in the clergy's eyes, were pagan routines. Those mummeries with animal masks, those wild fertility dances time and again got hold of the people, who would then try to invade the churches and disturb the services. An uncouth, illiterate mob would cry out for uncontrolled dancing, for their crude and often cruel customs of former days, for superstitious rituals instead of kneeling in church and listening to words they could not understand. These happenings were the rule in the early centuries of Christianity, but they recurred even after the twelfth century. Chroniclers write of such an incident in Paris as late as 1445. On this level, too, it was a slow awakening, with the Christian way of life only gradually taking root. But even when the heathen qualities were lost, the people retained what they liked about the past. And how many things in which we still indulge today have their roots in pagan rituals, such as the June wedding, Halloween, or Yuletide? Or how many of us would think nowadays of the Maypole as a phallic symbol and of the dance around it as a fertility dance?

Whatever evil became manifest, it was the devil's doing. The people's imagination visualized the figure of the devil as the "wild man" who seemed to come straight from the fauns and satyrs of antiquity. They had seen images of devils in mystery plays and pageants. Preachers often described them as having heads of cats with a huge mouth, sharp teeth, and bloodshot eyes. Their hairy animals' bodies were hideous. And the devil masks that people wore looked most fearsome and repulsive. The devil was also pictured as hiding in a seal-like costume—a concept borrowed from antiquity—with a frightening horned mask, a gruesome-looking animal head, and a huge tongue covering his genitals. Most of these masks stress the ancient idea of the demonic power alive in masks. All this bares the warped fantasies with which medieval people lived, the Gothic cruelty which indulged in self-flagellation as much as in the burning of witches and heretics and which made of executions a theatrical spectacle.

The medieval fools have an old tradition leading back to the classic stage fool. But it was in the Middle Ages that their raison d'être became weighty in meaning. Their very special costume and wit were their trademark and mask. The fool was usually clad in red and yellow, with a cap that fell over his shoulders in the form of ass's ears. The costume was often hung with bells, and there was an inflated bladder at the end of the fool's baton, or bauble, which he could use to underline his caustic remarks with light blows.

Fools formed important acting companies in France, and in their annual *fête des fous* they felt free to fool and annoy everyone. Neither clergy nor lords were safe from their ridicule on that day—reminiscent of the *Saturnalia,* the Roman festival in which the slaves were given temporary freedom to say and do what they liked. When the fools' merrymaking got out of hand, the Church had a hard time imposing a ban on what it was forced to sanction. Fools were also kept like symbolic pets in the households of the mighty and rich. They were tolerated, however painful their jokes and acid their wit may have been. It is characteristic of the Gothic mind that dwarfed or hunchbacked fools were given the greatest freedom. It was a curious mingling of masochism and superstition when the lords who kept them to be reminded of their follies and weaknesses pretended they believed their fools mad. Madness was holy in the Middle Ages. In the forty-one woodcuts of his "Dance of Death" cycle, Hans Holbein the Younger (1497?–1543) made death sometimes appear with a fool's cap. Did he wish to remind us how foolish it is not to think of death all the time?

DEATH, the devil, and the fool are the three common phenomena of the Middle Ages. The flagellants are a very special species, but a characteristic medieval aberration. They formed an anticlerical movement in the name of Christ, antedating the plague and danceomania. The flagellants moved in organized groups from place to place, doing penance in order to make God forgive all earthly sins, playing the role of redeemers who, by reenacting the scourging of Christ on their own bodies, tried to bleed and atone for humankind. Such self-flagellation was an improvised performance, usually in churchyards or city squares, with the townspeople watching this ghastly spectacle, weeping and sobbing over the actors' pain. A lay master headed such a group (which usually comprised hundreds of flagellants), seemingly a man with mesmerizing charisma whom they obeyed. They were forbidden to rest in beds or to talk, eat, or drink more than the needed minimum. These men, stripped to the waist, roamed all over Europe, imploring Christ and the Virgin for pity and God for help. Their trips lasted thirty-three and a half days, symbolizing Christ's years on earth. They were followed by a train of female flagellants who, though involved in the act of penance, were not permitted to enter the circle of the ceremony, as if their blood were unclean.

No chronicler described the physical movement of the flagellants in the act of scourging themselves, but the whipping gesture and the pain must have made them move. Since this performance was mostly done in a circle and could have only been possible as an act of mass hysteria, it is more than likely that the master may have directed the rhythmic process of self-torture. Flagellation dances are not uncommon among primitive people and, according to the musicologist Curt Sachs, their deeper meaning is "the magic consecration with the staff of life, a blow from which brings fertility and power and counteracts death."

In the beginning this was a well-organized movement of fanaticized men and women, sticking to their rules and taboos. At first they were not allowed to have intercourse in those thirty-three and a half days, but later reports found the flagellants combining the whipping orgies with orgies of sex.

In 1940 Martha Graham, who has often been attracted by the raw expression of the primitive and mysterious, created a scene of flagellation in *El Penitente*. Always interested in "the miracle that is a human being" and in making "visible the interior landscape," she tried to penetrate the hidden motivations behind the aberration.

If one tries to see history in its most far-reaching effects, then the movement of the flagellants is of serious import. The movement goes back to the apocalyptic prophecies of Joachim of Fiore, who died in 1202 and foresaw the coming of a new age in about 1260. He was a historian, philosopher, and biblical commentator, and as such he put a great deal of Byzantine feeling into his concept of the threeness of God: the age of the Father, of law and fear, was followed by the age of the Son, of grace and faith, and the Third Age, of the Holy Spirit, characterized by love and spirituality. Joachim predicted that the latter age would be ushered in about sixty years after his death. Violence would be a concomitant of its birth pangs, and before humankind would finally reach its highest destiny the Saracens and Jews would have to be converted.

Joachim's thoughts—not far from Hitler's messianic madness of his Third Reich—became the point of departure for the flagellant movement, which the Church soon recognized as a great danger to its own existence. The many charismatic masters of the movement, joined by dissatisfied priests, began to exert a fanatic influence on the masses, also making good use of the miseries of the time: famine, social disorder, and, later, the panic created by the waves of pestilence. The flagellants became a menace to the worldly and ecclesiastic establishments, but because of their claim to act under divine inspiration, Popes and cardinals soft-pedaled their restrictive pressures.

Sometimes history does repeat itself. The Jews were falsely accused of poisoning the wells during the many waves of the Black Plague in the fourteenth century. The pestilence originated in Asia and was brought to the European seaports, from where it quickly moved inland, afflicting parts of the continent more than others. It came and went, only to return; but the specter of its fear remained.

The Pope explained that the Jews would not poison the wells because they knew that they themselves would then have to die the Black Death. But the flagellants stormed the ghettos where the Jews lived huddled together, and the populace was behind them. Thousands of Jews were killed by the pestilence of prejudice and ignorance. Many hundreds of Jews burned themselves by setting fire to their houses. Most of those victims were in German lands. The year 1260 had passed without the advent of the Third Age, characterized by Joachim as the age of love.

Medieval men and women lived with the vision of death. Hell and damnation and the approaching Day of Judgment were as lively and concrete in their minds as the image of the Garden of Eden that they drew on their maps as if its earthly existence could be located somewhat to the east. The earth was flat, but their image of existence in this world was of a round oneness, with everything, whether concrete or symbolic, blurred. That medieval people had learned to live with extremes goes back to St. Paul's concept of divorcing the soul from the body, pitting the spirit against the senses. With such contempt for the body and its functions, with all human goodness assigned to the soul and all evil to the body, people could never escape mortification and sin. This dilemma was further hardened by St. Augustine's spiritual experience—of which he tells in the eighth book of his *Confessions* —when he was forced to open the Pauline Epistles and read the words "But put ye on the Lord Jesus Christ, and make not provision for the flesh, to fulfil the lusts thereof." It became the preamble for the Church's condemnation of all dancing.

But the people could not help dancing. Since it was a burst of running, skipping, and jumping, disharmonious, it often reached riotous proportions at the threshold of the churches. During the years of the plague such dancing was particularly wild, often reaching a point of hysterical gaiety, as if the people would have liked to trick death or laugh its frightening sight away. In an often cited game they played, someone would suddenly throw himself or herself to the ground and act dead, while the others would dance around in the manner of mock mourning. If it was a man, he would be kissed back to life by the women, whereupon a round dance followed. Then a woman would act out the plague-infected person, falling dying on the ground, and then be kissed back to life by the male dancers. They were playing "life and death" like a children's game, with a child's mentality, not realizing that through kissing they were spreading the plague.

IN the fourteenth century the plague killed about half the population of Europe. That the people should have been forced into a dancing mania during these years is understandable. But cases of dance hysteria were recorded long before the black pestilence haunted Europe—and long afterward. The Maenads were gripped by the same *enthousiasmos* in celebration of Dionysus as the people in their dance marathons in the 1920s and 1930s. Then people also danced for days and weeks, keeping awake through all kinds of tricks. These were the same symptoms of a similar malaise, even though at Madison Square Garden the dancers competed for a prize. This irresistible urge to dance, which may have its historic roots in the trance dances of earlier societies, has little to do with true ecstatic feelings and everything to do with a diseased, depraved, and desperate mind.

There are innumerable reports about outbreaks of wild, uncontrollable dancing since the eleventh century. There probably were many such occurrences during earlier centuries: we know of them only since chronicles have been written. No priest could stop these frenzied dancers. I doubt the stories about priests having cursed them "to dance the whole year through until a sympathetic archbishop removes the ban." These people were simply driven by the momentum of their madness and were felled by exhaustion or death. It makes good reading when Hans Christian Andersen has an executioner cut off little Karen's feet to stop her from dancing and dancing.

Usually dance hysteria breaks out when both the times and people's minds are disturbed. In the Middle Ages it mostly started in cemeteries and churchyards. These dancers may have believed in evoking the spirit of the dead or thought they were possessed by demons when they leaped and moved frantically in circles. They screamed and talked to their demons while groaning in agony. All this, as we know, is contagious. Some dancers formed groups, put flowers in their hair, had sexual intercourse, and roamed through the lands like the flagellants. Others had hallucinatory visions or laughed hysterically nonstop; laughter in a fit of melancholia or tears could be seen on their enraptured faces and in their gestures.

One never can say whether some of this dancing mania was in fear of the plague and death—in order to avert both—or as a consequence of being struck by the plague. One day it broke out in the Rhineland and spread all over Germany, spilling into the Low Countries. It was then known as St. Vitus's dance. Since it occurred before the plague had struck these parts of Europe, E. Louis Backman's idea must be mentioned; he suggested that these danceomaniacs were suffering from ergotism (a toxic condition caused by eating grain or grain products infected with the ergot fungus), which can make its victims react with involuntary, spasmodic movements.

In Italy, danceomania was popularly related to the bite of the Apulian spider *Lycosa tarentula*, supposedly causing melancholia, to which wild dancing (from which the dance *tarantella* took its name) was considered as bringing at least temporary relief. As we find so many medieval and Renaissance phenomena having their roots in former days, I refer to the authority of Curt Sachs, who pointed to the Roman *saltarello* and Tuscan *tresca* as dances most closely reflecting the original tarantella. He quoted Rainer Maria Rilke, who saw such a modernized version: "What a dance as though invented by nymphs and satyrs, old and as though rediscovered and rising up anew, wrapped in primeval memories—cunning and wildness and wine, men with goat's hooves again and girls from the train of Artemis."

Medieval people were told time and again that dancing is the devil's business, and the devil is the one dancer most often visually imagined and re-created. Salome is also looked upon as the devil's daughter, and as a dancer she takes a prominent spot in their astigmatic eyes. On the porch of the cathedral at Rouen she is shown turning somersaults; she is on the bronze door of San Zeno Maggiore at Verona and in the position of a "bridge" in a thirteenth-century cathedral sculpture in Brunswick. We have never quite lost sight of her depraved body-mind, and in our own days she was resurrected by Oscar Wilde and Richard Strauss as a harrowing image of total obsession in the truest medieval spirit.

Whenever the people were caught by the compulsion to dance, the whipping words of the priests' sermons still filled their ears. The condemnation of such trifling matters as the fashion of pointed shoes grew in the peoples' warped minds to tremendous taboos that were milestones in their struggle against temptation. The sermons warned them that Satan entertained sorcerers and witches, and people believed in witches riding on broomsticks and in the exorcism of devils. In 1374, the worst year of the plague, Pope Gregory XI stipulated that sorcery and witchcraft were the handiwork of devils and demons and fell within Church jurisdiction—which meant that the Inquisition would hold these trials or intervene in them, and also that such inspired people as Joan of Arc were then doomed, to be declared saints centuries later. One touching story, about the Tumbler of Our Lady, is retold in an old French legend about 1200. An aged minstrel, unable to sing, renders his ecstatic homage to the statue of the Virgin Mary through dancing for her until he collapses exhausted.

Through the ever-recurring pestilence over more than two hundred years, the notion of the Dance of Death became an indelible image. The visualized figure of Death was already known in antiquity. We find a dancing skeleton on Roman vases and on reliefs of Etruscan tombs. Death was a famous focal figure in dances of many primitive societies and, to this day, has a prominent place in voodoo dances. But it was left to the Middle Ages to glorify Death as the messenger of God. The symbols of Death's frightening power took on a variety of images. He was endowed with satanic reality; he gained social significance as the great equalizer. In the daily Dance of Death the poor could see the rich as their equal, and the dance itself gave those suffering at the bottom of the social ladder an opportunity to impersonate the rich, living and dying.

This *danse macabre—makabr* means churchyard in Arabic—found many visualizations by painters, writers, and choreographers. It may have reached a momentous vogue of personification between the fourteenth and sixteenth centuries, but ever since it has occupied the creative mind. There was no morality play without the parabolic character of Death as the central figure, and he has continued to play in a variety of disguises onstage down to Strindberg and O'Neill, Maeterlinck and Tennessee Williams. As mentioned, Hans Holbein gave this well-known motif the most incisive images in his woodcuts, and the death motif has fascinated painters and sculptors from Michelangelo in his "Dying Slave" to Ferdinand Hodler in his picture series of his dying friend and to the German expressionists.

The Dance of Death, in spite of all its frightening aspects, had stirred the imagination, creating visionary, dramatic, and even lyric components. The painter Piero di Cosimo designed a danse macabre pageant for the duke of Florence in 1507 while the city was besieged and disaster loomed. According to Vasari's description of this eye-filling pageant, there was a huge triumphal car, painted with skeletons bearing the gigantic figure of Death with scythe in hand. Skeletons sang songs, attendants wore the vestments of the grave, and voices sang in dismal unison the psalm of David called "Miserere."

In ballets, characters die both natural and unnatural deaths, but the figure of Death found no place in this art form until our own time, probably because ballet was always considered mere entertainment, an artistic means of escape. Ballet abounded in ghosts and specters during its Romantic era, and death could be implied through a fairy tale, but his appearance onstage came only with World War I and modern dance. The concept of death played a major part in Mary Wigman's dances, and from then on was no longer a figure excluded from dance creations. It triumphed in most dramatic terms in Kurt Jooss's *The Green Table* and, with sophisticated subtlety, in George Balanchine's *La Valse*.

The plague, of course, must have made a deep impression on the generation surviving its major assaults. Today we might speak of graffiti of death, but, in the late Middle Ages and the Renaissance, Dance of Death figures were seen on the walls of churches and cemeteries, and the theme was often treated in block prints and circulated among the populace. Christian art expressed far more serenity and hope before the plague; on most paintings of the fifteenth century the faces of the Holy Family have lines of deep despair. Like any human being, an entire era also has the right to be very human. In spite of its incontestable greatness, the Renaissance suffered from the scars of its medieval past.

There was one Renaissance painter about whose personality very little is known. One assumes he was born about 1450, and we know that he died in 1516, three years before Leonardo. He lived in the Dutch town of Hertogenbosch, and people called him Hieronymus Bosch. In his paintings he relived the nightmarish life of the medieval soul. He painted the horrors of hell with its torments and treacheries; he painted demons with human faces and humans with animal faces, a grotesque surrealistic bedlam, a devilish dance. Poor medieval people, punished for having been born into a time that finally gave birth to the Renaissance and such great artists as Hieronymus Bosch!

A Turn of Events

HUMAN BEINGS CAN BEAR LIFE ONLY BECAUSE—AS THE ONLY CREATURES aware of our mortality—we are able to forget that to live is, at the same time, a slow process of dying. We have religion in order to create a bridge from our subconscious into the unknown beyond. We have art in order to leave testimony with the world to witness our being and to help us overcome the thought of death through the power of our own creativity. But only someone with a terminal disease may better understand what a fourteenth-century person experienced, with death a daily guest or waiting around the corner.

Doomsday always seemed to be tomorrow. As long as humans cannot conquer death they will indulge in superstition. The ancient Greeks, at the height of their cultural accomplishments, were full of superstition, and so are we in a scientifically oriented age. Why should not medieval men and women have feared the days when the millennium would come, particularly with comets or the northern lights in the skies? The many itinerant preachers filled their ears with fearful diatribes against the vanities of the rich as much as those of the poor, and from the pulpit thundered a voice constantly evoking the image of the final judgment. When the day of reckoning—as the year 1000 was ominously prefigured—passed without any visible changes, then it had to be 1033, the millennium after Christ's death, or 1260, the advent of the new, the third, age. At the same time, the most often used theme in the Romanesque churches, in that style of simple calm and imposing gravity, was the Last Judgment. The fear that filled the people's life was also expressed by these churches themselves, which were referred to as fortresses of God.

In this state of relentless terror, dancing was a perfect vent for the people's pent-up feelings. What passed for dancing among peasants and artisans as well as at feudal courts or in the houses of the rich was a chain or ring dance that could last for hours. The endurance of the people, whether in listening to sermons or in dancing, was remarkable. The participants walked most of the time, interrupted by a short run or by a few hops and leaps. In his *World History of the Dance,* Curt Sachs described these dances as "continuous and uncircumscribed, as with primitive peoples. The knight does not grasp the maiden tenderly by the hand, nor yet by a kerchief that she holds out to him, but takes her possessively under his fur mantle. And often enough it does go as far as actual possession. . . ." Essentially, this dancing —to which the people sang and clapped their hands while moving—was determined by raw instinct.

From the mid-twelfth century, the fundamental changes that took place embraced the totality of life. It is the period in which the Gothic style emerged, trying to give the solemn symmetry of the past an emotional expression. The Gothic sculptor breathes life into his figures. The sacred story he tells is dramatically moving; it shows greater sensitivity than before and comes closer to the truth of nature. When we enter a Gothic church we can sense those invisible arms stretched out toward heaven, carrying us with them, a majestic lightness full of aesthetic impulses. Was it really little more than the translation of scholastic philosophy into stone or a well-calculated feat of an engineer's inspiration? No, this exhilaration and this ecstatic verticalism become the symbol of a new way of life. In a Romanesque church one can easily have the feeling of being sheltered like a monk in his cell. In a Gothic church one can perceive a dynamic flow, sense the entire dramatic process of life rising up in an ever-unfinished question, waiting and waiting for the silence of God to break and to reveal the secret of wisdom behind the eternal silence.

Medieval men and women were no longer necessarily a passive part of existence. Life set new accents and offered them new experiences.

This transition was best symbolized by the miracle of Chartres. The old Romanesque church burned down in 1194, only its precious relic being found intact in the crypt. Was it the will of a higher power or only the awakening will of the people that on the same spot and on the remaining foundation a new church had to be built that should rise above everything else in beauty and devotion? The chronicles tell us how hundreds of masons and thousands of workmen came from everywhere to build the cathedral of Chartres. It was the spirit of the people that made this towering, weightless wonder possible.

Much speculation was devoted to the sources and reasons for this spectacular change in history from a psychologically bewildering, austere, and ascetic outlook on life to one whose sensuous-emotional, sensual-erotic, and dynamic impact led to the foundation of a slowly reawakening world. There is no one-way solution to this marvel. It is, as always, rather a confluence of several sociopolitical events reaching out for new experience. But one thing is certain. While the Crusades came to their ignominious end in the thirteenth century because of their moral failure, they made Europeans rediscover the Orient and its pliant and poetic, colorful and meditative way of living. On the one hand, this moral disaster led to a booming trade of goods; on the other, to new aesthetic and social influences soon to bear fruit. The knight who set out to fight for the honor of God returned home to honor the woman whose uniqueness he discovered like a blind man whose eyes were suddenly made to see. For the many months and years of the lord's absence, it was the woman who ruled the castle and kept his position and possessions intact. This gave her a new freedom over life and herself that he could not help recognizing. It was the beginning of the age of chivalry.

A few decades earlier woman was a convenient commodity, a possession. Now she was idolized. Feminine influence was written all over twelfth-century court culture. The entire fabric of society began to change. The accent shifted to urban life. With the growing importance of a number of cities, patronage of the artists was no longer in the hands of the Church and the nobility alone. Architects were asked to design secular buildings, and one of the most famous and characteristic buildings of this kind was the Doges' Palace of Venice, which best shows the sweep and delightfulness of the Gothic style.

A gradual emancipation of thought from the Church went hand in hand with the secularization of culture. Until then, the Church Fathers tried to suppress any sense experience. Now, discovering that there was not only the one truth that came from the pulpit, but also a truth deeply embedded in nature, people affirmed nature as the phenomenon from which they could draw a new spirituality. Soon the antitraditional trend was noticeable on all cultural levels.

THE unfathomable turning point of European civilization was the twelfth century, a crucible from which emerged the impetus to a new way of thinking, acting, and being. Humanity gradually learned to use its intellectual energy on all levels of life. The traumatic experiences of the past did not disappear overnight—in Switzerland the last witch was burned in 1781—but the great breakthrough came with the realization that God could be reached through beauty. This new feeling of things began to make itself felt in the vibrant atmosphere of the Gothic church, whose windows told sublime stories through beautiful colors. It could be sensed in the way music changed its tune and in the joy of the people who could act out theatrically what occupied their minds.

Of all the changes, the most indicative of the coming of a new era took place in the Church itself, which, from about the tenth century, had created the liturgical play as another means of bringing the chief episodes of the Christian story to the people. The actors had come from the lower ranks of the clergy, and the locality of the action was first the altar, then the nave. For a long time these miracle plays were presented in Latin, of which the populace had no, or only scant, knowledge. It was not before the twelfth century that these plays, though still in the spirit of the Church, cut off their umbilical cord and became entirely vernacular in the hands of the laity. The origin of the theater may go back to the Dionysian festivals, but the modern theater had to be reborn, and it was reborn then and there.

The actors were now the burghers and artisans; the guilds became the producers paying for costumes and scenery. They worked with a number of decorated platforms, called *mansions,* adding up to a cyclic dramatic composition. Later the various mansions, usually presenting the Passion—which is why this type of theater became known as the mystery cycles, or *Passionsspiele*—were set upon wheels and, pageantlike, drawn from group to group of spectators. Heaven and hell, Angels and Herod, Judas and Lucifer were depicted. These plays became a higher reality of life for the acting artisans, who brought much gusto and probably little talent with them, as a chronicler expressed, saying that the performers

> are an ignorant set of men, mechanics and artisans, who know not an A from a B, untrained and unskilled in playing such pieces before the public. Their voices are poor, their language unfitting,

their pronunciation wretched. No sense do they have of the meaning of what they say.

However crude it may have been, a beginning was made, and many doors
were thrown open for the development of the theater. That Pope Innocent
III interdicted all dramatic performances in and around church buildings in
1210 helped the mystery play gather momentum.

A similar change occurred in music. The lyric poets of the late Middle
Ages were poet-composers, and the troubadour set the verses they wrote to
music. These popular singers may not have cared too much about regular
beats. After all, their message and entertainment value were in their
verses. However, our knowledge of secular music begins with documented
minnesinger melodies and the Goliard songs of the vagabond scholars and
vagrant monks, of whom there were many in the twelfth century.† It was a
singing era, one that loved stories, and many of them were in ballad form.
Until the twelfth century, people sang while they danced. Fiddles, double
flutes, mandolas, and small harps were in use, but mainly by accredited
troubadours.

During the centuries of ecclesiastical height the Gregorian chant was *the*
church music. In 1227 the Council of Trier deemed it necessary to point an
accusing finger at the secular trend that apparently had crept into church
hymns and Gregorian chants. The attack against the modernization of music
became even more vehement when, in 1324, Pope John XXII turned
against this "new school" in music. The Pope denounced its free-flowing
style; polyphony was then no longer the prerogative of the Church, for it
had become an artistic experience that wanted to please without necessarily
edifying.

Shortly afterward Philippe de Vitry (1291–1361) wrote his epochal treatise *Ars Nova.* The new art aimed at strictness and balance. It achieved a
novel rhythmic variety and subtleness, a harmonic flavor different from
anything known in the past, opening new ways through Vitry's isorhythmic
principle. The works of Guillaume de Machaut—the greatest French composer of the fourteenth century—or those of his Italian contemporary,
Francesco Landino, were based on it.

The entire ambience of hitherto unknown delight in life brought two new
musical types with it, the *madrigal,* a harmonically intimate fusion of
music and poetry, and the *chace,* or *caccia* (catch), whose structural principle was the canon. Love and the little joys of daily life were at the basis of
a new secular music.

A similar trend toward a new freedom also occurred in Italian painting.
A less perfect—sometimes impressive, sometimes lifeless—edition of Byzantine art, with its golden glimmering solidity of Eternal Truth, had been tra-

† Carl Orff's *Carmina Burana* is a true reflection of these songs.

ditional for a few centuries. Then the Florentine painter Giotto di Bondone (1266?–?1337) arrived on the scene. He changed the course of history in painting. He was able to breathe life into his figures and was the first to create the illusion of depth. He gave the old Byzantine forms a contemporary look. The gold ground expressing a stereotyped sacred feeling was changed to red and blue, to the reality of an early sunset or the imaginary blueness of paradise, to landscapes and church interiors. The shift from the sacred scenes to those representing a real world, from manifestations of God or the divine to scenes depicting such devotional subjects as the life of Francis of Assisi, was indicative of the new trend. As divine art became humanized and fictionalized, the imagination of the visual artist had a wide-open field to explore.

With the profane figure in the foreground, and with the general secularization of the arts, dancing also profited from this decisive emancipation from the past. The social dance, in its process of refinement and solidification, became, in the eyes of the new elite, a playful but vital symbol of humanity's self-awareness.

The Triumph of Illusion

THE TWELFTH-CENTURY COURT LIFE CREATED THE PHENOMENON OF chivalry, which resulted in some unique human experiences. It was the most flagrantly romantic period, of which the nineteenth-century version was only a pale facsimile. The pas de deux developed by the Romantic ballet truly reflects the inspiration for which it was indebted to twelfth-century Romanticism.

The most fascinating feature of the era was courtly love; and the most impressive character, the troubadour. He was the heart of an age whose intellectual and moral—or immoral—notions were a glorified *ars amandi.* There was no other period in history in which the ideal and perversion of love were so central to existence. It was more than the age of erotic poetry. It was a question of creating not only an ideal of love, but also the love of an ideal. Although basically concerning the nobility, it penetrated, in a diffused way, all channels of life and gave more than two hundred years the imprint of its beliefs and errors.

Love and knighthood were inseparable phenomena of the time. Walking through a museum and looking at a medieval armor collection, we first wonder at how short these knights must have been. But let us make no mistake

Giotto: St. Francis of Assisi receiving Pope Innocent III's permission to found his order. (Courtesy Istituto Italiano di Cultura)

about the courage it needed to be inside this hardware and to face enemies on all sides. Medieval warfare included some of the most vicious fighting in history. A true knight loved fighting for its own sake; he threw himself into battle without caring about the reason for the conflict. Some hated to miss any quarrel and traveled far in Europe to be part of a fight. In between, they would engage in tournaments.

Next to courage, loyalty mattered most to a knight. The phrase "a man of his word" goes back to those days when there were no written contracts, only a pledged word on which the huge pyramidal system of feudalism rested. Knighthood was a system of rights and duties, and also a spiritual way of being. Chivalry was full of unwritten rules and codes. A knight was always ready to fight the enemy of his feudal lord. It was a fight face to face, sword and shield against sword and shield. The concept of challenging and fighting another man in a duel became more popular then and began to die out only in our century.

Wars were mostly brief raids. Peasants were killed, their lands destroyed. The victor carried some loot home after having ravaged the enemy's source of income. Only war could fill the lord's coffers. With peace came poverty and idleness. Knight, horse, and sword were a hallowed trinity. The knight was fully occupied being a knight; fighting and hunting were substitutes for work. They gave his life some purpose.

Some cynical historians maintain that the concept of courtly love had its origin in the ennui of the knights. Others say it was in Persian literature, which, with its sensuous sighs over womanhood, infected the Crusaders. Others believe that it was a matter of transferring the adoration and deification of the Virgin Mother to a lady of one's choice. The strangest feature of the courtly lover was his service to fidelity and spirituality. The sensuous adoration of the beloved had to be halted before fulfillment of the lover's desire. This *amor purus* was in fact a mental coitus interruptus. The woman as the untouchable target of desire was resurrected as the unattainable object seven hundred years later during Romanticism.

Indeed, in front of everyone the troubadour—the poet disguised as knight, or vice versa—would pine for his lady, sing his verses of adoring despair, extolling her beauties while, at the same time, complaining about her chaste rigor. Her husband and all her friends would listen. Nobody's reputation suffered. On the contrary, everyone was happy, including the loving and suffering poet who, according to the rules, was not permitted to approach her in case he might meet her in the church or on the street.

The idea of courtly love was born in 1087. It was introduced by the first of the troubadours, whose name was Guilhem, ninth duke of Aquitaine and seventh count of Poitou. His description in an old Provençal chronicle could probably fit any other troubadour: "The Count of Poitou was one of the most courteous men in the world, and a great deceiver of ladies; and he was a brave knight and had much to do with love affairs; and he knew well how to sing and make verses."

Courtly love began at the court of Poitou as a parlor game and a literary exercise in flattery. The idea caught fire and was soon imitated everywhere, finally being supported as a social philosophy and known as *cortesia* in Italy and *Frauendienst* in the German-speaking countries. Its consistent inconsistencies, its duplicity acted out with a straight face, its praise of chastity and adultery at one and the same time are its remarkable features. To the many inconsistencies belongs the notion of the chastity belt, which came from the Orient with the Crusaders and about which much was written. But in Europe, as in the East, it was far more a literary flourish with symbolic meaning than actually in practical use.

Characteristically, in this era exaltation and delight were always paired with anguish and suffering. It was the age when Tristram and Isolt came to life—a theme revived in Richard Wagner's romantic opera: an old Celtic legend about two lovers united in life and death through a magic potion. This archetypal poem fitted the spirit of the twelfth century, when a French poet remodeled the legend as the triumph of true love over conjugal love.

This era of the late Middle Ages or early Renaissance brought forth three of the greatest writers of world literature, who, in their ways, reflected the character of the age. Carlyle said about Dante Alighieri (1265–1321) that "he gave voice to ten silent centuries." He certainly did to his own. He was married to Gemma Donati, who was betrothed to him when he was twelve years old, which was quite common in those days. Parents decided when you were a child whom you were going to marry. This was also behind Romeo and Juliet's traumatic problem, and to some degree it may explain the duality of feelings: on the one hand, the reality of life, the woman with whom you had children; on the other, the excitability of your senses and imagination which needed the dream image of an ideal love. Dante's great love was Beatrice Portinari, whom he met when he was nine years old; when he saw her again another nine years had passed. But this "wonderful lady" had greeted him, and he was beside himself—"intoxicated" was the word he used.

In his poetic vision the beloved is equated with the fleeting figure of a chaste and stately dancer. He said in his *Purgatorio:*

> *As a lady who is dancing turns her round*
> *with feet close to the ground and to each other,*
> *and hardly puts foot before foot,*
> *she turned toward me upon the red and upon*
> *the yellow flowers, not otherwise than a virgin*
> *that droppeth her modest eyes . . .*

It shows the ambivalence of the medieval mind that Dante is guided to heaven by a Florentine woman of flesh and blood whom his imagination must have coveted more than once, and not by the Virgin Mary. She was part of one's prayers, but life and art needed that other woman whom one adored and prayed to with songs and words and glances, the incarnation of all beauty and delight, goodness and inspiration. For Dante the inamorata became heightened to something divine as if his exalted love could turn her into a religious symbol. He was fascinated by the state of ecstasy reached through divine love. Beatrice was only the instrument through which he could transcend ordinariness.

For Petrarch (1304–74) the beloved already had human features. Laura was earthier than Beatrice, though still in the clouds, but brought somewhat closer to the touch of human understanding by the 366 poems he devoted to her. Most of them were sonnets, a verse form he popularized and, with it, the concept of love poetry in general. Laura is identified with a lady who had married into the Sade family, later made famous through the Marquis de Sade. She married young, had at least eleven children, and died young of the plague. Petrarch met Laura in Avignon, then papal territory, when he was twenty-three years old. She talked with the poet several times, outdoors and never unobserved. She was very beautiful and became his beloved inspiration. Thus it remained a romance never consummated: unfortunately for him but fortunately for world literature, which ever since has been enriched by poets and their unrequited love affairs.

Embittered over his way of life, he played the role of a recluse from time to time. What is most important about Petrarch is his discovery of a completely new world of physical beauty in which nature and nature's God shared in the divinity of the universe. In his old age he was attacked for having believed in Christian doctrines more than in those of Aristotle, but posterity has credited him with having been the first humanist, with his love for Vergil and antiquity and his frequent stressing of respect for the dignity and worth of the individual.

Giovanni Boccaccio (1313–75), nearly ten years Petrarch's junior, revered him as an accomplished master and became his lifelong friend. The subject matter of Boccaccio's work is medieval—the concepts of chivalry and love are all there—but the spirit of his work has Renaissance stature in emphasizing that recognition of our fortune and failings is part of human dignity, that we must accept life the way it is and also the consequences of our actions; that, in a truly Machiavellian sense, we must mobilize our intelligence and, while affirming all moral values, try to adjust life to our own designs.

The medieval fabliaux may have inspired Boccaccio to write his *Decameron*, in which seven women and three men flee plague-stricken Florence in 1348 to an isolated spot in the country, where for two weeks they take turns deciding the course of the next day. For ten of the days everyone had to tell a story, and each day ended with a canzone for dancing, sung by one of the storytellers—which only goes to prove that music and dance were part of the daily amusements of the privileged. "The queen [of the day] ordered Lauretta to dance and Emilia to sing a song," and on another day "the queen ordered Emilia to dance and Pampinea sang. . . ." The book ends on a noble note, with fidelity and constancy being praised in a chivalrous tenor. But Boccaccio was also pleading for womanly obedience. Here he deviated from the routine of his age. He had already deviated from the norm in his own life by having made his famous muse Fiammetta (who is thought to have been Maria, illegitimate daughter of the king of Naples) his mistress.

Boccaccio liberated the male from the game he played with his own desires and illusions. But undoubtedly both sexes loved to play this game, which must have left them enough freedom for the gratification of their needs. A clergyman who called himself Andreas Capellanus wrote a book about courtly love in the *court of love,* the strangest phenomenon to emerge from this age. This chaplain boasted, "We consider ourselves very expert in the art of love" and felt that clergymen are better lovers than knights, since more prudent—but then said apologetically that one must first know about it to be able to refrain from it in obedience to the dogma of the Church. He called it *Liber de Arte honeste amandi et de Reprobatione inhonesti Amoris* (*Book on the Art of Honest Loving and the Disapproval of Dishonest Love*) and tried to imitate Ovid. We learn from his work a great deal about the court of love and how it functioned. It started at the castle of Poitiers in the mid-twelfth century with Eleanor, countess of Poitou and duchess of Aquitaine, who, with her daughter Marie, countess of Champagne, reigned supreme over the procedures. At such a court of love either one lady or a panel of ladies decided in a kind of mock trial on the most serious love problems. A knight would present a problem, mostly his own, and the ladies would then open the debate on questions of love behavior until the female jury and judge would hand down the decision.

Our mass media often indulge in games of a playful nature whose interest lies in teasing curiosity, with a panel and a moderator. But although some of the questions to which the ladies of the court had to find an answer may strike us as grotesque today, and the judgment as predictable, there was always a serious debate with theatrical overtones through which the participants tried to come to a pedagogically valid pronouncement.‡ These noble people were baffled by their own attitudes and by the world that condoned them in the name of love and God. There may have been an inner need for clarification and further codification, and what the court of love probably did was create a dramatic situation leading to a desired resolution. The badly needed relief after such debates was a banquet, followed by dancing.

‡ Its scholarly counterpart was the many public disputations arranged by the universities where, so to speak, at a court of wisdom, bold theses were defended and challenged.

Some of these courts of love were blown up to great events. Matteo Villani's *Chronicles of Florence* tell us of such an upper-class experience:

> In June of the year 1283, at the festival of St. John in Florence
> . . . a social union was formed, composed of a thousand people
> who, all clad in white, called themselves the Servants of Love.
> They arranged a succession of sports, merrymakings, and dances
> with ladies: nobles and bourgeois marched to the sound of trum-
> pets and music in wild delight to and fro, and held festive ban-
> quets at midday and at night. This *Court of Love* lasted nearly
> two months, and it was the finest and most famous that had ever
> been held in Florence, or in all Tuscany.

The medieval mind preferred any event to last unduly long. When we think of the famous tournaments of that time (which later gave birth to the equestrian ballet), then we should not think in terms of a fight lasting a few hours only. The ancient Greeks had already proved that they could easily absorb five plays a day several days in a row; in fact, the nineteenth-century opera performances, mixed with ballets, could easily last from six in the late afternoon until long after midnight. Tournaments were not one-shot affairs: they could last as long as a week or longer, with each day reserved for prep- arations of all kinds and choosing the combatants for minor jousts before the final tourney, usually with a day of rest in between. These were active, noisy, and gay days, associated with feasting and dancing. The final fight was then the great event, with merchants and artisans invited as spectators. It was a brilliant spectacle to behold: the banners, the shining shields, the gilded or painted armor, with the horses decoratively draped and prancing to the sounds of trumpets, with flowers or scarves thrown at their favorites by the ladies seated on platforms.

Knighthood had a strange fascination for the people; it always had some- thing of triumph and a lost glory about it, even while it lasted. It kept up a resemblance of its presence when it had already become a vague image in people's memories. This is why, so many centuries later, Cervantes could not help immortalizing the deplorable and lovable knight in all of us and making it possible for all windmills to be giants, if we only wish to see them that way.

Some of the pessimism that overshadowed the fifteenth century—an other- wise exemplary era on all creative levels—was still part of the sunset mood of resignation and despair by which the people were beset toward the end of the fourteenth century. The majority of the populace took the scourge of pestilence as a warning, if not a beginning, of the final punishment for sin. A note of disappointment and mortified anguish also took hold of the poets.

Petrarch, writing to Boccaccio in 1366, could not suppress a deep sigh: "Such are the times, my friend, on which we are fallen." It was the more somber period of his later age in which he also chided himself for having ever loved women. "The world," his letter continued, "is perhaps depopulated of true men, but was never more densely populated with vice and the creatures of vice." His younger brother Gherardo joined the Carthusians, a severe order, and Petrarch confessed to him: ". . . I think it is granted to me to understand that there is no help in literature or in our own intellects, but all is the work of God, who will perhaps lend me his hand as I confess honestly my own helplessness." And in the same letter he spoke of "the deceptive sweetness" of love. It was more than the resignation of an older man when we read: "And I thought how, between one dip of the pen and the next, time goes on, and I hurry, drive myself, and speed toward death. We are always dying. I while I write, you while you read, and others while they listen or stop their ears, they are all dying."

Boccaccio reacted with even greater vehemence to the mood of the age. His health was failing him, and so was his beloved Fiammetta. He who had extolled womanhood in his younger years wrote a satire on women, *Il Corbaccio* (*The Crow*), in which he depicted them as lecherous, greedy creatures, constantly on the lookout for lovers and gaudy clothes. Besides this misogynistic sally, Boccaccio showed signs of religious scruples. The power of the Church and medieval thinking were still very strong. A Carthusian monk tried to persuade him to renounce the world and his studies; Petrarch, however, prevented him from burning his works and selling his books.

Its ambivalent feelings characterize this age as much as its excesses. We are used to thinking of the *Roman de la Rose* as one of the representative works of the era and the one most widely read and discussed; part of it was turned into English verse by Geoffrey Chaucer around 1370. This work contains a lively description of a medieval choral dance and many other references to dancing, proving what a significant part dance then played in the people's life.

> *And then a dance you might have seen,*
> *The maidens and the men in joy have been*
> *To tread a measure and to turn their rounds*
> *On grassy green of spring, and to the sounds*
> *Of flutists and of minstrels with a strain*
> *They sing of beautiful Lorraine. . . .*
> *Then came two damsels, young and neat,*
> *Their kirtles showed their forms sweet.*
> *In gaiety the two began to dance*
> *With queenlike leaps and furtive glance;*
> *Their bodies, lithe and limber, now advance*
> *And give their lips to kiss but half a chance.*
> *And then once more did they retreat*
> *To turn a dancing measure with their feet.*

‡ DANCE IN ITS TIME ‡

What more could I describe and tell
Of all their dancing, done so well?

The *Roman de la Rose* has over 21,000 lines, of which only the first 4,000 were written, as early as 1240 and in the belief of courtly love, by Guillaume de Lorris. It is full of allegorical figures in a pastoral setting. But what gave the *Roman de la Rose* its great success was the additional material of many thousands of lines written, toward the end of the century, by Jean de Meung, whom some called an enlightened man, others a dirty cynic. The fact is that he recognized the falsity behind the showy window display of faithful love and the chastity of women; he saw, as if with modern eyes, the pathological sickness behind the glorious gesture of self-delusion. He put "into the mouths of Venus, Nature and Genius the most daring apology for sensuality," as Johan Huizinga said. The book was attacked and defended for the right and wrong reasons. For decades and centuries people loved it—more than three hundred manuscripts survived—and apparently enjoyed its ambivalence: for the glorification of seduction as much as for the glorification of the knight's faithful love.

The allegorical tenderness of the pastoral scene, the loveliness of personified nature on a Vergilian scale has, in one way or another, remained with us. A pastoral element was never absent from court activities long into the mid-eighteenth century. Its arcadian mood fitted masques and masquerades. In the Middle Ages it could easily be related to the Christian faith: the prince as shepherd referred to the One who cares for his sheep. It mattered little to the surviving power of the pastoral that Jean de Meung gave the *Roman de la Rose* an ironic twist, or that François Villon (1431–c.1463), poet of the intellectual underworld, unmasked all picture-postcard ideals and idylls. He called a spade by its name, whether it was the fat canon amusing himself with wine and women, or the callous prince who was about to legalize the principle of *droit de seigneur*. Throughout history, reality has always had two faces.

. . . and a time to dance . . .

"To every thing there is a season, and a time to every purpose under the heaven," Ecclesiastes says. Through many allusions I have pointed to the need of medieval people to dance. This need had much to do with their illiteracy and their way of thinking in symbols. The written word had something exclusive about it during these centuries, and only the Renaissance made it into a more accepted common currency, in which humanistic refinement and the printing press were its greatest helpmates. In the Middle Ages the written word belonged to the priests, authorities, and ruling classes.* After all, this was the age of the scribes, and of the minnesingers and storytellers who were in great demand. Despite the great number of manuscripts in the monasteries and, later, in the libraries of some savants, despite the foundation of universities and the study of ancient writers, it was an oral age, with the town criers the living newspapers. True, the most beautifully illuminated manuscripts were written in the monasteries, and kings and lords vied with one another to present them to their peers or papal dignitaries. But in the oral communication of people the vocabulary was small and crudely rudimentary.

This gave expressive language great importance. Children who do not have the same language in common understand each other quickly. They seem to know the articulation of silence and the magic of symbolic expression. Life makes us unlearn these things with which medieval people could live so easily. Lack of a literate communication made people rely on symbolic gestures, with meaningful connotations. Everything physical and real was immediately translated into allusive and allegorical terms and moved into a distant world. Medieval people were afraid of the reality of everything real; they felt the need to relate it to what they envisioned as cosmic mystery. Yet the mystery of inexplicable phenomena had to take on a visible shape because the mind could grasp only what had a perceptible form. In this unconscious traffic between the dark and the light, the slightest sensation was raised to great significance. All sermons spoke to the people in allegories, and the personification of divine images was part and parcel of the mystery plays. It was only in a more sophisticated manner that a Renaissance mythology continued to personify such imaginative figures as Fortuna, Venus, or the Virtues. In fact, during the fifteenth and sixteenth centuries it became an intellectual pastime to create a system of symbolic conceptions in which any figure one chose found its place. This allegorical game reached a high point in Monteverdi's operas and never ceased to be practiced until the Age of Enlightenment tried to do away with it.

If one reads the lines "She soared high above him in a sky with clouds, she was bright like the morning star and shone like the radiant sun," one could easily think of a poet addressing his beloved. But it was the mystic Heinrich Suso (c. 1296–1366), a pupil of Meister Eckhart, who thus addressed his betrothed, Eternal Wisdom. The metaphor continued to thrive

---

* It was more frequent than we may think that even a troubadour could not read or write. He knew only the spoken and sung word. I offer as evidence Ulrich von Lichtenstein, one of the more important minnesingers and most flamboyant knight-errants who, in his later years, wrote the informative book *Frauendienst*. But did he *write* it? No. This illiterate knight had to dictate to a scribe the book that became an impressive record of his life and courtly love.

and triumph in mental ecstasy or in physical paroxysms. People loved to express themselves in metaphor during the Renaissance, too, and this is the frame of mind into which we must place the burgeoning court dancing in the mid-fifteenth century. The steps and gestures, turns and bows of the dancing couples in the halls of palaces and in those of rich middle-class homes were to them metaphors in which they spoke to each other without voicing a word. The ambience of romantic love hovered around them, and the approach to the dance was still based on the tenets of chivalry.

For a long time there had been no order or sequence of prescribed steps at any of the dance events during the constantly growing number of festivities and banquets arranged by the nobility and the well-to-do. The movements were simply thrown together without method or motivation, and everything was left to the mood and imagination of the dancers. But in the mid-fifteenth century these people were no longer satisfied with any extemporaneous "moving about"; they also wanted to cut a good figure on the dancing floor. Moreover, a new sense of order seen in terms of the reality of nature and geometric definitions began to be prevalent among the people and created a desire to be both entertained and instructed.

There were not many schooled dancers available who could teach people how to dance and how to posture while moving. What mattered was a question not only of good dancing, but also of etiquette. Already the troubadours had to play masters of etiquette, but in those early Renaissance days, with so many new self-styled dukes and princes, the need for behavioral guidance became paramount. Dancing masters were in great demand, learned dancers who could demonstrate and teach the steps while combining them in ever-new ways. A new profession came into being, today known as those of ballet master and choreographer.

With the emergence of the professional dancing master a decisive turn came in the development of the dance. What the dancers lost in spontaneity, they gained through discipline. Simultaneously, a clear cleavage began to separate folk dancing from the court dance, forerunner of theater dance. This separation functioned far more on a social level than on any aesthetic or artistic one, for the folk dance, constantly subjected to a process of refinement and theatricalization, has remained one of the important sources for theater dance to this very day.

ONE of the most curious phenomena of the time was the appearance of an unusual number of Jewish dancing masters, particularly in northern Italy, considered the cradle of the ballet. A unique type of entertainer emerged during the late Middle Ages. He came from the Jewish ghettos, of which there were many in Germany and France. A Talmudic legend envisions the Jewish *Spielmann*—they were called *Letzim*—being born with a fiddle in his hands.† Marc Chagall, who has constantly lived with the memories of his people, often includes a fiddling figure in his canvases.

The institution of the *Tanzhaus* in these ghettos became of intrinsic importance to the development of theatrical dance. The *Tanzhaus* was a building where Jews gathered for ceremonial dances on the Sabbath and on any festive occasions. At first the sexes were strictly segregated and the dancing restricted to religious purposes. But in such a narrow world of a lively people it was to be expected that in those dancing halls the ceremonial character of the dances would give way to recreational gatherings. In spite of the rabbis' efforts to prevent mixed dancing, it became unavoidable. It spontaneously happened that the best fiddlers would also be appointed as "callers," who had to arrange and oversee the dances. This was no slight feat considering the multitude of people on a dance floor of limited size and often strange shape. Sometimes the rabbis took it on themselves to space the dances and string the steps together.

The rabbinical efforts must of necessity have been oriented toward decency and refinement of whatever went into the social dances in the ghettos. The fiddlers were no doubt called upon to use their skill and imagination in polishing and elevating the style of steps and dance figures, which could only have been based on biblical descriptions. Nowhere is there any documentary proof of what the ghetto dances were like. But with the Bible and Talmud forming the pillars of existence of these people, both must have served as source material. Both contain unmistakable references to dances on the occasion of joyous family events, of public rejoicing, or of religious celebration. The Hebrew words used in the Bible mainly describe circular dances and moving lines, the two basic forms of early society. It was the rabbi's or the fiddler's task to invent steps and gestures within these two patterns, to control the people's predilection for spontaneity and the ecstatic expression to which they were prone. With a large crowd on a small dance floor it was the best training ground for the future dancing master.

AMONG the many Jewish dancing masters in northern Italy was Guglielmo Ebreo of Pesaro, whose greatest merit was to have written an important dance manual that not only characterizes the period and its dances but has the distinction of being the work of a great theoretician. He was born about 1440, possibly somewhat earlier. (Neither the date of his birth nor that of his death is quite certain.) But he must have traveled extensively, for he was known to have visited many places on the Italian peninsula. His work, *De praticha seu arte tripudii vulghare opusculum* (*On the Practice of the Com-*

---

† It may strike us as odd that a disproportionate number of world-renowned violinists are of Jewish origin. There can be no doubt that a hereditary thread leads back to the fiddlers in the medieval ghettos.

mon Art of Dancing), must have been used as a textbook by many of the dance masters of the time. This contribution is one of the earliest on which the huge pyramid of theatrical dancing rests.

There is little evidence about Guglielmo's life. We do not know where he came from and what made him settle in Pesaro, a small place on the eastern coast of Italy, or why he sought to perfect himself in the dance. But it is certain that he wandered northward, into the duchy of Milan, to become the pupil of Domenico, who lived in Ferrara, near the river Po, and had made a great name for himself as a dancing teacher in the first half of the century. Guglielmo was accepted and served his apprenticeship, not always easy in those days, involving sacrifices and many menial chores. In his own work Guglielmo referred to himself as the "most devoted disciple and fervent imitator of the distinguished gentleman Mr. Domenico da Ferrara, whose art is that of a virtuoso and an honestly matured dancer,"‡ and many of Domenico's dance compositions can be found in Guglielmo's compilation.

Of course, he was not the only pupil in Ferrara. Antonio Cornazano was there too; he was to become a well-known dance teacher and poet. He also wrote a book on the dance, with the simpler title *Libro dell'arte del danzare* (*Book of the Art of Dancing*), which bears a similar dedication to Domenico, whom they both adored and to whom they apparently owed a great deal. How difficult it is to write on an art as visual and fleeting as the dance was already recognized by Antonio when, after trying to make a dance clear to his readers, he retreated into the statement: "This cannot be well explained unless you are present to make you do it." Although both Guglielmo and Antonio tried their best to give in detail a choreographic technique, their explanations and some expressions they used remain rather obscure in places, but in those days the strangest specification must have been like the reading of a primer. How hard it was to keep the many variations of the dance forms in mind becomes evident through Guglielmo's stress on *memoria* as one of the essential prerequisites of the dancer. But Antonio bragged in his book that he needed to have a dance shown to him only once to be able to repeat it without the slightest mistake.

When Guglielmo left his master, he soon established himself as one who "excelled all men in the dance," and contemporary poets wrote flattering verses on his agility as a dancer and his skill as a musician. Giovanni Mario Filelfo, a well-known poet in his time, composed a long poem in honor and praise of Guglielmo, of which a few lines say:

> *Seeing him dance,*
> *Even Cato would have given up his legendary severity,*
> *While Diana herself would have been seduced by his skill and*
> *grace.*

---

‡ ". . . divotissimo disciepolo e fervente imitatore del diguissimo cavaliere, Messer Domenico da Ferrara, nell'arte del virtuoso et onesto danzare dotissimo . . ."

A man thus praised must have had access to the court of the Medici in Florence, and there can be no doubt about it, since Guglielmo's manuscript included two dances composed by Lorenzo the Magnificent (1449–92). Guglielmo was a familiar figure in other courts of Italy. He must have spent some time in Bologna, for one of his dance compositions reads: *"Alia nominata Caterva composta in Bologna."* Another entry proves that he knew members of the most powerful Roman family, the Colonna, although it is not certain that he ever went to Rome. But one of his famous dances, *Colonnese,* was composed for "Madonna Suena di casa Colonna," a relative of the celebrated poet Vittoria Colonna. In 1463 Guglielmo seemed to have been in Milan, where he was probably baptized as Giovanni Ambrogio— tired of bravely flaunting the epithet "Ebreo" in the face of the nobility and his envious Gentile competitors—and shortly after he was sent to Naples, where he was dancing master to the royal children, teaching them, among other dances, the then fashionable Milanese dance *ballo lombardo,* a forerunner of the famous *galliard.* Undoubtedly, for a longer period of time, Guglielmo lived and worked at Urbino, where Duke Federigo da Montefel-tro (1422–82) kept the most accomplished court in Italy, in which humanism was translated into reality.

Federigo was probably the most perfect representative of the Renaissance and of the self-styled aristocrats of his time. He had the political morality of the condottiere (or the Machiavellian amorality) as far as his "foreign policy" was concerned. But no other ruler of his time was so much beloved by his people, and it is said that he even dared to walk around among his people unprotected—a rarity in the days of the Renaissance. He kept an efficient household in which all had their tasks and all felt secure. His concern for the welfare of his people was so great and so modern in conception that he commissioned persons who were called revisers to travel about his dukedom for no other purpose than to find out the condition in which his people lived, what desires they voiced, and what improvements were necessary.

His palace, though not the most luxurious in Italy, was strictly classical in structure. Federigo prided himself most on his library. To speak of Urbino and not to mention its library was like speaking of Rome without thinking of the Pope. There were two wings. One contained the famous collection of manuscripts, the other printed books. In 1464 the first book was printed in Italy, and it was during the last ten years of his life that Federigo's library gained its reputation. He employed no less than thirty-four transcribers who worked throughout Italy and even went to France to complement his collection of manuscripts. As for his books, the Duke made it a rule that every volume must be bound in crimson and ornamented with silver.

All told, Federigo had between 350 and 500 people on his payroll, also two dancing masters, one of whom was Guglielmo.

Federigo da Montefeltro, duke of Urbino. (Courtesy Alinari/Editorial Photocolor Archives)

The Ducal Palace in Urbino, where the most exemplary Renaissance milieu could be found. (Foto E.N.I.T. Roma. Courtesy Istituto Italiano di Cultura)

GUGLIELMO'S manuscript shows that he was very much concerned with carriage and the general deportment of the dancers. According to Otto Kinkeldey's study *A Jewish Dancing Master of the Renaissance,* Guglielmo advised the young ladies how to conduct themselves:

> Her glance should not be proud nor wayward, gazing here and there as many do. Let her, for the most part, keep her eyes, with decency, on the ground; not however, as some do, with her head sunk on her bosom, but straight up, corresponding to the body, as nature teaches almost of herself. . . . And then at the end of the dance, when her partner leaves her, let her, facing him squarely, with a sweet regard, make a decent and respectful curtsy in answer to his.

Guglielmo's writings on the dance were not lightly undertaken, nor did he see their final aim as a mere compilation of dances and their instruction. Guglielmo tried to cover as much ground as possible; above all, he attempted to explain the fundamentals of dancing.

> Dancing is an action, showing outwardly the spiritual movements which must agree with those measures and perfect concords of harmony which, through our hearing and with earthly joy, descend into one's intellect, there to produce sweet movements which, being thus imprisoned, as it were, in defiance of nature, endeavor to escape and reveal themselves through movement. Which movement of this sweetness and melody, shown outwardly (when we dance) with our person, proves itself to be united and in accord with the singing and with that harmony which proceeds from the sweet and harmonious song or from the measured sound we are listening to.

He thought a great deal of the relation of the dance to music. At that time, music for the dance was based on four *voci principali,* which—like many other things of the time, as for instance the human temperament—were linked with the four elements of earth, air, fire, and water. Properly balanced, Guglielmo says, the four voices of the music fill the ears of the hearers with a most gentle sweetness,

> so that they often stand still and listen. For they are constrained by this sweetness and melody to make some bodily movement, some external demonstration that shows what they feel within. The dance is derived from this melody, as an act demonstrative of its own nature. Without the harmony and consonance the art of dancing would *be* nothing and could *do* nothing.

The teaching of the dances was not always simple. People were used to dancing spontaneously, with steps more or less dictated by the mood of the moment. But now for the first time the dancing teachers aimed at precision, striving for elegance of movement and the memorization of a well-defined vocabulary of steps. Any dance thus performed on a stage, instead of on one of the courtly ballroom floors, would have contained all the elements of theatrical dancing. Guglielmo must have given much thought to coordinating music and dancing, to making dancers more aware of what they heard, and to translating the imageless music into dance figures. He says, for instance:

> Let the dancer try a measure or two against the musical time. If he carries it through, it will afford him much pleasure, will sharpen his intellect, and make him attentive to the music . . . for everything is known and better understood by its contrary.

There were still other, though similar, tests. Particularly to test the beginner, have the dancer start against the time, Guglielmo suggests, and let the musician try to bring him into time. The skilled, of course, will not be confused. Likewise, someone who knows how to dance will keep time, even though the musicians do their best to put him out by every known device. All these tests will show whether or not the dancer has grasped the principles of *misuro:* that is, the ability to keep time.

Guglielmo helped to create a new style with which the foundation was laid for our ballet, a term derived from *balletto,* a diminutive for *ballo,* which in turn was a technical term for all livelier dances in contrast to the low, the *bassa,* dances. He outlined some of the prerequisites for dancers, when he spoke of *misuro* or *memoria,* or *partire del terreno,* the ability to judge the physical limits of the dance floor—briefly, the ability to do the right movement in space.

Guglielmo was probably unaware that he was outlining the basic necessities for the artistic dancer of any time. All he intended was to compose dances for courtly balls.

No time was ever better equipped to give theatrical dance its foundation than the Renaissance in Italy, even though this dance was destined to receive its polished stylization and, later, its baroque beauty in France. But a few little tyrants and self-styled aristocrats turned their social activities into stunning spectacles. Masquerades, mummeries, and pageants had regularly occurred at all levels of society everywhere in the late Middle Ages, but Renaissance nobility refined them and turned them into spectacular shows.

The productions at the interludes during banquets often grew into extravaganzas, with dancing as a focal point of interest. The earliest recorded pageant in London, in 1236, was in celebration of Henry III's marriage to Eleanor of Provence; it was totally dwarfed by the *trionfi* in Florence of the fifteenth century, with Brunelleschi and Leonardo designing visual wonders on floats based on classical models. If Lorenzo de' Medici did not provide some lavish masques, for which he loved to write frivolous songs exuding an unparalleled joy of life, then the guilds would arrange their pageants, the *carri*, with a multitude of people following their floats, symbols of their activities, singing, dancing, and roaming the city until early in the morning. Florence became a particular center of festivities beginning, traditionally, on May Day, with the young dancing in the public squares and filling the streets with boisterous songs and lusty movements. There were tournaments on the Piazza Santa Croce and colorful processions at the least provocation.

The carole or Reigen was the dance that came most naturally to the people, but leaping later became an important part of its performance, giving it more strength than in earlier centuries. Martin Luther referred to it by questioning whether one should step or jump—*ob wir treten oder springen sollen.** Another favorite of the time was the *morisca*, now better known as *morris dance*, done by the common people as much as by the nobility. It was a favorite for two hundred years, having been a part of all festivities between 1450 and 1650, still being danced as a solo by Will Kemp in 1600, when the comedian of Shakespeare's company stunned England with his nine-day morris dance from London to Norwich. His attempt to repeat this feat by dancing across the Alps to Italy ended as a fiasco.

The morisca has an interesting and varied background. *Moresco* was the Spanish name for a Moor who stayed in Spain and was Christianized after the country was partly reconquered by the Spaniards in the thirteenth century, the last Moors being expelled by 1492. Most sources claim that this dance emerged from romantic memories of the Moorish domination. It crystallized in two forms, as a solo and group dance. Its original form consisted of six dancers in two rows, with some having their faces blackened. Sometimes a man was dressed as a fool, a boy as a woman, and another would carry a hobbyhorse with him. All of them were usually costumed in an antic way with many bells around their legs. It was a dance of strength and precision with manly movements, vigorous thrusts, and high leaps. This dance reflected the reawakened strength of Renaissance man, the rekindled joy in his being.

We find the morris dance in a variety of forms, often mutilated and corrupted, in many countries. There is a hobbyhorse dance of the Javanese, and similarities with the Basque *zamalzain* are obvious. We can trace the influence of the morris dance on the French *fêtes des fous*, since masquers everywhere borrowed some of the characteristic features from the morris, with the hobbyhorse and the use of bells most often apparent. Resemblances could still be detected in many interlude entertainments during post-Renaissance banquets. Although the morris dance lost some of its popularity during the seventeenth century, it never died out. It kept its strongholds in England and the United States. Particularly, it has remained a favorite folk dance

---

* Erlanger Ausgabe, 67 Bände: *Schriften, Vorlesungen, Briefe* (1826–57).

with the British people after its revival in 1899, also being known as the English morris dance. Cecil Sharp, the famous folk dance expert, contributed greatly to its popularity. It is now still essentially the same dance as the moresca of the Renaissance days, when, however, it had weightier sociocultural accents.

We may encounter the moresca and other dances in the halls of the upper classes during the Renaissance, but the principal dance was the low dance, or *basse danse,* executed without jumps or any lively movements. Dances have their sociocultural reasons, as, later in the book, will be best demonstrated through the waltz. The basse danse is strongly related to the Renaissance emphasis on the dignity of humankind. The livelier and more vigorous dances, like the *saltarello* and the *piva,* never quite caught the imagination of the Renaissance as did the basse danse—referred to as the queen of the dance—and, whatever their movements, they were constantly combined in different ways and given fancy names, as if they wanted to deny their origin. The two important dances that developed from all this, the *pavane* and galliard, were closely identified with the court dancing characteristic of the sixteenth and seventeenth centuries.

What impresses most is the intensity, the diversity, and the casualness with which people danced until the dancing master brought order and system to their movements. It was not expressive dance in the modern sense that had made the people dance the way they felt. Their dancing was motivated by the need to escape a societal malaise. The dancing master could not remove the malaise or its symptoms, but he gave the ballet de cour its nobility of reason and purity of purpose.

SOME historians are inclined to see the fifteenth century as a period of discouragement and dwindling faith. But what accomplishments were crowded into this century, only comparable to our own! All the memento mori cries fade away in the scope of humanistic awareness that generated a surprising creative power. By some mysterious historic chemistry a revitalization took place and catapulted humanity in a new direction. This rebirth took place as an awakening in the full blaze of light and is perhaps best illustrated by the exclamation of François Rabelais (1490?–1553), the physician who was at heart a satiric writer: "Out of the sick Gothic night our eyes are opened to the glorious touch of the sun!" Seemingly unlimited energy and a burning curiosity drove men and women to the full realization of themselves.

I envision the ideal of this new man as powerful, resourceful, learned, impelled by an insatiable curiosity to experiment, to explore. He was graceful but had not yet lost the heritage of Gothic brutality and cruelty. He modeled himself very consciously upon the people of antiquity, or the way he imagined them to have been. There was, however, one difference: Renaissance man no longer believed in the inevitability of divine decisions, as the

Greeks did; he believed in the inevitability of human nature, which should do for him whatever he chose to do.

He tried to break away from his medieval past and to find the way to the imagined grandeur of antiquity. But he was not a revolutionary in our sense of the word; he did not intend to dethrone God and Christ, substituting for them Zeus and Apollo. To be occupied with antiquity, and its philosophers and writers, was not new at all. But in rediscovering the ancient culture, Renaissance man rediscovered the *humanness* in himself. In asserting the dignity and intrinsic value of man and his joy of being, he unwittingly set man's worldly potentialities against the Christian dogma with its promise of God's mercy after death. Humanity's temporal aspirations promoted the process of secularization. We cannot properly gauge how much Voltaire's and Rousseau's writings contributed to the French Revolution, yet no one doubts that they did. And equally no one can doubt that fifteenth-century humanism did not have its goodly share in preparing the revolutionary Reformation.

In sensing the beauty of his own being in a world of beauty and discovering the godlike power in his hands, Renaissance man pushed all gates open to prove himself, to best his fellows and to glory in his own greatness. Leonardo da Vinci (1452–1519) expressed this irrepressible ambition of his age when he said, "Wretched is the pupil who does not surpass his master!" Leon Battista Alberti (1404–72), that typical Renaissance genius known as *l'uomo universale,* addressed man in these words: "To you is given a body more graceful than other animals, to you power of apt and various movements, to you most sharp and delicate senses, to you wit, reason, memory like an immortal God." It was typical of a Florentine of the early fifteenth century to utter such self-confidence and to be so aware of his gracefully moving body.

Nature was seen in a different light, and through its close study the artist reached out to the expression of an ideal beauty. Curiosity led to experiments, and experiments to knowledge, which gave man a feeling of totality. "The love of anything is the fruit of our knowledge of it, and grows as our knowledge becomes more certain," wrote Leonardo da Vinci, who, in his restless search for the realization of his dreams, became the archetype of modern man.

But it was not merely Renaissance man's eagerness to accumulate knowledge or to enrich his visual power or to enjoy the beauty of life that distinguished him from the Gothic man of the previous centuries. It was this very preoccupation with discovery and experimentation. Fifteenth-century man learned to shake off the yoke of thinking in terms of symbols. He was no longer willing to accept the world as a sacred text which his logic might interpret but in which his heart had to believe.

Exploration and experiment made him become a man of action. It undoubtedly made him a new man who learned to handle experience and to view the world and the universe in a new way. Even though the modern scientific age began in the seventeenth century, it was Renaissance man who initiated it. Suddenly he saw the wonders of the world waiting for him, set sail to find new waterways to the East, and began to discover the world after first stumbling upon America. When Leonardo was young, he clearly expressed what the new age was all about when he jotted this note down: "I wish to work miracles!" The Renaissance did.

The knights were still with us then. Ulrich von Hutten (1488–1523), a gallant soldier and a gallant soul who fought against tyrannical and reactionary forces, taking up the struggle for Martin Luther, attacked obscurantism where he found it and wrote, still in Latin, dialogues à la Lucian, lashing out against all abuses and pretensions of princes. He was a medieval knight in humanist armor. He exuded a fighting spirit with his satires as much as the knights once enjoyed battles for the sake of the battle, but Ulrich's principles and purposes were those of the new man.

The Renaissance ushered in a new world that we may have buried in order to usher in yet another new world. But whatever we may think of then and now, let us echo Ulrich von Hutten's exclamation, so characteristic of his time: *"O saeculum, O literae! juvat vivere!*—O world, O letters! It is a joy to live!"

FROM MANNERISM
TO NEO-CLASSICISM

THE ARTISTIC PERIOD FOLLOWING THE RENAISSANCE, KNOWN AS MAN-nerism, produced, in its own way, works of some artistic magnitude. It was the era in which the commedia dell'arte came into being, a popular enter-tainment enjoyed for more than two hundred years; and the era in which the oldest surviving theater of modern times was built, in the spirit of the Renaissance but already bearing the marks of the beginning Baroque age, a theater with which we have lived happily ever after.

As if this were not enough, erudite gentlemen gathered in Florence in search of the way back to the ancient Greek chorus and—like Columbus wanting to sail to the Indies—discovered a new art form, which was to be-come our opera. And as if this, too, were not enough, on the occasion of a wedding celebration the Parisian court wanted to prove to the world that France was living in peace (which it was not) and that it was rich (which it was also not)—and in the process of proving both, its lavish festivity gave birth to what we know as ballet. What a century the sixteenth was, fathering so much that would give constant joy to humankind for centuries to come while its own time moved through the shadows of a violent religious war! It is worth our while to investigate the many channels leading to such great events.

The beginning of Mannerism is most often dated to Raphael's death in 1520, or Martin Luther's famous words "Here I stand. I can do no other!" on April 18, 1521, with which the irresistible movement of the Reformation started to cast over the world its blood-dyed gloom, which lasted for almost two centuries. Or was it the year of 1530, when Nicolaus Copernicus (1473–1543) circulated the summary of his ideas as a manuscript, ex-pounding his world-shaking heliocentric hypothesis? Or should we go back to 1513, when Niccolò Machiavelli (1469–1527) wrote *Il Principe* (*The Prince*), extolling the double standard and, convinced of human wickedness, issuing passports for free journeys into immorality to all men in power? Or was it when Michel de Montaigne (1533–92), summing up humanist think-ing and expressing a wide scope of contemporary experiences, created an es-sayistic springboard from which several generations of thinkers could take off?

Montaigne must be mentioned at the very outset of discussing this vital century. In saying that "every man carries in himself the entire form of the human state," he realized the free-flowing interactions between the manifold forces and forms of life to which the artist feels compelled to respond in a variety of ways. In bridging Renaissance learning and a new spirit of critical approach to questions of widely different significance, he injected a note of disillusionment, with emphasis on doubt and the contradictory nature of truth. "It is a thorny undertaking," he said in his *Essais,* "and more so than it seems, to follow such a wandering motion as that of our mind; to penetrate the dark depths of its innermost recesses; to choose and fix all the faint stirrings of its movements."

The sixteenth was not an easy century to live in. But which is? It was probably more exciting and challenging than many another period of transition. The wars of religion evoked a new specter of senseless self-destruction in the name of God. While this has not been a new experience for Europeans, the wars of Reformation and Counter-Reformation, with the Roman Inquisition established in 1542 to combat Protestantism, made life extremely hazardous.

In his *Civilisation,* Kenneth Clark stated that the age of Mannerism abandoned the belief "in the decency and high destiny of man that had been achieved in the Renaissance. Play it for kicks: that is the mannerist motto. . . . What could an intelligent, open-minded man do in mid-sixteenth-century Europe? Keep quiet, work in solitude, outwardly conform, inwardly remain free." Was to play "the intellectual recluse" really the only way out for Mannerists such as Torquato Tasso and Lope de Vega, or such outstanding figures as Shakespeare, Spenser, Marlowe, Francis Bacon and Walter Raleigh, those men of the brilliant Elizabethan Age, which, after all, was the most magnificent postscriptum to the Mannerism of the Renaissance? "No pleasure hath any savour unless I can communicate it," Montaigne said, and this statement is also quoted by Kenneth Clark. For so many intellectual recluses, the era of Mannerism was very articulate.

THE Renaissance was a period of prevailing optimism in believing in one's strength as a part of the greater order of things, of the divine harmony holding together the world that was thought to be the center of the universe, with the human race the privileged creatures of God, chosen, as none other, to imitate him in the act of creation. Then suddenly an assault on human beliefs, intellect, and senses came from all sides and spheres of activity during the sixteenth century. Suddenly there were two sides to the great truth that was God, and people fought and died for one of these truths. The outside world was shattered; people were either fanatics or lost without guidance in spiritual chaos. Belief in oneself was taken away, and the artist felt forced to reorient his artistic concepts as well as his entire vision of life.

One consequence was a flight into cynicism and satire; another, a recourse to critical evaluations. For the first time in history the desire to talk about the arts and the artist seemed more fascinating than the process of creation itself. This was the birth of art criticism and also of a character later so well acted by Dr. Johnson's Boswell and Goethe's Eckermann—the literary echo of greatness. Giorgio Vasari (1511–74) was the first art reviewer who wielded a frightening power by giving artistic and aesthetic value judgments. His critical evaluations of the Renaissance artists turned out to be the first best-selling book of its kind.

Another prototype of this era was Pietro Aretino (1492–1556) who, as a satiric writer, translated the Machiavellian principles into his life and art. Aretino, living by uncanny instincts and a merciless wit, once boasted:

> I am a free man. I do not need to copy Petrarch or Boccaccio. My own genius is enough. Let others worry themselves about style and so cease to be themselves. Without a master, without a model, without a guide, without artifice, I go to work and earn my living, my well-being and my fame. What do I need more? With a goose quill and a few sheets of paper I mock the universe.

Scorning society in his plays and epistles, he profited from people's weakness and corruption. He lived, as he put it, "on sweat of black ink." Popes, princes, and artists feared the power of his pen, and many were blackmailed with exposure of their private lives. He by far outdid Vasari as a gossip columnist, being the world's first yellow journalist. He is said to have died laughing too vehemently about a bawdy joke. It was the death best fitting the man who was the archetype of the bohemian and the greatest erotic sonneteer of all time.

The Age of Mannerism, with its exuberant use of images and metaphors, also created such types as Benvenuto Cellini (1500–71), who still had the daring of the Renaissance without the lofty purpose of its art. His statues of Perseus and Narcissus show him still to be the master of the human figure but no longer of its grandeur. There is an elongation here, a mannerism there. To him the human shape was an ideal form that one ought to appreciate, and some of this feeling could be noticed in the use of the body—however richly costumed it may have been—in the first attempts at choreography later in the century. But as a craftsman, Cellini cheapened the experience of the human shape by utilitarian purposes—by expanding the trend of embellishing door knockers, candelabra, forks, and knives with representations of the nude. Popularization of an idea seemingly goes hand in hand with a cheapening of taste and artistic vision. In Cellini's days people began to enjoy cutting their food or knocking at doors while fingering the figure of Venus.

Cellini lived and wrote about his life with many asides and with quite some flourish. He dictated his story (to a fourteen-year-old boy), by which

means it gained vividness and immediacy. Cellini, it seems, was a knave. Or was he the modern version of a medieval knight? He had a tumultuous zest for life; he was an adventurer who wallowed in excesses of self-satisfaction, no matter whether he stabbed someone in a brawl or indulged in endless wrangles with his patrons. Pope Paul III said of Cellini, "Men like Benvenuto, unique in their profession, stand above the law." And Francis I, king of France, when shown the model of Cellini's famous saltcellar, exclaimed, "The man is a wonder! He should never lay down his tools." In fact, Cellini never laid down his tools or his sword.

Yes, he was a knave and played with dreams of the past and the specter of the knight, or its modernized version with Renaissance veneer. It was the time when a revival of medievalism in literature made a strong show. Cervantes' creation of Don Quixote was the answer to it. And Don Quixote was only one of a few archetypes which were then born and with which we have lived ever since. With the renewed interest in medievalism, the figure of Dr. Faustus became popular (Marlowe wrote his version about 1592); its allegoric manifestation has haunted us as much as has the fictitious figure of Don Juan, who may have had a folkloric background until he received the stamp of literariness from the Spanish dramatist Tirso de Molina in *The Rake of Seville*. Erroneously thought of as a figure of libertinism, Don Juan, like Hamlet, is characteristic of the philosophy of that age and ours: both antiheroes. Don Juan's needs are deeply neurotic, his conquests forced upon by his imaginative and searching intellect. It is never the woman he longs for—as is the case with Casanova, who drowns boredom and despair in the carnal act—but the dream of the woman. Don Juan symbolizes man's self-imposed challenge to the world of his imagination and its limitation. A perfect post-Renaissance figure! And so is Hamlet. As Mark Van Doren said, "he is a soul in agitation," a noble man whose thoughts are lost in the turmoil of a time no longer attuned to itself.

No artist in any period creates in total freedom. Certainly the artist is directed by a mysterious inner force, but also by factual experiences and outside events. However, it is just as important to say that certain artists have always anticipated these changes, which would later have shaped their work. Even before Copernicus tried to make humanity believe that it is not the center of the universe and Luther taught us that the individual and not the Church mattered, Jacopo da Pontormo (1494–1557) started Mannerism in Florence. He did so gradually and before the impact of the rebellious thoughts could have been felt in Italy. Already by 1518 he had completed an altarpiece that no longer shows harmonic balance in form and content. In the grouping and the gestures he developed an agitation and emo-

Benvenuto Cellini: "Narcissus." (Courtesy Alinari/Editorial Photocolor Archives)

tionalism that became more and more outspoken. The changes that took place in conception and expressiveness led, on the one hand, to a point of distortion beautifully exemplified by El Greco and, on the other hand, to a delightful and sophisticated art, as Cellini proves.

In the sixteenth century the artist lost patience with such great ideals as self-discipline and self-control. The insecurity caused by political and religious upheavals created a heightened nervous sensibility leading to what today we would call anxiety. In his desire to step out of self-imposed classical ideas, the artist became bolder, more worldly, even in his religious themes, in paintings as well as in the morality plays like *Everyman,* which appeared in many versions in various European countries between 1495 and 1520. Already remote from the mystery and miracles plays, *Everyman* had realistic features. Although still religious in theme, it had all the necessary worldly and rebellious connotations of the time. As a sermon, allegorical of "every creature," its leading character is, for the first time, cast as the representative of a social class: a wealthy man.

There is no simple formula for the age that followed the Renaissance and found the realization of new truths. Mannerism was an age in which everything seemed to exist with its opposite. We have only to recall that Michelangelo Buonarroti (1475–1564) was a contemporary of Cellini and wrote a laudatory sonnet to Aretino in self-defense. Was he in any way a giant of lesser stature than Leonardo or other Renaissance figures? He simply followed—without being conscious of searching for a new expression—the inner law of time. His "David" (1501–4) still emerged as a figure of classic Renaissance ideals. But his explosive personality could not remain within the confines of restful serenity. When he painted the Sistine Chapel (which was finished in 1512), he already anticipated a new age. The eloquent energy and grandiose torsions of the bodies show the interplay of muscles as no one had observed and re-created since the Greeks. This was not only a work of supernatural beauty; it was of a rare dramatic—let us unashamedly use the word *theatrical*—power. Take only the one moment of the Creation, the divine hand as the central focus of the drama of Creation, and Adam's hand: a cathartic moment of dramatic magnitude, as if Michelangelo could foresee the longing of the age for theatrical expression.

Jacopo da Pontormo: one of the creators of Florentine Mannerism. His emotionalism, a departure from the High Renaissance, seems strongest in his religious paintings, as the example of his "Madonna and Child with Two Saints" proves. (Courtesy Istituto Italiano di Cultura)

The Players Are the Thing

THE TRAGEDIES AND COMEDIES WRITTEN AND PERFORMED DURING THE Renaissance and far into the Age of Mannerism owed a debt to the Roman playwrights. The triumph of humanism during the fifteenth century did not set on fire the imagination and dramatic inventiveness of the Renaissance poets. In their struggle with the rules of the unities and in their attempts to emulate the paragons of classicism, these writers failed; their dramatic works were doomed to remain stylized poetry with no dramatic life onstage. These plays lingered on for some time and found a highly select audience at some courts, in particular the one at Ferrara, which fostered the elegant classic drama and for which—the exception to prove the rule—the gifted Lodovico Ariosto wrote.

Early in the sixteenth century a growing impatience was felt with the flood of words that were alien to life, even at the halls of those courts where plays were staged. It was an elite theater for the elite. The actors were courtly amateurs who preferred Seneca to Sophocles and who had a condescending attitude toward everything theatrical. What they indulged in was more declamation than acting. It was medieval theater with a touch of learned humanism. It was called the *commedia erudita,* and it was erudite, no doubt, but amateurishly written and performed.

How about the populace? The mystery plays for so long enacted in the churches, the *sacre rappresentazioni,* became of less interest than the morality plays that were shown, in medieval fashion, on platforms in marketplaces. As was still the case in France since the Middle Ages, interlude players with crude little farces were seen in public squares, where pantomimes and jugglers mingled with them.

What were the sources of the players who developed into the strongest and most influential theatrical force in Europe for two hundred years? There had been rustic entertainments all along, the tenor of which was rough and merry, full of extemporaneous pranks and quite a bit of improvised dancing. Interest in the old Roman pantomime and in many features of the ancient Phlyakes and Atellan farces remained alive in Italy. These popular and down-to-earth entertainments of olden times were revived in the new street theater that came into being about midway in the century and was known as commedia dell'arte, or rather *commedia all'improvviso,* as it was called originally.

What began to develop in Italy was a unique experiment of a theater for

Painting by an unknown Flemish artist depicting a scene of the commedia dell'arte with the figure of Innamorata holding the spotlight. (Courtesy the Author)

theater's sake, completely divorced from literature. The old Roman farces worked with stock characters, easily identifiable by the audience; and so did the commedia. The players wore masks, mostly half-masks, further typifying their characters. The Atellan farces of Campania, like the Etruscan form of comedy, delighted in improvisations. The commedia in the sixteenth century was exclusively based on improvisation. After all, improvisation has been the lifeblood of the comedian from Will Kemp in Shakespeare's company to our days. No lines were given the players to study; all they had to go by was a brief scenario telling them of entrances and exits, with short instructions of what should or could happen in each scene. Each player knew a few stereotype phrases fitting his role, but they were their own authors and had to invent their lines while onstage. For instance, a scenario would indicate that Brighella and Pedrolino would have a scene together:

> Enter Brighella, from the sea after shipwreck which he describes. Enter Pedrolino from the other side, not noticing Brighella and telling the same story of his miraculous rescue and the loss of his comrades. They suddenly bump into each other on stage and make

the *lazzi* [slapstick antics] of fear. Then they touch one another, realizing that they both have been saved.

I have used the word *player* and not *actor* because they were musicians, actors, fencers, jugglers, and accomplished dancers, besides being their own dramatists and, as such, of no slight education. The essence of their performance did not lie in the telling of a story (which usually revolved around the burlesque theme of cuckoldry), but in the fun of farcical movement and stage trickery. The ability to move and express through gestures an entire register of emotions was basic to their profession. And professionals they were, long before Shakespeare and his actors excelled them by having profited from their example. Although all their players were trained comedians, every company had two or more Zannis (buffoons). Their *lazzi*—farcical interludes—were rarely verbal; most of the time they were physical tricks, ranging from grimaces to acrobatics.

The man who brought this movement into being—or at least the first of whom we know—was the playwright and actor Angelo Beolco. His stage name, significantly, was Il Ruzzante ("the one who tumbles and rolls around"). Together with a band of actors, he performed an improvised comedy in 1528. While the Renaissance was losing the chastity of classic form and embracing a playful artistic attitude, more than one company of players was probably experimenting with improvised comedy; the distinct consolidation of this genre can safely be dated shortly after 1550, when the first great companies were recognized as having established a new theatrical form.

Besides the typed players whom every commedia company employed, there were usually four actors engaged who took the parts of the lovers. Although the commedia kept away from the artificiality of its time and was the most earthbound artistic phenomenon of Mannerism, these four lovers were dressed either like the nobility or as shepherds and nymphs, recalling the arcadian world, a favorite escape of the time. These lovers were used as a social counterpoint to the robust world of the commedia players. They came straight from the pastoral romances and, in making up their speeches, they helped themselves by memorizing Petrarchan sonnets. They rarely relied on dance patterns and pantomime.

As in the morality plays, there were a few noteworthy social features about this new popular theater. Soon the lifeless, dull *commedia erudita* with its "closet atmosphere," as Allardyce Nicoll said, with "a preciousness, a smell of wax candle . . . heavy with perfume . . . stiff with brocade," had to give way to the commedia players, who were often invited to entertain the feudal lords and the nobility at court and castles. It was a brave new make-believe world which, for the first time, had women acting and dancing onstage, a revolutionary gesture in those days. More than a gesture were the commedia players' allusions to the social injustices, echoing the peasant revolts. Whether they played on the streets or at castles, they never hesitated to juxtapose well-to-do and learned types with the little man and his need to live by his wits in order to survive. In their plays it was always Harlequin, or Brighella and Columbine, the types on the lowest social scale, who inadvertently triumphed over Pantalone, Il Dottore, and Il Capitano. Thus it was the commedia dell'arte that introduced the clever servant types that we find in many plays of the seventeenth and eighteenth centuries, culminating in Beaumarchais' Figaro.

What marvels those performances must have been, marvels of pantomime and drama, music and grimaces, of verbal pirouettes, of somersaults of body and mind, perfection of foolishness, with the body speaking before the tongue could find the poetry of nonsense, kicking up the heels while looking for the lightning of a wild gesture to draw the caricature of a well-known man or thing or idea! And to complete this, all of a sudden Cantarina appears in the role of a dancer who is not in the scenario at all and presents a kind of musical intermezzo.

After its long life of about two hundred years the commedia dell'arte had to go the way of all make-believe. But the types it created have never died. Columbine, without a mask in order to show her pretty face, became, ever more refined, the soubrette in nineteenth-century operettas. Falstaff has many features of that braggart soldier Il Capitano, whom the commedia borrowed from Plautus' Miles Gloriosus and to whom it gave a Neapolitan mask. Or have we surfeited ourselves with old Pantalone, the cuckold figure of the *opera buffa* and of so much that has become drama and literature? Or take Il Dottore, the pedant, who appears in many disguises in Shakespeare's and Molière's plays, a type at whom nonintellectual audiences loved to laugh because they also saw in him the courtly bore. Who does not know the sentimentalized Pierrot, who once was Pedrolino? Endless are the metamorphoses of the main type Arlecchino, who lives with us in daily life as much as onstage in innumerable different masks; they may have changed in their makeup, and with it in their psyche behind the mask, but essentially it is the same Harlequin with the same or similar *lazzi*, pantomiming the wildest absurdities, evoking and conquering invisible obstacles, from Pagliaccio to Charlie Chaplin, from the early comedians in the silent movies to Marcel Marceau and every mime and clown in circuses all over the world.

THE commedia dell'arte was also called *commedia non scritta,* the unwritten comedy. But it was most often spoken of as the *commedia delle maschere,* the masked comedy. The player's mask characterized him as an easily recognizable type. In contrast to the mask of antiquity or of the East, the commedia mask was a half-mask, made of thin leather, leaving the mouth free and enough of the face for expressive grimaces.

The player of the commedia is unthinkable without a mask because it

Venetian maskers, after a painting by Pietro Longhi (1702–85), "Carnival in Venice." (Courtesy French Cultural Services)

gave him the strength of his own conviction, the power to believe in himself as Pantalone or Il Dottore beyond the immediate reality of being an actor who improvised. He needed the illusion of becoming in order to convey the illusion of being what he pretended to be. Briefly, the reality of a larger reality created for him the world in which he could do the most unrealistic things and make them believable.

The player's mask not only announced the character he was; it determined his movement language as it did the lines that would fit his type. Wearing a mask made it imperative that his gestures and body movements should be meaningful and evocative. Harlequin's black mask goes back to the ancient satiric plays in which poverty-stricken servants, thieves and panderers, or foreign slaves had to blacken their faces with soot. Pulcinella's grotesque mask was characterized by a huge hooked nose. Il Dottore wore either a black or a flesh-colored mask covering only his forehead and nose. Red spots on his cheeks and a short, pointed beard—which Pantalone also often wore—completed his mask. Add the characteristic costuming and the actor's dialect, and the audience could instantly identify him.

The commedia players knew how to attract audiences. If they were daring enough to have women onstage, then Columbine, Inamorata, and Cantarina wore no masks, the prerequisite for their roles being a winning personality and a beautiful face. Sometimes they sported a tiny black velvet mask, called a *loup*. But *loups* were then the fashion for ladies and can therefore hardly be considered a stage mask. Most ladies were seen on the streets in such masks; they wore them at home when receiving guests or when visiting, since they were a part of their dress or makeup; these masks enhanced, through the contrast with their skin, the ladies' complexion and added a touch of mystery to their coquetries.

It is interesting that masking and disguising should have played such a vital part in the life of an era keyed to individuality and the spirit of personal daring. The mask was associated with excitement, danger, and escape. In feudal Europe, but especially during the Renaissance, masking and mumming had serious as well as playful connotations. If you wanted to be incognito, you put on a mask. It was part of the social game and its conventions that you were seen but not recognized when hiding behind a mask. Wearing it, your incognito had to be respected. Masked, Romeo could enter the house of the Capulets and dance with Juliet. Everyone, even the Nurse, knew it was Romeo, the son of the hated Montagues, but Tybalt could not challenge him as long as he remained masked.

How does one explain the staying power of the mask? It began with early people's desire for transformation. Playfulness was added to it much later. To conceal human identity, to shake off corporeal existence in order to communicate with unknown powers, early people felt they had to wipe out their countenance. Since the spirit was thought of as living in the face, primitive people put on an artificial face, admitting with it another spirit. The animal masks were among the first and most logical images and disguises and they never lost their imaginative hold. They played a leading role in the festivals of Dionysus from which the Greek theater emerged.

There was rarely any early dancing without the use of a mask. Dancing was a ritualistic, compulsive manifestation of a way of life. Early people perceived rhythm as a constant phenomenon of nature and felt rhythm to be locked within them. They unlocked it on all possible occasions and for all decisive activities: birth and initiation, fertility and marriage, war and victory, harvest and hunting, healing the sick and exorcising evil spirits. Rarely could they do without masks. But in contrast to dancing, the creation of masks was a conscious act, executed in full awareness of rudimentary aesthetic principles. It was the first human attempt to give shape and meaning to mysterious visualizations, to reach beyond the ordinary for something of which people were only vaguely aware. Mystic and magic forces, often gaining demonic strength, played into the mask-makers' hands, and the mask was the first instance in the spiritual growth of humankind in which the synthesis of idea and matter reached an artistic form.

Mysticism and magic have remained vital powers behind the making and wearing of masks to this very day, as we find proved in the folklore of many peoples and their folk festivals, such as May Day and the Twelfth Night of Christmas, in the mummers' plays of England and in the *Fasnacht* (carnival) festivities in Switzerland. Much of the mystery in connection with the mask and ritualistic feelings is evoked by death. The mask is our most accomplished visual realization of our twofold existence: of day and night, wakefulness and sleep, life and death, the live and rigid face. The essentially immobile and unchangeable aspect of the mask—the face that lives without living—indicates that one of its original and strongest connotations has always been with death.

The mysterious spirit of the mask can be suppressed and diverted, but never silenced. Our century was destined to rediscover the inherent qualities of the mask, with Picasso's Congo masks and cubism, Hugo Ball and Dadaism, Mary Wigman's expressionistic dancing; with Oskar Schlemmer's Bauhaus experiments, Erick Hawkins's mystical earthboundness, and Alwin Nikolais' full-bodied masks in total theatrical function. Should we not link the reappearance of the mask to the first cataclysmic experiences in this century, to what preceded and followed it?

Death, devil, and fool—the most common symbols of medieval days— were realistically masked to stimulate and cater to certain images of the imagination. Death and devil remained recurring allegorical figures in the morality plays, and the devil never failed to appear fantastically costumed, usually in a grotesque animal mask. The great variety of intermezzi during the banquets, the carnival festivals, and outdoor pageants, all featured men and women masked.

The mask had a great vogue in those days. Something seriously meaningful becomes, in the wearing of it, a conventionalized and finally playful thing. Johan Huizinga, in his investigation of *Homo ludens,* pointed out how "in play . . . the distinction between belief and make-believe breaks down. The concept of play merges quite naturally with that of holiness." It does so with any experience that leaves its mark on us. The extravagance and playful trends in the era of Mannerism were ready-made phenomena to further the use of the mask.

For the next two centuries the mask was still in fashion, as a convenience, as a contrivance, in the streets, in the dancing halls, in the theaters, at all festivities. This lasted, characteristically enough, as long as the commedia dell'arte. In the 1760s the encyclopedists and with them the choreographer Jean Georges Noverre and the composer Christoph Willibald Gluck succeeded in stopping this fad. Playwright Carlo Goldoni, fighting along with them, wrote:

> Comedies without masks are always more natural and pithy. The mask always interferes with the actor's performance whether he be interpreting joy or sorrow . . . he always has the "leather" face. He may gesticulate and change his tone as often as he will, he can never communicate by the expression of his face the passions that rend his soul. . . . Nowadays the actor is required to have "soul," and the soul beneath the mask is as fire beneath ashes. That is why I conceived the idea of reforming the masks of the Italian comedy and replacing farces by comedies.

The Palladian Dream

THE THEATER BUILDING AS WE KNOW IT WAS SLOW IN DEVELOPING. THE medieval concept of a platform with its mansions or a scenic decoration built on floats was still quite common in the first half of the sixteenth century. The earliest English theater was copied from the courtyard of an inn, since the strolling actors were accustomed to such a surrounding. In France the earliest theater was modeled on a tennis court, for the same reason. The entire space was long and narrow, like most halls in the castles where the ballet de cour was at home and where sometimes plays were shown. The hall usually had a shallow platform at one end, which was, like a stage, decorated with as many mansions as needed. It was a limited space and as badly crowded for productions as once the chancel of the church was in the days of the mystery or, later, the miracle plays.

As with almost everything else, it was left to the Renaissance genius of the Italians to develop the physical image of our theater. We find its rudimentary beginnings in the cities of Rome and Ferrara, Venice and Bologna. Contemporary accounts describe the scenic devices in the courtyards. Such a setting usually consisted of a back wall composed of a few columns sup-

The erudite Renaissance theater was still based on the medieval system of the mansions. This woodcut, published in Lyons in 1493, shows a comic scene from a Terence play. (Courtesy French Cultural Services)

porting a number of arches. The spaces between the columns could be closed and opened by means of curtains behind which were tiny rooms, some with rear windows. It was still a poorly devised stage, with a touch of medievalism.

The event foreshadowing the great changes to come was the discovery in about 1484 of the ten volumes of Marcus Vitruvius Pollio's *De Architectura.* Little is known about Vitruvius the man, except that he was an architect who was born in the first century B.C. and lived through the era of Augustus. His book deals with building and city planning. With his Hellenistic approach, he tried to preserve the classical tradition. We can imagine how hungry the humanists of the quattrocento were for any bit of genuine information from beyond the Middle Ages. Vitruvius' book immediately became the Bible of the intellectual and artist. The tremendous progress that had been made in painting had heightened visual awareness, and in the same way in which the Petrarch wave caused everyone to write the greatest trivia in sonnet form, it became a parlor game of the intelligentsia to dabble in architectural design.

One should not sneer at all outbursts of dilettantism. We ought to be glad that people through so many decades endured their sonneteers so that Michelangelo and Shakespeare could give us the treasures of their thought in this poetic form. This is how history labors. The dilettante as architect finaly led to an Andrea Palladio (1508–80) and a Sebastiano Serlio (1475–1554).

Serlio first worked in Rome until it was sacked by the Spaniards in 1527. He fled to Venice, where he worked on his treatise *Architettura,* which he published in various parts between 1537 and 1547. Through it he is proved to have been a great student of classicism. He followed Vitruvius in providing scenic designs for three types of plays: comedy, tragedy, and the satiric or bucolic play. The scene for the tragedy was a street lined with lofty palaces and a statue above an arch in the rear; the houses for the comedy were of bourgeois style, with the house of a courtesan in the foreground. (In those days one would not dare to insinuate that a nobleman might ever be found there.) The satiric scene had the expected sylvan feeling, being full of trees, groves, and cottages on both sides of a stony path in the center. All this was painted on a backcloth in fine perspective at the end of a raked stage. As obvious and simple as these set designs may seem to us, they had the possible greatest influence on the European theater until the beginning of the eighteenth century.

They were more basic than revolutionary. Inigo Jones followed and perfected them in his sets for masques. The commedia dell'arte and all drama of the following two centuries were influenced by them. In Molière's and Lully's time, scenic designers still had to use them as guidelines. More than this, Serlio's threefold concept seemed to have forced the ballet to move along the same tracks, holding on to the "serious dance," the "comical dance," and the "pastoral." It was at the end of the seventeenth century that Louis XIV's choreographer, Pierre Beauchamp, tried to break away from this straitjacket and the painfully symmetrical patterns of the dance figures, which were the balletic echo of the rigidity of the pseudoclassic style then embraced by Corneille and Racine.

Compared to the erratic change of trends in our own time, any development then seemed hesitant in flowering into new directions. However decisive Serlio's contribution was, it still made use of the multiple setting known in the Middle Ages, which he classicized. The action onstage was still outdoors, taking place in front of the backcloth.

After Serlio had had his say, the physical image of the theater had not yet changed decisively, and it did not do so until Palladio, after a very long and successful career as an architect, received the assignment, late in 1579, to build a theater for the Accademia Olimpica in Vicenza. By then Palladio had designed and built many villas, palaces, and churches. He had called Vitruvius "my sole master and guide" when he wrote *I quattro libri dell'architettura* (*The Four Books of Architecture*), giving generations after generations of architects a manual which, to them, was the alpha and omega. This book contained clear and concise descriptions of his thoughts and rules, with most expressive plates drawn by the author, and was reissued several times.

When the academy in Vicenza decided to have a permanent theater built, Palladio felt that his selection as architect was an honor and the greatest challenge of his life. All he tried and accomplished so far ought to be crowned by this task. He wanted to restore antiquity in its purest form, but he always intended to fuse the forms of antiquity with the functions of modern life. He had taught the world by his example how easy it is—perhaps he made it look too easy—to make a new house appear as if it were an ancient temple, with many steps leading up to classical columns. The entire building would be placed on a high pedestal; there was a portico crowned with a triangular pediment and a few statues atop. Was the basic concept of his architecture really only symmetry, monumentality, and the skillful use of classical form? By the mid-sixteenth century Palladio had achieved a final wedding of antiquity with the needs of a time to come. It was a classic revival, but one that did more than evoke the past. With all its illusions, it showed the way for the grand gesture and Baroque theatricality. Some maintain that Palladio was the first step into the Baroque. And in even further distance his work cleared the way for Palladianism, for which he can be unjustly blamed, for the eighteenth-century architectural explosion à la

Title page of Book I of Sebastiano Serlio's famous book on architecture and scenic design, 1545. (Courtesy French Cultural Services)

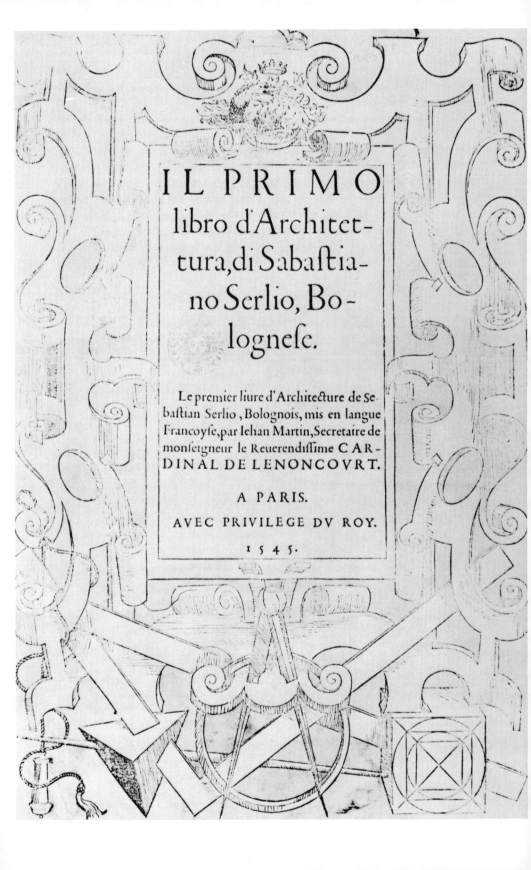

IL PRIMO

libro d'Architet-
tura, di Sabaſtia-
no Serlio, Bo-
logneſe.

Le premier liure d'Architecture de Se-
baſtian Serlio , Bolognois, mis en langue
Francoyſe, par Iehan Martin, Secretaire de
monſeigneur le Reuerendiſſime CAR-
DINAL DE LENONCOVRT.

A PARIS.

AVEC PRIVILEGE DV ROY.

1545.

Palladio and the Victorian errors that made every bank look like a Greek temple in a renewed revival of antiquity.

There were phases of gradual growth in Palladio's life. He journeyed to Rome. Seeing the past in its historical perspective and never losing sight of the reality that was the environment of his time, he early envisioned the scope of his calling. Central to his lifelong endeavor was the reconciliation of past and present. He may have best achieved it in the last phase of his life, in Venice. There he was charged with building churches. In his design of the Teatro Olimpico he came closest to the ideal of a Roman theater. It had unchangeable scenery, with forestage and proscenium compressed into a single architectural unit and a narrow acting area closely adjoining the auditorium.

Villa Rotonda near Vicenza is a characteristic design by Palladio. (Courtesy Istituto Italiano di Cultura)

Since his first great success with the Basilica in Vicenza, he had received many commissions. He always kept in mind practical issues such as the best materials and lowest costs. Whatever problems he tackled, whether designing trussed bridges—with which he was centuries ahead of his time—or inventing means to draw water from low places, he proved that idealism can be linked to realism. It was characteristic of his Renaissance character that he could absorb Mannerist motifs without losing the feeling for classic repose, balance, and order. The dualism of dream and reality, the wedding of aspirations to requirements, was strongest when he designed villas.

In the cinquecento, cities were growing with the increasing exploitation of commerce and craftsmanship. The idea of owning a villa outside the city became a realistic Arcadia, the "weekend" dream of the rich and their desire

The interior of the Teatro Olimpico at Vicenza. (Courtesy Istituto Italiano di Cultura)

to return to nature. Of all the Italian cities, Venice had become the richest and most powerful. The *Serenissima Repubblica* encouraged the building of villas but not of castles, of whose warlike menace the town fathers were afraid. To own a villa became the rage, and since there were many wealthy people in Venice the banks of the river Brenta and the entire province were studded with villas. The nobles from Venice, Padua, and Vicenza spent their free time and the hot summer months in the country. *Villeggiatura,* the Italian word for vacationing, is derived from *villa.* The rich and noble people lived a life of leisure there, with walks and hunting dominating. But they also brought with them their conversation, and their love of music and the dance.

Palladio was a master at building those villas, and their frescoes show the many amusements of those lords and ladies. These amusements seem to have been far more serene than those in the late seventeenth and eighteenth centuries in France, when everything began with a dancing gesture and ended with frivolity. Palladio's classical vision of his villas created the frame for the function of humanistic leisure. His architectural aim was to create an upward feeling, elevation in the truest sense of the word, for the enjoyment of the spirit. Height was emphasized at the expense of width; even the villas themselves were raised on a high pedestal. It was a symbol of Renaissance loftiness.

When Palladio was commissioned to build the Teatro Olimpico he had the wisdom of experience. He felt an inner readiness to resurrect the greatness achieved by antiquity: in fact, to continue where it had had to stop. He felt that "this blessed theater, in which I have made penitence for all the sins that I have committed or shall commit," would be the culmination of his creative genius. He could not realize that, after having finished the design and started to build the theater in 1580, he would no longer be able to commit any sins, artistically or otherwise. After his death, his disciple and admirer Vincenzo Scamozzi finished the building according to Palladio's plans. The physical image of the theater, as we know it, thus began in Vicenza.

Italian Genius in France

THE ITALIANS OF THE RENAISSANCE PROVED TO BE NOT ONLY GREAT HU-manists and artists, but also good business people. In the fifteenth and sixteenth centuries, Venice had accumulated great wealth from which the visual arts and the opera were to profit for centuries to come. All seaports gained in importance through the discoveries of lands soon to become colonies. Because of its central position in Europe, Italy had long enjoyed a flourishing business; by the mid-sixteenth century, profiting from the ships of the overseas trading companies going back and forth, it also became a place of lively speculation, of investment in ships with their cargoes and insurance. Companies offered the public unheard-of opportunities to participate in their enormous profits, and the moneylenders and the insurance business became very important features of commerce.* It was the time when modern capitalism was fully established and when, next to princes of the Church and of the world, finance capital became the third world power.

For a long time Italians felt strong enough to war among one another, princes against princes and Popes against both—while flourishing spiritually. Italy's wealth in finance and culture attracted the interest of the powerful nations surrounding it. Invasions of Spaniards, French, and Austrians were as innumerable as they were confusing, one power aiming at restoring or ruining the other or strengthening its might through intermarriage. Enmities, usurpation, and treacheries were, at times, of Shakespearean magnitude; nevertheless, all this warring was on a relatively smaller scale than we might imagine. While this political power game went on and great parts of Italy were dominated by foreign rulers, the Italian princes continued to preside over their courts, had beautiful buildings erected, and cultivated the arts.

During the late Middle Ages and the Renaissance, the French rulers strengthened their political potential and France developed into a center of Western civilization. The French had created treasures in Gothic architecture and sculpture. By the sixteenth century, with such minds as François Rabelais, Pierre de Ronsard, and Michel de Montaigne leading a host of other writers, a cultural awakening of ever-growing intensity foreshadowed France's cultural domination over several centuries. With an overriding ambition, the French were out to excel all other nations in the elegance of their language, in the grandeur of their court life, in the brilliance of their creative minds and artists—all converging in the creation of *la grande nation.*

The French, whenever invading parts of Italy, were skillful in taking with them, as loot, men of arts and letters. When the maréchal de Brissac, comte de Secondigny, conquered Milan in 1554, he found many extraordinary dancing masters there and induced Cesare Negri, among others, to come with him to Paris. The same campaign yielded another brilliant move on the

---

* Marlowe's *Jew of Malta* and Shakespeare's *Merchant of Venice* were sociologically conditioned plays. Shylock's antagonist, Antonio, is a romantically conceived character and totally unrealistic as a sixteenth-century businessman. Every merchant in Europe was accepting interest, which he refused to take. All continental shippers were insuring their cargoes at the rate of 10 to 15 percent, but Antonio sent out all his ships with precious cargo uninsured. Shakespeare may have needed such an all-innocent character as a dramatic counterpoint. The figure of Antonio nevertheless proves what a thriving business the discoveries brought about.

part of De Brissac when he spotted, among the band of dancers and musicians headed by the dancing master Pompeo Diobono, a violinist by the name of Baldassarino da Belgiojoso.

A CASE of intermarriage resulted in serious influence on the cultural scene. Lorenzo de' Medici, duke of Urbino and grandson of Lorenzo the Magnificent, had married Madeleine de La Tour d'Auvergne of the house of Bourbon. Their daughter Caterina (1519–89), or Catherine de Médicis, was married to the duc d'Orléans at the age of fourteen, and at the age of twenty-eight she became queen consort when her husband became Henri II. All her life—she survived three kings, two of them her sons, and was regent for some years—she strove to keep the warring factions in France, the Guises and Huguenots, from stirring up a civil war. Ultimately this was unavoidable. She was a Catholic herself, but in no way militant, and succeeded a couple of times in arranging peace with the Huguenots. But all failed, and the hatred and atrocities between the Protestants and Catholics caused a reign of terror. Emotions were constantly at the highest pitch; there were tragedies of violence that embraced all of sixteenth-century France and finally led to the ignominious Massacre of St. Bartholomew, to scenes of carnage only comparable to those of Hitler's *Kristallnacht* in 1938, with the one difference that the massacre in France was more passionate and less methodical.

Catherine had brought with her from Urbino and Florence a love of gaiety and splendor, of beauty and luxury. As wife of King Henri she had to play second fiddle to the king's mistress, Diane de Poitiers, until Henri's death in 1559, when she was forty. For thirty more years she reigned over a country that suffered nothing but agonies. As a young girl she had arrived for her betrothal in France convoyed by sixty ships, and her own ship's "sails of purple cloth" were "embroidered with gold. . . . On landing, a procession of unusual splendor took place through the city. . . ." Her start on French soil was as magnificent as the dream of her new life. But immediately life at court was misery and humiliation, full of intrigues against a foreign woman of bourgeois, yes, plebeian ancestry. Nine years without child, she was saved from divorce when she suddenly gave birth to an heir. She never lost her self-discipline, her dignity, and her love for the beautiful in life.

A bloodstained soil under dark skies brought forth a lovely flower. Of course, everything about this new flower of the dance had to be rudimentary. Nevertheless, it was a skillful, knowing attempt at a novel way of presenting theatricalized dance: The *Balet Comique de la Royne,* commissioned by Catherine, which was ruinously expensive for its time. Perhaps Catherine wanted to prove with it to the world that the country was again at peace with itself and that all the warfare could not impoverish France. In fact, this single production, heralded in the entire Western civilized world and watched by a thousand privileged people in the tremendous hall at the Petit Bourbon Palace, was a severe blow to the treasury. The ruling clique gave little thought to the specter of bankruptcy as long as higher taxation of an impoverished peasantry and the heavily burdened tradespeople could again fill the coffers. The Foreign Minister of King Henri III was grateful for this splendid event since it heightened the prestige of France.

It was a spectacular but not an isolated experience: humankind has always known how to fiddle while Rome burns. For Catherine there were many reasons for proving time and again to the French how impeccable the taste of a Medici can be, how thoroughly her eyes and heart were attuned to beauty and the arts. Catherine built and decorated the Palais des Tuileries and its gardens, where sumptuous festivities were held whenever the internal political situation permitted. Lavish entertainments were regularly arranged in Fontainebleau and in the Louvre. A year after the St. Bartholomew's slaughter, the *Ballet des Polonais* was given in honor of the Polish ambassadors who came to Paris to offer their country's crown to the duc d'Anjou, the future Henri III. The dancing became particularly famous for its complicated figures executed by sixteen ladies of the court representing the sixteen provinces of France. People were enthusiastic about the exact formation of the groups and the dancers' skillful interlacing, by which they created the image of complicated figurations of steps. Masks were also employed, of course, and one of the reports about this ballet said:

> The Nymphs descended, to dance a ballet twice; first masqued and then without masks. The Poles marveled at the orderly confusions, the well-formed numbers of the ballet, the different musics and said the dance of France was impossible to equal by all the kings of the earth.

For some time already—to be exact, since Cesare Negri was brought to Paris in 1554—figured-dancing had been the *dernier cri* in France; it was also part of the great success of the *Ballet des Polonais* in 1573. But this ballet de cour can in no way be compared with what took place on October 15, 1581, in the big hall of the Petit Bourbon Palace. The occasion was the arranged marriage between Marguerite de Vaudemont—Queen Louise's sister—and the duc de Joyeuse. Baldassarino da Belgiojoso, who had come to France not quite thirty years previously, had meanwhile gallicized not only his name, to Balthasar de Beaujoyeulx, but also his entire pattern of behavior and outlook on life.

We are told that Beaujoyeulx was "an excellent musician, a clever courtier, a man of ingenious wit and pleasing imagination," as Lincoln Kirstein characterized him. The great chance for Beaujoyeulx came with the acceptance of his plans for the major festivities, later known as the *Ballet*

Comique. He made a point of having given "the first title and honor to the dance, and the second to the story, which I designated 'Comique' more for the beautiful, tranquil, and happy conclusion than for the nature of its characters, who are almost all gods and goddesses or other heroic personages."

When he speaks of "a revival from such distant antiquity that it may be called modern," he does not think of a tragic ending. His reference is to the classic pastoral à la Vergil, whose arcadia was remodeled, domesticated, and vernacularized. It was the great rage all through the sixteenth century and far beyond, into the Rococo period. This vogue took such a hold that for some time one could not publish one's poems without having them pastoralized. From Tasso to Spenser, from Sir Philip Sidney to John Milton, literature was overcrowded with fairy queens, gods and goddesses, shepherds and nymphs. Shakespeare made fun of this craze in *As You Like It* at the end of the century.

Beaujoyeulx's setting was the pastoral, reflecting ephemeral happiness. His plans were accepted because they seemed sound for the occasion and in no way startling in the nascent stage of the scenario. It was certain that what he intended would please everyone and offend no one. Beaujoyeulx was not a deep thinker; he did not do anything particularly new, though he thought of his work as a "novelty." He simply joined together all the elements known to him, and to most everyone else, in an artistically valid and eye-pleasing whole.

He could proudly state in the printed libretto: "I can say that I have satisfied the eye, the ear, and the understanding in one well-proportioned creation." There were music, singing, and dancing, there were speeches and gorgeous costumes; the scenic designs overwhelmed the audience, which was stunned by floats reminiscent in their splendor of Lorenzo de' Medici's *trionfi.* One of the most exciting scenic images was the appearance of a fountain, which one could truly say was the most beautiful in superb design and artifice and the most magnificent in embellishment that had ever been seen, as he described it. There were three basins adorned with sculptures made of burnished gold and silver, with human beings imaginatively masked, beplumed, and hidden in white satin trimmed with gold tinsel. Scented water flowed down from the highest basin. The Queen was on this car, with eleven other royal ladies, representing naiads who "climbed down from their fountain," whereupon ten violinists entered the hall, richly attired, and "began to play the first entry of the Ballet." We are not told what they danced. It could not have amounted to much because their garish cos-

A scene from the BALET COMIQUE DE LA ROYNE *(1581). Beaujoyeulx: "The most exciting scenic image was the appearance of a fountain . . . the most magnificent in embellishment that had ever been seen." (Courtesy French Cultural Services)*

tumes precluded any particular movement that could be extended far beyond a pavane.

As on all such occasions, there was a presentation of gifts at the end, followed by a grand ballet de cour. The Queen and the other noble ladies, disguised as they were as naiads, "led out the princes to dance the grand Ball; and this ended, they began branles [the favorite sixteenth-century court dance] and other dances customary at great feasts and celebrations."

It was more than an eye-filling event ending in a joyful dance. The procedure of having a dance follow a theatrical production established a pattern for all balletic performances for the next hundred years, culminating in the English masque and antimasque where, as a grand finale, the dancing maskers were "taking the commoners out." Beaujoyeulx mentioned the branles, which were the favorite dances at the time—branles from the French provinces as far as Burgundy, Auvergne, and even from Scotland and Malta, where people had preserved the dances' exuberant vigor. Among the "customary" dances was the galliard, which, as early as the 1530s, was considered a mirror of the time's wanton spirit and which was indeed a dance of gaiety and strength. Queen Elizabeth I of England, as mentioned in Parnakh's *Histoire de la Danse* and quoted by most writers, was said to have exercised each morning by doing six or seven galliards. This is why Shakespeare wrote in *King Henry the Fifth:*

> . . . the prince our master
> *Says that you savour too much of your youth,*
> *And bids you be advised there's nought in France*
> *That can be with a nimble galliard won.*

Mythological figures and images, as well as such abstractions as Virtue, Fortune, and Chance (which we still find in Monteverdi's operas many decades later), visualized as goddesses, were familiar notions. Thus Beaujoyeulx dealt with concepts readily understood by his audience. Circe, the title role of the *Ballet Comique* (also known as *Circe*), was often considered to represent Fortune in life, who could transform people and objects. The ballet opens with a Fugitive Gentleman's complaint about Circe's power and wrath, which he barely escaped; the story then mobilizes goddesses and nymphs, tritons and sirens, even Mercury and Jupiter, who, as *deus ex machina,* finally uses his thunderbolt, striking Circe and freeing the captives.

Everything in this story is laden with symbols. The enchantress was understood as a figure of evil: the happy ending proved that it does not pay to be evil and that there is justice in Jupiter's thunderbolt. The Fugitive Gentle-

The opening scene of the BALET COMIQUE DE LA ROYNE *(1581). (Courtesy French Cultural Services)*

Luca Cambiaso (1527–85) anticipated twentieth-century cubism in this design. He called it "Seven Men at Play." Almost a dancing concept, it is a rhythmic-gymnastic idea carried to a climactic point. (Courtesy Scala/Editorial Photocolor Archives)

man was meant to be Time, wandering aimlessly in the realm of eternity. Circe holds him an entire year, the scenario says; we therefore have four Virgins and four Virtues in the ballet, allegorizing the four seasons. The fugitive is liberated by the gods Pallas Athena and Jupiter because, being the soul or essence of Time, he cannot perish; on the contrary, he must go on and on from each year's captivity and complaint to the next.

The *Ballet Comique* embraced the ever-growing interest in the metaphorical meaning of classical mythology, the arcadian concept of the pastoral, and the danced devices of the intermedia (interludes)—those mostly light entr'acte dance entertainments during banquet intervals. Another synthesis was closely related to this ballet, something that was attempted in a very practical way at Jean Antoine de Baïf's Academy (the first attempt by this sixteenth-century poet to found an academy) and was on everyone's lips when discussing the arts: their integration. Leonardo started this trend by saying that "painting is a form of poetry made to be seen." People began to realize the close interrelationship between the arts and—in anticipation of the Age of Reason—also related the arts to the sciences.

Beaujoyeulx flattered the ladies and gentlemen of the court: ". . . everyone believed that Archimedes could not have better understood Geometric proportions than these princesses and ladies employing them in this Ballet." Beaujoyeulx was greatly honored for his accomplishments, and in each laudation the comparison with Archimedes seemed unavoidable. In one of the sonnets written on this occasion and in his honor we read: "Thy Circe charms me less than the subtle movements of thy ballet even as Circe herself must yield to the celestial powers." Beaujoyeulx thought that these "subtle movements," as he wrote in his libretto, were, "in truth, no more than the geometrical groupings of people dancing together, accompanied by the varied harmony of several instruments."

The notion of geometry seems to have been uppermost in Beaujoyeulx's mind, since it was still a very fashionable term in his days. For medieval men and women geometry had divine connotations, with God envisioned as the great geometer and the universe seen in the shape of measured order, reflected in the harmonious architecture of the medieval cathedrals. Renaissance people, extending everything into worldly aspects, were heirs to the belief in geometry but could not help stressing its scientific implications. Without this mania for geometry, Brunelleschi could not have discovered the laws of perspective—and without perspective the first notions of choreography would have had to wait in the wings. The organic beauty of the human shape and geometry had reached their highest point of cosmic harmony in people's eyes during the Age of Mannerism.

As early as 1503 Pomponius Gauricus extolled this idea in his treatise *De sculptura,* in which the *exactissima harmonica* of the human body and the body in motion were relativized in regard to geometry and music theory:

"What a master of geometry, what a musician must He have been who shaped the human body in such fashion!" Some painters of this period, as the example of Luca Cambiaso (1527–85) proves, were obsessed with the idea of a measured sense of patterns. Cambiaso's figures often show the master's aim at stereometric forms, at a cubistic simplification, creating an impression that the organic dynamics of human bodies would throw them into a variation of playful movements. Beaujoyeulx, very conscious of the spirit of his time, translated the prevalent obsession with geometry into choreographic notions.

BEAUJOYEULX was not the producer of the *Ballet Comique,* only its scenarist and choreographer. He had to have someone write the verse and music as well as take care of the scenic design and the costumes. Queen Louise, or the court, must have decided on those matters. Pierre de Ronsard, France's greatest poet of the period, was still alive, but La Chesnaye, the King's almoner, was assigned to write the verse. Since the French did not mind making cultural loans from Italy, they might have gone, for instance, to Vincenzo Galilei, who had just published his *Dialogo della musica antica e della moderna,* in which he made a deep bow before Plato's principles and ancient Greek music. The Sieur de Beaulieu, however, a relative of the Queen, wrote the inoffensive music, assisted by Jacques Salmon. Only Jacques Patin, who designed the costumes and scenery, fully rose to the occasion.

After almost four hundred years, history remembers the *Ballet Comique* with due credit and some reverence. In its right perspective, without our overemphasizing the innovative character of its artistic statement, it has the place it deserves. It is maintained that the ballet was produced on too grand a scale and, for financial considerations, could not be repeated. What followed was not even a miniature replica of the *Ballet Comique,* since none of the ballets developed a story line or any coherence in their dance numbers. There was some masquerading and some dancing which was no longer really spectacular—just enough to deserve the name of *ballet-mascarade.*

The aristocracy and rich citizenry accepted a variety of *ballets-mascarades* because these entertainments adhered to no formulas and required no preknowledge of antiquity or mythology for better understanding. They were always a loose mingling of declamation, singing, and dancing, echoing the great example of 1581, but their lack of substance and direction was appalling. A production with more emphasis on music, singing, and pantomime was called a *ballet-mélodramatique,* a precursor of the English masques and the opera. All the variations of the *ballet-mascarade* brought forth the *ballet à entrée,* which consisted of dance numbers loosely held together. It was historically important for the development of the divertissements. This, of course, was dancing for the sheer sake of dancing, which was enjoyed by the aristocrats who performed it as it is still enjoyed by a majority of dance lovers to this day. Divertissements have been used from Lully to Balanchine, and they have always shown up the brilliance of a dancer's technique. Their inherent danger is the shallowness behind the bravura and their remoteness from the ballet's theme.

These *entrées* remained rather insipid throughout the seventy years following the *Ballet Comique*. The reasons can be found in the sociopolitical problems that prevailed in France for a long time. It would be unique in the history of the arts if after such a decisive breakthrough and such an impressive artistic statement as the *Ballet Comique* a yawning emptiness should have ensued, had not outside circumstances affected the development. The façade of the *Ballet Comique* was an extravagant showcase for political purposes, but the substance it contained was extremely valuable. How could this achievement immediately disintegrate into such faint facsimiles, into feeble exercises for relaxation? Did it come historically too early, being forced to wait almost a century for its reincarnation? It certainly did not take deep enough root in the feudal society for which it was created.

The Guise family opposed Catherine's attempts toward a tolerant policy. Her adversaries constituted a powerful Holy League in the 1570s and 1580s and swore to resist by force those who sought "to ruin the Catholic religion and the state." They kept their oath, and soon Henri de Navarre, the Protestant leader, Henri, duc de Guise, and King Henri III were fighting each other. They sought aid from abroad—from England, Spain, the Pope, the German princes; and all parties hired mercenaries from Switzerland. Henri de Navarre won the battle, but not immediately the war. The Parisians feared the Protestants, and the Guises entered the city with their forces in defiance of King Henri. There were barricades all over Paris. The King fled, but returned and had the duc de Guise and his brother the cardinal de Guise assassinated. He also put the cardinal de Bourbon, pretender to the throne, in prison. Henri III now had no choice but to ally himself with the Protestants. The two kings Henri moved with their armies to reconquer Paris. Soon, when King Henri III was assassinated, only Henri de Navarre was left. Navarre, now Henri IV, finally conquered Paris, having meanwhile become a convert to Catholicism. His war with Spain did not end before 1598, when he finally succeeded in restoring religious toleration through the Edict of Nantes.

Such was the political climate in the 1580s and '90s. In these tumultuous days of near-anarchy, the government lived on the sale of offices of state. The rural gentry was financially ruined and sold its castles and estates to prosperous businessmen who, with the acquisition of seignorial domains, acquired titles of nobility. They brought new blood into the aristocracy, which probably was badly needed. How much more difficult could a period be for the development of an art form than these two decades?

The concept and the promise of the *Ballet Comique* were lost in the civil strife and on the parvenus dominating the leisure class. They were content to watch the entrance of a few musicians who were foolishly masked, followed or preceded by torchbearers; then dancers would enter, beautifully or oddly dressed or masked, stepping in unison right or left, bowing toward each other, moving gracefully back and forth. This was repeated until everyone joined in the social dancing. Sometimes acrobats or pantomimes performed instead of dancers. There were no theaters as yet, so performance and dancing took place in halls, the bigger events at the Louvre, the Hôtel de Ville, or smaller halls, public or private. Early in the seventeenth century little theaters were built, and the entertainments shown there returned to the pastoral and mythological subjects of former times, themes also seen in the *ballets-mélodramatiques*, which favored more music. It was from these minor productions that the *ballet à entrée* evolved.

Despite all the wars and turmoils, these performances went on everywhere in France. A statistically inclined mind maintained that there were somewhat more than eight hundred of those minor events between 1581 (the *Ballet Comique*) and 1610, when Louis XIII performed in *Alcine*. Against a pastoral background, this ballet combined features of the *ballet-comique* and *ballet-mélodramatique*. Torch-bearing pages disguised as green snails came out of the wood, and violinists dressed as Turks danced and played. It was the way it had been for the past three decades. When the enchantress Alcine left the forest and approached the King's throne to sing verses, echoed by her chorus of nymphs, it seems little more than a weak imitation of Beaujoyeulx's triumphant statement of 1581. It took ballet a few more decades to liberate itself from dilettantism and to enter into a more serious phase.

WE know more about people's general behavior and the social dances that brought them together because toward the end of the fifteenth century the first printing presses began to work and many books were then printed about these subjects. It is surprising how many there were since the hesitant beginnings with Gutenberg's Bible around 1455. One of the first books on etiquette was Count Baldassare Castiglione's *Cortegiano* (*The Courtier*) of 1528, a treatise on the perfect courtier, sketching an ideal image of nobility in chiseled style and in harmony with the most moral aspirations of the Renaissance. Castiglione had his asides on the dance; he thought, for instance, of the branle as a dance that should be performed only in private (*in camera privatamente, ma in publico no così, fuorchè travestito*), where he can dare show himself in a more forceful dance—unmasked.†

† The full text of this passage reads: "There are certain other exercises that can be practiced in public and in private, like dancing; and in this I think the Courtier ought to have care, for when dancing in the presence of many and in a place full of people, it seems to me that he should preserve a certain dignity, albeit tempered with a lithe and airy grace of movement; and although he may feel himself to be very

Nicholas Hilliard's "A Young Man Among Roses": a characteristic image of the perfect courtier. (Crown Copyright. Courtesy Victoria and Albert Museum)

Among many books for a relatively limited readership, another book of the greatest importance was published sixty years later, in 1588. Thoinot Arbeau, canon of Langres—his real name was Jehan Tabourot—recorded the dances known in the sixteenth century, adding historical comparisons with antiquity and an evaluation of the dances from the aesthetic and moral viewpoints. *Orchésographie* is a treatise in the form of a dialogue between the author and an imaginary pupil, Capriol, "whereby all manner of persons may easily acquire and practice the honorable exercise of dancing."

Arbeau was a humanist, interested in mathematics and astronomy. In his old age, and probably prompted by the *Ballet Comique* as well as by the failure of his contemporaries to live up to its lofty aims, this Catholic priest merely put down his "scribblings to kill time" while remembering the dances of his younger years. This dialogue, reminiscent of Lucian's dialogue on pantomime, was accompanied by drawings that were descriptive and even hinted at the five basic positions that the *danse d'école* (the school of classical dancing) would develop. His other writings are long forgotten, but his *Orchésographie* has remained memorable to us as it seems to have been vital then.

Curiously, during the Age of the Baroque many theologians wrote about the dance. Above all there was Father Marin Mersenne (1588–1648), a mathematician and philosopher, born as Arbeau's *Orchésographie* was published. His most important work was *Harmonie universelle,* full of searching thoughts about music, dance, and life. Descartes said that in him "was more than in all universities together." He believed in the performer's expressive ability to force his way into the spectator's or listener's soul, but, as the rationalist he was, distrusted any artist's sole reliance on imagination and illusion. For Father Mersenne the "principal end" of all art "was to delight the cultivated listener, and not to rouse his passions."

In 1658 the Abbé Michel de Pure wrote in his *Idée des Spectacles* that *le sujet est l'âme du ballet,* a dictum in which most of us still believe. Pure wrote about dancing at a time when each *entrée* was still accompanied by a *récit:* that is, by one or several voices. But he must have envisioned ballet as a far more independent art form, since he referred to it as an "expressive pantomime," believing that it could represent through gestures and movements "that which could be expressed by words." His ideas were formulated three years before the French academy for dancing, L'Académie Royale de Danse, was founded in Paris. He helped prepare the right ambience for it by siding with the professionals against the noblemen who, he

---

nimble and a master of time and measure, let him not attempt those agilities of foot and double steps which we find very becoming in our friend Barletti, but which perhaps would be little suited to a gentleman. Yet in a room privately, as we are now, I think he may try both, and may dance morris-dances and brawls [branles]; but not in public unless he be masked, when it is not displeasing even though he be recognized by all."

felt, participated in ballets for the sake of "vanity and personal interest." He expected the dancing master to make a clear distinction between the social dance and ballets as a new art form.

Some time later, at the height of the Baroque era, the Abbé Jean-Baptiste du Bos (1670–1742) also discussed the dance in his *Réflexions Critiques sur la Poésie et la Peinture*. He saw dance as an "animated and mobile painting" and pointed to the ancient Greek dance as an expression that "had to signify something," in contrast to "the gestures of our dancers," which are "attitudes and movements that serve naught but gracefulness." His criticism moved, as we shall see later, in the direction of the *ballet d'action*— ballet with a plot. When Du Bos spoke of the dance as *"le langage du coeur,"* he felt that in people's expressive movements lies the secret of their being and becoming.

These theologians were fascinated by movement, dance, and mime, by all that reveals human beings and by what we can reveal without words. Like Arbeau, they were humanists and came, through the study of antiquity, to think of movement and dance in their own time. They also may, in an age and in a world torn by religious strife, have looked for a unifying gesture that *one* God gave to all of us: movement and the ability to make people move to their hearts' delight and by the will of their minds.

They were aestheticians, but none of them was as practical-minded as Arbeau. His *Orchésographie* moralizes somewhat, as all earlier dance manuals do, but it not only describes the dances of the time with the help of drawings, it also establishes that until the end of the sixteenth century the stage dance was identical to the social dance; it has its own system of dance notation, made comprehensible with letters; and it defines the principle of turned-out legs and feet which, a hundred years later, Pierre Beauchamp was to make a necessary part of the *danse d'école*. In all the modesty of its presentation, it laid the foundation for France's predominant position in this art form.

From "Dramma per Musica" to the Opera

WHEN THE FRENCH HAD BUILT UP THEIR BALLETIC DOMINANCE THROUGH the Renaissance genius of the Italians, it was an Italian poet, Ottavio Rinuccini, who saw some *ballets-mélodramatiques* in France and took his impressions with him as inspiration to write the text for a few *drammi per musica,* as the early attempts at opera were called. He and his friends in Florence were interested in reviving Greek tragedy. They were under the impression that the actors in ancient Greece did not actually speak but sang their lines. These gentlemen met regularly in Florence, and their meeting place was known as the *Camerata fiorentina*. They were militant in their rejection of the *rabies barbarum* by which they referred to everything Gothic and to counterpoint. Totally caught up in the wake of humanism, they envisioned every step in their artistic endeavor as one toward the renascence of the chorus in Greek tragedy. But they were also well aware that sacred music dramas had existed for a long time and were performed by the clergy on feast days, possibly in costumes. These were certainly sung to some kind of instrumental accompaniment, probably with a built-in sermon. We only have to remind ourselves of *The Play of Daniel* (c. 1140), which has been successfully revived in our day.

These Florentines were erudite men and very much engrossed in what was then creating the greatest interest in learned circles: Neoplatonist philosophy, a mingling of Platonic thinking with early Christian theology that emerged in the third century. The original writings of the Neoplatonists did not become available in Italy again before the second half of the sixteenth century. Only selected groups and a few individuals had had access to these Greek texts, certainly among them the noblemen of the Camerata, who read and discussed Greek mythology, tragedy, and philosophy. Neoplatonism had permeated the thinking of that dying ancient world in which Christianity was born; in whatever diffused and diluted form Neoplatonism had been absorbed by the early Christian theologians, historically it was a bridge from a dying into a growing world, and therefore also of great importance in the studies of those interested in Greek tragedy.

Who were those noblemen of the Camerata? Above all, there is the glamorous figure of Vincenzo Galilei. In 1581—the year in which the *Ballet Comique* set an example for the future art of ballet—Galilei wrote his *Dialogo della musica antica e della moderna,* in which treatise he developed the theoretic basis of the Camerata. In it he attacked polyphony and descriptive music. He advocated vocal monodies to the accompaniment of viols. In other words, what he aimed at was recitative. It was experimented with at that time and also occurred in the *Balet Comique de la Royne.* Galilei may not be as important as his son Galileo, who decisively changed our outlook on our world's position in the cosmos, but we ought not to minimize his merits. While others were probably more explicit in outlining the route to be taken, his *Dialogo* inspired the noblemen who gathered in the house of Giovanni Bardi, count of Vernio in Florence.

Polyphony, as Galilei explained, was considered responsible for the deterioration of music, and the members of the Camerata gradually hit upon a single-voiced melody. The counterpoint—voice against voice, tone against tone—was discarded and a new monodic style was sought. What was finally to flower as a new art form in the seventeenth century had various roots, some reaching back to the medieval liturgical plays, which employed a chanting delivery of lines. Opera developed in an atmosphere of pastoral tableaux and madrigal spirit. The madrigals became an aristocratic form, an elegant fusion of the smooth polyphony of Flemish motets with the chordal style then prevalent in Italy. The text, mostly of pastoral subject matter, dealt with delicate sentimentality and wit. If we can see certain roots of the opera in the madrigals, then it is mainly because the music was wedded to the text, which preceded it. Wherever we look, we find a single-minded interest in the word, which the music had to accentuate. Emilio de' Cavalieri, one of the esteemed composers of the time, still thought in 1600 that music without words was totally lacking in interest.‡ Even the principal creator of the opera, Claudio Monteverdi (1567–1643), echoed Plato and Cavalieri in his *Scherzi musicali* when he maintained that "speech be the master, not the servant of music."

The work of Orazio Vecchi (1550–1605), a master of the polyphonic style, is also often cited as a harbinger of the opera. Vecchi created what could be called a *madrigal* or *a capella opera,* if it is not a contradictory term. He combined fourteen madrigals for five voices (one of them for four voices) without instrumental accompaniment. He called his work *L'Amfiparnasso.* It had two parallel plots, and was a comic opera (*grottesco comico*), for which Vecchi borrowed a few commedia characters, such as Pantalone and Pedrolino, and a commedia plot line, juxtaposing it with a *lirica tragica* involving the love story of Isabella and Lucio. Vecchi published this work in 1597, a time when the musical intermezzi, the favorites of Renaissance banquets, had matured and could assist the composer of *L'Amfiparnasso* in building his theatrical concept. Since the action pretended to be extemporaneous, like any other commedia production, Vecchi had to write his own text. But were it not for the stress on the text and the theatrical action in this work, it could hardly be considered a forerunner of the opera.

SEVERAL men participated in the heated debates taking place in Bardi's academy: Jacopo Peri, Emilio de' Cavalieri, Vincenzo Galilei, the singer-composer Giulio Caccini, and, above all, the poet Ottavio Rinuccini, who indefatigably produced one libretto after another. From time to time these gentlemen assigned a *dramma per musica* to one of their composers. Peri's *Dafne,* based on Rinuccini's text, was the first opera on these lines, produced in Jacopo Corsi's palazzo in 1597. Unfortunately, it has been lost. Rinuccini

‡ In many musical quarters this concept was kept alive. In the days when the singers, particularly of the Neapolitan school, reigned supreme we can read in *The Spectator,* in 1712, that music is "only valuable as it is agreeable to and heightens the Purpose of Poetry . . . ; to say it shorter, mere musical Sounds are in our Art no other than nonsense verses are Poetry."

then wrote a libretto called *Euridice,* which both Peri and Caccini set to music.

Peri's work was performed on the occasion of Maria de' Medici's marriage to the French king Henri IV, just as other operas and ballets were mostly occasioned by such festivities in the seventeenth century. The opening scene is set in a bucolic environment with shepherds and nymphs. The announcement is made that Orpheus and Eurydice have married, a typical opening and an obvious reference to the royal wedding. Just as characteristically, there is a happy ending with the message of a female voice that Orpheus and Eurydice are reunited.

Rinuccini may not have been a bad dramatist in writing his many libretti, but the first *drammi per musica* were performed in halls without any decoration to speak of. He did not yet have any theatrical means at his disposal, or else he did not perceive how even a hall can be dramatically exploited for a music drama. Moreover, the Camerata was interested only in telling a story, clearly articulated, the words sung with exaggerated inflection and accompanied by a small orchestra of flutes and harpsichord. In these beginning stages, opera consisted of little more than a declamation in the form of recitatives. The productions may have looked like bas-reliefs. Much of the action was related, mainly by messengers, and not acted out onstage. The Camerata members handicapped themselves by slavishly adhering to what they thought was the right way of reviving the Greek chorus.

Plato had already done some mischief by making it easier for the Church Fathers to condemn dancing. When the Camerata now came upon Plato's dictum "Let music be first of all language and rhythm, and secondly tone, and not vice versa," they were guided by him into a dead-end street. Moreover, when these gentlemen read the Greek philosopher Aristoxenus' advice that any song should be patterned after speech, they were convinced that the chorus of Greek tragedy, if not the entire play, was presented in a singsong pattern, neither speech nor song, since the actors had to articulate each phrase rhythmically.

THE subject matter of the first operas is the myths of Daphne and of Orpheus and Eurydice. This is significant for the era and especially the Florentine scholar-artists, intent on recapturing the spirit of antiquity. Obviously the subjects they hit upon first were of mythological origin. Moreover, the myth of Daphne has a pastoral background, of great importance in sixteenth-century life. This story of a beautiful girl, the daughter of a river god, living a bucolic existence, has features of later Romanticism. She is the symbol of the unattainable spirit of peaceful seclusion. When Apollo pursues her, she prays to Earth and her father to rescue her, whereupon she is transformed into the laurel tree, whose leaves were formed into garlands, and later poetic laurels.

This story was dear to the Florentine intellectual elite, but it was eclipsed by the intriguing attraction of the Orphic myth. Superficially, the men of the Camerata, as well as Monteverdi and Gluck, may have been fascinated by the triple image of the poet-singer-lover embodied in Orpheus.* These composers found a ready-made situation in which to echo the magic power of Orpheus' lyre and voice onstage. Furthermore, he is the lover whose devotion is so strong that it enabled him to charm the nether deities into consenting to Eurydice's return from the dead on condition that he would not look back at her until reaching the light of the sun again. But the desire of the lover for the beloved finally forced him to disregard this condition. Was he to trust the deities implicitly? Or had they known in advance that Orpheus' great love would be his and Eurydice's undoing? Was their mercy, then, only pretense, since they knew too well that nothing could ever upset the laws of death? The myth leaves this question unanswered, and all we realize is that Orpheus' desire for his beloved forfeited her.

The spectator of this tragedy enacted onstage may wonder at Orpheus' impatience, but the way back from Hades into the world of the living is in fact arduous and long. Symbolically, the road back to life is so long that it never ends (except through reincarnation). Orpheus reputedly could work miracles with his lyre; those who heard him play and sing worshiped him, his voice tamed wild animals, and trees and rocks left their places to follow the sound of his harp. He charmed Persephone in the underworld. The legend tells us that he found a violent death at the hands of the Thracian women who, according to Aeschylus, tore him to pieces in Maenad fashion because he worshiped Apollo more than Dionysus, or rather because the Orphics added to the Dionysian worship the Apolline notion of purification.

The Orpheus operas had an early precedent when the humanist poet Angelo Poliziano (1454–94), a protégé of Lorenzo de' Medici, wrote *La Favola di Orfeo* for a court occasion in Mantua in 1480. It was a dramatic poem permeated with the humanist ideal of beauty. It was used as a libretto and set to music with solos, dialogues, and a chorus, the music derived from favorite dance and carnival songs. In its time it had great influence on musical intermezzi.

In Poliziano's version the audience is shown Orpheus' death. The Thracian singer experiences death in losing his beloved. When he returns without her, he decides to live among males only, renouncing any relationship with women. Poliziano's *Favola di Orfeo,* a product of the early

---

* The erudite Florentines also hit upon a kindred spirit in Orpheus as the patron of a religious movement. In ancient Greece, Orphism stood outside the state-approved religious ideas, knew no moderation, and was guided by an authoritative priesthood, believing in personal independence and individual salvation. This paralleled the many sects going their own religious ways at the turn of the sixteenth century. Orphism was bound to arouse the interest of the Camerata and, with it, interest in the legendary figure of Orpheus.

Renaissance, particularly stressed the experience of male prowess and strength. It reflected the twofoldness of the Apollonian and Dionysian in human beings. Both Ottavio Rinuccini, writing his text for Peri's *Euridice,* and Alessandro Striggio, doing the same for Monteverdi's *Orfeo,* were, however, imbued with the spirit of Mannerism. The conception of the tragic Dionysian elements were no longer acceptable to the courts of the Baroque era.

The ideals of aesthetic harmony were then prevalent, and the happy ending or some form of reconciliation was expected. In Monteverdi's opera, Orpheus is taken by his father, Apollo, to Olympus—"against my will into the hated light," as Monteverdi has him sing. His audiences can accept the tragic pain of loss that Orpheus suffered because they are reconciled through the ending. Gluck's version is characteristic of the late Baroque, when Amor, almighty god of the Rococo, saves Orpheus. Correspondingly, we find Poliziano envisioning no dancing in his *favola,* whereas Striggio and Monteverdi created a pastoral *dramma per musica* in which the shepherds and nymphs are seen, realistically, expressing themselves through dance in Act II and particularly in Act V. There, at the conclusion of the sung dance chorus of the shepherds, a wild morisca is indicated, probably in reminiscence of the Maenads. For the noblemen in whose honor this opera was performed, dance was too familiar to be left out. For Gluck, who believed in simplicity, truth, and naturalness, the function of music, as he stressed, was "to serve poetry by means of expression and by following the situations of the story, without interrupting the action or stifling it with useless superfluity of ornaments." Gluck could therefore include dance as if a part of the action, furthering the plot as an expression of dramatic truth.

The Opera's Progress

THE NEW KIND OF MUSICAL DRAMA, WITH WHICH THE ITALIAN PEOPLE fell in love at first sound, was an art without a home. The Camerata's works were, in the beginning, produced in the palaces of the nobility. It soon became obvious that such a sung drama needed a stage, an environment worthy of its potential significance. The people of Venice, who have always had a flair for the spectacular, rushed into building opera houses, which were public theaters for a paying audience. It was a mixed, a new audience. Writing for it, the librettists were freed from courtly obligations, such as the happy ending. Theatrical elements dominated the dramaturgy: there were human beings, and no longer mythologized types; there was dramatic development within the scenic action, and no longer a narration of the story in tedious reports of what had happened offstage.

The dramaturgic development went hand in hand with the change in scenic imagery, and both were best mirrored by the tremendous progress made between Monteverdi's first and last operas, his *Orfeo* in 1607 and his *Incoronazione di Poppea* in 1642. *Orfeo* has its root in the madrigal and a pastoral atmosphere, whereas *Poppea*, which tells the story of Nero's mistress replacing the Empress Ottavia, tries to stay away from too much mythology and the unreal, introducing human characters that experience the effects of their passionate makeup against a fully realized historical setting. Within about one generation, or Monteverdi's working lifetime, the Italian opera was born.

Its setting was no longer a court, like the one of Mantua, where on March 1, 1607, *Orfeo* was presented for the first time, after having been shown in a rather private circle at the Accademia degli Invaghiti on February 24 of the same year; nor was the setting a wedding, such as that of the prince of Mantua Francesco Gonzaga with the Infanta Margherita of Savoy, on which occasion *L'Arianna* had its premiere (of which opera the lyrical "Lament of Arianna" survives). *Poppea* was first heard at one of Venice's many newly built opera houses, the Teatro SS. Giovanni e Paolo. "The figure of Orfeo inspired me to a true prayer," Monteverdi could say in a letter written to his librettist Alessandro Striggio on December 19, 1616. In *Poppea* he achieved the humanization of his dramatic and historic material.

Francesco Busenello, the librettist, a lawyer by profession, did not have to think of celebrating a royal wedding. He could be true to history and create in the Empress Ottavia a schizophrenic figure crying out as an innocent victim, while scheming Poppea's murder. Seneca appears as the voice of conscience, but his reasoning is full of empty intellectual sophisms. The court life of *Poppea* is seen through the eyes of the merchants of Venice, a place of arrogance and deceit, a city of ducal grandeur but with all the middle-class attributes. The social accents are set. The world of king and courtiers who share the heroic-tragic passages and that of soldiers and servants who envision the royal love affairs and historic events from a realistic and even ironic viewpoint are pitted against each other. On the one side we find Poppea's sentimental outbursts as she expresses her intent to become Empress by hook and by crook, while Arnalta, her servant-companion, sees only the reality of the situation: she, too, will belong to the clique of the courtiers; they will flatter and admire her, but she won't believe that suddenly she has become beautiful. Yet she will pretend to accept their compliments in good faith. This down-to-earth realism is juxtaposed to Nero's passion for Poppea, and his words in Busenello's libretto show the entire Machiavellian cynicism that the Baroque age inherited from the Renaissance.

A revival of Monteverdi's Eighth Book of Madrigals by the Zürich Opera House, arranged by Nikolaus Harnoncourt, staged by Jean-Pierre Ponnelle. The picture shows the scene of IL BALLO DELLE INGRATE. *Choreography by Max Natiez. (Photo: Bild + News Photoservice, Zürich; courtesy Zürich Opera House)*

THE *dramma per musica* had come a long way. With *Poppea,* Monteverdi gave the opera a solid dramatic foundation. From then on, Italians were all ears for their operas and the interest in theatrical dancing was more or less drowned in bel canto. There was a sociocultural justification for opera's triumph. In the early seventeenth century, opera was a new experience and burst upon the scene with great impetus. By then ballet ought to have found its way artistically and aesthetically: it had anteceded opera by several decades. But in France, where ballet had such a promising start in 1581, it remained in the hands of a playful elite for the purpose of self-amusement, after having had to weather political and societal changes. For the greater part of the seventeenth century the court dance continued in a poor technical and intellectual state. The shallow concept of the *ballet à entrée* impeded any progress. A grand ballet had up to thirty *entrées,* as Nicolas Saint-Hubert tells us. He was a court painter who staged ballets during Louis XIII's reign and left us a valuable little document on *La manière de composer et faire réussir les ballets (How to Compose a Successful Ballet).*

But there was an appalling lack of coherence and depth in the subject matter. It was a theatrical triumph of trivia in an age of preciosity. The quick success of opera as a new art form meant that for almost two hundred years theatrical dance remained dependent on its sister art.

INITIALLY, opera also faced difficulties, but—in contrast to the many decades of stagnation in the dance—within about a decade it overcame the tediousness of the recitative, that musically heightened singsong and the composer's major obstacle. The change came with the emergence of the genius of Claudio Monteverdi, who turned the awkwardness of the recitative into a workable miracle. His pupil Francesco Cavalli (1602–76) used the term *opera* for the first time, specifically *opera scenica* instead of *dramma per musica,* when, in 1639, he composed his *Le nozze di Teti e di Peleo.* From then on, the opera as an "extravagant and irrational entertainment," as Dr. Samuel Johnson reputedly called it, triumphed as the new art form that immediately caught the fancy of *Homo ludens.*

In the beginning, and later in different forms, the opera created the feeling of a solemn celebration, a churchlike sensation that went well with the tumultuous events of religious fanaticism during the entire century. Not only was opera discovered in Italy, the Italians took it to their hearts with such intensity that it soon grew there to a point of excess. About 1685 the Neapolitan school of composers emerged with its guiding spirit Alessandro Scarlatti (1660–1725). The aria and the tenor became the domineering features. The Neapolitans established the importance of the *da capo* aria— repeating an aria from the beginning—and composers vied with each other in writing highly decorative melodies for the display of vocal virtuosity. These laryngeal excesses overshadowed everything else in importance on the operatic stage into the forties of the eighteenth century.

Ridicule was heaped on these vocal orgies by John Gay in his *Beggar's Opera* (1728). But it only proved the popularity of the prima donnas and the craze over castrati† with their sensuous vocal charm, of the coloratura,

† The development of the opera could also be described as the story of the tenor's triumph. It started with the Neapolitan school and has not yet left the operatic stage. During the era of Neapolitan predominance, baritones and basses—however important they may have been—were considered necessary evils. The highest pitch reigned supreme. Although castration was legally punishable, it was practiced and desirable in order to achieve something beautiful because unnatural. A boy's vocal purity expressed with male strength became the most adored nonpareil. It fitted exactly in the era of preciosity, and the society ladies worshiped the castrati, who were among the most famous singers of that era. Gluck wrote the role of his Orpheus for castrato voice. The cry for a third sex was also gratified through the concept of the transvestites. The parts in which ladies acted in boys' clothes and boys in ladies' clothes were conditioned by time and convention from the Renaissance far into the second half of the seventeenth century—to be more exact, until women as professional actresses and dancers were seen onstage. Among the serious arts, the opera continued this playful disguise as a theatrical gimmick in our century. Transvestites and female impersonators have been favorites in music hall entertainments ever since.

whose tonal richness corresponded so excessively beautifully with the rich ornaments of the scenic designs by the family Galli-Bibiena or the many Baroque churches in their opulence of detailed splendor.

It seemed as if Catholic churches almost wanted to compete with the theaters in visual abundance during the Baroque. From the last decades of the seventeenth century until 1750, the year Johann Sebastian Bach died, the major stimuli for most of the arts were religious in inspiration, and opera unfolded its tonal majesty in these decades like a new profane religion. Opera was apparently not only a pleasurable toy in the hands of the aristocracy; it flourished mainly in Catholic Italy and north of that country in a few cities dominated by Catholicism, such as Vienna, Prague, and Munich. Of course, it existed in France, too, which was ruled by cardinals until Mazarin's death and where the Jesuit influence was strongly felt. There is an unmistakable kindred spirit between the ritual solemnity of church service, culminating in the liberating music inherent in organ and chorus, and the musical magic that voice and orchestra can convey in the opera house. However this may be, opera's flamboyance in its initial stages disturbed the Protestant mind. Its dislike of opera only gradually gave way to acceptance during the eighteenth century.

We may blame the Neapolitans for their vocal and tonal oversupply, but we must admit that such self-indulgence brought about some rewarding by-products. To train and harness those overflowing voices, hundreds of music academies and schools sprang up in Italy at that time. With the composers' servitude to the singers, their creative ego cried out for recognition. There was no better way out for them than to preface an opera with an instrumental prelude. The Italians called these preludes sinfonias or toccatas. Scarlatti's overtures—which, by the way, bore no direct relationship to the main work—started with a fast section, generally in a fugal style, followed by a slow one, and then closed with a fast movement again. The French overture, introduced much later by Lully, differed in that its opening movement was kept majestically slow, the second section moving fast and mostly in fugal style, while the final part was a popular dance, generally a minuet. This is an important point because it sheds light on a principal difference between the development of the opera in Italy and France. In the beginning the overture had little thematic connection with the opera itself. To accomplish this was left to the great reformer Christoph Willibald Gluck in the latter part of the eighteenth century: "My idea was that the overture ought to indicate the subject and prepare the spectators for the character of the piece they are about to see. . . ."

THE Italians, so completely engrossed in the opera, relegated ballet to short productions performed between the acts of an opera (as in Shakespeare's days a dance would be shown to fill out the intermission for relief). This habit continued in Italy into the nineteenth century. Stendhal, typically French but imbued with great admiration for some Italians ("Canova, Rossini, and Viganò—they are the glory of the Italy of today!"), gives us a telling account of how the Italians treated opera and ballet in their theaters in his *Vie de Rossini:*

> On February 1, 1818, the show at La Scala contained the first act of *The Thieving Magpie* played from 7 to 8:15, followed by Viganò's ballet *The Vestal* from 8:30 to 10, then came the second act of *The Thieving Magpie* from 10:45 to 11:15 and finally Viganò's little ballet buffoonery *The Shoemaker's Wife* which was booed by the public—as though it felt it had to uphold its own dignity. But the same public saw it again performed with great pleasure, for it had meanwhile found out that there was something new in it. The performance closed with this little ballet which reached its end between midnight and one o'clock. Each week these little ballets show a new pas.

There is the difference: ballet sandwiched between the acts in Italy, while the French, whose kings were addicted to the dance, could not envision an opera without a ballet as part of the action and preferred the overture to end with a minuet. Opera knew professionals only, while ballet was still dominated by amateurs. In the 1640s opera was a developed art form, thanks to the uniqueness and the intellectual drive of the Camerata, followed by the genius of Monteverdi. Although there had been staged dancing since 1581, it would be justifiable—at least, from an artistic viewpoint—to date back the birth of ballet to the foundation of the French Académie Royale de Danse, in 1661, rather than to the *Ballet Comique* in 1581. The *Ballet Comique* may reasonably have been called ballet, but in fact it was a musicodramatic synthesis of all the then prevalent forms of entertainment, skillfully presented. As an integrated work based on the ballet de cour it was, and to this extent only, a point of balletic departure.

WHAT is the magic of the opera that flowered in the Age of Reason, in an age torn by religious and political strife? In spite of the fact that the dance was gradually forced into a corset of aesthetic principles, it has never lost the reality of its physical being. It is at its best when it has a touch of the poetic, the secret of elusiveness, the mystery of its own magic. The magic of opera is different. Opera is theatrical, vocally articulated drama, even when the bravura and beauty of the voice drown out the word itself. It pretends to represent life, but its artistic elements are directed toward escape from reality. "In opera," Tchaikovsky said, "everything is based upon the not-true." We may close our eyes and still hear drama elevated to a high C. Laryngeal acrobatics may hold us spellbound. It is the realism of untruth that takes us away from ourselves and into a world of enchantment that rings true in all

Of the many members of the Galli da Bibiena family, `Giuseppe
(1696–1756) was the most inventive and imaginative scenic designer; he

also designed the sets for many dance creations. (Courtesy French Cultural Services)

its absurdity. And the seductively sensuous accents of bel canto make us forget whatever may be absurd in it. Voltaire thought of opera as a bizarre and magnificent spectacle that gratifies eye and ear more than the mind.

By the second half of the eighteenth century, opera had overcome its first crisis. Composers no longer bowed to the dictates of singers. The Neapolitan school then gave the world the light, farcical opera called *opera buffa,* and its master, Giovanni Battista Pergolesi, gave it *La Serva Padrona,* which was destined to play a great role in opera history. The philosophers of the Enlightenment, strangely enough, accepted opera as the unrealistic and irrational art form it is, without reservation, whereas Diderot, speaking about the dance, referred to the prevalent pastoral scenes peopled with nymphs and shepherds and thundered that "the enchanted world may serve to amuse children. The real world alone pleases the mind."

The same Diderot invited Rousseau to write the articles on music for the *Encyclopédie,* and Rousseau could write: "Opera is a dramatic and lyric work of art combining all charms of the fine arts in a passionate action in order to arouse sympathy and illusion by means of pleasant sense perceptions. The composite parts of the opera are the poem, music, and decoration. Poetry speaks to the mind, music to the ear, painting to the eyes; and all must become one to move the heart. . . . An aria invented by a genius and composed with taste is the masterpiece of music: here unfolds a beautiful voice, here shines beautiful instrumental music, here, as if unnoticeable, passion touches the soul through the senses." And how Rousseau loved the Neapolitan school! "Don't look for what genius is. If you have it, then you feel it yourself; if you don't, you'll never experience it. . . . If you want to know whether even a spark of that mighty fire quickens you, then rush, yes, fly to Naples and listen to the masterpieces of Leo, Durante, Jommelli, Pergolesi. . . ."

The Germans came rather late to opera because their lands were devastated by the Thirty Years' War, while the French and Italians developed culturally in an atmosphere of relative peace. The first German composer of international magnitude, Georg Friedrich Händel, was born in Halle in 1685 and, as Sir George Frideric Handel and one of the most important English composers, was buried in Westminster Abbey in 1759. From church to ballet music,‡ from opera to oratorio, Handel left his imprint on the Baroque Age, and to this very day his *Messiah* and *Water Music,* among other works of his, are cherished experiences.

At this time Handel's popularity on the Continent was overshadowed by that of Johann Adolph Hasse (1699–1783), the only other German opera

‡ The famous English producer of pantomimes and ballad operas John Rich, who also founded and directed Covent Garden, later London's great opera house, assigned Handel to compose music for Rich's protégée the then famous ballerina Marie Sallé in 1734. Handel's operas *Ariodante* and *Alcina* are Italian in character, but they contain some beautiful dance music in the French style.

composer of the Baroque who achieved international recognition. While Handel lived in England, Hasse veered toward Italy. He wrote a great number of operas—some sources give fifty-six, others more than a hundred—besides oratorios, masses, and instrumental works. The Caruso of that time, Carlo Broschi Farinelli, made Hasse famous as an opera composer and is known for having sung two of Hasse's airs to the melancholy King Philip V of Spain every evening for ten years. Hasse's name stands as an example of how little an international reputation during one's lifetime is sufficient guarantee for survival.

Germany may have lost about a hundred years in creating its own opera tradition, but certainly made up for it in the eighteenth century. Then the thoroughness of the German mind took up the historic and aesthetic studies of music, and the greatest of its early classical writers devoted their thoughts to various aspects of the art.

In comparison to the very few champions of the dance as an equal to the other arts, opera was unmistakably moved into the foreground of interest in the eighteenth century. Gotthold Ephraim Lessing (1729–81), dramatist and scholar, who opened the gates to German Enlightenment, was interested in all forms of stage presentation. He did not deny dance its aesthetic due. In fact, he properly evaluated Jean Georges Noverre's significance in the fight for the new ideals of his time by combining Enlightenment rationality and intuitive insight. It was Lessing who translated Noverre's *Lettres* into German. Having been primarily interested in drama, Lessing included Noverre's concept of the ballet d'action as an important part of his own aesthetic tenets. Nevertheless, he saw greater potentialities in opera than in ballet: in his essay on "Laocoön"—the well-known Greek statue now in the Vatican—he envisioned the concept of the totality of the arts in which one art form would no longer help or support the other but in which all would strive together toward an artistic entity; and he thought that a combination of poetry and music ought to accomplish a particularly perfect piece of art.

His younger contemporary Johann Gottfried von Herder (1744–1803) combined the progressive and reactionary tendencies of his time, expressing the ideological conflict in turning against the cool rationalism of the Enlightenment, and became a leader of the Sturm und Drang (Storm and Stress) movement—that radical movement of German youth at the beginning of Romanticism. Similarly to Lessing, Herder touched upon the dance while treating *Plastik* (*Sculpture*). With the body as focal point of his investigation, he saw in it the natural expression of life and vigor, and therefore to him the body was beauty per se. The human body became alive, exciting, and convincing through its gesture. Movement was the annunciation of life, and life the annunciation of movement. "In this way," he said, "and in this way only the soul speaks through the body."

Herder was, far more than Lessing, the torchbearer of a new era in which classicistic and romanticized trends ran parallel to each other. Herder was strongly influenced by Rousseau, whom he called a "saint and prophet." We can, therefore, easily see why Herder felt he was doing a great service to the arts and culture in salvaging opera "from the mistaken vanity of singers and the unwise compliance of composers," as Gluck was to term it. Yet Rousseau remained opposed to classical influences on opera when he said, "They want to judge the old music of the Greeks and do not have the guts to appreciate the modern Italian melody." Herder saw opera as a synthesis of classic and romantic sources:

> Unnecessarily, one has tormented oneself about the wonders of the opera, about how people can relish such dreams of irreality and the supernatural. Are we not in our personal dreams just as much in a magic world? And how true are our dreams! Shouldn't then any art entertain us with the most beautiful dreams in a most beautiful way when we are awake? —Once put into a world in which everything sings and dances, then the world around it ought to correspond with this mood: it may enchant us.

Herder had the better of two worlds: classicism and Romanticism. So had opera at a magnificent time of transition, and it profited from it to this very day.

The Splendor of It All
or
Poetry versus Carpentry

> *Painting and carpentry are the soul of masque.*
> *Pack with your peddling poetry to the stage,*
> *This is the money-got, mechanic age.*

THESE LINES ARE TAKEN FROM BEN JONSON'S "AN EXPOSTULATION WITH Inigo Jones" at a time when Jonson's imaginative invention had to acknowledge defeat by Jones's magnificent splendor of stage designing. How familiar are the words "money-got, mechanic age" and his accusations, as if a contemporary critic were to complain about the extravagance of showy costumes and decor onstage while the content was left without substance! This complaint was made in 1631, when the English masques and antimasques began to die of their own spectacular grandeur. But England and Jonson were not isolated cases. By 1622 Lope de Vega had already attacked the stage magicians with their cloud machines and other visual tricks in a prologue to a book of *Comedias*. The dialogue runs like this:

THEATRE: Can't you see that I am injured? My arms and legs are broken. I am full of holes made by a thousand trapdoors and nails.

STRANGER: Who brought you to this miserable plight?

THEATRE: The carpenters—at the orders of the theatre managers. . . . The managers depend on machinery, the playwrights on the carpenters, and the spectators on their eyes.

When, in 1605, Jonson's and Jones's collaboration began with *The Masque of Blackness,* this new form of social entertainment for the elite of the nobles and well-to-do had a long past. The word *masque,* originally Arabic *mashara,* was used by the French, and the English adopted and used it in the French spelling for such entertainments, in which masks played a major part.

King Henry VIII—whose lust for life became notorious—and his maskers asked the ladies of the court, present at a Twelfth Night masquerade, to dance with them at the end of the masque. The ladies, however, refused, since they knew about these fashionable *masquerades,* a favorite entertainment in Italy's Ferrara and Modena and a custom marked by wanton wit and licentious gallantry with their obvious consequences. (Shakespeare has Henry VIII say to his chosen maid, Anne Bullen, in such a masque, "Sweetheart, / I were unmannerly, to take you out, / And not to kiss you.")

This was not the entertainment we know from Florence and the brilliant days of Lorenzo de' Medici. Henry, loving the pleasant paraphernalia of life more than its poetry, combined the ruthlessness and the magnificence of a medieval knight—somewhat imitative of Emperor Maximilian I, who earned the epithet of the "Last of the Knights." Henry had the boldness of a Renaissance figure but "delited in feats of chyvalrie." He loved the symbolic gesture of the tournaments, and loved the sumptuous pageants preceding them even more than the excitement of the tournaments themselves, and the disguising game connected with them more than anything else. He was fond of the lusty dances, but he did not dance as well as his daughter Elizabeth, who began her day with six galliards. Elizabeth inherited from her father a gift for poetry, music, and the dance. It was left to her to give the masque a triumphant note. And then there was Anne of Denmark, who joined James I on the Scottish and then the English thrones, who had an admirable flair and feeling for the arts, and the masque in particular.

England was not the only country in which court entertainments flourished. The rivalry between the European courts reached a feverish pitch on more than one level, with religion playing a major role in the political game of chess. But the religious issues leading to thirty years of bloodshed in 1618 were mere pretense. The real cause was a struggle for the European balance of power in which all of Europe was involved and in which wars were conducted and peace after peace concluded only to incite new battles for political predominance. In the metaphor of the chessboard, all knights were called into action, castles were besieged or liberated, and even bishops were moved for the aggrandizement of the House of Hapsburg in Spain and Austria. As always in history the pawns were the major losers: they were the common people on German soil. When it all ended, the German lands were devastated, Spain's power was gone, the United Provinces of the Netherlands had finally shaken off the Spanish yoke, England had begun to rule the waves, and France had become the established political and cultural power on the Continent.

Throughout history, what is so amazing is that half the world may bleed to death while the other half wishes to attest to its power through lavish festivities. No overall economic consideration kept the Stuart queens from squandering fortunes in order to prove them. On the other hand, to be willing to spend a great deal of money for the glory of a day does not guarantee artistic creativity. The English did not mind learning and borrowing from the French and Italians. What was known in France as *le grand ballet* became the main feature of the masque, the grand masque dance. Also, the costumings of the maskers were similar in both countries. Only the sequence of events was different: *le grand ballet* was placed at the very end of the festivities as the grand finale, while it occupied a central position in the English masque, followed by revels in which the dancers "took out" the members of the audience for a dance.

The magic of the stage design was borrowed from Italy. The Italian masquerade could easily be adopted and adjusted to anyone's national temper. It lent itself beautifully to wedding ceremonies or celebrations of all kinds, especially the arrival of foreign dignitaries—briefly, to any pretext for displaying the visual splendor of dresses and dances with a flourish. And yet with all the borrowing from foreign genius, the greatness of the English masque could not have been achieved had it not been for the presence of native genius at the right moment and the right place in Ben Jonson and Inigo Jones.

GREAT accomplishments in the arts often depend on the curious coincidence of circumstances seemingly beyond the control of those involved in them. Everything in life may be chance, but what we make of chance becomes destiny. Such a moment occurred in 1603 when Sir Robert Spencer was charged with preparing an entertainment at Althorp for Queen Anne and her son Prince Henry, who were scheduled to pass through Northamptonshire on their journey from Scotland to London. Sir Robert was aware that his entertainment might be a trivial affair, but he nevertheless thought of the poet Ben Jonson, whom he commissioned to put together a brief rustic drama for the Queen's reception. It seems Jonson did such a marvelous job that he was offered the position of purveyor-in-chief of the court amusements. This is all the more surprising because he was not an easy man to get along with. He had many notorious brawls behind him, nor was prison an alien experience to him. But by about 1602 he had many friends among the members of the Inns of Court. He was a plain-spoken man, sneering at flattery and knowing no compromise in a society in which wealth and name began to matter more and more. As a man of intellectual integrity, he had wit and charm hewn of rough vitality. What probably got him the position was his ability to overcome the barriers that normally separated his like from intimacy with court circles.

He called the entertainment he wrote for the occasion *The Satyr;* its nucleus was a speech of welcome. This minor effort must be distinguished from the masques he was later to write, in which he saw a vehicle that should combine the poetic gesture with the gaiety of whatever the festive occasion was, mainly expressed through the dance. One cannot claim that Jonson invented anything new. He only added to the many strains of the masque a poetic touch and the brightness of his inventive mind.

Had anything really changed so much when we compare the motivations for the masque with the customs of early peoples who celebrated with dance periods in the year's cycle and important passages in the life of the individual or tribe? The court masque was a direct descendant of those ancient traditions. It was related to seasonal festivals such as May Day or the Twelfth Night of Christmas as much as to royal betrothals and weddings. But Ben Jonson did not have to go that far. The nearest links to the English masques were the Renaissance intermezzi, outdoor pageants, and the variety of ballet-masquerades.

Dancing and *disguising* were the two key words for all these entertainments, and the common custom developed of having a dramatic interlude of light allegorical value or the performance of a weightier morality precede the disguising. What the masque finally accomplished was to bring all parts of the entertainment into a coherent story, generally borrowed from mythology and related to the occasion. Ben Jonson poeticized the text and gave it literary solidity.

From the very beginning, Jonson's aims for the masque were high. He wanted to bring to it the same moral purpose behind his bitter and biting comedies without curtailing the amusement through instruction. In the preface to his second masque, *Hymenaei* (1606), he refers to his patrons as being "curious after the most high and hearty inventions . . . and those grounded upon authority and solid learnings; which though their voice be taught to sound to present occasions, their sense doth or should always lay hold on more removed mysteries."

It was this belief in the "more removed mysteries," in the depth of the poetic image, that made Jonson write masques. Long after he became disgusted with what usually went into the writing of masques and at a time when he wrote one of his last masques, *Chloridia,* at Shrovetide 1630, he still stated emphatically his belief in a more meaningful work to be presented: "All representations, especially those of this nature in court, public spectacles, either have been, or ought to be, the mirrors of man's life, whose ends, for the excellence of their exhibitors (as being the donatives of great princes to their people), ought always to carry a mixture of profit with them no less than delight."

Jonson never turned against the dancing. He acknowledged the importance of the dancing masters who drilled the aristocratic amateurs, rehearsing with them for weeks—one record speaks of fifty days. The dance steps were not altogether unknown to them. Most of the time the dancing was an imaginative attempt at creating, with the steps used in social dances, something that came close to a choreographic conceit. The dancing masters had a somewhat easier time with the professional dancer-actors, to whom the parts of the antimasques were usually assigned. Jonson had no quarrel with the composers of these masques, although only second- and third-rate composers wrote the music. Here—with the English offering their most accomplished contribution to dance development—we find a curious parallel to those minor composers of the Romantic era of the nineteenth century.

According to the published version of Jonson's *Masque of Queens,* one must assume that all the aspects of its performance, besides the basic concept, were envisioned by the author—verse, costume, music, and the choreographic notions—when he wrote:

> At which, with a strange and sudden music, they fell into a magical dance, full of preposterous change and gesticulation, but most applying to their property: who, at their meetings, do all things contrary to the custom of men, dancing back to back, hip to hip, their hands joined, and making their circles backward, to the left hand, with strange fantastic motions of their heads and bodies. All which were excellently imitated by the maker of the dance, Mr Hierome Herne, whose right it is here to be named.

However potent Ben Jonson's influence on such productions may have been, no one—not even at his time—has ever doubted that he came close to the high goal he had set for himself, except Inigo Jones and one minor writer of masques, Samuel Daniel, who assailed Jonson's pretensions to literary ambition and dramatized erudition in the writing of masques. Daniel wanted to free himself from the tyranny of antiquity and did not see any "reason why we may not emancipate our inventions, and be as free as they to use our own images." But it was not only the high and holy function of the poet, as Jonson envisioned it for all writers of masques, that would have separated him from Daniel; it was rather Daniel's total subservience to Inigo Jones when he spoke of "the art and invention of the architect" that "gives the greatest grace, and is of most importance: ours, the least part and of least note in the time of the performance thereof. . . ."

Daniel's was only one man's voice, and, at that, the voice of a minor poet (or "no poet," as Jonson retorted), but in the years between 1604 and 1640, the years in which most masques were produced, Daniel's attitude came closest to the sentiment of the courtiers in whose behalf the masques were arranged. It is the irony of fate that Jonson's inventiveness contributed to the deterioration of this art form that was brought about by the inclusion of the antimasque, although this did indeed heighten its effect. This process began in 1609, when Queen Anne voiced the general feeling of the court— certainly her own—that weariness may set in through the display of so much beauty and of such an incessant parade of grandeur; "the nobility of invention" and "the dignity of their persons" made such a masque too uniformly solemn. Ben Jonson lets us know in the prefatory remarks to *The Masque of Queens* that "Her Majesty had commanded me to think on some dance or show that might precede hers and have the place of foil or false masque."

This was the beginning of the antimasque. Jonson thought of twelve hags, "not unaptly sorting with the current and whole fall of the device," who were the very opposite of the twelve queens of the main masque. The antithesis of characters was beautifully employed in this masque and served to relieve the exaltation of beauty and the solemn formality of the main masque. Since so often the opposite helps create the right balance and strengthens purpose and affect, the antimasque accentuated the leading idea and gave it the life and new glamour it did not previously have.

The experiment was justified by its success. Jonson foresaw, however, the dangers inherent in the entertainment value of the antimasque. He permitted himself the inclusion of only one antic scene—for which he had a particular flair—and this scene had to be well placed. He realized that such gaiety could easily have a demoralizing effect on audiences that merely flirted with the seriousness of life and in whose hands the antimasque would be a welcome toy.

The transcript of *The Masque of the Inner Temple and Gray's Inn*— which was danced on February 20, 1613, as part of the celebration for the wedding of the Princess Elizabeth and the Elector Palatine—gives a clear account of how the antimasque soon began to defeat the very thing it tried to enhance. It was written by Francis Beaumont and dedicated to Sir Francis Bacon, that eminent philospher of the Baroque, the only one of the time who was not a mathematician and who believed in the need of destructive criticism as much as Descartes believed in doubt. This philosopher, who asked in his investigations for material evidence and not blind judgment, was called the "chief contriver" of this masque; moreover, Beaumont addressed him personally in his dedication, saying:

> And you Sir Francis Bacon especially, as you did then by your countenance and loving affection advance it, so let your good word grace it and defend it, which is able to add value to the greatest and least matters.

However insignificant this matter must have been in the eyes of those learned men in the Inner Temple and Gray's Inn, they did not foresee that the production of the masque would put both inns deep into debt. But what did these exorbitant expenses mean in the face of the great pleasure that this masque afforded His Majesty! There were two antimasques providing much of the fun, and these interludes were seemingly so impressive that "it pleased His Majesty to call for [the second] again at the end, as he did likewise for the first anti-masque. . . ." Never in history have the members of any court failed to love what His Majesty loved, and this meant the beginning of the end for what was to be a unique contribution of the English to the development of the dance. Jonson was not willing to give in, and when he introduced two antimasques in *Neptune's Triumph for the Return of Albion* in the year 1625 it was only to ridicule this outrage that was in such great demand. Jonson held on to his poetic principles against "progress." He even went so far as to ask that the dances—and there he allowed as many as seemed necessary—be made to fit the action.

We must wonder that Jonson should not have been able to measure the temperature of the social body in England correctly. After all, this was the same man who, in 1606, had come out with his masterpiece *Volpone,* satirizing greed incarnate, and shortly after with *The Alchemist,* adding gullibility to greed. Was he not irate about the acquisitiveness of the age? Did he not fume with fury while watching how London turned from a cultural into a mercantile center? We cannot blame history with its Puritan wave sweeping over the land, carrying with it all things evil and good, for having stopped the masque and antimasque. In a mood of anger, Jonson often exposed "the time's deformity." Why should he think that the taste of the courtiers would show no moral and intellectual decline when, in fact, it was the aristocracy that set the tone in England in the first half of the seventeenth century? With so many victories won, with the rapid growth of their fortune and fortunes, the populace, the powerful bourgeoisie, the arrogant courtiers all went through the normal process of losing within while gaining without. With Jonson's poetry less and less in demand, everyone wanted to be dazzled by the display of visual splendor.

The Triumphant Machines

THERE WAS NOWHERE A GREATER RENAISSANCE THEATER THAN THE Elizabethan, rivaling in depth and scope the drama of the Sophoclean age. Besides the unfortunate fanatic Oliver Cromwell, England gave the seventeenth century Francis Bacon, John Milton, and Henry Purcell; Sir Christopher Wren and Inigo Jones, two architects who made the Italianate Baroque look English; and above all, Sir Isaac Newton.

The words *science* and *mathematics* will always be used when the accomplishments of the seventeenth century are discussed. Our modern age began with the search for scientific truth at that time. It did not happen in only one nation. The search for the reality of facts could be found in all European countries and the exchange of ideas from country to country was slowed down only by the difficulty of communication. The word *science* was on everyone's lips—as *geometry* was in the Age of Mannerism—and, naturally, overused. In a treatise on dancing and deportment, published in 1623 by F. De Lauze under the title of *Apologie de la Danse,* we find "The science of behavior (or civility) should be necessary to youth" and "I do not spare many worthy people who have conversed so long and happily on this mountain, so greatly renowned of the God of the Sciences, and who have so justly discoursed upon that which they have undertaken. . . ." The word *science,* then a common household word, only signified that people were thinking along scientific lines. But behind all this grand quest for truth stood the belief that everything in the world and the cosmos is harmoniously arranged, that there is somewhere a symmetry ordained by a higher power—a thought lingering from earlier days. Even though people still sought the truth of man's "thinking heart"—to use Donne's phrase—a rational approach to the phenomena of nature characterizes the seventeenth century.

This entire process of getting a firm grip on the facts of appearance led to the setting up of rules and academies to enforce them. These belong with the great achievements of the century, and there can be no doubt that the classical dance, also, could only begin to unfold in such a scientific atmosphere. Rules gave the dance its backbone. When Françoise Prévost succeeded the first ballerina, Mlle Lafontaine, as première danseuse at the Royal Academy of Dance in 1705, Pierre Rameau, the author of *The Dancing Master,* could write that Prévost "put into one single dance all the rules we are able to give in our art and she puts them into practice with such grace, justness, and activity that she may be looked upon as a prodigy of her kind."

THE man who contributed most to what he termed *Rules for the Direction of the Mind* during this century was René Descartes (1596–1650), generally considered the father of the modern science of thought through his belief in the possibility of mathematical exactitude in metaphysical reasoning. He discarded the authoritarian system of the scholastics, introducing the thought of universal doubt. On the premise that there is one thing only that cannot be doubted, namely doubt itself, he cleared the road for the advance toward truth. If one can say that the eighteenth century is the age of Voltaire, then the seventeenth is the century of Descartes.

It was the era that celebrated "Reason" like a goddess. Hand in hand with the most spectacular advances in science came the invention of instruments and machines that helped create a new world. The Dutch invented the telescope, which Galileo (1564–1642) improved to such an extent that he could study the skies and—with his confirmation of the Copernican thought—upset the world with the news that the earth revolves around the sun. The thought that the world of mankind could no longer be considered the center of the universe was an assault on the Aristotelean professors in Italy and on Christian teaching, which believed in the Ptolemaic system. The cardinals, supported by the Jesuits, were convinced that Galileo's ideas would have graver consequences than those of Luther and Calvin put together and be of much comfort to the Protestants. Whatever immediate struggles ensued between the beliefs of the past and the new forces, the greatest incentive for a daring advance of science was Galileo's proof that the "book of nature is written in mathematical characters," as he said in *Il Saggiatore*.

Then came Newton and gave us an exact, logical, mathematical account of the cosmos, notions with which people lived for two and a half centuries until Einstein's theories superseded them. We know from our experiences in our own time what fascination light can have, how it can awake untold illusions and even make us believe it can move and dance. Newton discovered the theory of the spectrum and the Dutch scientist Christiaan Huygens the wave theory of light.

With light becoming a focal point of scientific investigation, it could not fail to attract the attention of the scenic designers and, above all, the painters. It was the time when the drama of light against darkness was discovered, leading to a new vision of tangible reality. Michelangelo da Caravaggio (1573–1610), breaking away from Mannerism, was the first to find a new way of seeing nature and, like the scientists of his day, had a burning passion for the face of truth. He dared to give his characters the plebeian expression they actually had. His cheats and rogues prepare us for the faces Frans Hals would soon paint, or Hogarth several decades later.

Caravaggio's "The Musicians" characterizes the degree of reality that this painter brought to Italian visual arts in the early seventeenth century. (Courtesy The Metropolitan Museum of Art, Rogers Fund, 1952)

LIGHT began to play a decisive role in the way it fell through a room or moved across a face or drapery. It evoked a realistic feeling, which the Dutch painters perfected to such an extent that their paintings often make you think you can walk into a room and visit with the people whom Jan Vermeer, say, painted with endearing love for the most minute detail. While Caravaggio was infusing his Christian stories with a down-to-earth spirit whose extremism often angered the Church authorities, the Dutch painters mainly remained in the reality of their little world. Only Rembrandt van

Rijn (1606–69) dared to break through the naturalism of his compatriots to a deep understanding of and sympathy with the human being. His unique greatness lies in the fact that he never painted for the sheer virtuosity of his craftsmanship but that the pictorial was never separated from human compassion, whether he painted portraits or re-created a scene from the Bible. The realism of the drama in life found its expression in the contrast of searching light and deep shadow that he caught on his canvases.

THE simultaneity of divergent trends flowering at different places is in no way surprising since the various European peoples had different backgrounds in past experiences, character, and tradition. The Dutch skillfully built up a small empire of enlightened mercantilism in a living democracy in which the intellectual and artistic life reached rare heights in the seventeenth century; and while a dazzling world of masked make-believe enchanted the English nobility, Italy gave birth to the opera as well as to the physical wonders of the theater. For most artists from all over the Western world, Italy was still the place to be visited, the place where they hoped to experience the great revelations of the day and to meet some of the finest creative minds from all over Europe.* Among them was also Inigo Jones, of whose stunning creations for the English masque we have heard. By the year 1603 he journeyed south to witness the new surprising developments in scenic designs. Everything Jones created for the masque was extravagant in the Baroque sense; only his architectural work introduced a classic style to England, "solid, proportional according to the rules, masculine, and unaffected."

Jones's enthusiasm brought him back to Italy, where he spent the winter of 1613–14. There he may have heard about the French engraver Jacques Callot, who at that time lived in Florence, where he was employed by the Medici to make pictorial records of their lavish entertainments. Jones may have learned more about the commedia dell'arte from him than from seeing their performances. Callot mastered to translate those mannered, artificial court festivities—which had a recognizable touch of the Baroque—into a very personal and naturalistic style. Callot's etchings were popular because he also had a special gift for the grotesque. With a few lines he could conjure up an elongated figure of the commedia and make it memorable. Dance enthusiasts can learn far more from Callot's etchings about the movements then employed than they can from any verbal description.

* There were exceptions. Shakespeare, Rembrandt, and Bach never set foot on Italian soil, nor did Sir Christopher Wren, to whom English architecture is deeply indebted. But Wren managed to go to France, where he met Bernini. Florence, Mantua, Bologna, and Venice in the north and Rome and Naples in the south were important cultural centers. While Claudio Monteverdi was still working for Duke Vincenzo I, Peter Paul Rubens was court painter at Mantua. Traveling artists have always been important links in a cultural exchange that speaks all languages.

WHAT were the theatrical wonders by which the Italian scenic designers and architects proved their post-Renaissance genius? The concepts of the theater buildings changed from decade to decade. First, about 1606, wings were added, which made the behind-the-scenes activities easier for the performers. With the completion, in 1619, of the Teatro Farnese at Parma, one of the first more elaborate stages was created. It had a permanent proscenium, but the idea of a decorative frame had been known for some time. By the beginning of the seventeenth century most theaters worked with backdrops and sky borders masking the flies and lighting units. In general, greater mobility brought about an until then unknown scenic splendor.

One of the famous etchings by Jacques Callot of a typical commedia dell'arte scene. (Courtesy the Author)

*The Drottningholm Theater near Stockholm is the only extant Baroque the-
ater producing opera and ballet the way it was done at the end of the eighteenth century. (Courtesy Swedish Information Service)*

Giacomo Torelli (1608–78) was one of the most important masterminds
behind theater machinery. There was no end to magical effects: devices to
stage a city in flames, to simulate waves onstage, to have wing flats move
quickly in grooves. Torelli, in his Teatro Novissimo in Venice, constructed a
revolving stage. He had a device for quick scene changes: wings moved
from below the stage with the help of a drum through slits onto the stage.
Some of the stages were raked to create the impression of a deep perspective.
Chandeliers hung over the stage. Most of the action was first carried out on
the forestage, but over the years the actors moved into the area of the scenic
display.

There were stage technicians who performed scenic miracles. They delighted in stunning images of moving clouds and scenic changes with rocks shifting, and people and scenery being lowered and raised with the help of machines. Everyone used trapdoors. Platforms could be brought in behind gossamer veils so that no one would notice the trick. Entire palaces and ships mounted on wheels rolled onto the stage. Torelli's stunning system of wheels and rollers enabled one man to change the wings in a minute. A fine example of a Baroque theater still in working condition can be found in Drottningholm near Stockholm, Sweden.

Quite a few scenic artists left their imprint on the Baroque theater, which is mostly the theater we still know. Besides Torelli and Jones there were Bernardo Buontalenti (1536–1608), Ludovico Burnacini (1636–1707), Giambattista Piranesi (1720–78), and three generations of the Galli da Bibiena family, the oldest born in 1657, the youngest dying in 1787. Their influence on painted scenery was especially remarkable. Opera houses have made use of it all along the centuries. The painter's scenery came back with Diaghilev's Ballets Russes, and the décors, from Léon Bakst's sumptuous colors to Pablo Picasso's mocking style, reflected this company's traditional and experimental years.

Of course, one could claim that the Baroque did not really start all these stunning effects through stage machinery. Vitruvius maintained that Aeschylus introduced scene painting, although we know from Aristotle that Sophocles should be credited with it. The ancient Greeks used machines that could roll out platforms and others to facilitate raising and lowering divinities. In Aristophanes' *Clouds,* Socrates is hung in a basket by such means. The phrase *deus ex machina* derives from the use of the *mechane.*

Vasari tells us in his famous *Lives* about stage machinery used in the *sacra rappresentazione* during the Florentine religious festivals in the days of the Renaissance. He credits two architects with having engineered these mechanical contrivances: Filippo Brunelleschi and Francesco d'Angelo, called La Cecca. Vasari speaks of this machine, referred to as the *gloria* or *paradiso,* as it was used in the Teatro San Felice in Piazza in Florence for *The Annunciation:*

> The paradiso was really a wonderful thing, displaying the ability and industry of the inventor, for it presented the spectacle of Heaven full of living figures that moved about amid an infinite quantity of lights which appeared and disappeared like lightning.

Brunelleschi also placed two large doors moving in grooves on rollers above the *paradiso,* sliding open to each side. A cord could pull these doors open and close them. Vasari underlines that, because of their weight, they sounded like thunder when they moved.

Vasari also lets us know that La Cecca invented similar contrivances for another spectacle, called *The Ascension*. With the help of this machine "Christ was raised from a mountain marvellously constructed of wood, and carried to Heaven by a cloud full of Angels, leaving the Apostles on the mountain." At the end of his description Vasari reiterates that "these ingenious things and many others" were invented by Brunelleschi, although some people maintained that they were introduced long before. In an earlier and similar production such contrivances may have been used. But Vasari leaves us vague about it.

The production of BELLEROPHON *in Venice (1642) is a good example of seventeenth-century scenic splendor, with a palace in heaven and a descending chariot. (Courtesy French Cultural Services)*

"Design for Cloudwork and Divinities," which may have been done by Buontalenti. (Photo Victoria and Albert Museum. Devonshire Collection, Chatsworth. Reproduced by permission of the Trustees of the Chatsworth Settlement)

WHATEVER scenic accomplishments there may have been in the past, the Baroque theater perfected them. These stage wonders belonged to the essential nature of the age, for the theatricality in the playhouses only reflected the theatricality of all facets of life. Feudalism could not help showing off the splendor of its power, and the splendor had to increase with its outside power and inside weakness. Since the early Renaissance and the first pageants it had been a question of theatrics. The scientific trend in the early Baroque inevitably led to the building of theaters. While ballets were still performed in the halls of palaces and mansions, the opera, with its professionalism, created an ever louder demand for a theater. Venice, which first became the focal point of opera productions, is a good example of this. Venice had a musical tradition of long standing and, since Aretino's days, the joy of life as the major motivation of its people was well known. The people crowded the churches, but not so much to participate in the service as to hear good music.

In 1613 Monteverdi left Mantua and became maestro di capella at the Basilica of San Marco. The San Cassiano, the first European opera house, opened its door in 1637. In the course of the seventeenth century, Venice offered operas and plays in sixteen theaters simultaneously, not including the many private little stages in palaces and the itinerant troupes that found a rich and art-interested public there. To go to the theater was a way of life. The Venetians loved disguising, so they went to the theater masked, and everyone came, the nobleman and the gondolier, the working woman and the doge's wife. In Venice, theaters were still considered a property and showcase of feudalism, but in the Republic of Venice there was a touch of democratic life—naturally, in moderation only: the boxes were the sole property of rich patricians. It was not before 1651 that an ordinary burgher could also be registered as the owner of a loge. This custom was started by the then newly built opera house Sant' Apollinare.

Venice was the first city in which the theater turned into show business. The Grimani family became the most powerful impresarios, owning several theaters. Their most spectacular stage was the San Giovanni Crisostomo, which took only four months to build and turned out to outdo all others in size and splendor.†

Venice and Holland, republics in their fashion, burgeoned with pen and brush, with theatrical and vocal ecstasies. They remained almost untouched by the political upheavals and the religious strife that marked the century,

† In comparison, most of the French theaters were court theaters, like those in the Louvre and Versailles, or the Salle du Petit-Bourbon, which was later turned over to acting companies, as were the Palais Royal and Théâtre du Marais, opened under Richelieu in 1634.
    Mazarin brought Giacomo Torelli to France in 1645 to stage operas at court and, fourteen years later, Gaspare Vigarani to build the Salle des Machines and its stage machinery in the Tuileries.

The equestrian ballet was one of the favorite feudal entertainments that disappeared in the seventeenth century when the opera gradually took its place. Only the Hapsburgs in Spain and Austria preserved the tradition of four hundred years. Vienna's Spanish Riding School with its amazing race of Spanish-bred horses has kept up the quality of technically dazzling performances. (Courtesy Austrian Press and Information Service, New York)

while Spain experienced nostalgically the sunset of its glory, while the German lands were bleeding in a life-and-death struggle, while France secured its authoritarian grandeur and England its splendid isolation. The Italians made their last great contribution to the civilization of the Western world with the opera and scenic machinery.

The rejuvenation of the theater in the early Baroque was not the work of the dramatic poet or of the professional actor. It was created by Italian architects and painters and thus was the most logical finale to the Renaissance dream. A visual image was created to serve a social purpose and function. No doubt it was a new beginning with a beautiful, dazzling-looking shell. No one really cared about the content of the plays. The theater was eye- and ear-filling. It was keyed to magic, mystery, and illusion. After all, there is such a thing as visual poetry. How often to this very day a rising curtain reveals the stunning pictorialization of a mood, an amazingly painted statement of a situation! Does not the audience applaud it—before a single word is yet spoken or sung, before the first dance phrase commences? Why should we then blame the people of the seventeenth century for acknowledging the enchantment the Italian stage magicians prepared for them?

The Thinking Heart in the Great World Theater

THERE IS ONE ASPECT OF THE BAROQUE THAT HAD A DECISIVE INFLUENCE on the arts of several countries as a deterrent rather than a stimulation. In the wake of the Reformation a variety of new sects emerged, of believers in God in their own fashion. As if the world badly needed a counterpoint to its reasoning and rationalizing attitude, a turmoil of disputes over religious questions arose and was fought out on the battlefields with cannon and sword as much as with speech and pen. It was a great time for the preacher and his sermons on death, damnation, and decay. John Donne (1572–1631), poet and priest, or rather poet because priest and priest because poet, was one of the outstanding preachers of his age, followed by the Germans Angelus Silesius, who wrote some of the most pensive poetry, and the remarkable Protestant hymn writer Paul Gerhardt. Yet Donne's "naked thinking heart," whose voice had the power of passion from the pulpit or the written word, best reflects the metaphysical poetry of those days in which feeling and thought, the spirit and the flesh, were poetically blended.

The poetry, however, was lost in dispute and persecutions, with the flesh paying a heavy penalty for the people's spirit in uproar. The principal thought of the Pietists that the Reformation is not something that can ever be completed but must renew itself constantly led to an individual outburst of sectarianism lasting well into the eighteenth century. The irony was that all the groups desired basically the same things: liturgical reform, a purification and simplification, as well as a heightening of inwardness. It always began with the notion of finding mystical experiences outside the ordinary ecclesiastic channels or an immediate experience of oneness with Ultimate Reality.

Quietism, a movement issuing from and within the Roman Catholic faith, postulated tenets parallel to those of the Pietists and Quakers, seeking perfection in the passivity of the soul. Such an interior way of contemplation and such a desire of opening one's soul to a superior being—in other words, the pure and quietistic elements—can be found in many beliefs, certainly in Buddhism and even in Gnosticism. However pious and pure these concepts appear to be, in the eyes of the worldly and ecclesiastic powers they contained irksome, if not revolutionary, elements that had to be suppressed. The political mind knew how to play on the delusion and passion of the people and how to profit from schisms. The Thirty Years' War left Germany devastated and retarded its cultural rise for at least a hundred years. It strengthened France, which could fortify its leadership in all spheres of human activity, while liquidating its own religious dissenters perfidiously but skillfully. In England, also, open conflict was inevitable and soon turned into political battles between the old and new forces and spiritual concepts, between the relative importance of the King and the people. After 1620 many Puritans began a new life in the New World and took their religious world with them.

Those who stayed in England finally became followers of "the great Independent," as Oliver Cromwell was called, who favored sectarianism. His fatalistic and fanaticized religious beliefs made him appear as a man of fierce passions who interpreted God's will for himself. An ardent Puritan he felt it divine justice that the theaters be closed in the wake of internal strife. The year was 1642. That the London theaters had been on the wane since the 1630s was not something he was concerned about. Certain amusements were incompatible with the spirit of Puritanism. Accordingly, there was little public dancing in Cromwell's revolutionary days—the period of the civil war and the Commonwealth—but the interest in the art did not vanish. Cromwell himself, who was a great lover of music, did not mind dancing at his daughter's wedding, and he presided over an official production of a masque in 1653, honoring a Portuguese ambassador.

Also under the Commonwealth, John Playford published *The English Dancing Master: or, Plaine and easie rules for the Dancing of Country Dances, with the tune to each dance,* an anthology of 104 social dances of the time, and a book of some influence on future generations. There was dancing during the reign of the Puritans. There even was dancing in New

England among the early Puritan settlers because we know of a dancing master who dared to set up a school of "mixt dancing," moreover on Sundays, and who created a scandal. As some scholars suggest, he may have precipitated Increase Mather's famous tract *An Arrow Against Profane and Promiscuous Dancing Drawn Out of the Quiver of the Scriptures,* which was issued in Boston in 1684. Certainly the Puritan spirit suppressed theatrical experiences in New England, but could not prevent casual performances —mainly of amateur actors—in other parts of the country or the appearance of the professional Hallam Company from London, which presented *The Merchant of Venice* as its inaugural production in Williamsburg in 1752. Not until after the Revolutionary War and the repeal of the antitheater law in 1789 did European-trained artists begin to appear more regularly in America, giving the first impulses to a histrionic development in the United States, even though the Puritan prejudice was noticeable well into the nineteenth century.

That dancing in general, but particularly theatrical dancing, is now overflowing the United States is as if history would like to make up for lost time and early Puritan mistakes. It is amazing to think that in 1785, about two hundred years ago, when the theater dance was a self-understood feature of the theatrical entertainments all over Europe, John Durang, the first famous American-born dancer, had to disguise his dance performance in Philadelphia as a lecture—in the same way that a production of *Othello* in Newport, Rhode Island, had to be advertised as a "Series of Moral Dialogues" a few years previously.

The great number of reformers after the Reformation who followed an inner voice compelling them to better all reformers did not have only a negative influence on the development of the dance. There were two groups which, almost at the same time—though with different religious roots and for different reasons—made dancing one of their outer ways of inner experiences.

The Shakers were an offshoot of the Quakers in England, led by one of them, "Mother" Ann Lee, daughter of an English blacksmith, to the New World in 1774 in order to escape persecution and, most significantly, in response to a revelation. They lived in the style of a commune, separated from the world and its sinful ways, and also separating the sexes among them. Similar to Christian Science doctrines, the Shakers believed in the power over physical disease. The "shaking" was a bodily response to religious ecstasy, and ritualistic exercises were central to their belief. Their dances were sometimes circular, sometimes in lines, standing dances and shuffles as well as elaborated marches. Their religious philosophy made them incorporate gestures, such as bowing, stamping, and whirling, reminiscent of the ecstatic dances of early peoples—with the difference that the Shakers were aware of the symbolic meaning of their gestures, which were termed "gifts"

"Shakers near Lebanon," a lithograph by N. Currier (undated). (Courtesy the Museum of the City of New York, the Harry T. Peters Collection)

according to the scriptural meaning of "gift." For instance, one might have the gift of shaking or turning like a wheel. The Shakers' dancing was all more or less improvised.‡

The dancing of the Pietist movement of the Hasidim who protested the orthodox system of Judaism was also basically extemporaneous. Hasidism goes back to the Jewish mystics in the twelfth and thirteenth centuries, but this modern spiritual revolution took place in the eighteenth century when Israel ben Eliezer—or Baal Shem-Tov, "Master of the Holy Name"—became the focal point of a new mystic interpretation of Scripture among the Jews of Eastern Europe. He turned against the Talmudic withdrawal from the world and spoke of the immanence of God in all existence. A

‡ Doris Humphrey created an artistically impressive version of a Shaker dance in which she made use of the ritual of "dancing one's sins away" for a theatrical presentation, accompanied by speech, song, and accordion. This dance, whose first professional performance was at the Craig Theatre in New York City, 1931, and which was a year later inserted in the Broadway musical *Americana,* has become one of the classics of the modern dance in America.

stronger awareness of communion with God related to all activities in life permeated with joy, with the pursuit of a pious but also living happiness. Religious songs and especially dancing belonged to the ritualistic features for which the Hasidim were known.

The Shakers and the Hasidim both sought a sense of spiritual liberation. They renewed an experience known to the shaman and to King David dancing before the Lord, to prophets and dervishes. At all times it has been the raw feeling of aloneness and the desire to link our littleness with the cosmic powers that has made us move our body to make manifest the soul.

Tremendous forces of spirituality accumulated during the seventeenth century. People tried to escape the hierarchic, orthodox confinement of the established religious powers in a variety of manners for the sake of what they felt to be true faith. The century faced the challenge of and struggled with phenomena determined by their contrasts: illusion and reality, doubt and absolutism, the desire to transcend one's being by the means of reason or religion. There was something theatrical about the greatness of its achievements as much as about its disasters. It was an era for which Calderón found the most telling description when in 1649 he named one of his *autos* —his dramatized religious allegories—*El gran teatro del mundo*. Indeed, the seventeenth century was God's greatest world theater, a spectacular and an extravaganza par excellence.

Audiences

THIS CENTURY WITNESSED A DECISIVE CHANGE IN THE AUDIENCE-ARTIST relationship. There had been a long period in which the ballet de cour was an exclusive affair of the nobility, acting as both performers and watchers. As dancers the nobles were amateurs in the best and worst sense. The only professional outsider was the dancing master. Even in the days when the dancing master began to fulfill the duties of a choreographer—as was the case with Beaujoyeulx of the *Ballet Comique* or such minor maîtres de ballet as Thomas Giles and Hieronymus Herne choreographing most of the masques and antimasques in England—the participants were members of the aristocracy. The exception were those antic characters of the antimasques with which no nobleman wanted to be identified and which, moreover, only a professional actor could properly perform.

In the course of time more and more ballets were produced, particularly in France, whose nobility associated itself ever closer with this art form as if it were their private possession. Performances took place at the court and in private homes. The golden age of the ballet de cour lasted from 1581, when the *Ballet Comique* established the art of theater dance, until 1681, when the first professional ballerina, Mlle Lafontaine, appeared onstage. These hundred years saw the tremendous transposition in which noblemen gradually relinquished their role as active participants in the various ballet performances, exchanging it for the part of patron. Onstage, the courtiers realized that they depended on the professionally trained dancers and that they could never compete with them. There were, of course, as many exceptions as any rule needs, and to prove the contrary one can easily cite the example of such an impressive dancer as the duc de Luynes, Louis XIII's favorite "gentilhomme de la chambre," who not only took over the leading roles, but practically was the soul of all ballets in the years 1615 to 1621.

The feudalistic society had made proper use of the dancing master since the early days of the Renaissance, but the growing need for technical proficiency and elegant eloquence made the acceptance of dancers of the less privileged classes necessary. The foundation of academies in the latter part of the century was but a confirmation of the general trend toward professionalism, to be expected in an age that so strongly believed in a rationalized process of thinking.

THE conventions of what constituted an audience and who was to be seated where changed with the centuries. The nobility hardly ever visited public theaters in sixteenth-century England, and no woman was seen there if she cared for her reputation. In case she nevertheless desired to attend a performance, she wore a mask to avoid recognition. The aristocrats had their private theaters. In Elizabethan England and well into the seventeenth century the public was admitted to the theaters according to class distinction. The galleries were reserved for the upper classes, while the lower classes were crowded into the pit, where seats were rare and thus the pit could hold a large number of people. For some privileged gentlemen, seating was provided on the stage itself whenever necessary. This habit, a great nuisance for the actors, was strangely enough continued into the eighteenth century in some smaller theaters.

As we know from the seating arrangement on the occasion of the *Ballet Comique,* there was a throne or thronelike seat, often with a velvet canopy embroidered with gold and silver, reserved for the King or any prince, who was surrounded, at a certain distance, by his courtiers and bodyguard. This central and sheltered position of royalty was a continued practice even when the opera houses were built and the horseshoe theater came into fashion. Then the royal box faced the stage, as did the royal seat in the princely halls of the earlier centuries. The King could observe the stage action most conveniently and—just as important—he could conveniently be observed by the audience. In the era of the Baroque, when many horseshoe theaters were built for the art-supporting aristocracy, the boxes on the same level as the royal box were reserved for the highest-ranking nobles. Reversing the practice of the Elizabethan stage, the more expensive seats for the lower-ranking nobles were created where once there was standing room only; the middle class was forced into the balcony and galleries. The fashion of hooped skirts dictated that only two ladies could be seated in a box, while the gentlemen usually stood behind them to have a decent view of the stage.

The gradual change from the amateur dancer to the professional artist had its counterpart in the composition of the audience. The English masques were exclusively arranged for and by the nobility. This type of entertainment was imitated by wealthy citizens on a smaller scale, but there was little mingling of the classes. The spectators were made participants of the affair when the masquers "took out" the spectators of the other sex. This "commoning," as it was also called, was for many the favorite part of the spectacle, a kind of well-defined audience participation. Ben Jonson says in his famous *Masque of Queens* that after the masquers' second dance "they took out the men and daunc'd the *measures,* entertayning the time, almost to the space of an hower, with singular variety"—which also informs us that the performing dancers were female members of the nobility.

The gradually progressing colonization made the merchants and townspeople in most European countries, and particularly in France, prosper in the seventeenth century. A well-to-do middle class became more and more acceptable to the lower-ranking aristocrats who frequently mingled with them in their playhouses, although the courts had their own theaters. The exalted members of the aristocracy hardly ever visited private theaters. There were private performances for them in the Louvre or Versailles, in Fontainebleau or St.-Germain, as well as in the theaters in the palaces of those who held high positions. The less privileged person tried to play the gate-crasher and participate in ballet performances of the upper classes. With more and more theaters being built after 1637, more well-to-do citizens were welcome as ticket purchasers since the upkeep of the court theaters was quite expensive. Toward the end of the seventeenth century and more so in the first half of the next, all court theaters were forced to open their doors to a paying public. But the festive mood of theatergoing was kept alive. One not only paid a high entrance fee but also wore one's best Sunday suit. Our gala performances have retained this festive spirit, to which also belonged the desire to be seen as well as to see the stage action.

At the same time a broadening of the audience also took place in the playhouses. Despite his absolutist mentality, Louis XIV had a unique attitude toward the arts and the Parisian public. While keeping up his entertaining productions at the Louvre and in Versailles for his courtiers and their ladies, he turned two theaters over to the public and acting companies, the Palais-Royal and the Petit-Bourbon. Moreover, he spent considerable sums on subsidizing his Italian players as well as Molière's company, which, after Molière's death, was amalgamated with the company at the Théâtre du Marais. Thus he created a new audience that was to become highly sophisticated. When Molière died, Lully and the French opera took up the greatest interest of the theater-loving public. In 1680 the King unified the various acting groups into a single company, to be seen at one playhouse only. Again, this was a first for the growing cultural dominance of France: now it had a national theater—the world's first—which was to be known as the Comédie-Française. This grand gesture of the King proved his ardent love of the stage.

Like his academies, however, the Comédie-Française was also strong testimony to his love of ordered power. The state-supported theater was a product of absolutism as much as was the whole of France. The arts cannot necessarily flourish in a climate of rigid rules and regulations from which any healthful competition or rebellious thoughts are barred. Conversely, the public could depend on high standards in its acting and in the cultivation of the classic repertory. For another hundred years the French language and culture reigned supreme. Only the English theater kept its independent development (while failing to develop any remarkable dancers). Theaters in the German-speaking lands remained Gallicized until Lessing's essays *Hamburgische Dramaturgie* and the attack on the critic Johann Christoph Gottsched's domination of the literary scene and advocation of French pseudo-classicism. The Comédie-Française remained true to its principles, supported by an audience reared in the spirit of Corneille and the style of Racine.

The arts were far more broadly based among the people in Italy than in France. They reached a wider spectrum there, as if a public had grown during the Renaissance into something that could truly be called native, whereas art came as an importation of Italian genius to France and mainly with the intention of pleasing the upper classes. But toward the latter part of the seventeenth century the French bourgeoisie also came to appreciate the arts. They gained more and more access to the sources of the arts, they could prove their appreciation of what they were shown, and, with the human gift for adaptation and need for imitation, they had soon adopted the characteristics of an aristocratic outlook on life.

WHETHER the spectators belong to the aristocracy or the bourgeoisie, the crux of any theatrical performance has always been the interaction between stage and public, however uneven and complex the relationship of these two partners may be. Theater is a malleable notion. From time to time we may have to decide on what constitutes theater, each period creating what it needs and deserves. With its stress on the contemporary, theater cannot easily divorce itself from the experience of the day.

Bravos and boos will resound in the theater as long as theaters exist. They are as old as the East Indian dance-drama where we seem to find the first evidence of applause, acclamation, and refutation. The audience plays a double role: giving and receiving. This raises the question of whether the theater is a shrine of amusement or, as Friedrich Schiller thought, a moral institution. Or is the purpose of the theater, as Bertolt Brecht believed, not only to educate but to act as a tribunal, demanding a verdict from the audience? I have seen stunned, bewildered-looking audiences faced with experimental productions and audiences mesmerized or emotionally whipped up to ecstasies by subcultural experiences.

What lucky people, what a fortunate era in which the arts can arouse as much fanatical interest as any vital issue in the political arena of a nation! And woe to an epoch in which no one is scandalized in theaters, in concert halls, or at exhibitions! Indifference and polite applause drive nails deep into the coffin of the arts. Flaubert said that theater is not an art but a secret. He was right, however we wish to interpret it. And the key to this secret has always been the audience.

Academies

THE SPLENDOR AND WASTE OF THE BAROQUE WAS NOTICEABLE IN ITALY and England as well as in France, but with different accents, and in different decades. We have seen, however, that the seventeenth century belonged to France. One speaks of *le grand siècle,* which I would like to extend to the 1760s, including the age of Voltaire and of the philosophes.

The glory of this century was a French court culture par excellence. But this century falls into two very distinct parts, changing its face with Cardinal Mazarin's death in 1661. It was as if destiny wanted to change horses in midstream. Monarchic absolutism before this year was marked by a comparatively relaxed, almost liberal form of government. When Jean Baptiste Colbert took over the reins for Louis XIV, a period of strict reforms changed most aspects of life. During the first half of the century, France was practically ruled by two cardinals. In this Age of Reason "the reason of state" was for Cardinals Richelieu and Mazarin to make France the politically strongest and culturally most important country.

While France brought forth such philosophers as Descartes and such poets as Corneille, the society atmosphere was dominated by the *précieuses* (highbrow ladies), whom Molière mocked in his *Précieuses Ridicules,* imitating their "precious" language. A chair was "a commodity of conversation" and a shirt "the eternal companion of the living and the dead." This was also the time of the clever and imaginative marquise de Rambouillet, whose house became the meeting place of the best Parisian society between 1620 and 1650, marking the beginning of the salons. A member of the Rambouillet coterie, Madeleine de Scudéry, wrote ten-volume novels. The one entitled *Clélie* was the apotheosis of preciousness. She recommended love as an art without a heart, letting the lover wait in a state of hope, despair, and servitude as long as possible. In the first volume of this much-read novel she explained graphically the various roads a woman may choose on the *Map of Loveland:*

> . . . as there is no road where one cannot get lost, Clélie has arranged the map in such a way that if those who are at New Friendship go a little too far to the right or to the left, they likewise can get lost. For if upon leaving Noble Mind, one goes on to

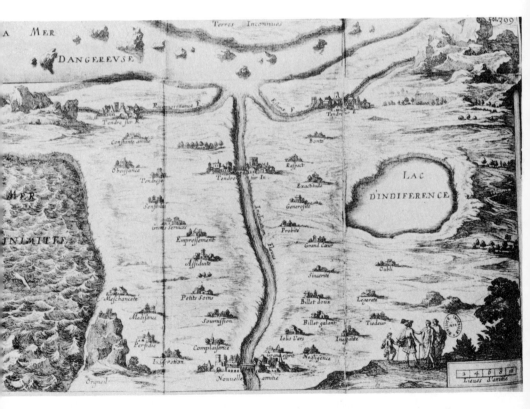

The Map of Loveland from Madeleine de Scudéry's novel CLÉLIE. (*Courtesy Photo Giraudon*)

Negligence, which you see close by on the map; if then, continuing on this wrong road, one goes to Fickleness, from there to Tepidity, on to Inconsiderateness and to Forgetting; one ends up in the Lake of Indifference, which you see marked on this map and which, by its calm waters, certainly illustrates the thing it is called after. . . .

Madeleine de Scudéry was also an excellent mistress of dialogue. These ladies of the Hôtel de Rambouillet created the atmosphere of literary trivia that spilled over into the ballets.

In those days the French ballet vacillated between the ballet de cour and a variety of *ballets-mélodramatiques*. It tried hard to achieve a more definite form, but in the 1630s it reached its lowest level, declining into insipid comedies incoherently interspersed with *ballets à entrée*. The dances serving as basic stage material were those described by Arbeau, but the content of the *entrées* was mainly on a childlike level, with impersonated animals, always danced by children, and clowns cavorting, a whimsical world of inanimate objects embellished and disguised.

It was not until Cardinal Richelieu's death in 1642 and the rising importance of Cardinal Mazarin (he was originally Giulio Mazarini, of Sicilian parentage) that the Italian genius began to be strongly felt again in Paris. (This was when Giovanni Battista Lulli, later called Jean Baptiste Lully [1632–87], was brought to Paris at the age of fourteen.) That Mazarin was one of the most skillful diplomats when France went through a difficult time of internal strife is recorded in history; that he and the Queen Mother were lovers, secretly married, and that the Sun King, Louis XIV, was the result of their love is historic rumor; that Mazarin had one of the greatest private libraries, now attached to the Bibliothèque Nationale, is as important as his understanding of and interest in the arts.

In 1661 Mazarin recommended to the King that he grant permission for the founding of a dance academy. Its immediate prototype was the Académie Royale de Peinture et de Sculpture, founded as a free society of visual artists in 1648, but soon afterward administered as a state institution by an authoritarian board of directors. After all, the funds came from the King's treasury, and with Louis XIV the absolutist tendency became more and more evident. In the preamble of the new academy he made it known that "dancing has always been recognized" as an honorable art and most necessary for the training of the body; but that during the last wars a number of abuses became noticeable:

> Many ignorant people have tried to disfigure the dance and to spoil it, as exhibited in the personal appearance of the majority of people of quality; so that we see few among those of our Court and suite who would be able to take part in our ballets. . . . It being necessary, therefore, to provide for this, and wishing to re-establish the said art in its perfection, and to increase it as much

as possible, we deemed it opportune to establish in our good town
of Paris a Royal Academy of Dancing. . . .

The dancing masters were dependent on the musicians' guild, since all
theatrical dancing had been a part of either operatic trifles or scenes of repe-
titious fantasy. The new Académie Royale de Danse was to give them their
desired freedom. The dancing master to the King was the head of thirteen
academicians whose task was to supervise and instruct aspiring dance
teachers and to keep alive the knowledge of both existing and new dances.
They were supposed to meet and decide on important issues in a salon at the
Louvre every Saturday. For the codification of dances and debates on the art
they gathered more frequently at *L'Epée de Bois* tavern. But in this early
stage the duties of the academicians were not too many or rigidly defined,
except to provide excellent dancers for the King's ballet and to prevent
dilettantes from teaching.

Lully took over the leadership of the academy in 1672, uniting the dance
academy with the *Académie Royale de Musique,* which was founded a year
before this important change in leadership. It was not until then that the
academy was a thoroughly professional institution, forming the basis of the
Paris Opéra.

THIS academy had a predecessor in the mid-sixteenth century when a
group of seven French poets founded a literary society called the *Pléiade,*
whose spiritual leader was Pierre de Ronsard, called "prince of poets and
poet of princes." He studied with Jean Antoine de Baïf (1532–89), a minor
poet but a major scholar of the classics. The musician J. Thibaut de Cour-
ville encouraged Baïf to create quantitative verses using Greek meters and
have them set to music. Baïf's passion for poetry and antiquity made him try
to reconquer classic ground by harmonizing music, verse, and movement in
a manner lost since the days of Sophocles and Euripides.

At that time France's intellectual elite and politicians were eager to establish their own humanism independent of Florence and Rome. This—besides
personal enthusiasm—was the hidden motivation behind the poets of the
Pléiade, whose manifesto clearly stated their objective, which was the
Défense et illustration de la langue française (*Defense and Illustration of
the French Language*). But beyond the aim of purifying the language was
an intent to create an instrument with which to rival Italian humanism.

In the beginning, Baïf attempted to find the way in which Greek tragedy
was really done. What was the actors' speech pattern? Did the chorus sing
or speak, or both? These questions haunted the intellectual poets during the
waning days of the Renaissance—and with frantic ardor—until the Florentine Camerata was to smooth the way for Monteverdi and the opera. Baïf
tried to transpose the iambic meters of the classical chorus into a corre-

sponding French idiom. The sung music had to conform exactly to the metrical regulation of the poetry's rhythm. What harmony could be achieved, he felt, when the duration of each note would be minutely translated into steps of equivalent length! There it was, a harmonious balance between musical-verbal rhythm and the complementary gestures and steps. In more than one way, Baïf anticipated what Émile Jaques-Dalcroze could fully realize 350 years later. Ideas do not seem to die out. History makes it plain that we must learn to believe in intellectual-artistic reincarnation.

Also, there are no isolated phenomena. Fabritio Caroso from Sermoneta was dancing master at many a palace in Rome and wrote a treatise on the dance of his time, *Il Ballarino*, published in several editions in 1577 and 1581. What interests us about him here is the one ballet of his, *Ballo del Fiore*. In this treatise he, too, described steps that ought to fit Ovid's meters and be the equivalent of spondees and dactyls, a *contrapasso "con vera mathematica sopra i versi d'Ovidio."*

In 1570 Baïf had received permission from Charles IX to found an Académie de Poésie et de Musique in order to study and promote his ideas. The religious wars put too quick an end to Baïf's dreams, but neither the idea of an academy nor the desire to create a dramatic synthesis of music, dance, and verse died with Baïf's attempt. Some of Beaujoyeulx's ideas in the *Ballet Comique* reflect those of Baïf, and a generation after the dissolution of his academy the new music drama, later known as opera, followed similar concepts. The preface to Marco da Gagliano's *Dafne*, produced in Mantua in 1608, asked for a strict synchronization of music and action, with every step and gesture slavishly following the orchestra. The minutest details indicate how the singer may pause after the opening strophe, make three or four steps (but always in time with the music), and begin his step with the sustained penult,* the next to last syllable.

THE Renaissance genius already knew that there was no art without the mastering of one's craft. The Baroque experienced a precipitation of a new awareness toward an elevated, controlled, and controllable level of instruction to make the way safe for adherence to the classical ideals. Academies have to chart ground rules, prepare precepts for pure art or what art ought to be, and delineate how human passions, sentiments, and thoughts may be expressed and creative energy put to use. Academies are a pool of information and a solid basis for the practical accomplishments of technique. They are indispensable, as all learning is.

However, true artistry will always experience academism as a straitjacket.

---

* In 1852, Richard Wagner also used such detailed synchronization in his *Remarks on Staging the Flying Dutchman*, in which the singer is told how to time each movement and what kind of step or posture should coincide with which notes.

Critics of the academic artist felt justified in sneering at art institutions when expressing their disbelief in the creative power of artistic prescriptions. Disintegration of codes into rigid codification, of standards into empty formulae, is an obvious danger. Wherever demarcation lines are drawn, then the best impulses are stifled, the flow of imagination restrained, any daring silenced, any attempt at breaking out of prescribed routine frowned upon.

In the seventeenth century the academies clearly reflect the philosophy of absolute rule. For Louis XIV, academies were a matter of personal prestige to intensify and secure the splendor of His Majesty and his court. Academies have always served the aggrandizement of the establishment; the spiritual-humanistic purpose was always subjected to the glory of a Renaissance prince—by 1600 there were seven hundred academies in Italy alone—or to a Tsarina when, in 1735, the Russian Academy was founded, the basis from which emerged the Bolshoi Ballet. As long as princes and kings, empresses and queens vied with one another to prove the magnificence and grandeur of their state, the dance, with which one could so easily display a sumptuous background, profited from it.

The academies were wonderful instruments in the hands of an absolute monarch like Louis XIV or of his right-hand man Colbert. They appointed the heads of the academies and could not have wished for a more loyal and capable man than Lully. His counterpart in the field of the fine arts was Charles Le Brun (1619–90), who became the guiding and despotic spirit of the Académie Royale de Peinture et de Sculpture and director of the Gobelins tapestry factory.

Le Brun was even more ruthless than Lully in serving his masters as much as his own position, but far less accomplished in his craft. Le Brun the artist paled in comparison to his contemporary Nicolas Poussin, the master of French classicism, who, together with the poet-dramatists Corneille and Racine, was the most civilized expression of those Gallic classical ideals within a Baroque world. But it was Le Brun on whose decisions so much depended (as was the case with Lully)—commissions, exhibitions, positions, awards, and pensions. Lully and Le Brun were the dictators of taste and talent and thus charted the direction the arts should take. In one of his academic lectures, Le Brun advanced special rules for the correct delineation of all human passions and sentiments in art—"correct" in the way he envisioned—and, in accordance with the scientific trend of his time, he stipulated that painting be "founded on a demonstrable science," namely, geometry.

LIFE at court was also determined by rules and regulations, reduced to or exalted by etiquette and ceremony to the minutest detail. It was a life-style in which form meant everything and content little, in which the most contemptible immorality was gilded by a punctilious and pompous ritual, however elegant, precise, and solemn the manners may have been.

This court ritualism reaches far back into the medieval days of feudalism. With religion eyeing everything beautiful in life at that time, everything beautiful had to be heightened to images of the ideal. A life of heroism and probity was elevated toward the sublime. All this finally led to strict ceremonials of feudal life, with etiquette receiving the stamp of solemn ritual. Even certain aspects of religion, then playing a part in all forms of life, can be detected in these formalities. For instance, during the ceremony of meals the *panetiers* and cupbearers ranked highest in the service because, being in charge of bread and wine, the very things they were in charge of had a holy character.

The way the ceremonial etiquette developed at the courts in Spain and France—also imitated by the ruling circles in England and the German-speaking countries—had something theatrical about it. A formalized pattern of behavior prescribed the exact numbers of steps when someone approached a royal ruler, and the depth of his bow. In fact, even the facial expression and hand movements during a levee in the King's bedroom, at a gala dinner at the Tuileries, or merely during a conversation with dignitaries were subject to strict rules. When and how far you stepped forward, and who could present the napkin when Her Highness asked for a drink, and how you drew your glove from your hand before reaching for the napkin or handing the King his nightshirt were matters of prestige and protocol.

These codified social attitudes were close to choreographed patterns, which were adhered to with imitative zeal down to the lowest aristocratic circles. How correct was Balzac's definition of ballet as "a manner of being"! On all levels of existence the nobility was governed by an etiquette that never loosened its grip and was only modified from grave dignity and chivalrous arabesques in the seventeenth century to frivolous dignity with a touch of boudoir grace and gallantry in the era of the late Baroque and Rococo, until the guillotine put an end to this feudal ritual.

Submissiveness reached a point of excess with everything keyed to "the liturgy of court ceremonial, infused with the awe-struck reverence of the subjects," raising "the King to the equal of a god," as Carl J. Burckhardt said in his *Richelieu*. People never uttered "anything that might displease the King," we read in Pierre La Porte's *Memoirs*, published in 1755. He was the First Valet of Louis XIV. "When His Majesty called him, saying: 'Monsieur le Maréchal,' he would reply: 'Yes, Sire,' even before knowing what it

A dancing school of eighteenth-century England. (Courtesy New York Public Library Dance Collection)

GROWN GENTLEMEN taught to DANCE.

Engraved after an Original Picture of M.ʳ John Collett, in the Possession of M.ʳ Smith.

Printed for Jn.ᵒ Smith, N.ᵒ 35, in Cheapside, & Rob.ᵗ Sayer, N.ᵒ 53, in Fleet Street, as the Act directs 20.ᵗʰ Aug.ᵗ 1768.

was all about, so afraid was he to refuse him anything." In such choreo-graphed existence the dance could not help but flower. When the time was ripe to harness court dancing and to have it subjugated to academic rules and prescribed artistic aims, its development had to come out of the spirit of this hierarchical society, as a mirror image of a generally recognized form of etiquette.

The dance of the time was the minuet, originally a folk dance from the region of Poitou. Before the minuet caught the fancy of the ruling class in the seventeenth century it was described as a very fast and gay dance; it was tamed for use at the French court. Lully and the academy gave the minuet that courtly polish which corresponded with the "noble dance" of the ballet then taught at that institution. Jean Jacques Rousseau was therefore justified in defining the minuet for Diderot's *Encyclopédie* (1751–72) as a dance of "a grave and noble simplicity; the movement of it is rather moder-ate than quick, and one might say that the least gay of all the kinds of dance used in our balls is the minuet."

This dance of mincing steps—its name is derived from *menu,* small—became *the* symbol of the ceremonial attitude so characteristic of feudal so-ciety with its stress on dignity, and accentuated charm, with play-acted re-straint and gallantry. Those dainty little steps and glides, interrupted by stereotyped bows, fitted exactly, as a stylized, refined dance play of courtship and symbolized love, the age of powdered wigs. Despite a certain limitation in the dance pattern, the minuet nevertheless demanded great skill in the ex-ecution of its gestural and mimic playfulness, in the theatricality of its un-derstatement.

To be able to dance the minuet well was the passport to enter the higher and well-to-do society, and the dancing masters profited from it. Since the basse danse, particularly the pavane, in early Renaissance days there had been no dance as intellectualized as the minuet. It was still danced in the first decade of the nineteenth century when Beethoven com-posed a "minuet à la Viganò." Goethe took dancing lessons from his father, who "instructed us most precisely in the positions and steps, and when he had brought us far enough to dance a minuet, played some pretty thing in three-four time on his *flûte-douce,* and we moved in time as best as we could." The minuet continued to reflect the spirit of the Baroque in the era of Enlightenment, even at a time when the waltz had already made its claim for predominance. On his second Italian journey in 1790 Goethe remarked that "especially the minuet is really considered a work of art and

Giovanni Lorenzo Bernini: "The Ecstasy of St. Teresa." (Courtesy Alinari/ Editorial Photocolor Archives)

only performed by a few couples. Such a couple is encircled by the rest of the party, admired and, at the end, applauded."

THERE are moments of history that deserve to be known as Golden Ages, such as Periclean Athens, Augustan Rome, Elizabethan England, and the France of Louis XIV.

He and his court formed a spirited *haut monde:* they were noblemen of a questionable nobility, they were more cultured than civilized, they cherished and challenged creativity, even though they simultaneously threw it into chains of rules and regulations. They incontrovertibly had charm, taste, elegance, and, above all, they loved the dance.

In contrast to that of the Renaissance, we must call Baroque art a popular art. Of course, the inclusion of the widest spectrum of the population through the mass media in our time dwarfs the appeal of Baroque art. But through emotional channels far more than through the then tremendous intellectual advance a rather large audience participated in the results of the creative mind, especially if we contrast it with the in groups of the intellectualized humanist elite during the Renaissance.

Baroque parallels to our own time also lie in changes in which doubt of established facts spurred action and stimulated a frantic search for truth about nature and humanity; they manifested themselves in a race for progress at any price; in the destruction of the old universe (vide Galileo and Kepler) and of the influence of scholasticism; in the disbelief in yesterday's authority; in deifying scientific discoveries which were at that time in their way as fantastic and overwhelming as twentieth-century ones are now to us. A maddening and awe-inspiring progress for the sake of progress had then begun. Moreover, all these wonderful thoughts and explorations must be imagined against a political background which, with its senseless raging of religiously motivated wars, was as frightful and frightening as has been the ideological struggle in our own time. Contrasts in the arts were then as strong as they are today.

The entire period is called the *Baroque,* a word borrowed from the Portuguese *barroco,* denoting an irregular or rough pearl. It implies something intriguing and lustrous, something having a smooth, rounded form of iridescent color, fragmentary, bulging, and straining outward. All this leads us to expect restraint and excess, with restraint tied to the power of reason, excess reflecting the emotions. The nature of their temperament meant that the Italians would indulge in excess, while the French, far more inclined toward reason, indulged in the elegance of restraint. Early in the century, the Italian stage designers developed, as we have heard, a dazzling splendor of inventiveness. In 1646 Giovanni Lorenzo Bernini created the powerful sarcophagus for Pope Urban VIII in St. Peter's, full of Baroque exuberance, and, shortly thereafter, the bulging tabernacle with "The Ecstasy of

St. Teresa," with sunrays in the background breaking through marble clouds, and the angel piercing her heart.

Bernini captured that moment in stone when the arrow is readied to reach St. Teresa who, in the ecstasy of pain, expresses that "infinite sweetness" and the wish for "the pain to last eternally." I cannot think of any sculpted scene which, in its arrested movement, would indicate a more passionate dance. In this profusion of ecstatic expression there is nevertheless quite a bit of restraint, the same restraint that we find in all the sensuousness of Monteverdi's operas, mainly in his *Orfeo*. Let us juxtapose to it the minuet with its mincing steps and many bows, a dance that quickened the hearts of the French nobility, all the more when it was danced with self-possession and poise.

CHANGING SCENARIOS

THE AGE OF LOUIS XIV BROUGHT FORTH THE PERIOD OF FRENCH CLASSICISM
that later generations would call pseudoclassic. There was a renewed power
of imagination at work in this early part of the Baroque, which was coincidental with societal conflicts and restrictive measures.

With the world full of dissensions and coalitions, intellectual life in
France was a perfect mirror image of the world at large. A struggle between
the conservative and progressive forces turned into lively public debates.
What has been recorded in history as the *Querelle des Anciens et des
Modernes* was a convoluted struggle between those who believed in the supremacy of the classics and those who challenged it. This sounds as simple
as any fight between an avant-garde movement and the established forces,
yet it was anything but a clear-cut controversy between two polemicizing
parties.

The discussion began as a diatribe against those who loved all languages
but their own and admired the history of other eras more than the contemporary. The immediate attack was motivated by a purely patriotic viewpoint, with the "Moderns" taking a nationalistic attitude. In fact, the struggle was like a rekindling of the flame once ignited by the men of the Pléiade
some decades previously. But in the mid-seventeenth century the Moderns
felt philosophically supported by the voice of doubt in all authority: the
voice of Descartes.

The difficulties with the Cartesians, as his followers were called, resulted
from both sides claiming acceptance of at least some of Descartes's ideas and
making use of the same terms. At that time no Frenchman would have liked
to be caught off guard without *le bon sens,* the Cartesian good sense. It
finally boiled down to the question of how to define and interpret Descartes's
ideas and how to give them the meaning one desired to see in them. Someone known for standing on one side of the fence would suddenly use the arguments of the opposite faction. The situation was worsened by the many
personal friendships and antagonisms, and by dependence on the goodwill of
the ruling authorities and the patronage going with it.

Descartes turned the French into a nation of philosophers. The war of
words and definitions created a cultural environment that affected all the
arts. It was an open invitation to everyone to use his own mind, and some

more than others helped to build a lofty edifice from which not only France but the entire world profited.

François de Malherbe (1555–1628) was a link between the sixteenth and seventeenth centuries. He prepared the French poets and artists for academicism, dismissing emotionalism, extravagance in metaphors, and mythological obscurity, yet demanding structural harmony and firmness. As a true academician, he sought a substitute in dignity for his lack of transcendental imagery. This dignity may have had rhyme and reason, but the prophet in the poet was sent back to school.

In the year in which Malherbe died, Charles Perrault (1628–1703) was born. An outstanding controversialist, he was on the other side of the fence, writing many fairy tales, among them *The Sleeping Beauty,* which provided the story for one of the enduring Classic ballets. Perrault, although a member of the Académie Française since 1671, was the most articulate defender of the Moderns. He believed in the evolutionary progress of the human mind and thought that every civilization has the art reflecting its own state; with progress, modern literature and art must be more refined than their ancient counterparts. However false his thinking, he made his point with his essayistic poem *Le Siècle de Louis le Grand (The Century of Louis the Great),* which antagonized the Ancients.

Perrault was supported by Philippe Quinault (1635–88), who would be long forgotten were it not for the fourteen librettos he wrote for Lully's operas. In his day, Quinault was a respected author whose word carried weight. That master of intrigue Lully sided with Quinault whenever convenient and changed his opinion in favor of those at whom the King and his minister Colbert might have smiled. He cheered Perrault when, in 1675, he came out with an appeal to patriotism with his essay *Defénse de la poésie et de la langue française (In Defense of Poetry and the French Language),* saying in it that to follow the classics was to disregard the glory of France.

This controversy did not pass unnoticed in other countries. By the turn of the century it also caught fire in England, where one no less than Jonathan Swift (1667–1745) became involved in it. His loathing of emotionalism and his witty ridicule of irrational human conduct made him use this controversy in his mocking allegory *The Battle of the Books.* In the opening scene between the bee and the spider, Swift identified the Moderns with the spider "feeding . . . on itself" and "producing nothing at all" and the Ancients with the bee which, bringing home honey and wax, gives "mankind . . . sweetness and light."

Swift was quite serious about how this issue had gotten the better of so many emotions. The best example was the French poet-critic Nicolas Boileau-Despréaux (1636–1711), who was the most polemical opponent of Perrault and knew how to set himself up as the great authority on French literature of seventeenth-century France. In 1674 he came out with his *Art poétique,* written in verse, in which he defined literary forms and laid down the rules for the writer who, according to his laws, ought to "follow nature" as the ancient writers did. Boileau felt more at home with the Romans than the Greeks, who he felt were too often their own true selves, too Dionysian and individualistic for comfort. When he spoke of nature, he mostly thought of the nature of the court, which he advised all artists to observe as closely as possible. In principle, he held up the Ancients, in whom he saw reason, nature, and harmony. Later in life he was under the impression that women were the strongest defenders of the Moderns, so he wrote a satire against them, *Contre les femmes* (*Against Women*). By then, of course, he no longer needed a female patron.

Careers were then made by patronage, and it needed skill, as well as talent, to secure as a patron the King's mistress, the one person wielding the greatest power in the land. The marquise de Montespan—whose beauty and high birth were matched only by her wit—was the patron of Corneille, Racine, and La Fontaine. Shortly after having published *L'Art poétique,* Boileau was also favored with her patronage and received a position as historiographer royal. This enabled him to acquire a country house to which he retired, to play the part of the grand old man of French literature to his last days.

The great controversy ended in 1700 when Boileau apologized to Perrault, admitting that there are some virtues in the modern as in the ancient writers, after all.

When Louis XIV asked Boileau one day, "What writer has most honored my reign?" Boileau replied without hesitation, "Molière, Sire!" This must have come as a surprise to the King, for not so long ago he had told Molière, "Smile. Write comedies. Use if you must the blackest stuff of life. But smile. Write comedy." And Jean Baptiste Molière (1622–73) obliged the King. He accepted the role of a jester in subservience to his royal master, but he played the role of the fool to perfection.

The King wanted to be entertained, and that was all that really mattered. Temperamentally, Molière did not fit into the rather formal and reasonable era in which he lived, but his philosophy and sense of humor made it possible for him to adapt to the golden mean. In his plays he avoided excess, usually juxtaposing any tragicomic excess in one of his characters with the goodness of the others. "This is a strange business," he once said, "this business of making gentlefolk laugh."

He learned fast to oblige the King and, in the truest sense of the word, to humor him. He did so with the first *comédie-ballet, Les Fâcheux* (*The Bores*). Lully, from whom Molière could take a few quick lessons on how to please without humiliating himself, immediately recognized the potentialities of this new genre. Molière envied Lully for his buoyant lightness and the talent of a comedian onstage and in life, which Louis appreciated most.

Lully was always at ease and popular with everyone, covering his ruthless ambition with natural gaiety. For six years he worked with Molière on the *comédies-ballets,* which, as the term indicates, were musicals in which play, ballet, and music were to be equal partners. They were an important contribution to danced theater.

The genre was, however, not entirely new. Molière wrote that it "is new to our stage, but one might find authority for it in antiquity. . . ." In the verbal duels between the Moderns and Ancients, Molière was a follower of the latter, as his reference to antiquity shows. The lightweight *ballets-à-entrée,* which could not be envisioned without *récits,* sung words, did not live up to his dramatic expectations. He sided with some of his contemporaries in asking for some significance in dance movements and gestures onstage. Already in one of his early comedies, *Les Précieuses Ridicules (The High-*

vray Portrait de Mʳ de Moliere en Habit de Sganarelle

Molière in his role as Sganarelle. (Courtesy French Cultural Services)

brow Ladies), written and produced in 1659, he mocked the shallowness of the stage dance, which reflected its triviality as social entertainment, when valets disguised as aristocrats arrange a ball for the pretentious ladies, Madelon and Cathos.

> MASCARILLE: This is a kind of extempore ball, ladies, but one of these days we shall give you one in form. Have the musicians come? [*Dancing to himself and singing*] La, la, la, la, la, la, la, la.
>
> MADELON: What a very elegant shape he has.
>
> CATHOS: He looks as if he were a first-rate dancer.
>
> MASCARILLE: [*Taking out Madelon to dance*] My freedom will dance a courante as well as my feet. Play in time, musicians, in time. Oh, what ignorant wretches! There is no dancing with them. The devil take you all, can you not play in time? La, la, la, la, la, la, la, la. Steady, you country-scrapers!

Molière's aim was to expose absurd affectation and superficiality, which extended to the treatment of the dance. For a time this comedy was forbidden, since the noble ladies felt they had been laughed at. Two years later, Molière had prepared a three-act comedy in verse. Dances thought of as being most appropriate for the material and occasion ought to have been highlights of the comedy, and some songs by Lully replaced the customary *récits*. *Les Fâcheux* was skillfully put together, yet it wasn't until 1664 that their collaboration on *comédies-ballets* actually started with *Le Mariage Forcé* (*The Enforced Marriage*), followed by many more. The best known is *Le Bourgeois Gentilhomme,* though whenever it is produced today the dances are unfortunately omitted. Molière was not always happy in this collaboration, since the dances and Lully's flair for light dance music must often have taken the spotlight from his words. As the dramatist he wished the dancing to be more closely related to word and action, which it rarely was.

When Molière toured the provinces in his youth, he must have been aware of the troubles plaguing the country while Louis XIV was still a minor: the wars fought by France in Spain and Holland; the growing disparity between an impoverished peasantry, a money-minded middle class, and an oversophisticated court living in splendor. Nothing of this turmoil, corruption, and injustice is reflected in Molière's work. Of course, he saw the weaknesses and vices, the flaws and foibles in human beings, whoever they were. He made fun of their perennial shortcomings and their various conceits. But he never attacked institutions, neither the monarchy, nor the aristocracy, nor the clergy.

There were two exceptions: *Le Misanthrope* and *Tartuffe,* in which plays Molière points an accusing finger at sore spots of society. In *Tartuffe* he attacked Pietism, but, accused of being an atheist, he revised the play and re-assured the world he never intended to attack religion or God—only those who pay lip service and use piety to conceal their self-interests. Molière was frightened that the King would be frowning because his jester showed his teeth while smiling.

In his *Misanthrope,* Molière shed a merciless light on his age and contemporaries. The central character, Alceste, has many autobiographical features and is comic because he is so utterly tragic. He is a man disgusted with ignoble nobility, with schemers, bootlickers, and aristocratic philanderers, loathing the affectations and follies on which everyone else seems to thrive. To see how people pay their way through life with counterfeit money turns his repudiation of the world into an obsession. He spurns the well-intended counsel of his loyal friend Philinthe to come to a compromise with the world and himself. The Misanthrope must have appeared comic to those who believed in reason and in nothing done to excess. To renounce humankind and the world and withdraw from both must have seemed ludicrous to people who were convinced that their world was the best of all possible worlds. They laughed at Alceste and did not see their own mirror image in the other characters.

Obviously, Molière was angered. However, as the product of his time he could not help keeping his satiric fury muted. He always tried to apply balm to the wounds of those he injured. Alceste recognizes the artificiality and corruption of the world, but he is partly mastered by the very things he loathes—as was Molière. In using Philinthe as his mouthpiece, he himself condemned his own hero:

> *This world requires a pliant rectitude;*
> *Too stern a virtue makes one stiff and rude;*
> *Good sense views all extremes with detestation,*
> *And bids us to be noble in moderation.**

Noble was the key word of the age. And so it was for the dance. In his *Lettres sur la danse et sur les ballets,* published in 1760, Jean Georges Noverre (1727–1810) sneered at it: "That dance which they call *noble* was denuded of expression and sentiment." Not that he could have been blind to the technical progress made at Lully's Académie over the figure dancing used by the ballet de cour! On the contrary, Noverre was only too well aware of the admirable technical progress the dancers had made, of their surprising elevation, ballon, and entrechats. But that was exactly what disturbed him: people in love with their technical proficiency, the pretentiousness of the glamorous gesture, the meaningfulness of expression not measuring up to the artist's physical abilities.

* Translation by Richard Wilbur.

By the time Noverre voiced his critical remarks an entire century had passed since the Académie's foundation, and this institution was in bad shape in the mid-eighteenth century. Noverre's claim that "they neglected to form pupils and failed in their duty which was to improve the art of dancing," was correct from his viewpoint, one of deep concern about the shallowness of the art, even though it seemed to impress by leaps and bounds almost everyone else. One of Noverre's competitors, Gasparo Angiolini (1731–1803), had a different reaction. Angiolini happened to be choreographing Gluck's *Don Juan,* "a pantomime ballet in the manner of the ancients," in 1761 when Noverre's *Letters* stirred the excitement of the art-interested world. He wrote Noverre that in his opinion the duties of the academy "were to teach and to produce good dancers and good teachers for the ballets. It has not failed in its mission."

True, in the late seventeenth century the academy was doing what it was expected to accomplish. The King needed trained dancers for his varied entertainments, and in this respect the academy was doing its best according to the rules it had set up. By 1660, many reports mention, there were about two hundred dancing schools in Paris alone. The academy was charged with keeping the level of teaching as professional as possible. Of course, when we read what a Dutch scholar, Isaac Vossius (1618–89), wrote, we must doubt that the dancing masters did a good job. A humanist interested in the dance of antiquity and also in the theater dance of his time, he maintained that none of the dancers, not even the professional ones, were sufficiently equipped to make their movements meaningful. The lavishness of the theater dance may dazzle the eye for a moment, but though there may be some rhythm and harmony in the movements, the presentations have no substance. Referring to the ancient pantomimes, he asked, "Where, today, would one find a dancer or mime who simply by bodily gestures could express things with the clarity of an orator, and in such a manner as to seem to possess as many tongues as limbs?"

Dance as an art had a confused and slow beginning; it was not yet of age when it entered the academy. It also had to overcome the handicap of growing up in an atmosphere of brilliant superficiality. While serious advances were made in scientific thinking and most of the literary products were on a high level, the performing arts were still made for and depended on the upper classes of society who insisted on the grand, heroic, and flamboyant gesture, on refinement at any cost. With pretension and pleasantry as guiding principles, spirituality or any spontaneous artistic expression came, if at all, as an afterthought. The ruling circles tried to perpetuate the present, since, from their viewpoint, they rightly felt that it was their *grand siècle.* But neither time nor progress can be locked into a room—or into a palace. And if we speak of human progress, then it was certainly accelerated in the seventeenth century.

The Spirit of the Early Eighteenth Century

WITH THE DEIFICATION OF REASON AND THE RATIONAL ORDER IN NATURE and philosophy, the autocratic government of Louis XIV continued into the early eighteenth century, creating political stability. Culturally, the various academies fared well as far as the personality of the idolized King and those who promoted his image were concerned. On the surface, one might not have noticed anything pointing to important social changes in the making. Although some of France's power was slowly frittered away through unfortunate political maneuvers, the French nation retained its *gloire*, its reputation for cultural predominance. However, with the middle class becoming a dominant force in the Anglo-Saxon countries as well as in the Netherlands, France, too, was soon to feel the pressure from below.

Most critics of Louis XIV's regime had to leave the country to make themselves heard: for example, Pierre Bayle (1647–1706), who defended Protestantism valiantly after the King decided to revoke the Edict of Nantes in 1685, turning 400,000 Frenchmen into émigrés overnight. Bayle compiled his *Dictionnaire historique et critique* in 1697; it was the first attempt at editing an encyclopedia. His method of subversive criticism was unique and was imitated by Denis Diderot about half a century later. Bayle would define a subject very briefly, but annotate it in small print, quoting profusely and stating by innuendo what the authorities would not like to hear.

One of Bayle's subjects aroused a violent reaction at the time: King David—about whom we are used to reading only laudatory comments. David danced, as the Bible says, in a religious procession in honor of the Lord, on the occasion of the removal of the Ark. He was dressed in the official robe of a high priest. Dancing in ecstasy before the Deity "with all his might," he uncovered himself. Saul's daughter saw and despised him. King David rejected such reproof, saying that "it was before the Lord" that he danced as an expression of religious joy.

Pierre Bayle asked himself, in his small-print annotations on his entry on David, how God-fearing was this ancient King of Israel who is called, in the biblical phrase, the "man after [God's] own heart." His conduct, Bayle intimated, was often immoral, barbarous, and cruel. Bayle demanded ethics before orthodoxy and said that David was "a sun of sainthood in the Church, . . . but he had his spots." Did David not admit the sin of adultery with Bathsheba, the sin of murder of Uriah, and many other deeds which— in the true spirit of Scripture—we should not forget to interpret? Then

Bayle's bitter criticism of Louis XIV is added: "The history of King David may reassure several crowned heads against the fears inspired in them by severe casuists who maintain that it is almost impossible for a king to be saved!"

We may recognize similar Voltairean cynicism in another critic of the Sun King: François de Salignac de La Mothe-Fénelon (1651–1715). The mystical theologian Fénelon, who got into trouble with the Pope because of his belief in Quietism, also had his difficulties with his King. When engaged as tutor to the duc de Bourgogne, the King's grandson, he gave him political advice, indirectly reproving Louis XIV for his policies. Regarding the authority of an ideal ruler, Fénelon wished to see the King's freedom of action limited by a body of law. "He has absolute power to do good, but has his hands tied the moment he wishes to do evil. Nothing offers so great a threat of a fateful crash as authority pushed too far." Did he see the signs of revolution on the invisible wall of the future? Small wonder that one day the King ordered him not to show himself at court any longer.

However isolated and sporadic the voiced criticism of the Roi Soleil may have been toward the end of his reign, it was nevertheless an indication of the court's losing its prerogative of being the sole cultural center. The rich bourgeoisie solidified its position while the feudal nobility became more and more impoverished through a constantly growing inflation during *le grand siècle*. On the one hand, these two layers of society were rivals; on the other, they had common problems and interests that drew them more closely together. The Crown and the approximately four thousand families sponging on the country came to live and act as if they were a nation within a nation. No one could hope for reforms in France under Louis XV and Louis XVI, a period that Mme de Pompadour so succinctly characterized with the words "Après nous le déluge."

Gradually, the upper layer of the bourgeoisie and the lower aristocracy began to form a single cultural elite sharing the same ideas and the same taste. In the previous century French writers emerged from the ranks of the aristocrats and the clergy; in the eighteenth century their origin was the middle class. The bourgeoisie read their books and bought their paintings. Boileau or Pope, for instance, still wrote their essays on the arts and man in verse. Now, however, prose took over, and the mannerism of writing in letter form. The turn of the century also witnessed the growing importance of the *salons,* which, in many respects, were destined to take over the role of the court. The people frequenting the salons during the seventeenth century belonged to the aristocracy and clergy almost exclusively, but in the Age of Enlightenment class distinctions were loosened. The salons became a gathering and rallying point for everyone talented and brilliant who had made a name for himself or was well on the way to leave his mark on history.

The salons also reflected changes in the structure of society Early in the

A poet reading at Mme Geoffrin's salon in 1725. (Painting in the Musée des Beaux-Arts, Rouen. Courtesy Lauros-Giraudon)

eighteenth century, women appeared on the stage for the first time; they were legitimate actresses and dancers who had studied their crafts in academies or had made their way onto the stage through the sheer power of a native talent. The salons, always presided over by women, may not actually have helped the female reach this state of accomplishment. Rather, it was an inevitable development of history that paralleled the significance of the salons. But the Académie Royale de Danse started in 1661 with more male than female students, a ratio that quickly changed in favor of the ballerinas who after the 1720s took the spotlight.

Also, the salons were no longer necessarily run by aristocratic ladies. Mme Geoffrin, for instance, presided over one of the most fascinating salons of the time. She was the daughter of a *valet de chambre* at court, definitely a bourgeoise. Her mother died a year after her birth, and Marie Thérèse was brought up in her grandmother's house. At the age of thirteen she was married off to a rich businessman, François Geoffrin, who was forty-eight years old. He soon left her a wealthy widow. Then, at the age of thirty, Mme Geoffrin opened her salon to the artists and aristocrats, to poets and philosophes. Everyone thought of as important came to dine with her.

Her salon won the highest repute because she had grace and the intelligence to gather around her the greatest minds and most charming women. Her warmth as much as the unobtrusive manner in which she managed her wealth made friends for her. Her tact and insight into human beings gave her the strength to steer friendships and to keep flirtations from becoming passions and public nuisances. She found out that it was better to entertain statesmen and members of royalty separately from artists, who were strange, egocentric, and tempestuous people, while the former stressed good manners and discretion; only the philosophes mingled well with both groups.

When one of her rival *salonnières* died in 1749, the writer Fontenelle, who was then ninety-two, sighed, "What a good woman! She had been a veritable synthesis of sin!" But he had no reason to worry where to dine now; Mme Geoffrin was only too glad to take him into her fold. She was a great patron besides being a hostess. When Diderot started his *Encyclopédie* she contributed over 500,000 livres to its costs, admiring, as she did, the courage and wisdom of these philosophes. She bought the works of her painter friends, and Jean Baptiste Siméon Chardin (1699–1779) has left us her image—just as Picasso painted Gertrude Stein—as a plump and kindly-looking matron in a lace bonnet. One of her weekly guests was another painter, Charles André Van Loo, a favorite of Parisian society. A story has it that, when he died in 1765, she bought two of his paintings for 4,000 livres and resold them to a Russian prince for 50,000 livres, sending the profit to the painter's widow.

Some of the greatest luminaries of her time considered it an honor to be received by her, second only to being received by the King. The ambassadors attached to Versailles would be frequent guests and bring along the royalties of their countries. Mme Geoffrin was befriended by Catherine II of Russia and Gustavus III of Sweden. The King of Poland invited her to visit him and his country when she was already over sixty years of age. It was a long, tiring, but triumphant journey through Vienna and other capitals, where she was received with honor. Her letters sent from this journey to Paris were read and reread by her friends, and Baron Friedrich Melchior von Grimm mentioned in his *Correspondance littéraire,* reporting about interesting events going on in Paris, that "those who had not read Mme Geoffrin's letters were not fit to go into good society." When Catherine II asked her to let her know more about her childhood, Mme Geoffrin spoke about her grandmother:

> . . . she taught me to read . . . to think, and made me reason; she taught me to know men, and made me say what I thought of them, and told me how she herself judged them. . . . She could not endure the elegancies that dancing-masters reach; she only desired me to have the grace which nature gives to a well-formed person.

ENCYCLO
PÉDIE
ÉLÉMEN
TAIRE.

ENCYCLOPÉDIE,

OU

DICTIONNAIRE RAISONNÉ

DES SCIENCES,

DES ARTS ET DES MÉTIERS,

PAR UNE SOCIÉTÉ DE GENS DE LETTRES.

Mis en ordre & publié par M. *DIDEROT*, de l'Académie Royale des Sciences & des Belles-Lettres de Prusse; &, quant à la PARTIE MATHÉMATIQUE, par M. *D'ALEMBERT*, de l'Académie Royale des Sciences de Paris, de celle de Prusse, & de la Société Royale de Londres.

Tantùm series juncturaque pollet,
Tantùm de medio sumptis accedit honoris! HORAT.

TOME PREMIER.

A PARIS,

Chez
{
BRIASSON, *rue Saint Jacques*, *à la Science.*
DAVID l'aîné, *rue Saint Jacques*, *à la Plume d'or.*
LE BRETON, *Imprimeur ordinaire du Roy*, *rue de la Harpe.*
DURAND, *rue Saint Jacques*, *à Saint Landry*, *& au Griffon.*
}

M. DCC. LI.

AVEC APPROBATION ET PRIVILÉGE DU ROY.

Title page and frontispiece of Diderot's ENCYCLOPÉDIE *(1751)*. *(Courtesy Photo Giraudon)*

Next to the salons, the coffeehouses began to play an important role. They were introduced in Paris in about 1700, and more than three hundred cafés opened up within a short time. Voltaire noted that the city had become a single huge coffeehouse. The Procope, opposite the Comédie-Française, was frequented by artists mainly; the Café Gradot was preferred by the scientists and philosophers and honored by the members of various academies. But all this was still a far cry from the bohemian life of which the coffeehouses became symbolic in Central Europe in the nineteenth century.

This animated and democratized life should not make us believe that etiquette and ceremony had disappeared or that the new cultural elite would not have continued in some ways to imitate and perpetuate courtly habits. Only the grandeur and solemnity of former times had vanished under Louis XV and his successor. On the contrary, etiquette was then in everyone's possession. *Noblesse oblige* became a general concept, the trademark of the well-educated Frenchman. Everyone sought to show *complaisance,* a telling word then used by French and English alike describing a clearly defined and definable behavior pattern of refinement, self-assured nonchalance, and controlled vitality. It was a way of being: court life and courteous life embracing the upper middle class, those who belonged or pretended to belong to the ruling class. They were the vestiges of yesterday's ceremonies continued in a more relaxed manner; but the ideal of the *honnête homme* of the seventeenth century, the perfect courtier, conforming to the graceful customs of a genteel life, was still desired. The term *grande* or *douce manière* described the desired behavior.

A good posture, keeping the strict vertical line of the torso, and the small but embroidering hand gestures were a part of complaisance on the dance floor, in the salons, and on the streets. They went well with powdered wigs, hose, doublets, and ribbons, with heeled shoes, underskirts, hoops, and decorative laces. Clothing had not only become a body mask, it was utterly theatrical. All this was as if based on a tasteful, elegant vocabulary of comportment, and many self-instruction manuals, mostly written by dancing masters, were published at that time. People were so preoccupied with etiquette that advice on how to conduct one's social intercourse slipped into even more serious manuals. Thus John Weaver (1673–1760) said in his *Anatomical and Mechanical Lectures upon Dancing,* published in London in 1721:

> . . . from the Regular or Irregular Position, and Motion of the Body, we distinguish the handsome Presence, and Deportment of the fine Gentleman, from the awkward Behavior of the unpolish'd Peasant; we discover the graceful Mien of a young Lady, from the ungainly Carriage of her Maid. . . . how advantageous is it, for a Gentleman, or Lady, to be Adroit at every Step, and, that every Motion, and Action of the Body, be consonant to Symmetry and Grace.

The house concerts became an institution in eighteenth-century France and were of equal importance to the salons. (Courtesy French Cultural Services)

The Viennese Schloss Schönbrunn is one of the characteristic Baroque gardens of feudal society. (Courtesy Austrian Press and Information Service, New York)

THERE are a few more features of this Age of Enlightenment that round out the varied panorama of its background. Let us move through the gardens of a past world, which can still be seen at Versailles or Vienna's Schönbrunn in their most perfect condition, gardens in which the trees and hedges are adorned with Baroque statues and rhythmically cut and trimmed in geometric lines.

The carefree world of the nobility is associated with the Rococo. The painters who celebrated the niceties of this privileged society on their canvases were Watteau, Boucher, Pater, Lancret, and Fragonard. Jean Antoine Watteau (1684–1721) was able to transcend the sparkling scenes of frivolity and graceful gallantry. He knew how to make the flesh come alive and how to turn triviality into the vision of a dream. All five painters dealt more or less with the same subjects. What sets Watteau's work apart is a touch of sadness over the transience of beauty, the delicate sentiment with which people are placed in their landscape, with man matched to woman as if the whole scene were an afterthought of the Creator.

Such a painted *fête galante* is a bucolic world in which shepherds and shepherdesses reappear in human shape and stylish costumes. The mind's eye sought again the Arcadian ideal of remoteness from the real—and what better age could there have been for it than the one in which the spirit of the minuet could be found symbolically everywhere? In a glamorous superficiality, civilization and nature were identified with a contemplative and idyllic life. This explains much of the playfulness and apparent frivolity of the paintings, reflecting a lack of sincerity, little more than a flirtation with life.

This very same lightness found expression in a renewed joy in the pastoral. The period was marked by a renascence of escapism, which found a strong expression in literature and the arts. Escapism has always been reflected in the arts, but there are certain moments when it becomes unavoidable for certain layers of society. The first half of the eighteenth century was such a time.

Some writers celebrated nature with idylls of great sensuous love. It was their way of finding the promise of liberation from the fetters of a civilization that was growing ever harsher. This was like a prelude to Rousseau's more serious realization that "our existence is nothing but a succession of moments perceived through the senses." Before Rousseau saw in man's return to nature a return to a livable simplicity and one's better self; and before the Romantic poets Wordsworth and Coleridge claimed Nature as their mystical experience, men like Alexander Pope (1688–1744) wrote idylls crowded with spirits, demons, fairies, and sylphs as if they would sketch a ballet tableau.

Or take the Swiss scientist Albrecht von Haller (1708–77), one of the last great polyhistorians, who, while collecting plants in the Alps to prepare a book on the Swiss flora, wrote his famous poem *Die Alpen* (*The Alps*). Another Swiss, Salomon Gessner (1730–88), enjoyed international fame that can hardly be fathomed today. He is often mentioned in books on music because this gracious old man was visited by the young Mozart in Zürich. Gessner's revival of the idyll and his short bucolic stories, which he also illustrated, were characteristic products of the Rococo atmosphere, with a touch of the sentimental and the romantic yearning for man's return to nature:

> . . . . Oh, how beautiful you are, Nature! In your littlest ornament, how beautiful! He who passes your beauties carelessly misses the purest joys; he whose mind is spoiled by raging passions and

false delights is incapable of the purest joys. Blissful is the man whose . . . senses always find endless sources of joy on every path he walks, in the shade in which he rests; gentle delights bubble from each well, exhale fragrances from each flower, sound and whisper out of each bush. . . .

How unreal was the reality of this world of the idylls? In certain instances we cannot claim that it was remote from life. There were places and people who could experience a perfectly tranquil and secure joy of being. In those days such people were not troubled by world events, since news traveled slowly. On the other hand, people were gripped by a letter-writing fever that coincided with the opening of post offices and the use of mail coaches.

The writing of letters had, in fact, become such an obsession that it was the fashion to write novels or a book of essays in the form of letters. In 1740 Samuel Richardson published *Pamela, or Virtue Rewarded,* probably the most widely read novel of the mid-century. It made dramatic use of the letter form. With pent-up emotionalism forcing its way into the most direct communication, this literary form with its touch of confession easily revealed the drama of the Self. In Goethe's *The Sorrows of Young Werther* (1774) the letter form triumphed. Satires like Montesquieu's *Persian Letters* and such a work as Noverre's *Letters on the Dance and Ballets* also made use of this device.

Criticism in periodicals or newspapers was penned as if letters sent from the scene of action. A touching event took place in the home of the critic Johann Jakob Bodmer, who received the German poet Christoph Martin Wieland in 1752. At a certain point of their conversation they decided to continue it by writing letters to each other. Perhaps someone played the flute while this curious conversation in letter form happened. The flute was then the favorite instrument, also used to accompany dancers. (The piano was not introduced into bourgeois home life before the late 1760s.)

With the growing vogue of everything Chinese from the early 1730s on, porcelain became the most appreciated object of decoration in the home. The Chinese had achieved an enviable mastery in the creation of porcelain, conjuring up beautiful colors and delicate shades. The early eighteenth century wanted to get away from the grandeur of the noble dance to reach the lightness of elevation; it wanted to leave the imposing, heavy classicism of Versailles behind it, and there was nothing more expressive of the somewhat exaggerated elegance of French Rococo than porcelain. Whoever did not buy porcelain in the factories at Sèvres was not a good Frenchman, thought Mme de Pompadour, who cared for Sèvres and porcelain with a loving passion. But then did not the Germans feel similarly about their Meissen porcelain, and the English about their Wedgwood? There was no Rococo life without one or the other.

The marquise de Pompadour took a personal interest in supervising the state china factory at Sèvres. (Courtesy French Cultural Services)

Jean Baptiste Joseph Pater caught the spirit of the Rococo in his painting "La Danse dans un Pavillon," the dance being a minuet. (Courtesy The Cleveland Museum of Art. Gift of Commodore Louis D. Beaumont)

A New Era of Entertainment

THE GREAT REIGN OF LOUIS XIV HAD LOST SOME OF ITS MAGNIFICENCE BY the time Jean Racine (1639–99) withdrew from writing for the stage in the 1670s after having created some of the best tragedies in a language of "pure poetry." His withdrawal—whatever private problems may have motivated it —coincided with the paling of Louis XIV's lustrous regime. Later, Racine did—to please the King—a few minor jobs, such as writing the words for an *Idylle sur la Paix,* which was set to music by Lully and performed at Sceaux. However minor this work may have been in literary and musical value, it was noteworthy because it did not take place in Versailles or the Tuileries, but at Sceaux, in the castle of the duchesse du Maine, who from then on was hostess to the more important fetes.

What had happened to Louis was not his age as much as Mme de Maintenon's influence. Brilliant and beautiful, she advanced from mistress to his secretly wedded wife, practically running the affairs of state from the 1680s. She was a devout and bigoted Catholic who engineered the persecution of the Huguenots and injected gloom and gravity into the character of the court. Closest to her heart was the convent at St.-Cyr, founded for the education of orphaned or poorer girls of the nobility or of officers killed in Louis's several wars. Mme de Maintenon approved of the production of plays performed by the girls, since she wanted them to improve their language, elocution, and memory; the right plays might open a beautiful world of pure thoughts for them. She approached Racine with the request to write a play for her pupils, but nothing unseemly like his *Andromaque* or *Phèdre,* in which love was an overriding motif.

Racine obliged her and decided on a dramatic poem about Esther, certainly a religious subject. Although the play was a resounding success, the pressures from Church dignitaries and educators at St.-Cyr, who saw in any spectacle only impious distractions for the girls, made Mme de Maintenon stop public performances altogether. It was a bad time for the arts, and particularly for the theater arts. The masterminds who had created a sound foundation on which to build left the scene. The year that Lully died, 1687, Pierre Beauchamp (c. 1639–c. 1705), the choreographer of King and academy, retired. The first generation of academy-trained dancers were ready to take over: among many others, Jean Balon, Raoul Auger Feuillet, Marie Thérèse Subligny, Françoise Prévost, and Louis Pécourt, who became premier danseur and Beauchamp's successor as choreographer.

Much had been done by Lully in preparation for a great future for his Académie (read: Opéra), for a thorough schooling of the instrumentalists, singers, and dancers. He was an organizer par excellence, overseeing the entire scene and devoting his energies to the smallest detail, and a strict disciplinarian who achieved results. He was a musician before anything else and would insert recitatives in his ballets wherever he could. He made the ballet an important feature in his operas; ever since, no operagoer in Paris would have wanted to miss a ballet, chiefly in the second act. He soon realized that coherence was the key to creation, and coherence meant a unified dramatic subject produced by one composer, one librettist, one designer, one choreographer. He was fortunate in finding the very best men with kindred enthusiasm, such as Jean Bérain as scenic designer, who toned down the Italianate effects, and Pierre Beauchamp as ballet master. When Louis XIV could say, "L'état, c'est moi," then Lully could say with even greater justification, "L'art, c'est moi."

We have it on the authority of Pierre Rameau and his account of the early-eighteenth-century dance scene—his book of social dances, Maître à danser (The Dancing Master) was published in Paris in 1725—that Beauchamp was a first-rate choreographer: "I cannot praise him enough for the justified reputation he acquired. He was knowledgeable and original in his compositions. He needed skilled dancers to perform whatever he invented." We have no way of knowing how accurate this evaluation is, but we have no reason to doubt it. If he needed skilled dancers, then, as the Académie's ballet master, he had to create them. We know that Beauchamp developed the figured dance of the ballet de cour into the technical nuances of what turned out to be the danse d'école. He set down the important principle of the turned-out leg and made the five fundamental positions of classical ballet an irrevocable point of departure. Beauchamp's direction was toward technical perfection, toward the classical ideals of clarity, balance, and proportion. After all, he, too, was the product of his age, which had faith in mathematics.

Despite the technical brilliance with which everything started at the Opéra, a long interval set in after Lully and Beauchamp were gone. Music had received a tremendous impetus through the novelty of vocal bravura with which the Italians impressed the so-called civilized world. The poetic and artistic level was low, whatever was being produced. Ballet was strongly featured in the opéra ballets that became fashionable, but these had neither plot nor ideas. They were held together in a peculiar way in which one never quite knew whether the ballet was there to frame the operatic scenes, or vice versa. But every scene seemed to be a pretext for something that lacked any concept and that was without the least semblance of any character. Whatever the audiences sensed as novelties were minor embroideries on tired academic clichés, mainly in the direction of technical improvement. There was a need for more rewarding entertainment.

The Italian commedia players were the theatrical artists most preferred for the unexpected and undemanding in entertainment. Their improvisational acting style left everything open to surprise, and more so in their pantomime than in verbal communication. The range in their unconstrained bodily expression and the ease with which they conveyed ideas through gestures caught the fancy of the people in France as much as in England at the turn of the century. This is best illustrated by an evening at the château of the duchesse du Maine in 1708, when two celebrated dancers of the Opéra, Françoise Prévost and Jean Balon, performed the final scene of Act IV of Corneille's *Horace* as a pantomime. It was expressed through gestures and bodily movements. An attempt was made to have dancers trained in the vocabulary of the classical dance to forget their dance steps and use their subtle bodies to make them speak. The only help these dancers had came from the audience, which was quite familiar with every line of the scene. Was it a conscious imitation of the Parisian Comédie-Italienne, a company for which mute scenes were a daily occurrence and for whose members the language of gestures and movements was their working material?

It was an experiment with little consequence, except that it proved how the nobility was eager to escape presentations caught in the snares of the academic cliché and to participate in the more popular fun offered by the pantomimes. These Italian players simply stepped into a vacuum and filled it with great skill. They were often blamed for having lowered the public taste, but it rather appears as if the lowered taste welcomed them. Their effect on the English scene was also of great importance. The Pietist movement had brought with it a kind of pseudoclassic and pathetic tragedy in both England and France, and, what was worse, the decay of true comedy and the growth of sentimentalism.

Of course, sentimentalism was everywhere to be found in this Age of Enlightenment—probably as a badly needed antidote—but it cannot be condemned wholesale. On the contrary, in its wake most significant art experiences emerged and even reached human greatness and compassion in a man like Rousseau. George Lillo's play *The London Merchant,* produced in 1731, was dripping with false sentiment, but it ushered in the bourgeois drama. The interest in the common man onstage was echoed by painters like Chardin, who, in the 1720s, began to depict day-to-day scenes of ordinary people. Jean Baptiste Greuze shortly followed him, painting scenes of actual peasant life, and this at a time when Fragonard was still perpetuating Watteau's Rococo feeling. Bourgeois realism went along with sentimentality, a trend that lasted to the end of the century, only to be embraced and revarnished by Romanticism. It was a trend of superemotionalism, of emotions rising to passion in works which are, as Denis Diderot said, "terrible or sensuous, at the same moment that they charm the ear, carry love or terror to the depth of your heart, dissolve your senses and purge your very soul." This was the same Diderot, the guiding spirit of the Encyclopedists, who reproached the dancers for being children who long for an enchanted world to amuse them. He could thunder verbally in the *Encyclopédie* that "the real world alone pleases the mind," while admiring passion and delighting in melancholy sentimentality, sadness, and solitude. And in the 1760s, with the Italian excavations in fashion and a run on ruins, Diderot anticipated all later Romantics when he said, "A palace must be in ruins to be an object of interest."

Let us not denounce the trend of sentimentality that started early in the century and led to a pseudophilosophical and lachrymose drama. This type of theatrical fare developed realism to the point of the absurd and laughable in the course of time. It resulted in the melodrama, which attacked human emotions with violence and jazzed up its incidents with the sensational and spectacular. The characters were shaped in terms of romanticized sentimentalism—stock characters in thrilling episodes with a contrived ending. It all cried out for musical accompaniment. This very melodrama had great influence on nineteenth-century theater and particularly on ballet. One may be surprised to discover threads leading from the melodrama to *La Sylphide;* nevertheless, they are clearly marked.

Sentimentality was only one of several trends dominating the first decades of the century. Music stood in the foreground of interest, surging forward and breaking the barriers against a free-flowing artistic expression. By 1711 a new musical instrument was born, unique in every respect. Bartolommeo Cristofori is usually credited with the invention of the piano, but, as is mostly the case with inventions, other models came into being simultaneously in France and Germany. The Neapolitan school was not alone in making people think that this was the age of music. Bach and Handel were at work at the same time. Bach's universality was accomplished, like the work of a medieval artisan, behind a provincial organ, while Handel was a man of the world, a theatrical entrepreneur. Also, writing operas brought him closer to the realities of the theatrical world. He was the right man to come to London at the right moment. Neither Queen Anne nor George I had any interest in the theater, but George loved operas and, if there was any patronage forthcoming, it would only have been for the opera.

Since the actors could not expect royalty to patronize their playhouses, they had to turn to the public, which loved the commedia players. And English pantomime was soon the great theatrical event. The public expected a farcical afterpiece to be added to any play production; and more and more, people came to like a mixed program with songs and dance, and even acrobatics. A great ballerina like Marie Sallé (1707–56) had to appear between circus acts.

The best-known name on the London theatrical scene at that time was that of John Rich (1692–1761), the most outstanding talent among the native pantomimes. This little-educated man, uncouth in speech, was a brilliant performer and shrewd manager. In fact, he was one of the first international impresarios in history, importing dancing and dumb-show entertainments from the Continent. His most memorable hit was John Gay's *Beggar's Opera,* which he produced in 1728. It had sixty-two performances, phenomenal for that time. Its success ushered in a wave of ballad operas,

Bartolommeo Cristofori built the first pianoforte in Florence in 1709. He had perfected it by 1720. (Courtesy The Metropolitan Museum of Art, The Crosby Brown Collection of Musical Instruments, 1889)

also inspiring the *Singspiel* in Germany. John Christopher Pepusch put together a tuneful score which contributed to the lightness of this genre. The show made fun of the excesses of Italian operatic style and lampooned Sir Robert Walpole's corrupt government. The people, tired of the regime's chicaneries, enjoyed the political references and the farcical daring that ripped into the fanciful artificiality of the time.† All of London spoke of it, a sequel was quickly concocted, and the comment making the round was that *The Beggar's Opera* made Gay rich and Rich gay. But John Gay was not alone in his attack on the social conditions of his time. A far more mordant indictment came from the canvases of William Hogarth, on which he caught life in its very act of being.

In the year 1717, when John Rich began to present his annual pantomimes, of which *Harlequin Sorcerer* (1741) was his greatest success, John Weaver choreographed a dramatic pantomime: to be exact, "A Dramatic Entertainment of Dancing," called *The Loves of Mars and Venus*. Weaver was an oasis in an artistic desert—the word *jungle* might be more descriptive, if we consider that an accomplished actress and dancer like Hester Santlow appeared with great dexterity on one and the same evening in 1710 as Ophelia in *Hamlet* as well as in a dance sketch, *Dutch Skipper*.

In this context, how good a dancer Weaver was is less important to us than how his mind worked as a writer and choreographer. He seems never to have pursued dancing and choreographing as other artists of his caliber would. *The Loves* must have been successful since Rich found it expedient enough to burlesque Weaver, and Colley Cibber, that famed actor, dramatist, essayist, and poet laureate of the first half of the eighteenth century, gave a good account of Weaver's position:

> Dancing therefore was now the only Weight in the opposite Scale [reference is to Italian Opera] . . . to make it something more than Motion without Meaning, the Fable of *Mars and Venus* was form'd into a connected Presentation of Dances in Character, wherein the Passions were so happily expressed, and the whole Story so intelligibly told, by a mute Narration of Gesture only, that even thinking Spectators allow'd it both a pleasing and a rational Entertainment. . . .

Weaver followed it up with a "Dramatick Entertainment in Dancing," *The Fable Orpheus and Eurydice,* and another pantomime, *Perseus and*

† Gay's story of the underworld was again popularized through Bertolt Brecht's adaptation, *The Threepenny Opera.* Gay's prison pastoral received two hundred years later, in 1928, through Brecht, unmistakable twentieth-century and Marxist connotations.

Frontispiece of THE FABLE ORPHEUS AND EURYDICE, *"with a Dramatick Entertainment in Dancing thereupon; Attempted in Imitation of the Ancient Greeks and Romans. As perform'd at the Theatre Royal in Drury-Lane. Written, Collected and Composed by John Weaver, Dancing-Master (London 1718)." (Courtesy Harvard Theatre Collection)*

Andromeda, themes proving his vital interest in the ancients. As a dancer-choreographer he was adamantly opposed to easy tricks and technical efficiency without meaning, and also therefore very much opposed to the Italian type of pantomime of which John Rich was a master. That he created relatively few works and was rarely seen as a dancer on the London stage may have been prompted by his disgust at the easy victories won by Rich and his ilk.

The Spectator—which often dealt with the problems of the theater—raised the question why "dancing, an art celebrated by the ancients in so extraordinary a manner, be totally neglected by the moderns, and left destitute of any pen to recommend its various excellencies and substantial merit to mankind." The answer to this question why dance had remained a nonliterary art form was, in the words of *The Spectator* that "the low ebb to which dancing is now fallen, is altogether owing to this silence. The art is esteem'd only as an amusing trifle; it lies altogether uncultivated, and is unhappily fallen under the imputation of illiterate and mechanick. . . ."

The year in which *The Spectator* ceased publication, 1712, Weaver's *Essay Towards an History of Dancing* was issued. In it, he projected a far-reaching idea that he described as "scenical" dancing, which corresponds with the term *ballet d'action,* or ballet with a plot, too often referred to as the invention of Noverre. Weaver was the Newton of the dance. He was caught in that feverish thirst for knowledge, characteristic of his time, for investigating the laws of nature and theorizing about the arts based on investigation, the very same pursuit here described as so essential during the Age of Reason.

Time and again, Weaver points to the dual task of the dance of aiming at pleasure *and* instruction, and numerous are his references to the laws of nature. In the preface to *The Loves* he pointed to the fact that "Nature assign'd each Motion of the Mind its proper Gesticulation and Countenance. . . ." His appeals to the laws of nature became strongest in another book, written nine years after the *Essay: Anatomical and Mechanical Lectures upon Dancing,* which for the first time clearly established the anatomical basis for proper dance instruction. In the second lecture of this book he referred to the rules of dancing as being "built upon the Fundamentals of Anatomy; agreeable to the Laws of Mechanism; consonant to the Rules of harmonical Proportion, and adorn'd with the Beauty of a natural and cultivated Gracefulness."

With the systematization of knowledge in the sciences and arts, this new approach to the dance had to come about. It also seems natural from an artist who detested the low state of artistic expression. About half a century later, Jean Georges Noverre continued Weaver's revolutionary thoughts. Noverre was prompted to act in this direction out of aesthetic dissatisfac-

but scarcely rising from the ground; yet she was received with fervent applause." But a beginning was made. The concept of the *danse terre à terre* (steps on the ground) was destined to become a thing of the past, as was nobility. The *danse haute* or *verticale* was in.

But there were dancers who still had a feeling for the noble and stately in their movements. Louis Dupré belonged to them—*le grand Dupré*, the prototype of the danseur noble. Noverre was his pupil, and for an eyewitness account we may again call on Casanova, who had seen him in *Les Fêtes Vénétiennes*, reminiscent of Watteau's painting. The time was about 1745:

> . . . I saw that fine figure coming forward with measured steps, and when the dancer had arrived in front of the stage, he raised slowly his rounded arms, stretched them gracefully backward and forward, moved his feet with precision and lightness, took a few small steps, made some battements and pirouettes and disappeared like a butterfly. The whole had not lasted half a minute. The applause burst from every part of the house; I was astonished, and asked my friend the cause of all these bravos.
>
> "We applaud the grace of Dupré and the divine harmony of his movements. He is now sixty years of age, and those who saw him forty years ago say that he is always the same."
>
> "What! Has he never danced in a different style?"
>
> "He could not have danced in a better one, for his style is perfect, and what can you want above perfection?"

Dance dynasties rivaled those of the enlightened kings in the eighteenth century. Experience and technique were handed down from one generation to the next: from Beauchamp to Pécourt to Dupré to Noverre. Another disciple of Dupré was Gaetano Vestris, whose son Auguste, taught by his father, was considered the greatest male dancer of the century. The Vestris (there were several other dancing members of the family) dominated the dance scene for most of the century. They were also known for their arrogance. Father Vestris called himself "le diou de la danse," and admittedly all contemporary reports indicate that Auguste added virtuosity to his beautiful line and style.‡ The epithet *divine* was usually reserved for the female dancers, and the age abounded with them, from La Barberina to Marie Madeleine Guimard.

Marie Sallé and Marie Camargo were the most striking opposites as personalities and artists. They came to symbolize two worlds and stood at ex-

‡ Gaetano Vestris supposedly said about Auguste: "He is more skillful than I am, and the explanation is simple: I am his father, an advantage nature denied me." Auguste is credited for having introduced multiple pirouettes and the entrechat huit. He is proof of the constant progress made from master to student. Among Auguste's pupils were Charles Louis Didelot (who laid the foundations of the great Russian ballet tradition), August Bournonville (father of the Danish Royal Ballet), Jules Perrot, and Fanny Elssler.

Nicolas Lancret (1690–1743) was best known as the painter of fêtes galantes. This is his portrait of the famous ballerina La Camargo. (Courtesy the Author)

treme poles in the struggle that ensued between the Lullists and Ramists, the followers of Jean Philippe Rameau (1683–1764), Lully's heir. Since Camargo was identified with Rameau, his new music, and his leanings toward the vertical dance, while Sallé, being a dancer of the noble school, was typed as a Lullist, it would be simple to say that Camargo typified progress and Sallé the past. This, however, was not so.

Casanova was dumbfounded by Dupré's noble gestures and Camargo's seeming elevation. She had shortened her skirt to bare her ankles and show her footwork, but this was not really what impressed the audience. It was

Marie Sallé. (Courtesy New York Public Library Dance Collection, gift of Lillian Moore)

her temperament, her stage magnetism that fascinated the public. Voltaire wrote that Camargo danced like a man. He recognized the aggressiveness in her brilliant technique—compared to that of other ballerinas—as a turning point in balletic history. Camargo wrested the supremacy from the male dancer.

While Camargo pointed into the future, Sallé projected beyond it: as the eternal rebel against cliché and conformity. She surprised rather than shocked the dance world when she turned to the ancients and gave her ballet-pantomime *Pygmalion* the simplicity of outer and inner expression. She told this classic story without the customary paraphernalia of the ballet and with the expression of one whose inner experience motivated each gesture and movement.

In 1734, the year of *Pygmalion,* she was able to theatricalize fully John Weaver's dream of a ballet d'action. Her art had nothing to do with the ideals of the Lullists, although they saw in her "the muse of modest, gracious gesture." She stood alone as that singular artist who cannot help but further the art form. For the first time we find dance for the sake of dancing pitted against dance that gains meaning through expressiveness. Sallé had to be her own choreographer, because no one else could have found the way to the realization of her "soul." And it had to happen in London, whose theaters were open to reason and experiment, particularly when the artist came from France.

"We live in a strange time and under surprising contradictions; Reason on the one side, the most absurd fanaticism on the other . . . *sauve qui peut.*" What Voltaire said here was, of course, motivated by the world-shaking issues of the eighteenth century. Reduced to the dance scene, his saying loses nothing of its poignancy or piquantness.

From "Les Indes Galantes" to "Les Fêtes Chinoises"

IT ALL BEGAN WITH THE RESTLESSNESS OF THE RENAISSANCE, WITH A wave of enthusiasm for discovery that had started in the late fifteenth century. Notwithstanding all the wrong perceptions of how to reach India by sea or how to get to the east coast of Asia, the dream of ages came ever closer to fulfillment. One could easily say that the improvement of the magnetic compass made these long voyages out of sight of land finally possible. Nevertheless these explorations were daring feats. Within two centuries most of the world was known to Europeans. Exploration brought with it colonization and exploitation, their benefits and curses to be harvested over the centuries.

In Lully's days there was some interest in the East, with Turkey in the foreground. But by a few decades later the trade with Eastern countries, particularly China, had grown immensely. Around 1720 everything "Chinois" became fashionable, as Baroque style turned into what was then termed "modern"—picturesque and full of fanciful forms. Toward the end of the century this trend received its historic label *Rococo,* which by then was assuming a derogatory meaning.

The rich fabrics, the porcelain, and, above all, the bold yet symmetrical designs of the carved lacquer, delicately wrought in most minute detail, corresponded with the people's predilection for the minuet and the playfulness of their bucolic fêtes. The spell that an alien culture could cast on the West was stupendous in its impact on the total style of life. The French took to it with great flair and ingenuity.

It was not the first or the last time that the East exerted an influence on the West. The ancient Greeks borrowed many things from many lands, but, within their great cultural advance, soon made these their own. Dionysus— whose cult not only is associated with the first significant signs of danceomania, but also initiated our form of theater and with it theatrical dancing—came to the Greeks from Thrace, according to Homer, or from the Babylonians, Chaldees, and their nomad tribes, according to some modern scholars. The continuity of culture proves the timelessness of our ritualistic needs and artistic experiences. When Emperor Leo III drove the icon worshipers out of Byzantium in A.D. 730, many of them escaped to Italy and the Frankish territory between the Loire and Rhine, where their influence on Romanesque art was quite noticeable. Byzantine ivories, elegant in their expression, became models for all carvings in the West. The austere atmosphere in architecture, also, was from then on loosened. After the inevitable impact in the seventeenth and eighteenth centuries of the Renaissance expansion, the East decisively affected Western civilization in two separate waves: one at the end of the nineteenth century and the other in the twentieth, with No drama and Zen Buddhism.

Until the mid-1750s French literature chose for its environmental background Persia, China, and many other Middle or Far Eastern countries. Antoine Galland (1646–1715), Orientalist and writer, who traveled extensively in the Near East for Louis XIV, was one of many who became enamored of Arabic literature. His was the first translation into a European language of *Les Mille et une nuits (The Thousand and One Nights),* the last volume of which was published posthumously in 1717. These stories appeared in all European languages and became the most famous reading material of their time. They became a part of the mental climate of the Rococo. They inspired writers, painters, and dancers.

That this Eastern craze would be an open invitation to all hack writers to publish books on the East is obvious. A series of genuine and fantasized travel books were available for pleasant armchair voyages. A minor writer, Charles Rivière Dufresny, came up with an excellent idea. He introduced an exotic traveler to Paris in his *Serious and Comical Amusements of a Siamese in Paris,* which gave Dufresny the opportunity to contrast two different worlds and take a satirical look at French society. But he did not have the wit of Baron de Montesquieu (1689–1755), a man of many titles and far more brains. In Montesquieu's *Persian Letters* he had two Persians come

The set for Les Indes Galantes, *the epochal ballet of 1735.* (*Courtesy French Cultural Services*)

to Paris and reveal through their amazement at what they encountered the inadequacies of the French regime. The book was issued in 1721 and became an immediate international success. It started the interest in comparative culture. A libraryful of imitators followed in its wake, writers who pleased the pockets of their publishers with Turkish, Persian, and even Iroquois letters. One of the more famous imitators was Oliver Goldsmith, who in his *Citizen of the World* had a Chinese sage cleverly comment on the Western way of life.

Not even François Marie Arouet Voltaire (1694–1778) could withstand the magic attraction of the East. He gave it a prominent place in his historic *Essai sur les moeurs* (*Essay on Manners and Morals,* 1756). He also wrote a minor Oriental fantasy, *Le Blanc et le noir* (*The White and the Black*), late in his life, and scored a resounding success in a tragedy called *L'Orphelin de la Chine* (*The Orphan of China*).

Until then, in all plays—in whatever period and region they may have taken place—the actors' costumes were always the dress of eighteenth-century Paris, with hoop skirts and powdered wigs. But on August 20, 1755, the famous actress Mlle Clairon (legally Claire Josèphe Hippolyte Léris de La Tude, born out of wedlock) startled her audience by appearing onstage in a dress and hairstyle that fitted the time of *The Orphan of China*. She insisted that all costumes and the decors should be Chinese. She triumphed in the play, and so did her daring changes. It probably was the mood of the time, assuring us that Marie Camargo did nothing outrageous when she shortened her skirts.

THE craze for everything Oriental also left its mark on two men and mainly on two of their works, signposts in the development of the ballet: *Les Indes Galantes* (*The Gallant Indies*), composed by Jean Philippe Rameau, and *Les Fêtes Chinoises* (or *Chinese Metamorphoses*), choreographed by Jean Georges Noverre. Before Voltaire could say, "Rameau has made of music a new art," it was an arduous uphill fight for Lully's successor. When he was fully established as a composer and theoretician, Jean Le Rond d'Alembert praised Rameau in his *Preliminary Discourse* written for Diderot's *Encyclopédie* in 1751. He called him an *artiste-philosophe* who had brought laws to the art of music and had thus established it as a science. The gospel of Enlightenment was science. Most of Rameau's critics maintained that his theoretical work was more significant than his compositions, and he might have agreed, since he himself said that "it would be most desirable to have the musical knowledge of this century's composers equal their capacity to create beauty." He was a theoretician before a composer, writing his first serious opera at the age of fifty. In 1722 he had published his *Traité de l'harmonie* (*Treatise on Harmony*), in which he extols the mathematical principles of music:

Music is a science which ought to have certain rules. These rules should be derived from a self-evident principle which cannot become known to us without the help of mathematics. I must concede that, despite all the experience I acquired in music through its practice over a considerable period of time, it was only with the help of mathematics that I was able to unravel my ideas, that light replaced an obscurity I had previously not recognized as such.

In another theoretical work, *Génération harmonique* (*Harmonic Generation*), he defended the notion that melody derives from harmony, whereas Rousseau asserted in his article for the *Encyclopédie* that melody is free and expressive. Rameau had many enemies—the Lullists, because they thought he betrayed Lully's legacy, and the Encyclopedists, who saw in him the old-fashioned representative of the Rococo. When, in 1735, he composed the opera-ballet *Les Indes Galantes,* he explained apologetically where he thought he stood:

Forever occupied with fine declamation and the lovely melodic line which reigned in the recitatives of the great Lully, I attempt to imitate him, not as servile copyist, but availing myself, as he did, of fair and simple nature as my model.

Singers and instrumentalists complained about the difficulty of interpreting his music; they called it too rich and complicated, in fact cerebral; the critics reproached him for his many daring instrumental tricks; and finally, he was assailed by the proponents of Italian opera for being behind his time in not recognizing the melodic genius of the Italians. When Giovanni Battista Pergolesi's *La Serva Padrona* was performed in Paris in 1752, the *guerre des bouffons* broke out, lasting for two years. Battles in the Opéra and street fights were part of this controversy, fought harder by intellectuals than by musicians.

Rameau's most merciless adversaries were Rousseau, Diderot, and Baron von Grimm. They only halfheartedly granted that he was at least a theoretician. Also, the Lullists did not accept his claim that he worked in the Lully tradition. Being of his time, his orchestration could not help but show a more striking counterpoint and his harmonies had to be more complex. Nobody, of course, could surmise that in his nobility and clarity he anticipated some of Gluck's reforms. In 1725, when Rameau was forty-two years old, he arranged his *concerts spirituels* for the general public; they were performed during the twenty-four days of each year when opera productions were forbidden and were the first modern kind of public concert performances.

Montesquieu thought of music that "of all sensible Pleasures there is none that less corrupts the soul." But the historic events proved him wrong when, in mid-century, a violent quarrel broke out with Rameau as the central

Costume design for a dancer in LES FÊTES CHINOISES *by Jean Georges Noverre. (Courtesy New York Public Library Dance Collection)*

Rameau's opéra ballet La Princesse de Navarre *features a scene of a ball at court. Voltaire wrote the libretto, and the first production was at the Palace of Versailles. Drawing by Cochin. (Courtesy French Cultural Services)*

figure. It was no longer a fight between the Lullists and Ramists. The question arose whether people ought to follow Rameau as the first native French composer and creator of a French opera or blindly believe in the melodic Italian school. How vicious his enemies were can be seen from Diderot's posthumously published *Neveu de Rameau* (*Rameau's Nephew*), in which he depicted a man, eccentric in every respect, whose miserliness had features of a Molière character. When introducing his hero with the words "He's the nephew of that celebrated musician who delivered us from the plain-song of Lulli that we had been chanting for more than a hundred years," he was scarcely hiding that the nephew was a stand-in for Rameau.

The great misfortune for Rameau was that he never found a librettist who had the qualities of a dramatist. A third-rate writer, Claude Pierre

Fuselier, concocted *Les Indes Galantes* for him. The noble savage—a beautiful image for the white man's collective guilt—was exalted in many ways, as Turks, Incas, and Persians were indiscriminately thrown into one opéra ballet. Some of Rameau's finest music went into this hodgepodge idea, typical of the mentality of the time. What finally made this opéra ballet a historic event was not only Rameau's new style of music, but also the dancing, with its accent on sensuous excitement. Louis Dupré choreographed the ballet and had the best dancers at his disposal, among them Marie Camargo and Marie Sallé. Rameau's operas show that he cared too little for dramatic structure and was easily satisfied with whatever text he was given. Not even Voltaire, who wrote the book for his *Princesse de Navarre,* did more than a fair job. In this collaboration the dancing triumphed—Rameau's choreographer was Dupré again—and, some time later, Rousseau helped Rameau fuse the three major divertissements of this *comédie-ballet* into a consecutive work which was then called *Les Fêtes de Ramire.*

This entire period was dominated by one librettist, Pietro Metastasio (1698–1782), whose works were set to music by practically all the composers of his time from Pergolesi to Gluck and Mozart; many of his libretti were composed more than once. In 1730 he became poet laureate to the imperial court in Austria, where he considerably contributed to making Vienna a new European cultural center. What made his work so highly recommended was his ability to mingle artificiality and delicacy with operatic bathos, a tight dramaturgic structure with absurd plots. The major theme of the age, reason versus emotion, played an overriding part in his conceits. Obviously, he was attuned to the time, and Voltaire's cynical remark "What is too silly to be said is sung" fits perfectly the description of Metastasio's libretti.

NOVERRE'S first professional dance experiences were associated with the name of Marie Sallé. This was of the greatest consequence to the direction in which his artistic temper developed. In 1743, when the Opéra-Comique was granted the concession to produce entertainments of music and dancing, Marie Sallé was the leading ballerina of fourteen dancers, one of whom was Noverre. The impresario Jean Monnet asked a baker boy turned poet and playwright, Charles Simon Favart, to put together a one-act vaudeville, which was called *Le Coq du village (Cock of the Village).* A few interludes, songs and dances, were thrown in for good entertaining measure—which only goes to show that the state of the dance was still in a haphazard condition. Noverre may have made his debut in one of the dances with which the season opened, but he certainly danced in the following premiere, at the end of August 1743. It was called *L'Ambigu de la Folie ou le Ballet des Dindons (The Ambiguity of Madness or the Ballet of the Dupes)* and was a parody of *Les Indes Galantes,* which was then again playing at the Opéra.

We next find Noverre with another company in Germany. With Voltaire's help, Frederick the Great engaged a group of French actors and dancers. But the maître de ballet, Sieur Poitiers, refused to work with amateurs in the corps de ballet, and since there was not enough money allotted for professional dancers, Poitiers soon left, and with him a number of dancers. A new ballet master was engaged. It was Jean Barthélemy Lany from the Opéra-Comique, who brought Noverre with him. Barbara Campanini, known as La Barberina, was the prima ballerina, making her debut in Berlin in 1744. She was soon the rage of Berlin, received a fantastic salary, and insisted on the corps de ballet with which she wanted to show off best her own virtuosity. That she would become the enlightened monarch's mistress goes without saying (although some maintained she was in name only). Noverre danced in several ballets with her. He was known to have amused the King by imitating leading danseuses and also entertained Voltaire with "wicked stories." However, the dancers did not enjoy the military tone then prevalent in Berlin and left the city toward the end of 1747.

Noverre finally landed in the city of Lyons, whose opera house enjoyed a great reputation. It was a wealthy city, and its Académie des Beaux Arts arranged musical concerts; Rameau was often seen there, also in his capacity as master organist, and Rousseau taught at the Académie in 1739. For several years Noverre headed a company of dancers there, choreographing ten ballets each season. At that time he gained greater insight into the tasks of the choreographer.

In February 1752 the Opéra-Comique was refurbished and reopened. François Boucher painted the ceiling; the ramp that had connected the auditorium with the stage was removed; candles were replaced by oil lamps backed by reflectors. (These important technical improvements impressed David Garrick [1717–79], and he ordered such lamps from Paris for his Drury Lane Theatre.) Noverre designed the ballets for this new undertaking, and in July 1754 one could read about the premiere of this ballet master's *Fêtes Chinoises* in the *Journal,* as observed by Charles Collé:

> . . . my adversion to dancing has greatly increased since all the theatres have become infected with ballets; but I must admit that this Chinese ballet is unusual, . . . designed by a certain Noverre, a young man of twenty-seven or twenty-eight years. He seems to have a wide and agreeable imagination for his profession. He is novel and prolific, varied and a painter. It is not by the *pas* and the *entrée* that he pleased, it is by the variegated and novel tableaux that he achieved this prodigious success. If there is anyone who can drag us out of the childhood in which we are still in the matter of ballets, it must be a man such as this Noverre. The Opéra should secure and pay well such talent; but for the very reason that they should do so, they will do nothing of the sort. . . .

The *Mercure de France* referred to the extraordinary luxury with which this ballet was staged and, in a later issue, it said that "the multitude flocked to see it with unprecedented furore."

DAVID Garrick thought highly of Noverre, and since the theater world, whether Baroque or Romantic, is generous with epithets, Garrick referred to Noverre as "the Shakespeare of the dance." In turn, Noverre saw in Garrick "the Proteus of our own time; because he understood all styles and presented them with a perfection and truth. . . . He was so natural, his expression was so lifelike, his gestures, features and glances were so eloquent and so convincing that he made the action clear even to those who did not understand a word of English. . . ." This shows the mutual admiration these men felt for each other; it also recalls the tremendous impact that the commedia dell'arte had on the European theater. Garrick's style directly emerged from the enthusiasm the English developed for the art of Italian players early in the eighteenth century.

In the previous century, as a natural result of the repression under which the London theater had suffered for many decades, most plays and players in the Restoration period—after 1660—produced a toughness in tone, a pleasant vulgarity to tickle the jaded palates of the playgoers. Out of this arose a renewed interest in the commedia type of acting, the edges of which were as rough as ever. As a consequence, sentimentality, squeamishness, and puritanical hypocrisy overtook the theater without uprooting the joy of the rougher Italianate play. All this led to superb acting but to a barren dramatic period in England, which ended only with Oliver Goldsmith's *She Stoops to Conquer*, produced in 1773, followed by the plays of Richard Brinsley Sheridan's genius. Wit was now offered without lubricity, and the satire on the man of sentiment, on parvenus, on all foppery and coxcombry, was done with a scintillating fancy.

By then one other feature of the earlier eighteenth-century theater in England had disappeared: the row of strong iron spikes running along the front of the stage, necessitated by the frequent riots in playhouses. Some of the roughnecks even belonged to the nobility. There were riots at Drury Lane in 1744 when the management dared to raise the entrance prices; as late as 1763, there were riots when Covent Garden tried to abolish the curious custom of letting people in at drastically reduced prices after the third act, still giving them the chance of seeing two more acts and some dancing.

David Garrick had his own run-ins with violent crowds. He invited Noverre to bring *Les Fêtes Chinoises* to Drury Lane. It was an ill-fated undertaking. Noverre's company came to London at the eve of the Seven Years' War, which started with Britain's being pitted against France to secure the former's position as the greatest trading nation of the world. An invasion of England was feared, and the London mob was aroused to a rare patriotic pitch. Even though Garrick did his best to prepare a lavish production and to soothe the chauvinistic waves, the calls from the galleries of "No French dancers!" persisted from one performance to the next. The King, attended by the entire court, honored the first performance with his presence. The nobility, and particularly the ladies of society, still had strong links with France. They tried to ensure the continuation of the production, but during the sixth performance the violence took on disastrous proportions and the ballet was withdrawn. David Garrick's own home was besieged and its windows were broken. Noverre and his family had to go into hiding.

Noverre stayed on for some time in England during the war, doing odd choreographic jobs. When he left London in March 1757 he was an embittered man. There was nothing for him to do in Paris, where the coveted position of ballet master at the Opéra was denied him. So he left for Lyons, where he again headed a company, and he worked there for the next three years, choreographing many ballets. But he also used the leisure of these years to write down his thoughts about dancing and dancers. He felt stimulated by Garrick's natural and convincing art of acting and miming; but he also felt certain that at long last he had found himself and was able to break with the past. Until then he had staged spectacles startling in their visual beauty and pleasing pattern. Now he was resolved to paint human passions through movement. He envisioned a heightened pantomimic dance drama of which the plot would be made visible through the revelation of body movement and gesture. In desiring to make the soul dance, he was convinced that new aesthetic tenets had to be postulated.

The 1750s: Spiritual Watershed

IT HAD TO HAPPEN IN THE MID-EIGHTEENTH CENTURY. ALEXANDER Gottlieb Baumgarten (1714–62), a German philosopher, created the term *aesthetics,* with which he embraced the study of beauty and the theory of art. Of course, many thinkers since Plato have dealt with ideas of beauty. But in his two volumes of *Aesthetica* (1750–58) Baumgarten created the framework and the unity of aesthetics as a philosophical discipline. It was a pioneer work in the development of modern aesthetic theory, forgoing, however, any popular value by being written in Latin.*

* As an apology for Baumgarten it must be said that since the fourteenth century

To this very day it has been a long, slow process to circumscribe perceptions of beauty and to establish principles of art. The study of aesthetics progressed more decidedly in some disciplines, such as music, literature, or painting, than in others, such as dancing. Even today, dance aesthetics is, according to Edwin Denby, "in a pioneering stage." The reason for this slow development of dance as an art form based on aesthetic principles is that it had been in the hands of aristocratic dilettantes for too long. Also, dance has been thought of by many as light entertainment rather than as art.

This retardation occurred despite the fact that the entire character of the Baroque and certainly of the Rococo Age was that of lightness and movement. Dance was very much on everyone's mind. It was the desired entertainment at courts, with plays taking a secondary place. Yet dancing inside and outside the theater must also have been ever present; as Noverre wrote, "Today, sir, dancing and the ballet are the craze; they are followed with a kind of rage, and never has an art been more encouraged by applause than ours." About the time he made this statement, Diderot's *Encyclopédie* was put together. Noverre rightly complained that no one with deep insight into the craft was asked to write about dance. Hurt pride and vanity have often been great stimuli for creative minds, and this may have been one of the many incentives for him to get his own thoughts down on paper and to publish them.

Diderot took it upon himself to write the articles on the *Beau* (the beautiful, an equivalent of what is now known as aesthetics) and the mechanical arts for the *Encyclopédie,* which started publication in 1751. Diderot may not have exhausted the subject, but by defining ballet as "an action explained by a dance" he stated in essence what Noverre had in mind when he advocated the ballet d'action. Furthermore, Diderot wrote: "A dance is a poem. This poem should have its independent representation which presupposes the collaboration of poet, painter, musician, and pantomime-dancer." Thus he pointed to the need of the ballet to be an "independent representation," another principal idea that Noverre promoted. Aristotle had already defined dancing as the "presentation of passions, actions, and manners" that should avoid "fine steps which represent nothing." Noverre stated, in the terms of his age: ". . . renounce cabrioles, *entrechats,* and over-complicated steps; abandon grimaces to study sentiments, artless graces and expressions . . . put judgement and sense into your *pas de deux.* . . ."

Again, Noverre was not alone in feeling urged to dissect, analyze, and formulate the technical and artistic elements of his craft. Of course, Leonardo was the prototype of the investigating, restless mind—the first scientific

Latin was the language to be known and used by humanists, savants, and scientists, until the eighteenth century, when this proof of scholarly learning lost its significance. But the study of aestheticism would have hardly coalesced and advanced much faster had Baumgarten used his vernacular.

William Hogarth was the great satirist of English society during the early eighteenth century. From his election series: "The Polling." (Courtesy The Metropolitan Museum of Art, gift of Sarah Lazarus, 1891)

researcher who tried to understand the secrets behind natural appearances and who already realized that "where the spirit does not work with the hand there is no art." In the century of reasoning, when scientific truth became the unhaloed goddess, it was to be expected that the artist would call himself to account for what he was doing and why.

This trend was strongest among the visual artists, who were governed by classical ideals and an almost enigmatic feeling toward nature. At a time when portrait painting was strongly in demand in England, Thomas Gainsborough (1727–88) was drawn to nature, even though he achieved perfection in society portraits, then the bread and butter of the artist. In contrast to Sir Joshua Reynolds (1723–92), his counterpart, his was not only a love of nature but also an enthusiastic struggle for its expression, in the course of which he approached the subject in a variety of techniques. He achieved a Wordsworthian poetry while catching nature in paint. The fusion of Baroque classicism with idolization of nature was one of the marked developments in the mid-eighteenth century.

Despite serious differences between Reynolds and Gainsborough, they were both products of their time. So, a generation earlier, was William

Hogarth (1697–1764), who had the courage to break away from conformity. John Gay's *Beggar's Opera* inspired him to a satirical painting, and it was such a success that he was asked for repetitions, which determined his future direction. In his reminiscences he wrote that the theater influenced him to "compose pictures on canvas similar to representations on stage," expecting them to be "tried by the same test, and criticized by the same criterion. . . . I have endeavored to treat my subjects as a dramatic writer: my picture is my stage, and men and women are my players, who by means of certain actions and gestures, are to exhibit a *dumb show*." Theatricality remained Hogarth's trademark as a painter. And what a lovable, roguish spy on humanity he was!

About 1750 Hogarth was discouraged by the reception of his work and withdrew for some time from painting, composing instead his *Analysis of Beauty*, written with a view to fixing the fluctuating "Ideas of Taste." In the writing of this book, Hogarth's tone tried to be scholarly.

He believed in the gracefulness of the undulating line and saw in the pyramidal and serpentlike form the ideal beauty. Did he not thus prefigure Isadora Duncan's basic movements or the intricately interwoven figures and the intertwined arm and hand movements of George Balanchine? An economy of simplicity was just as important to him as variety: "Simplicity without variety is wholly insipid. . . . There is no object composed of straight lines, that has so much variety, with so few parts, as the pyramid. . . ." Even though some of his ideas border on the absurd—most of his contemporaries thought of him as an arrogant ignoramus—he delved with loving care to find a new method of acquiring easy and graceful movements of the body. He devoted quite some time to discussing dancing, in particular the minuet:

> The minuet is allowed by the dancing-masters themselves to be the perfection of all dancing. I once heard an eminent dancing-master say that the minuet had been the study of his whole life . . . the minuet contains in it a composed variety of as many movements in the serpentine lines as can well be put together in distinct quantities. . . .
>
> The other beauties belonging to this dance are the turns of the head and twist of the body in passing each other, as also gentle bowing and presenting hands. . . .

Neither Reynolds nor Hogarth closely adhered to his own theories in his creative efforts. More important, however, was their endeavor to search for truth and to bring systematized order into the world of thought and the arts. It was symptomatic of this era of a growing neoclassicism with scientific accents. The time was ripe for definitions and the organization of studies. A series of dictionaries were then edited. Dr. Samuel Johnson's was the one that is mentioned in the schoolbooks, if for no other reason than for Johnson's erudition and brilliant personality. Encyclopedias were often called dictionaries and lexicons in the seventeenth and eighteenth centuries, the terms being interchangeable. Bacon's *Novum Organum* (1620) has been looked upon as the first encyclopedia of modern times and, when, in 1745, Denis Diderot (1713–84) was charged with the supervision of an *Encyclopédie*, he used the opportunity to turn the pursuit of knowledge into a dissemination of revolutionary thoughts. There was enough material to go on.

A two-volume *Cyclopaedia* (1728) by Ephraim Chambers was to have been translated into French by Diderot, but because of a quarrel between the publisher and those who held the English rights, Diderot changed the nature of this undertaking by broadening the scope of the project and gathering around him a team of the most outstanding minds. These included Voltaire, Rousseau, and his co-editor Jean d'Alembert, the well-known humanist and mathematician. In 1750 Diderot published the prospectus for this project. He went back to Bacon's concept of envisioning knowledge as an intricately structured whole, but, since he backed it up with a philosophy of faith in human progress, his rational approach had a radical ring.

Diderot's last words, "The first step toward philosophy is incredulity," join the ages of Reason and Enlightenment. Descartes's thought "that all things must be doubted" and Diderot's "incredulity" are related. The progress that doubt and incredulity engendered up into our own time led to Alfred North Whitehead's saying that "all philosophy starts with wonder." What a long and triumphant way we have come—finally to wonder about the mystery there is!

Noverre's Triumph and Tragedy

THE ENCYCLOPEDISTS DEMANDED THE ELIMINATION OF THE FANCIFUL world of make-believe; they wanted to liberate the stage from the caprice of enchanted figures and create a reality of make-believe. Noverre was their brother in spirit when he advocated "less of the fairy tale, less of the marvelous, more truth and more realism," and when he said that "the passion of Merope for Aegisthus, the submission of Iphigenia, and the eternal love of Clytemnestra will arouse our feelings much more than all the magic of our Opéra." But Diderot, who as a playwright favored the bourgeois drama, went far beyond Noverre in demanding realism onstage.

While Noverre was putting together his *Letters* with all his exhortations and formulations of tenets, he choreographed *L'Amour Corsaire* at the Opéra in Lyons for the season of 1758/59. In it nymphs and naiads, tritons and Cupid appear, and, as a deus ex machina, "an arm is upraised, the blow is about to fall when a god, who is a protector of lovers, stays the arm of the sacrificer and casts a spell over the island. . . ." As Noverre himself describes the ballet, Diderot might rightly have said that such an enchanted world is too infantile for an enlightened mind. Later in his career, Noverre admitted that he did not think highly of his *Chinese Metamorphoses,* with which he succumbed to the fad of the time, and he may have been unhappy about these early ballets as well.

When Noverre left France in 1760 to turn Stuttgart into a balletic center, he lived up to his own principles and from then on stayed mainly with classical material, with what he called tragic and heroic ballet themes. These included *Antoine et Cléopâtre, L'Apothéose d'Hercule, Der gerächte Agamemnon,* and *Iphigénie en Tauride.* The works were marked by dramatic coherence and by the use of the corps de ballet as an integrated part of the action, giving it the status of a Greek chorus.

In this, Noverre anticipated the trend of neoclassicism when in his early Stuttgart period (the early 1760s) he created a series of "heroic pantomime ballets," before the impact of Johann Joachim Winckelmann (1717–68) and his *Geschichte der Kunst des Alterthums (History of Ancient Art),* published in 1764, could have been felt. When Winckelmann was about to pronounce that the essential qualities of Greek art were "a noble simplicity and tranquil loftiness," "a beautiful proportion, order, and harmony," we find the same notions expressed and published by Noverre four years earlier. Translating them into dance terms, Noverre considered the importance of how "to make your gestures noble"; he exhorted the dancer to take off "those enormous wigs and those gigantic headdresses which destroy the true proportions of the head with the body." Where Winckelmann felt that "the depths of the sea are always calm however wild and stormy the surface," Noverre stressed that action did not mean a "bustling activity," but "the art of impressing, by truly significant movements, gesture and facial expression, our feelings on the minds of the audience."

In 1765 Diderot read Winckelmann's *History of Ancient Art* in its French translation and reacted to it with the words: "It seems to me that we must study the antique in order that we may learn to see nature." Nature was the *primum mobile,* the spring of action, for Noverre, and it had been the key word of the age. He wrote that "poetry, painting and dancing are, or should be, no more than a faithful likeness of beautiful Nature," and that there is "but one rule common to all the arts and which we may depart from only at the risk of being misled, and that is the imitation of beautiful Nature."

Of course, "imitation" in the idiomatic and learned use of the word contained a creative, formative, in fact dynamic, potential. Imitation was considered the artistic means of stirring the soul of the onlooker. The image of *"l'imitation de la belle nature"* can be found in many books published in the first half of the century. They all stress the need to translate (read: imitate) "human actions and passions" into pantomime dance. The phrase that the dance ought to express, paint, outline "to the eye some affection of the soul" is recurrent. Noverre also emphasizes that a choreographic work worthy of its name ought to be capable of "stirring and captivating the spectator, of speaking to the soul."

"To speak to the soul through the eyes" gave the metaphor of the eyes being the windows of the soul more than a symbolic meaning. The spectator's pleasure at having the soul touched through the eyes' perception presupposed the ability of the dancer-choreographer to imitate nature in the same eye-soul process. In the Baroque Age, it was generally thought that the sentiment rather than the intellect is the artist's link with nature, and it is also through the sentiment that, in the last analysis, Noverre wanted to lift the mind to the vision of spiritual beauty.

Noverre worked successfully in Stuttgart and Vienna, but what he desired all his life was the position of ballet master at the Paris Opéra. It would have bolstered his prestige, crowned his life's work. He had to wait until 1776 and his fiftieth year, when a former pupil in Vienna, Marie Antoinette, now Queen of France, named him after Vestris' resignation to the coveted position. History and its recorders—André Levinson wrote a most beautiful essay about him—made a regretful note that his appointment became Noverre's greatest disappointment.

It would be wrong to assume that Noverre, while in his self-styled exile in Stuttgart, was never produced at the Paris Opéra. Vestris, who danced the title role in his ballet *Jason et Médée* in Stuttgart, was so enthusiastic about this work that he made its production in Paris possible. The celebrated Madeleine Guimard danced the role of the shepherdess in the third act, wearing a dress that immediately became the rage of Paris. To Noverre's chagrin, however, Gaetano Vestris made a few unauthorized additions of his own. The ballet may not have been improved by Vestris' ideas, but it impressed the audience by its very novelty. The fact remains that the Parisian balletomanes could see Noverre's ballet d'action in action before he had returned to the Paris Opéra as ballet master.

Noverre's *Letters on the Dance and Ballets* were written with a candid enthusiasm that never hides the fury animating his words. The work was epochal in the way it encompassed in full detail and knowledge of the craft what had become the revolutionary trend in Noverre's time. When Noverre sent his *Letters* to Voltaire soon after their publication, with the wish to fashion a ballet after a section of Voltaire's *Henriade*, he received nothing but praise from the man then considered to be the "dictator of opinion": "Your work of genius, sir, lies in front of me; my gratitude equals my admiration. The title of your book speaks of the dance only, but you throw light on all the arts. . . . In my opinion, you are such an excellent representative of your genre that the injuries and disappointments which you suffered, and which forced you to seek use for your gifts far from your native land, in no way surprise me. I think your merits will find the necessary understanding where one loves Nature; but will you find the actors able to realize your ideas?" This letter, written on October 11, 1763, was cherished by Noverre to his last days; it ended with the often-quoted phrase: "You are a Prometheus, you must mold men and move them." Such a pronouncement must have helped him to strengthen his belief in himself and, in his bitter days at the Opéra, retort, in self-defense, to a Minister of the Crown: ". . . I am as much a dancing master as Voltaire is a writing master."

We can easily imagine the traumatic insults, humiliations, and difficulties caused by the intrigues of the all-powerful prima ballerina Madeleine Guimard, who hated Noverre with a vengeance, dancing indifferently in some of his ballets while reaping ovations in others. Also, we must understand the brothers Gardel, Maximilien and Pierre, who both coveted the position of ballet master and who offended Noverre since they felt offended by him and the Queen, having made Noverre "master over those who thought to be masters." How difficult Noverre's struggle as the head of the Opéra Ballet was and how defeated he must have felt can be seen from a letter he wrote to his friend Fabre in 1790 from Clermont-Ferrand, where he withdrew after his forced retirement from the Opéra in 1781. It was a note accompanying a condensed version of his famous *Letters:*

> I send you, my dear Fabre, the ramblings of a young man of twenty-five, or the dream he then had to raise from the cradle a weak and languishing art. May you embellish it by following a career which I have lived with sorrow. May you harvest flowers where I have found but the thorns and the brambles of intrigue; may you be as happy as it is possible to be in a bawdy house where they sing of a happiness which has never been seen there, where esteem and friendship find no refuge. . . .

Since Noverre aimed high, he cannot be blamed for not always having reached what he preached. He clearly separated the execution of mere dance movements from expressive pantomime, thereby unavoidably creating many empty stretches in his ballets in which stately walking predominated. He saw in the pantomime dance the heart of the ballet d'action, and pantomime was elevated to an amazing height by Salvatore Viganò (1769–1821), often considered to be a masterly disciple of Noverre, when he was choreographer at La Scala, Milan, from 1813 to his death. Historically seen, Viganò was the great afterthought to Noverre's choreographic concepts and seems to have overworked the emphasis on pantomime. His work is best recorded by Stendhal, and even if we overlook that writer's romantic raptures, there would still be left enough greatness in

Viganò's work. Three years after Noverre's death, Viganò began his career at La Scala, but he had staged ballets from his own imagination since 1790, undoubtedly aware of Noverre's ideas.

Stendhal's remarks about Viganò's work and some descriptions by his contemporaries give us a rather clear idea of what his choreodrama was like. It apparently combined emotional expression through pantomime with pictorial visualization through the movement of groups and solo dancers; the music not only served as stimulation but was first of all vigorously translated into movement patterns and gestures. Viganò aimed for the total orchestration of a movement idea, with each dancer expressing individually the inner experience of the music, reducing solos and pas de deux to a minimum, thus achieving a natural flow of the dramatic action. He worked indefatigably on shading the facial, pantomimic expression of each individual dancer, also using the then unconventional "natural" gesture, meaningful in its expressiveness. Viganò had taken Noverre at his pantomimic word and created a composition of utter plasticity evoked by the power of those Greek and Roman sculptures with which the neoclassic decades had been familiar. Some people, among them Rossini, may rightly have complained that there was more posing than dancing, which had to be the result when Noverre's pantomimic concept was taken to its ultimate point.

Neither Noverre's nor Viganò's works have become part of the ballet repertory. It is as if Romanticism swept them off the board. The only ballet of this classic era still performed from time to time is Jean Dauberval's *La Fille Mal Gardée,* first produced in 1789. What speaks for Dauberval is the fact that, as a pupil of Noverre, he tried to further his master's ideas and that he introduced with this work the genre of the comedy ballet. What speaks poorly for the classical era of ballet is the theatrical oblivion in which all its balletic productions drowned. Théophile Gautier, foremost critic of the Romantic era, vaguely referred to Viganò once or twice, probably having read Stendhal's accounts of the choreographer, but he never mentioned Noverre, simply because he may never have heard of him. We cannot blame the lack of dance notation (in which, incidentally, Noverre did not believe), as none of the many Romantic ballets profited from it, and yet survived. And is not the music, are not some of the operas and plays of the seventeenth and eighteenth centuries often revived and enjoyed?

Viganò's choreodramas are as good as forgotten because they are badly constructed and, despite their classic themes, did not have lasting validity. Also when one studies Noverre's scenarios, one notices a certain slowness in the flow of his dramaturgic structure, which André Levinson called "unvivacious weightiness." The shaping of the various scenes was mostly praised, the motifs often criticized.

After forty years, Noverre revised his concept of identifying ballet with pantomime. When he revived his ballet *Euthyme et Eucharis* in London in

1788, he spoke of ballet as a complex art form in his preface to the printed libretto. Pantomime, he said, is only the art of expressing emotions and inner experiences through gestures determined by passion. But dance, being the art of the pas, of beautiful movement and poses, of shapes and figures, is determined by rules of grace and taste, by the creative genius of the choreographer, by his gift of recognizing the interrelation of movements and combined figures. Each of these things differs from the others, but, fused together unnoticeably, they constitute the ballet d'action or ballet-pantomime-drama.

At the very end of his career, after having said farewell to his dreams and ambitions, he envisioned the formula for the ballet which, to this very day, has hardly changed. This realization came too late—too late for him in his career, too late to give ballet the timelessly valid imprint it needed so badly during its classical period.

Granted, Noverre's fate had its tragic features. Yet in the late 1750s he played the part of a receptacle gathering the experiences of the preceding fifty years, redesigning, planning and arranging, recasting the parts, adjusting some basic ideas to new trends, and adding his own conclusions. His great merit was to have been fully attuned to his time and to have written down with conviction that the world of the arts was about to change.

The New Grand Simplicity

THE CHANGES WERE SOON QUITE NOTICEABLE, AND BARON VON GRIMM could report in his *Correspondance littéraire* in 1763:

> For some years now the forms of ancient times are much in favor. Taste has benefited thereby, and everything is *à la grecque;* exteriors of buildings, their interior decoration, furniture, fabrics and jewelry. Thanks to this we now have beautiful and noble forms instead of the eccentricities which offended us ten or twelve years ago.

The swinging back of the historical pendulum from something so playful and artificial as the Baroque and its Rococo excesses to a more form-fulfilled serenity could have easily been predicted by anyone used to observing the motion of these proverbial pendulums. Usually, as if it were all a matter of chance, many unexpected events began to corroborate in this tremendous change.

But the Baroque world from which the pendulum swung was so complex in its multiformity that it brought with it another movement—as it were a concomitant—that gathered a portentous power running underground or undercover for some time. It is no surprise, therefore, that Jean Jacques Rousseau (1712–78) began as a man of the Enlightenment, or that Johann Joachim Winckelmann was all his life a romantic neoclassicist. The escape into nature in an arcadian manner changed from its bucolic gesture to Hellenic beauty. The cry for nature and the longing for "the grand subject matter" were never divorced. The rediscovery of antiquity brought with it the notion of a grand simplicity, unique to the ancient Greeks, which Winckelmann articulated and Gluck embraced. "Nature! Nature!" said Noverre. "And our compositions must be beautiful; let us renounce art, when it is not simple."

Neoclassicism did not appear overnight and did not issue from one country only, although the spiritual reawakening of the German-speaking people helped remarkably. If one looks at the themes of plays and paintings, at certain books such as Fénelon's *Télémaque,* and at the superficial use of dance subjects from antiquity, then one could say that the interest in the ancients had never ceased since the fourteenth century (and was kept alive by the clergy during the medieval period). But all of a sudden, as if time wanted to rid itself of its flirtations with life and put on a more serious mien, the interest in antiquity gave the world another look. Between 1734, when the Society of Dilettanti was formed in England, and 1768, the year of the foundation of its Royal Academy, the changes in interior decoration and architectural designs, in fashion and the theaters, were remarkable.

One usually takes the year 1748, the beginning of the excavations at Pompeii, as the point of departure when a new mental climate seized Western Europe. Systematic excavations had started, as a matter of fact, some ten years earlier in Herculaneum, an event that did not have the same marked impact. It was like a play that failed on opening night and, some time later when the moment was right and the audience mentally ready, turned into a lasting success. During the first half of the century the European world was still caught in the scintillating web of its Baroqueness. But then, around 1750, there was, in effect, a spiritual watershed.

Winckelmann did not discover or usher in the renewed interest in antiquity. But at that time he wrote best about it, and his enthusiastic style proved contagious. In his first essays he contended that the Greeks understood nature better than the moderns, and that therein lay the secret of their accomplishments. "The only way for us to become great, indeed, to become inimitably great . . . is through imitation of the ancients." His first essays began to appear as early as 1755. Did Noverre know about them? Hardly; even Diderot learned about Winckelmann only five years after Noverre had published his *Letters.*

Winckelmann's first contact with the Greeks was through their literature and his own observations of the Roman copies. His misfortune was that he never had enough money to travel to Greece, and when he did, he was murdered while on his way. The murder had something to do with his homosexual leanings, which in a way influenced his artistic judgment. He claimed to have forgone any preference for sex, but his aesthetic predeliction for the beauty of the muscular male figure rather than the rounded female contours is obvious. On the other hand, he extolled the fluid, softly curved line and abhorred angularity and tension. The highest form of beauty existed for him only in consistent smoothness, in, a refined line, in restraint and nobility, above all in the harmonious proportions of a unified whole. There it was, the source of the "grand simplicity," the noble grandeur. Winckelmann wrote to a friend in Germany from Rome: "If you wish to learn to know men, here is the place; here are heads of infinite talent, men of high endowments, beauties of the lofty character which the Greeks have given to their figures. . . ."

What a romantic led us back to the classic form and vision, away from all the sophisticated insincerity and empty brilliance of the preceding years! And what a persuasive man he was, who even invented the term of *Kunstgeschichte* (art history) for us. In short time, the style of the ancient temples triumphed, with the Madeleine and the Pantheon in Paris, the many triumphal arches mushrooming in Europe's cities. What did it matter that it was not Phidias who stood at the cradle of the 1760s rebirth of antiquity! The models were those of Rome, and Rome became the Mecca for the artists and the intelligentsia. To have journeyed to Italy and to start collecting antiques was part of the *bon ton*. It became the rage of the time. Viganò's choreographic conceits came right out of this climate. There were more books about all aspects of antiquity than there were readers. Antiquity was in.

One of the best sellers of the time was the many-volumed *History of the Decline and Fall of the Roman Empire* by Edward Gibbon (1737–94) which he began to publish in 1776; it was a rare accomplishment. Voltaire had begun the study of history, and books on the past considered history to be a constant continuum. Gibbon summarized what he was doing with the famous words "I have described the triumph of barbarism and religion." He showed the causes of decay in the Greco-Roman world, but it was left to Hegel and other thinkers in the Romantic Age to realize that, as Arnold Hauser pointed out, "historical development represents a dialectical process, in which every factor is in a state of motion and subject to constant change of meaning, in which there is nothing static, nothing timelessly valid, but also nothing one-sidedly active, and in which all factors, material and intellectual, economic and ideological are bound up together in a state of indissoluble interdependence, that is to say, that we are not in the least able

Francesco Guardi: "Classical Composition: Ruins and Figures." Characteristic of the late-eighteenth-century interest in ruins. (Crown Copyright. Courtesy Victoria and Albert Museum)

to go back to any point in time, where a historically definable situation is not already the result of this interaction."

Wedgwood's porcelain began to feature classic designs by the sculptor John Flaxman, whose work rivaled that of the two great masters of this neoclassic time: the Danish sculptor Bertel Thorvaldsen (most of whose figures are reinterpretations of Roman themes of classic antiquity) and Antonio Canova, a celebrated neoclassicist esteemed by Stendhal. Women were walking around in togalike dresses, with long skirt and high waist, almost baring their breasts. A classic simplicity was added to this everyday fashion when high-heeled shoes were replaced by heelless slippers. Because of the scantiness of the dresses, shawls and wraps of different fabrics and shapes became *le dernier cri*.

The movement "back to antiquity" also caught up with Christoph Willibald Gluck (1714–87) when, in the year 1754, Count Marcello Durazzo engaged him as kapellmeister with the understanding that Gluck would compose for the court in Vienna. Durazzo had become tired of the conventional Italian opera and put together the text for a musical drama he called *L'Innocenza giustificata,* for which he took some material from Metastasio, mixing it with some of his own. Gluck's music harmoniously blended with the text, and there were logic and simplicity in the way the arias were fitted into the plot. This work, produced at the imperial castle at Laxenburg in December 1755, was a harbinger of things to come.

Coincidences prepare the great chances for history. Raniero da Calzabigi, a friend of Casanova's, published that year an edition of Metastasio's *Poesie drammatiche*. In it Calzabigi pointed to the need for an opera that would be "a delightful whole resulting from the interplay of a large chorus, the dance, and a scenic action where poetry and music are united in a masterly way." He had spent some time in Paris, where he exchanged ideas with Baron von Grimm, Voltaire, Diderot, and Rousseau; the probability that he had read Noverre's *Letters,* which were then creating quite a stir, is great. At any rate, Calzabigi was full of reforming ideas about operas when he came to Vienna and met Durazzo, who asked him to write a new version of an opera about Orpheus for Gluck. The result was *Orfeo ed Euridice,* produced in 1762. Simplicity, truth, and naturalness were the key words for their collaboration. "Beautiful simplicity," as Gluck wrote on the occasion of his second collaboration with Calzabigi, on *Alceste.* All decorative flourishes were gone. Gluck's manifesto for this work could just as well have come from the pen of Noverre, who did the choreography for it:

> When I undertook to set the opera *Alceste* to music, I resolved to avoid all those abuses which had crept into Italian opera through the mistaken vanity of singers and the unwise compliance of composers, and which had rendered it wearisome and ridiculous, instead of being, as it once was, the grandest and most imposing

stage work of modern times. I endeavored to reduce music to its proper function, that of seconding poetry by enforcing the expression of the sentiment, and the interest of the situations, without interrupting the action, or weakening it by superfluous ornament. . . .

With such grand simplicity a new era was entered in the field of the opera. Winckelmann's spirit may have played the prompter, for all we know, on December 16, 1767, when *Alceste* was premiered at the Burg Theater in Vienna. Also, there was some housecleaning to be done on the legitimate stage. The influence of the commedia dell'arte had lasted long enough, more than two hundred years. The wearing of masks was condemned by Noverre in his *Letters;* however, the prolific Italian playwright Carlo Goldoni had already, in the 1740s, started his attacks on the actors' habit of wearing masks. He simultaneously objected to leaving any parts in the plot for extemporizing.

Gotthold Ephraim Lessing was a German writer who symbolized the awakening of his people. He was a dramatist and essayist, and his voice was the first to be heard beyond the German border. A man of the Enlightenment, he was a militant humanist, writing the first play—*Nathan the Wise*—against racial and religious prejudice, one of the noblest expressions of eighteenth-century idealism. Heinrich Heine (1797–1856) said about Lessing's work that it "breathes the same grand social ideas, the same progressive humanity, the same religion of reason, whose John he was and whose Messiah we still await."

This writer became a foremost fighter for artistic reforms. He was strongly impressed by Noverre's *Letters*, recognizing their epochal meaning. His comedy *Minna von Barnhelm*, produced in 1767, was the first play in any language to change sets for every act. In his critical studies in *Hamburgische Dramaturgie (Hamburg Dramaturgy)*, he attacked the predominance of the pseudoclassic school of the French and prepared the way for the romantic revolt by extolling Shakespeare as the ideal dramatist. He echoed Noverre's sentiments when he tried to free the writer from the straitjacket of the three unities of time, place, and action. "The only inexcusable fault of a tragic poet is to leave us cold," he said. "If he interests us he may do as he likes with the little mechanical rules."

Under Winckelmann's influence, Lessing wrote his famous essay *Laokoon: oder über die Grenzen der Malerei und Poesie (Laocoön; or, on the Limits of Painting and Poetry)*, in which he turned against the Baroque and Renaissance concept that poetry and painting can be equated. He admired the emotional and artistic restraint of the sculpture depicting the suffering of Laocoön and his two sons. This sculpture group became the point of departure for his investigation, in which he came to the conclusion that poetry is essentially movement and therefore has the freedom of developing action organically within time, while painting depends on proximity in space. "The wise Greek," he said, "confined painting strictly to the imitation of beauty. The Greek artist represented nothing that was not beautiful. . . . Nothing in his art was dearer to him or seemed to him more noble than the ends of art."

Lessing may have been an innate rationalist and neoclassicist, but through many of his writings he showed Romanticism its way. It so happened that Frederick the Great won decisive victories against the French in the Seven Years' War at a time when Lessing turned against the yoke of French pseudo-classicism. But it was more than coincidence that when Lessing began to write, the first signs of the waltz became noticeable.

Rousseau and the Waltz

THE YEAR 1750 WAS A POINT OF DEPARTURE FOR MANY SEARCHING MINDS. In July 1749 the newspaper *Mercure de France* announced that the academy of Dijon was offering a prize for an essay dealing with the question of whether the sciences and arts were instrumental in purifying or in corrupting morals. Rousseau read it while on his way to visit his friend Diderot. They had become friends when Rousseau arrived in Paris with high hopes— an opera, a play, a new system for musical notation, and a few poems in his pocket. A year later, in 1743, he had met Diderot in the Café Procope.

Rousseau was quite excited about the notice he had just read. Diderot, the enlightened rationalist, supposedly urged Rousseau to compete for the prize, proving that science and art can, indeed, corrupt human morals. And so he did. However great Diderot's share in it may have been, he never mentioned it, and with good reason since the attitude Rousseau took turned against Diderot and the enlightened thinkers who believed that accumulated knowledge would liberate humankind.

Rousseau stressed that human beings are unhappy, feeble, and frustrated. He saw them trapped in a social environment of their own making. "God makes all things good," he said; "man meddles with them and they become evil." The inequalities of wealth and the growth of society with its mushrooming intricacies are beyond human mastery. People can be happy and free only in a community small and simple enough to be within their grasp. Rousseau's essay *Discours sur les sciences et les arts* won the first prize, and when it was published in 1750 he became famous.

Rousseau was a born outsider and dissident in an age in which dissident intellectuals, doubters from the cradle, were the order of the day. He was not an easy person to get along with; he even quarreled with his best friend Diderot. If we take his *Confessions* as a measure of the man, he must have had a hard time living with himself. He went through a rough childhood and badly needed affection. But after his initial success he decided to remain emotionally and socially independent, aloof from all worldly hustle and bustle, although he needed approval as much as love. In his excessive self-centeredness his demands on others were high. His emotional balance sheet of give and take was as much in disorder as his whole life. He was sentimental and impulsive, solitary and suspicious. Strangely enough for one of the world's most potent thinkers, his thoughts were often muddled and his reactions self-contradictory. For instance, Rousseau who wrote plays and operas, yearning to be a man of the theater and winning fame through it, spoke out vehemently against opening a theater in Geneva. He was, nevertheless, a man of genius, burning with hopes and ideas in a most unorthodox and romantic manner, a dreamer who managed to push his dreams to the edge of fulfillment.

And yet he seemed ill prepared for his high goals. With scant knowledge of music, he taught it and composed. He thought of himself as a musicologist and became a contributor on music to Diderot's *Encyclopédie*. Of all his works in the theater, only his pastoral opera in the style of Pergolesi, *Le Devin du village (The Village Soothsayer)*, met with great success and is still remembered today. It was produced in 1752 and must have made quite an impression, since Gluck wrote in his dedication to *Orfeo:* "The accent of nature is the universal language: M. Rousseau has employed it in a simple manner with great success. His *Devin du village* is a model that no author can help but imitate."

When we think of Rousseau, the cliché of "Back to nature!" comes immediately to mind, but this makes sense only if we take it as a means to an end and not as the end itself, if we see it in the context of the thoughts of Rousseau the great social reformer. The French Revolution would undoubtedly have taken place if there had been no Rousseau, but its declaration of the rights of man was based upon his *Social Contract,* which passionately defended the viewpoint that all government must rest upon the consent of the governed. Benjamin Franklin, Thomas Jefferson, and the other revolutionaries who founded the United States of America took their cue from Rousseau.

His *Émile* was an amazing book, pretending to be a novel while being a treatise on education. He favored what we could call "permissive" freedoms for children, a thought that fitted his romantic concept extolling nature and the natural man. *Émile* was also critical of the Church, and the book was condemned in Paris and burned in Geneva. Rousseau had to go into exile and wrote the greatest part of his *Confessions* in England. The eighteenth century saw the beginning of the writing of autobiographies. Casanova's

Memoirs turned out to be an important social history with a great deal of self-revelation. But Rousseau's *Confessions* started the "self-revelation" books, so characteristic of Romanticism, in which the brutal assault on the central mystery of the human heart became an exploitable safari into the Self. Here Rousseau showed the way: "I desire to set before my fellows the likeness of a man in all the truth of nature, and that man myself."

We must see Rousseau within the frame of his time to realize his alienation from it and the power emanating from such estrangement. The credo of his time was *sociabilité,* and even a Voltaire or Diderot believed in the necessity of being social. This was characteristic of the lightweight Rococo existence; when the Enlightenment discovered the pursuit of personal happiness, presupposing close contact with one's fellows, sociability remained a part of it.

It is one of the many ironic touches of history that Rousseau never wrote the phrase "Back to nature!" in any of his works or letters. He celebrated the natural man and pitted the noble savage against the savage in man covered with a veneer of civilization, whose victim man himself is. He introduced a new awareness into the world that much is wrong in the concept of our culture, in our inherent conflict between convention and spontaneity, tradition and inner freedom.

Rousseau personified Romanticism, with his excessive sensibility and ambivalence. His was a passionate individualism and rebellion against the established social order; he glorified instinct, introspection, and imagination; his ideals were simplicity, primitivism, sentiment, sensual and platonic love; he championed escape from reality into solitude and nature. He had the loftiest ideals and was an impressive phrasemaker, which gave the power of his convictions a compelling sound: "Man is born free, and everywhere he is in chains." He was the first romantic outsider, and his schizophrenic frenzy became flagrantly obvious. He went mad, mad over himself and the world—but not quite as mad as other romantics from Novalis to Nietzsche. Toward the end of his life he found solace in his lonesome walks among nature, and his only serene and tenderly written work was the reflections he made during those walks, his *Rêveries du promeneur solitaire* (*Daydreams of a Solitary Stroller*), a reconciliation with man's fate and his own.

So much has been said about Rousseau because to understand Romanticism and the power of the waltz as its symbolic prelude we must give credit to this lone and suffering figure, a modern seer and prophet. About 1750 Rousseau rushed in on the world of feudalism with then frighteningly new ideas, which remain revolutionary to this very day. His thoughts shook the foundation of an age doomed to fall apart and destined to ascend to new heights. More often than not, history has moved in strident contrasts, but two elementary phenomena simultaneously surprised the established powers in the mid-eighteenth century. As Rousseau's concepts attacked feudalism, the waltz turned against the minuet as a symbol of feudalistic society. An intellectual-emotional thrust was paralleled by an emotional-physical one. They were unrelated and yet motivated by the same antagonism to existing conditions and propelled by nature-oriented feelings. They had the stamp of Romanticism, its power of persuasion and emotional appeal. They both happened because the time was ready. Voltaire, Beaumarchais, and Rousseau may have contributed a great deal to the French Revolution. But the waltz symbolized that intoxicating, expansive rhythm, that artless abandonment, that youthful desire which in the beginning carried with it the courage of defiance, and then became a gyration into oblivion, a joyful, almost ecstatic expression of escape from reality.

What the galliard was to the fifteenth and sixteenth centuries, the waltz was to the eighteenth and nineteenth, mirroring a new mood. The word *Walzer* was first heard in the early 1750s. The equivalent of the colloquial idiom in the German language was "tramping," but the word was also used for "gliding" and "sliding." In the Old High German, *walzen* meant to turn, to roll. Paul Nettl found the word used for the first time onstage about 1754, when the Viennese clown and dramatist Joseph Felix von Kurz appeared in his comedy *Bernardon,* entering in a waltzing mood while singing a few lines in which there is a reference to *walzen.*

The waltz, like any dance, has had its precursors in folk dances going back to the sixteenth century, in the *Ländler, Weller,* and *Spinner,* dances performed with strong, impetuous movements, with jumps and forceful sliding. There was an invigorating, natural spirit in this fast, sliding peasant dance, a simplicity in its execution, in utter contrast to the minuet which, despite its limited range of movement, had to be studied meticulously. To waltz was an open invitation to break with the routine of the past, with the protocol of formality, with etiquette often bordering on exaggerated subtleties. In its close embrace, the waltz defied such studied politeness. It held out a personal freedom, an individual pursuit of happiness, because its intoxicating rhythm in 3/4 time and its closeness, as much as the couple chose, offered an ecstatic experience.

The ancestry of the waltz can be found among the peasants of the mountains in Austria. The dance was robust and, with its emphasis on the first beat, had a connotation of challenge, of assertion of the ego. In its stress on the inherent joy in life it embraced everyone and anticipated the revolution. Undoubtedly the minuet was, in its stylized artificiality, a dance of courtship, but the waltz was a total release from inner and outer confinement, it had the exuberant feeling of communal festivities.

This new dance followed the pattern of the time in which the trend toward simplicity and the vernacular triumphed in literature; in which the *opera buffa* challenged the French Rococo composers in 1752, with the *guerre des bouffons;* in which the notions of nature and passion were equated. Noverre said: ". . . we must not merely practice steps; we must study the passions." And the waltz was the most expressive gesture of human passion.

Even in its most refined state, this deep-rooted peasant dance has never denied its past, its native strength and capacity for evolution. The waltz has survived more than two hundred years, outliving the quadrille and cancan, both children of the minuet. Its climactic highlights were in the nineteenth century, with the Viennese genius of Johann Strauss, Jr., and Josef Lanner; it ran its course with the skipping French *valse* and, in our century, with the Hesitation and Slow Boston waltzes.

The waltz has inspired composers from Mozart to Chopin to Richard Strauss. There was hardly an operetta from Jacques Offenbach to Franz Lehár without its waltz. Pierre Gardel was the first choreographer to use this dance, in *La Dansomanie* in 1800. Since then it has appeared and reappeared in ballets from *The Sleeping Beauty* to Balanchine's *Liebeslieder Walzer*. The waltz has gone through many metamorphoses, but basically it has never changed its true face as the symbolic expression of the bourgeoisie.

In 1797 a booklet was published in Germany that purported to have proof for the waltz's being one of the main sources of the weakness of body and spirit of the generation. The list of the waltz's condemnation is endless. England did not accept this dance before 1812, and for a long time it was forbidden in many parts of Europe. France, whose cultural reign was identified with the past, was most strongly opposed to the new dance; its dance teachers, of course, disapproved of it most vehemently. If we try to be honest with ourselves and them, we will understand that, at that time and with their cultural accomplishments, they must have envisioned those boorish dancers as ghosts or throwbacks from the late Middle Ages, with their originally hobnailed boots and gestures of ill-breeding. This dance was done in the mountains at a time when the French had built up an astounding culture of hierarchical magnitude. Not only the French, but also the German bourgeoisie, wishing to distinguish itself from ordinariness, was horrified by the vulgarity of the waltz for many decades.

Only the Austrians and particularly the Austrian aristocracy were enamored with the waltz as soon as it was cleansed of most of its uncouthness. There had always been a few popular elements in the fetes of Baroque Austria, whether they were inspired by the pastoral or those so-called *Wirtschaften*—happenings, as translated in modern idiom—where there was much down-to-earth masquerading. We know of a *Wirtschaft* given in Vienna in honor of Peter the Great of Russia where the Austrian majesties welcomed their guest disguised as the host and hostess of an inn. The waltz was then danced. The Austrian love for the dance also had political connotations. In many ways the Hapsburgs had felt all along culturally inferior to the French and only reluctantly relied on the French language, etiquette, and manner of being. But with the waltz also becoming accepted at court, the Hapsburgs could claim to be with the present—and future— rage. The waltz was one of their cultural trump cards and reached a climax symbolizing Metternich's triumph when all the dignitaries waltzed at the Congress of Vienna in 1814.

THE waltz became popular at a time when an interest in folklore began to flourish. In the last third of the eighteenth century, poets, musicians, critics, and philosophers became fascinated by the inexhaustible well of folkloric material and began to collect and study it. One of the foremost scholars among them was Johann Gottfried von Herder, who helped prepare the groundwork for Romanticism, to which belonged his endeavor to locate the roots of a nation's poetry in its folksongs.

Herder wrote that people think with *Gefühl* (feeling), that feeling has an immediate experience of reality, as direct as the sense of touch. The experience of one's individual body and the awareness of its vital power help one to assert oneself. It is a very romantic thought. Something analogous happens to us through the inherent potency of the waltz. In his evolutionary approach to history, Herder visualized humankind in a continuous flow of progress toward the creation of a perfect humane being. And with gesture being of the greatest significance to him, he saw in movement or dance a means to achieve human happiness.

Simultaneously, a larger section of young German intellectuals embraced the waltz as a means of demonstrating their rebellious spirit. They were dreamers, ill at ease with society, escaping into all vagaries of emotional disenchantment. Genius and originality were the only two things this "Storm and Stress" generation believed in, extending originality to the point of the macabre. What they had in common with their age was love of nature, which they deified and called the "living garment of God." Young Johann Wolfgang von Goethe (1749–1832) was their leader.

The first and foremost novel of this movement was Goethe's *Sorrows of Young Werther,* one of the several starting points of Romanticism. This novel, written in the conventional letter form, was an immediate success. It is the story of an oversensitive man who committed suicide out of frustration. It is also the monumental expression of *Weltschmerz,* by which young people were then consumed. There is a neglected social connotation to *Werther.* The hero belonged to the bourgeoisie and was prevented from advancing in his diplomatic career, which, at that time and long after, was considered the prerogative of the aristocracy. Werther's suicide is mistakenly seen as caused only by his emotional impasse. But the young Goethe had both causes in mind.

It was the time in which the bourgeois began slowly to replace the aristocrats in the social structure. They were the new readers, they were the upcoming patrons commissioning and buying works of art, and they shared in the patronage of the theaters. Toward the end of the eighteenth century the bourgeoisie became very self-conscious and, as the class destined to rule to-morrow, it began to build a new image of itself. The malcontent young people were products of the well-to-do middle class (much as were the hippies in the 1960s). It was the young dissatisfied bourgeois and his aristocratic sympathizer who became the self-styled outsiders, harbingers of the Romantic hero. Goethe soon severed his umbilical cord to the movement and saved himself by joining the establishment. Werther had to commit suicide in order to save Goethe.

Many writers on the dance pay tribute to Goethe's interest in this art by citing these passages from *Werther:* ". . . they whirled round together like the spheres, it was certainly a little rough to begin with, because so few knew how to dance it [the waltz] . . . I moved so lightly. I was no longer a human being. To hold the most adorable creature in one's arms and fly around with her like the wind, so that everything around us fades away . . ." But these quotations are only passing references in the climactic chapter of the novel. For several pages Goethe described the dances at a party to which he went, the minuets, the waltzes, the English contra dances, and the Teutsche. Werther's love is projected into the dancing, and dance reflects the beauty and grace of the woman he adores. It is the decisive event in which his beloved Lotte, while dancing in his arms, moving to another partner, and returning to him, tells him about that other man, Albert. Twice in passing "she mentioned his name with much significance," Goethe wrote. "Albert," she said, "is an upright man to whom I am betrothed."

Goethe once advised a young poet only to write what he had experienced, and he said later in his olympian life that all his works were only the "fragments of a great confession." Before becoming *Hofrat* (councillor) in Weimar, Goethe revolted against the prosaic world in *Werther,* when the discrepancy between dream and the reality of his own experiences seemed to crush him. In the letters of this novel (which Napoleon claimed to have read seven times during his campaigns) Goethe used the dance as a means of revelation.

Goethe's generation was caught up in the historic transformation from a feudalistic to a bourgeois society, from a rational to a romantic spirit. The Machiavellian French minister Charles Maurice de Talleyrand-Périgord said, "He who has not lived in the years around 1780 has not known the pleasure of life."

Toward the end of his life in 1778, Voltaire still took note of *Werther's* impact and implications. But he was too feeble and embittered to share Talleyrand's pleasure, of which he had his good share in his younger years. He was no longer there to watch Talleyrand's and the world's macabre waltz into another era.

BALLETOMANIA

A RUSSIAN BALLETOMANE BOUGHT A PAIR OF TAGLIONI'S BALLET SLIPPERS for 200 rubles to take to a farewell dinner celebrating the dancer's departure for France in March 1842. This gala dinner featured as the main dish Taglioni's slippers, which, expertly cooked, were served with a special sauce. One can hardly imagine a more spectacular outburst of balletomania.

Individual balletomanes—people possessed by a crazed love for the dance and particularly its balletic form—have existed in all countries where ballet flourished. Danceomania in the Middle Ages and dance marathons after World War I have been explosive expressions of frustrated, desperate people and, like the frenzied embrace of rock 'n' roll, reflect phases of our long age of anxiety. But balletomania as a special group affliction could originate only in Russia.

Many people need to create their own private myths, to live within invisible walls papered with pinup images. People cannot exist without love or without borrowing some starry glitter from imagined glory. Matinee idolatry has always filled empty rooms of life. Francis Bacon classified the errors of our beliefs under four different idols. Had he lived in the nineteenth century, he would have added a fifth: ballet. The direction in which enthusiasm runs amuck makes little difference. The idols may be politicians, actors, mimes, or dancers.

There have been classic examples of idolatry. Ancient Greek actors were exempted from military duty, permitted to cross enemy lines in days of war, and, during the Dionysia, regarded as sacred. Two pantomimes, Pylades of Cilicia and Bathyllus of Alexandria, had all of Rome at their dancing feet in 22 B.C. In 1771 a costume worn by Madeleine Guimard became, as the robe à la Guimard, the great fashion of that year. The success of Salvatore Viganò and his wife, Maria Medina, dancing at Vienna in 1793, was sensational. To do things à la Viganò was the vogue. In the turbulent Viganò furore it seemed a minor event that Beethoven, who later wrote his *Prometheus* for him, composed a minuet à la Viganò, based on one of the couple's dances. Everything from clothes to coiffures, from bonbons to cigars, bore their name. When Maria Medina was pregnant, it even became fashionable for a lady to run around with a false stomach. Fanny Elssler stayed in America for two years, although she had intended to stay for two

Frontispiece of a theater magazine published in Vienna in 1842 showing
balletomanes in action. The caption reads: "Careful that the flowers don't
land on the contrabass!" (Courtesy the Author)

weeks only, because for the first time the New World became acquainted with great ballet performances and the audiences' enthusiasm knew no bounds. Anna Pavlova's popularity gave rise to Pavlova perfume and stockings. The Germans called Isadora Duncan "the Divine Isadora" and carried her triumphantly through the streets of Berlin.

What a short page of a huge catalog listing many cases of idolatry lavished upon fascinating stage personalities! But the Russian balletomane was quite a special species of the Romantic era. Basically, he was a balletophile with maniacal propensities. At this point it is difficult to say whether he loved the ballet because he was in love with the image of the ballerina, or whether the physical appearance of the ballerina drew him to the esoteric potentialities of the ballet. But the unquestionable corporeality of the dance itself and its latent erotic qualities cannot be erased from the balletomane's picture.

In 1700 the Russians lived in conditions close to the Middle Ages. Then, within a few decades, Peter the Great imposed the era of the Baroque and forced Western culture on them, just as the Russian Revolution of 1917 turned an agricultural people into a technological one within two generations. Intensity, sacrifices, and brutal hardships imposed upon the people have never been a matter of concern to Russia's rulers. In the year 1700 Russia was a backward country. A century and a half later it brought forth such giants as Tolstoi and Dostoevski, Gogol, and Pushkin, and, in a convoluted haze of sophistication, the balletomanes.

Peter the Great had seen ballets and masquerades in the capitals of Western Europe. He himself loved to dance and contemporaries said about him, "He made caprioles that any dancing master might envy." It was soon making the rounds at European courts that the most elegant minuets were danced at St. Petersburg. In 1703 he had a wooden theater built near the Kremlin. It burned down, so he immediately built a new one. He arranged lavish balls. As has always been the case in hierarchic social structures and particularly at that time in Russia, the male courtiers were ready to imitate the Emperor, and so was the entire aristocracy down to the rich landowners, the not yet crowned princes of the future bourgeoisie, the *noblesse de bourse.* And the reluctance of females—on the highest and lowest levels—was quickly crushed when Peter's guardsmen were ordered to drag into the ballroom any women who had tried to ignore and evade his invitation. Considered second-rate individuals, women were used to being ordered around and to obeying.

In other words, Peter began to Westernize Russia in Russian fashion.

All the reigning heads who followed him were equally enamored of the dance. Empress Anna Ivanovna ruled that all cadets of the military academy had to take dancing lessons from ballet masters whom she hired in France, Italy, and Germany. During her reign, in 1735, the Russian Imperial School was founded, the home of the later Kirov Ballet. From then on, interest in the dance did not wane either in St. Petersburg or in Moscow. Dance was soon to be used by Russia as a part of the political play of power. It was recognized that nothing could have better served the country's influence than balls of festive magnitude.

When, in 1762, Catherine the Great ascended the throne, her coronation was a huge dance spectacle for which about four thousand people were employed. The events were arranged by such first-rate ballet masters as the Italian Gasparo Angiolini, the French Charles Le Picq, and the Viennese (of Dutch extraction) Franz Hilverding. Le Picq, Noverre's pupil and known in Louis XV's Paris as the Apollo of the dance, spent several years in Russia (1786–98). Russia had by then become famous for its eccentrics, and Prince Grigori Potëmkin was certainly one of the ablest and most extraordinary of all eccentrics. "Extravagant" would be a fitting epithet in the light of a famous party he gave shortly before his death. Le Picq was asked to stage it for him at the estimated cost of more than half a million rubles. Was it one of Potëmkin's grand gestures with which to regain the Empress's love and to overthrow her new and last favorite? Or, since Potëmkin was then busy crushing the Turkish Empire, was it a symbolic gesture of power and a signal directed at France that Russia also could unfold its splendor to the point of dancing at the brink of bankruptcy? No matter, it was all in the line of excess at all costs.

The nobility and officials of the government, the military caste, and the rich landowners and serf-owners, all took their cues from the Czar and his intimate entourage. Ever since Peter the Great discovered his love for the dance and liked to have dance productions in his house theater, everyone else in the country who thought highly of himself went out of his way to do as the Czar did. These house theaters were soon to be seen everywhere. Every aristocrat and landowner created little ballerinas selected from the "corps" of his serfs' daughters.

Anatole Chujoy, who founded *Dance News* in the 1940s, stated that "attractive and well-formed people from among the house servants or orphans" were chosen to form a serf ballet for the amusement of the guests. Since the performers were serfs they were rarely paid, but when a landowner discovered an outstandingly beautiful dancer among those he owned he would very often sell or donate the dancer to the government's imperial theaters. One of those girls, Pauline Kovalevsky, became the first Russian prima ballerina. She called herself "Fine Pearl," and it was said of her that she wore a necklace worth a hundred thousand rubles. Everyone knew about the interest that influential gentlemen of the aristocracy took in girls from the ballet, considering ballet an art form for the exclusive entertainment of the upper classes. This caused an interrelation between petty politics at court and intrigues at the academy. About the mid-nineteenth century the house theaters all over Russia numbered several thousands. Balletomania had then reached a culminating point in numbers and fervor.

The question has often been raised as to how it was possible for the ballet —originally a feudal institution and theater for an elite audience—to survive the Bolshevik Revolution in 1917. Since the overwhelming majority of the dancers had always come from the bottom of the social strata, this art form had never been thought of as aristocratic or bourgeois. No one questioned who these daughters of former serfs had been dancing for, only who the dancers were. An analogous case is the French Revolution, another historical hurdle that ballet easily overcame, even though it had to endure a few insipid choreographic notions extolling Reason and Revolution. But these nonsensical, aesthetic derailments passed with the spent fury and enthusiasm for a new era, and ballet moved on in its traditional groove.

The attitude of the Russian revolutionaries toward the ballet is all the more surprising when one realizes that the imperial theaters in St. Petersburg and Moscow were run first of all for the pleasure of the royal family and only as an afterthought for the benefit of the populace. Long after the French Revolution had shaken the foundations of feudalism in the Western countries it was still very much alive in Russia. The theaters were headed not by a man whose profession was the stage but by a courtier appointed by the Czar. The courtiers and the men in uniform reigned supreme. The entourage of the Emperor drew wide circles and in its full strength could easily fill the three theaters that were used to show ballet productions, above all the Maryinsky, with about 2,500 seats. In both cities the ballet sold out long in advance and only a few balcony and gallery seats were on sale for the general public. The subscribers for the orchestra and loges formed the hard core of the balletomanes, never failing to attend any production or any performance of a favorite ballerina.

There is a characteristic passage in Vladimir Telyakovsky's *Vospominania* (*Reminiscences*), published in 1924, about the balletomanes. Telyakovsky was the last director of the Imperial Theater before the Revolution, occupying this position for fifteen years. He wrote many not too flattering things about this conservative-minded group, which always interfered whenever he tried to enforce a reform:

> The most influential and outstanding balletomanes enjoyed special privileges on performing nights. . . . During each intermission they congregated in the study of the chief of the theater police . . . animatedly discussing ballet events. . . . The conversation would begin with an analysis of the female personnel. . . . New dancers were treated with special attention. . . . When one appeared on the stage, the balletomanes analyzed in detail her legs and feet (for size and form), shoulders, waist, her whole figure, her face, smile, manner of holding her arms, balance at the end of a pas, self-con-

trol, confidence. In short, everything was analyzed, evaluated in detail, and an oral record was made, on the basis of which the further career of the debutant was decided. Marius Petipa had always been on friendly terms with the balletomanes. . . . The favorites, entering the rehearsal hall with Petipa, sat down by the mirrored walls, and in agreement with him selected the dancers for a particular ballet. One can imagine what motives guided the selection of this or that girl. . . . The balletomanes, firmly allied with Petipa and the press, made any protest whatsoever impossible. . . .

By 1880 these balletomanes had become a tightly knit group with extremely conservative leanings both in politics and the arts. They acted as if they owned the ballet, resenting any changes that could affect their status and objecting to artistic reforms or the substitution of a new variation for a familiar one.

We may have our own opinion of these balletomanes but must not underestimate their power. The officer who adores the ballerina onstage and from there all the way to his bed; or the little dreamy-eyed ballerina standing in front of the stage door hoping to step out from there one day and into the arms of an admirer; or the poet who with his words, in prose or verse, transcends all realistic confinements in his homage to ballet and a ballerina —all three types are the patrons of the art, carrying it from one performance to the next through the decades and centuries. They may not be aware, however, of defying the limitations of reality and searching for a fairy-tale life full of sweet light and a touching beauty of otherness.

A Fairy-tale World

THE NUMBER OF WRITERS ENAMORED WITH THE DANCE—FROM LUCIAN to Cocteau—has been astounding. Euripides, Socrates, Plato, and Vergil were hardly balletomanes, but they realized the deep-rooted sources of dancing and discussed its aesthetic and ethic principles. The writers and poets who have associated themselves with the dance have been spiritual anchors of this fleeting art form.

Those who never muster sufficient liking for any theatrical form of dancing are the same people who will rarely be found in a lonely corner reading poetry. For dance, like poetry, penetrates the mysterious world of our emotions, fantasies, and dreams.

Somewhere there is always a child's soul in the poet. Both the child and the poet are really at home in fairyland, in a world of make-believe. With a flourish of trumpets princes appear, sleeping beauties awake to new life through the surprise of a kiss, a beast turns into a prince in the eyes of another Beauty, little Cinderellas triumph over the ugly and wicked in human beings, and a simple country girl, deceived by a fickle male, joins a band of spirits to take revenge on males and dance them to death when they can get hold of them in the woods. It is all make-believe, ranging from sweet ecstasy to accentuated pathos, from the supernatural to the weird.

The fairy tale is the handmaiden of Romanticism, a literary apotheosis of mankind's flight from reality; without it, the classical and Romantic ballet would have been lost. But visual beauty and sensual excitement cannot exist in a vacuum. Théophile Gautier, the author of *Giselle,* was fully aware that a ballet needs a story, and that "for a ballet to have some probability everything in it must be impossible. . . . Legends, fairy stories, hashish- and opium-inspired dreams, all the fantasy beyond the realms of possibility are the true sphere of ballet." Although the Romantic ballet stressed and finally overdid the sheer virtuosity of dancing, it is generally identified as the ballet of fairy tales in all its varieties.

Did the strongest influences on the Romantic ballet, then, come from literary sources? For one thing, they certainly cannot be found in music. Ballet could seemingly get along with very minor music for inspiration, with the exception of Tchaikovsky, Delibes, and Glazunov. The most uninspiring music was acceptable as long as it delivered the beat on which the ballerina could turn and leap. To make her shine in heaven-born virtuosity was all that mattered.

When the great breakthrough of the Romantic ballet came in 1832 with the ballet *La Sylphide,* certain influences could immediately be recognized. The most direct inspiration came from melodrama and the opera. The theater, like all the arts, remained neoclassic after the French Revolution. The populace went to see what was then in vogue on the Parisian stages: the opera, vaudeville, sentimental comedy, and, above all, melodrama.

Melodrama remained the rage for a long time. Much later, Émile Zola called it "that bourgeois offspring of the Romantic drama," when, in reality, he might have better referred to the Romantic drama as the bourgeois offspring of the melodrama. The most skillful of all the melodramatists was the German August Friedrich Ferdinand von Kotzebue (1761–1819), who wrote a large number of highly undistinguished plays that were lasting hits on many stages in many countries.

The melodrama worked with stock characters who were all painted in black and white and thrown into a plot whose realism reached the possible limits of reality, often becoming a caricature of itself, placing the expected where least expected and always moving on the brink of absurdity. The basic theme of these plays was for the virtuous to suffer all imaginable vicissitudes because of starkly villainous characters, but there was a stereotyped happy ending with the virtuous triumphant. Two generations of theater-goers had learned to accept the irrational and sensational onstage, which played on their visual receptivity and sensitized them to accept heightened stimuli, so that finally the weird and grotesque, mystery and medieval horror, a fantastic world full of fairies and ghosts, seemed to become the normal histrionic diet. This is where the Romantic ballet came in, with its love for supernatural effects and the eerie, for the unreal treatment of dramatic realities. Sir Walter Scott (1771–1832) unknowingly contributed to it with his flair for incidents in the history of Scotland. His *Tales of a Grandfather,* stories of his homeland, were published only a few years before *La Sylphide* was mounted. Can it be mere coincidence that the background of this ballet should be the Highlands of Scotland, with a touch of medieval magic?

Long before the Romantic ballet came into being, the melodrama reached great popularity and finesse. Guilbert de Pixérécourt (1773–1844) developed this theatrical genre with Gallic esprit. His *Coelina, ou l'enfant du mystère (Coelina, or the Child of Mystery)*, produced in 1800, immediately caught the fancy of the world. Pixérécourt gave the melodrama its final face, although he was less prolific by far than his German counterpart, Kotzebue, whose life was as romantic and melodramatic as his more than two hundred plays. Kotzebue was a one-man melodrama factory that could deliver the goods on demand. Like him, another German dramatist, Friedrich Maximilian von Klinger (1752–1831), also wrote numerous plays. His heroes were the dream image of the Romantics: action-driven, hot-headed men with strong convictions and great potentialities. Klinger's early plays were written in revolt against routine and man's fate; they were written at great speed, flippantly, and in a fury of intoxication, all characteristic of the era. The hero of Friedrich Schiller's first play, *Die Räuber (The Robbers,* 1781), was a Robin Hood figure. Johann Wolfgang von Goethe chose at the start of his career as a dramatist a medieval figure as central character, *Götz von Berlichingen.* Moreover, a work pursuing him into his late age was *Faust,* the story of the famous medieval magician, a work of the greatest accomplishment in dramatized philosophy and one that found its way into ballet and opera in several versions.

The yearning for the mysterious aura of everything medieval was a characteristic feature of the romanticized past. The spirit of the melodrama had strong roots in the Gothic novel, a popular literary entertainment in the latter half of the eighteenth century. These novels were marked by violence and terror and a taste for an idealized image of the Middle Ages, for the pointed and arched grandeur of the Gothic, with gloomy castles in moonlit nightscapes.

It was this scenic image which appeared in the opera *Robert le Diable* and was most directly responsible for *La Sylphide.* This opera was composed by a German, Jakob Liebmann Beer by name, who settled in Paris after

Marie Taglioni as the Sylphide. (Courtesy French Cultural Services)

many journeys to London and Italy, where his failures as a composer accompanied him. In 1831 Giacomo Meyerbeer, as he was then called, wrote this, his first French opera, based on a libretto by Eugène Scribe and Delavigne. It took Paris by storm and became a model for the French grand opera for the next few decades. Its impact was enormous because it was skillfully calculated to appeal to the current Romantic taste for medievalism and the supernatural and macabre. Moreover, it lingered in the memory of the Parisian opera devotees because of its extremely lavish stage image.

This event coincided with a change in the management of the Paris Opéra. Dr. Louis Véron was now at its helm, a shrewd businessman hiding behind artistic pretensions and aesthetic gestures, a master at never losing control over the customary and intricate Opéra intrigues. He more often than not insisted on avoiding any serious themes in ballet: "Dramas, comedies of manners do not belong to the domain of choreography. The audience wants first of all variety." This may very well have been the case—as it is today. But, time and again, at certain points in theatrical history something unexpected happens in the chemistry of this impure art form—and art triumphs through the sheer momentum of its being what it is. And this happened with *Robert le Diable* and *La Sylphide*.

Opera and ballet have always needed their Maecenases. Probably Louis Véron knew the patrons of the Opéra very well, those aristocrats of the bourgeoisie. In catering to their taste he undoubtedly helped form it. Heinrich Heine also recognized the taste of the moneyed theatergoers for what it was when he wrote in his report on the French scene: "Most people go to the Opéra for a show of prosperity and are satisfied only if beautiful scenery, costumes and dancers hold their attention to such an extent that they entirely forget the beautiful music."

They probably applauded enthusiastically a stunning decor and virtuoso dancing, and the Opéra director was intent on offering both. *Robert le Diable* featured two ballets, one of which was the famous *Ballet of the Nuns*. It was a scenic triumph, with costumes of rare beauty. The entire corps de ballet appeared for the first time in ballet history in costumes of such translucent, all-white texture and delicate shape as to evoke with every movement an esoteric, ethereal feeling. This unrelieved whiteness and gossamer subtlety gave the onlooker a sensation of total escape; the awareness of being carried away had such an impact of surprise on the audience that it was as though one's own being would tumble into a state of nonbeing. It was a new theatrical experience, what the vernacular calls a smash hit.

In the light of this success Louis Véron welcomed Adolphe Nourrit's idea of creating a full-length ballet in which the focus would be on something ethereal, with a witch and a magical scarf, against a background remote from anything well known and with a supernatural motif in a fairy-tale atmosphere. He trusted the costume designer Eugène Lami and hoped for a new triumph with Pierre Ciceri's scenic notions. In fact, he trusted both of them as much as the choreographer's daughter, Marie Taglioni, who had made her debut at the Paris Opéra in 1827. She had been received with great admiration during the five years previous to her triumphant success as *La Sylphide* and had established herself as the leading ballerina. Véron bet on a successful repetition of the *Ballet of the Nuns,* and his gambling instinct paid off handsomely.

Adolphe Nourrit, who was a tenor at the Opéra, found the right story with all the necessary ingredients. He was not a great librettist any more than Jean Schneitzhoeffer was an impressive composer. It has always been important which sources dramatists take their ideas from and what they do with them. Nourrit went to the most logical source he could find at that time and, from the viewpoint of a ballet scenario, did amazingly well with it.

Charles Nodier (1780–1844) played a fascinating role in the development of the Romantic movement in France. An intellectual snob, he was not an easy man to get along with. Yet he was a man with great charisma. He was a novelist, botanist, journalist, philologist, and bibliophile, and in 1824 he became the librarian of the Bibliothèque de l'Arsenal in Paris. While attached to the library, he attracted the most significant artists and intellectuals, such as Hugo, Sainte-Beuve, Dumas père, Lamartine, Vigny, Balzac, Delacroix, Liszt, and Gautier.

Nodier soon established himself as the leader behind the scenes of the Romantic movement. Alfred de Musset referred to his salon as *la boutique romantique.* Nodier was somewhat older than most of the artists who frequented his place, and acted as their mentor and patron. He once defined Romanticism as *la liberté régie par le goût,* and he really meant utter liberty ruled by taste, or rather by one's personal desire. He usually showed a very critical and arrogant attitude toward human accomplishments. He considered himself as an intellectual, a man of letters, and went to the Opéra only when he could not avoid it. As far as we can gather from reports, he seems to have looked down on ballet as a minor art form titillating the senses. But fate would have it that one of his novellas, *Trilby: ou, le Lutin d'Argail,* published in 1822, should have caught Nourrit's attention, and this elf of Argyll became the source and inspiration of the ballet *La Sylphide.*

Nourrit's balletic version has a much stronger dramatic plot than the original story by Nodier, in which Trilby is a male spirit that attaches itself to a fisherman, falls in love with his wife, and performs all kinds of services for her. Nodier's story fascinated other writers, among them George du Maurier, with his popular *Trilby.* In his version, young Trilby (now a girl) falls into the hands of a Hungarian musician who calls himself Svengali—a name that became a household word at the turn of the century. Under Svengali's mesmerizing spell Trilby becomes a world-famous singer. At one of her concerts in England Svengali, sitting in the loge as always, suddenly dies of a heart attack, and at this very moment Trilby loses her voice forever.

In all three versions we find, above all, the elements of the supernatural, the power of love, and the desire to reach out from the ordinary into the dream of the unknown.

La Sylphide is the story of James, a young Scotsman whose mind seems divided, his psyche in a state of unrest. He does not quite feel at home in the bourgeois setting of his sweet Effie, whom he is supposed to marry.*

We find the characteristic problem of the romantic in James, who seems sure of his love for Effie, but in the back of his mind has the nagging feeling of uncertainty that this marriage may not be the fulfillment of his life. The true romantic always lives with his dream of something different and bigger, more exciting and rewarding than his very existence—and with a touch of sadness, the reasons for which he cannot find nor define.

It is another life experience, another world, of which James dreams. And in comes the Sylphide, the very creature of another world. James cannot help falling in love with her, the apparent incarnation of otherness. Obviously she must lure him away, spiriting him into the woods. The romantic is traditionally fascinated by the child's soul, and woods convey to children something sinister, impenetrable, while they are drawn to the seeming secrets hidden there: the wind playing symphonies of eerie sounds in the trees, sylvan animals and unknown beings hiding everywhere. Nature has always held out to the romantic an enigmatic key to a mysterious freedom.

James has no choice, he must follow the Sylphide into her woods. There he finds himself alone with the fallacies of his desires. Whenever he is close to her, close enough to touch and embrace her, she escapes. At this point of the story demonic elements are added to the supernatural. James meets his witch (as Oedipus once encountered his Sphinx). We are facing a fairy-tale world, and witches belong with the image of medievalism and woods. The appearance of a demon or something demonic in the Romantic era was the equivalent to the deus ex machina concept of antiquity, of the riding messenger in later days, or the arriving letter as the denouement in Act IV of the well-made play of the same period. Moreover, the word *demonic* was as fashionable in the 1830s as *neurotic* is today. It was overused and always pointed to something wrong in a human existence—another form of the hero's hubris—something that might disrupt the harmony of his life.

The witch, Madge, hands James a scarf and advises him to put it around

---

* Two years previously, in 1830, students and workers had lost a revolution to the bourgeois establishment, gradually replacing a worn-out aristocracy. A disappointed youth faced a reality in which the machine more and more encroached on their daily existence. Rebels and poets like Georg Herwegh and Georg Büchner became refugees haunted by the brutality of Metternich's notorious police.

the Sylphide's shoulders. Then she will be his forever. But when he throws the scarf around her shoulders, her wings fall off and she dies in the arms of her sister sylphs. In the Romantic language, wings are symbols for ecstatic moments in life, for ephemeral beauty, but also for the fulfillment of our dreams. James is unable to reconcile reality with his dream. Can we ever experience or live the dream of our reality? There is always the danger of the scarf forcing us back into our actuality. In most versions of the ballet, at the end we see Effie passing by in the background, on her way to marry another man. Another romantic hero is defeated, and the life of ordinariness remains triumphant.

Elfs, good and wicked fairies, spirits of all sorts are the stock-in-trade of fairy tales. Sylphs are a special kind of imaginary creature, mortals without souls, elemental airborne beings. Since they are thought to inhabit the air, our imagination has to see them with wings. Sylphs are all lightness and whiteness, certainly incarnate luminosity. They are the saleswomen of the unattainable, the dream images of the romantic hero.

The man who invented these creatures was a great romantic of another era: Theophrastus Bombastus von Hohenheim (c. 1493–1541). He wanted to be known as Dr. Paracelsus, choosing this epithet to demonstrate his superiority to Celsus, an eclectic Platonist who lived in Alexandria or Rome in the second century A.D., one of the first iconoclasts, who represented the most powerful pagan reaction against Christianity. Paracelsus hoped to outshine Celsus's rebellion against all norms and standards of his time. He was one of those romantics who pushed his dreams to the very edge of reality. As a Romantic of the Renaissance, there was nothing morbid about him. His dreams had something of the action-driven daring that characterized the Renaissance. Paracelsus still mingled the physical sciences with alchemy, but in his preparation of new medications concocted of opium, mercury, iron, sulfur, arsenic, and copper sulfate he was on the right track.

Paracelsus may not have found the philosophers' stone, but he almost touched it. Still tortured by medieval concepts, he wanted to escape the past and never gave up hope of coming upon the wonder of tomorrow. Only such a daring dreamer could envision the imaginary creature he called a sylph, three hundred years before she slipped into the unreal-real gestalt onstage as well as into the minds of theatergoers. It should be stressed that Paracelsus believed people were inseparable from the universe, as an extract of all beings previously alive. Small wonder, then, that he should also have believed in a sylphlike creature with the power to transmute from a state of being into a state of nonbeing, and vice versa. In a mystical sense, it is little more than the ultimate principle of spiritual regeneration. And in the depth of his frustrated ecstasy, this was the romantic hero's final desire and his last hope.

WE are in the world of the fairy tale that gave the Romantic ballet its raison d'être, the garment in which to wrap the arabesques of its thoughts and the pirouettes of its hidden morals. It would be wrong to assume that fairy tales are written for children only. They are written for the child in us all and have been more or less popular, depending on the mood of history. Fables have always been used by writers to convey a moral sub rosa. La Fontaine spoke of the moral as "the soul of the fable." From Aesop to George Orwell, writers have depicted fantastic situations in faraway lands, often using animals or inanimate objects to convey some worldly wisdom. Animals are friends of the child, who sees the human creature in them. For the adult mind it is the metaphor that is inescapable. La Fontaine was a sophisticated master at telling simple fables, the rage of the French court toward the end of the seventeenth century; and Charles Perrault told those familiar stories of *The Sleeping Beauty, Cinderella,* or *Bluebeard,* all ballet material.

The images of strange creatures have haunted people to this day, when some of us are still puzzled by objects from outer space. In fact, the more miraculous our scientific progress becomes, the stronger must be our belief in the wonders of nature that elude our minds and our technological skills. In former days a vague notion was very much alive that there are other creatures beside human beings: creatures without souls, real in an unreal way, possessing magical skills, doing good and bad things to us. They acquired folkloristic features. Sometimes they were of a solitary nature, like the Irish leprechaun. Trolls, fauns, dryads, and nereids were kept alive in our memory and have played a major part in theater dance. Ghosts have never stopped haunting people and literature, and with the growing power of Christianity the devil was endowed with the most sinister traits of human evil. The theater arts have always shown a weakness for the devil. One has only to look through the balletic repertory in the early years of Romanticism to find such titles as *Le Diable boiteux, Le Diable amoureux, Le Diable à quatre,* and *Robert le Diable.*

Fairy tales again moved into the foreground of literary interest with the social changes in the eighteenth century, with Rousseau's stress on the need of the child to become morally and intellectually self-reliant, and with the romantic's fascination with the child's soul as the mysterious source of becoming. Romanticism was a fertile ground for the fairy tale. But this literary genre can prove its validity only if it goes beyond the child's receptivity, when it touches, in its allegory, our life's experiences while escaping with us into the state of lost innocence.

Of the many writers of fairy tales the Russian Ivan Andreevich Krylov is the least known. He wrote nine books of fables, after having translated La Fontaine in 1809. His stories have an authentic national character. Besides having been Russia's most brilliant teller of fairy tales, he was an archetypal romantic hero—with a Russian accent. Krylov was very much in demand in the salons at St. Petersburg. There he played the role of a bohemian, appearing slovenly-dressed as if being unkempt and untidy were the trademark of genius. He was self-indulgent and self-centered, and no one could ever be sure what to expect from him next, a pose he used to his advantage. At parties he could be content to just sit there as though demonstrating his boredom, or he could lash out with malicious wit against everyone.

With Pushkin, Krylov belonged to the group of ardent balletomanes. From its earliest stages, the Romantic ballet exerted a great fascination on the poetic mind. When Charles Louis Didelot was called from Paris to St. Petersburg in 1801 to give the Russian ballet a new choreographic face, Pushkin, in romantic exaggeration, declared that there was more poetry in Didelot's ballets than in all French literature of that time. And Stendhal's analytical mind lost its bearings in Milan a few years later when he downgraded Shakespeare because Salvatore Viganò's ballets rose in his eyes to Olympian heights. Hans Christian Andersen joined these poets when he exclaimed in *The Story of My Life:* "There must be youth, and that I found in Fanny Cerrito! It was something incomparably beautiful, it was a swallow flight in the dance, a sport of Psyche, a flight!" What a grand jeté of the Romantic mind!

Hans Christian Andersen's stories are about human problems of a universal nature, and they all deal with or have elements of the outcast or outsider, a role that Andersen saw himself play all his life. He loved to write about people seeking happiness in vain. Essentially, he envisioned two groups of people: those predestined to be happy and those longing for the happiness they must dream of or that which they have lost around the corner of life. So much of Andersen's spirit is echoed by the spirit of the Romantic era of ballet. What life meant to him in 1835, and what ballet was about at that time, he caught in and between these lines, quoted from *The Improvisators:*

> It was a fairy world, the strange realm of the mind. . . . Here had we once been before—here had the sea-robbers forgotten their treasure, when no one ventured to approach the spot. Now was every supernatural appearance cleared up in reality, or reality had passed over into the spiritual world, as it does always here in human life, where everything, from the seed of the flower to our own immortal souls, appears a miracle; and yet man will not believe in miracles!

In many ways our own time has proved that what seemed a miracle only yesterday has turned into reality today. We have learned to live in a world of science fiction, which has become the fairy tale of our time.

The balletic use of stories proves their romantic genuineness. One writer closest to the Romantic ambience of the last century was E. T. A.

Hoffmann, who wrote stories of grotesqueries, horror fantasies, and the bizarre. Time and again, his stories have found their way onto stage or screen. There is the perennial *Nutcracker* (incorporating "The King of Mice"), the imaginative *Coppélia*, Offenbach's *Tales of Hoffmann*, Busoni's opera *Die Brautwahl*, Hindemith's opera *Cardillac*, and the silent movies *The Doll* and *The Cabinet of Dr. Caligari*.

In his *Complete Stories of the Great Ballets*, George Balanchine said how important it is to feed the child's mind with fairy tales:

> I would suggest reading the child fairy stories . . . of E. T. A. Hoffmann. . . . And by all means read the stories of the great Hans Christian Andersen. And I don't mean Andersen's stories, or any others, as they are watered down, especially translated and condensed for children. Good fairy stories were always written for intelligent people. Children are more intelligent than many of us think. . . . They don't like to be talked down to; they like it very much if you respect their capacity for new experience.

Children are true romantics. They can experience the fairy tale as the reality it is not, and they can experience the *real* as the mere appearance it may, in its ultimate consequence, be.

The Romantic Hero

FRIEDRICH LEOPOLD, FREIHERR VON HARDENBERG, KNOWN AS NOVALIS (1772–1801), was one of the great German poets who gave the Romantic movement its philosophical profile. He described the fairy tale as the dream of "that homeland which is everywhere and nowhere." He saw the need for "all poetry" to be "akin to the fairy tale." His reason: "Because the poet adores chance." It does not bind him in any mental straightjacket, or to any burden of logic and causality. This is why the Romantic dramatists had to overthrow neoclassicism and rebel against the "old-fashioned" Aristotelean set of unities, and this is why they adored the Shakespearean genius, setting up his own laws for his individual dramatic poetry.

In his most important prose work, *Heinrich von Ofterdingen*, Novalis created a medieval environment, poetically idealized. *Dream* was one of the key words of the era. Novalis began his story with a symbolic dream of his hero, a minnesinger, who, after walking through dark forests and passing the mossy rocks of a steep gorge, enters a cave. He then encounters rapturous landscapes, mountains and streams and most brilliantly clear skies. He falls asleep and, on the threshold of awareness, perceives a beautiful pale blue flower. But the very moment he tries to grasp the flower, it suddenly vanishes. Now that he is fully awake, it dawns on him that all his life he would have to search for this blue flower, even though in the back of his mind he would know only too well that the quest must be in vain.

Novalis was a rare figure, a solitary spiritual tower, the intellectualized hero of Romanticism. He lived only twenty-nine years. As fragmentary as his life was his work. But out of his excruciating experiences emerged a philosophy he termed "magic idealism." His aphoristic notes proved him a visionary. He jotted down as if in passing: "I am not to accomplish anything here, I am to be cut off in my flowering-time."

Often we find references in his work to the mysterious way toward human inwardness. "Within us, or nowhere, is eternity with all its worlds, the past and the future. The external world is the world of shadows, it casts its shadow into the realm of light." It is characteristic of his personal fate that he always felt like a citizen of two worlds, of light and shadow, or rather, life and death. But this was a common notion of so many during the Romantic movement. One must become attuned to their yearning cries, often poetically phrased. Only a genuinely tormented soul as that of Novalis can cry out:

> By giving a lofty sense to what is vulgar, a mysterious aspect to what is commonplace, the dignity of the unknown to what is familiar, an infinite extension to what is finite, I romanticize them.

Novalis strongly believed that "our body is absolutely capable of being set in desired motion by the spirit." This was a novel thought at the threshold of the nineteenth century. Today it has become a psychosomatic truism that our mind may exert an obvious—and yet still obscure—influence on our physical being. Novalis believed in the power of the human spirit in a metaphysical sense, and he foresaw that we would be able to separate mind from body at will; we would reach that enviable state of experiencing the world to the utmost, of being able to decide on how to absorb our sense experiences and in which context. To set our mind free is to set our body and the entire physical world free.

The ballet dancer's accomplishments at that time were symbolic representations of Novalis' mystical speculation. To find freedom and lightness of the body meant to Novalis, first of all, to acquire a lightness of the soul, to experience reality as though in a state of dreaming. It would then ennoble and enable the individual to penetrate the physical world and become lost in it in joy.

The idea of the lightness of the human body and soul calls to mind two other German writers, separated from each other by more than half a century. In both their genius is as unquestionable as their morbidity and madness. They are Heinrich von Kleist and Friedrich Nietzsche. We can see in Kleist another type of Romantic hero unable to cope with life, lost in day-dreams ("When I shut my eyes, I can imagine anything I please"), a writer far ahead of his time in psychological penetration of his subjects and a human being ever more despairing over the failure of his life. The image of death is common currency with the Romantics, Novalis' spiritual bedfellow; and Kleist remarked in one of his letters that death was little more than "only walking from one room into the next." When he met an incurably sick woman who begged him to kill her, he committed suicide with her. Shortly before, he had written: "My soul is so sore that—how can I put it?—when I stick my nose out of the window, the daylight that shines on it hurts."

We have a twofold interest in Kleist. He was a well-drawn example of a certain type of Romantic hero. In his quest for truth—for *the* truth and not for the many little truths—we can see him grope in the dark but time and again come up with concepts of deep insight into the complexities of the human machinery. Like Hamlet, he was thrown from indecision to indecision; he was hopelessly disoriented in a seemingly incomprehensible world. He was a Romantic with a sense of profound isolation and alienation from society.

Kleist was also fascinated by the problem created by the interaction of the subconscious and the body. He wrote an essay—a masterpiece—which he called *On the Marionette Theatre*, in which he raised the question of the center of gravity and grappled with the problem of unawareness and inno-cence in a dancer. Kleist was "fully aware of the disorder and destruction wreaked by man's intellect upon his native, God-given grace. . . . Every first impulse, all that is involuntary, is beautiful and everything is crooked and cramped as soon as it understands itself." This is why "grace in its most exalted state" can be found in primitive instinctiveness (as Kleist illustrates with his story of the bear that outfences the best fencing master) or in the state of complete innocence. He concludes that "if he could have a mario-nette built according to his specifications, he would be able to create a dance which neither he nor any other great contemporary dancer, including even Vestris, could duplicate."

In his *Gay Science* Friedrich Nietzsche maintains that "one thing is need-ful . . . 'Giving style' to one's character." It is needful that "a human being attain his satisfaction with himself. . . . Whoever is dissatisfied with himself is always ready to revenge himself therefor; we others will be his victims." The true Romantic hero takes revenge on himself. Kleist was his own victim. He suffered from self-inflicted wounds his entire life in a struggle to liberate himself from his own mental heaviness. Nietzsche also suffered almost all his life. But the Dionysian power of his pen danced with lightness and clarity into obscurity and finally into a total darkness of mind. Nietzsche used the dance as a simile only for the lightness of being. To him the essence of the art of life was a dance in which the dancer rises to inner freedom and rhythmic harmony, overcoming the ordinariness of existence. In a neo-Romantic era he was an afterthought to the Romantic hero; he was the personified trauma of a decade dying in cancan gaiety.

ROMANTICISM was a worldwide movement. It was not something the Germans invented for themselves and indulged in, although the German brand of Romanticism was the most colorful in texture and gave it its philosophic backbone. True, the French were hesitant about embracing this new movement, which was alien to their mentality. After their great Revolution they were thrown out of gear culturally, and as soon as they had recovered from their political shock they reversed direction and tried to hold on to their prerevolutionary institutions.

The revival of neoclassicism made it difficult for a new idea to generate or for any rebellious voice to be heard. There were no significant writers or composers; however, some painters of stature emerged in post revolutionary France: David, Houdon, Gérard, and later Ingres. But the Revolution had either decapitated or driven their wealthy buyers and knowledgeable connoisseurs into exile. The surviving middle class, which now began to replace the aristocratic establishment, was slow to cultivate its own and recognizable taste. In fact, it took an entire generation. Toward the end of the 1820s it was in the cultural saddle and even strong enough to profit from a second revolution, the one in 1830, also taking the bombardment of its senses by the assaults of the Romantics, of a Victor Hugo and Théophile Gautier, in its bourgeois stride.

As all the other arts after the Revolution, the ballet settled down to business as usual at the Paris Opéra. It indulged in superficial brilliance. Madeleine Guimard—for many years the uncrowned queen of the Opéra—danced the main parts in most ballets; she also danced in some of Maximilien Gardel's. His choreography was pleasantly pale; it could not hope to survive the momentary triumphs that Guimard gave it. Noverre, disgusted by the turn of his nation's history and his personal destiny, lived in his modest retreat at St.-Germain-en-Laye until death liberated him from his grief-stricken state in 1810. In 1803, in a preface to a new edition of his *Letters*, he wrote:

> However, as in all arts, observations and principles drawn from nature always end by conquering. My opponents, although exclaiming that I was wrong, and rebutting my ideas, yet adopted them gradually. They came over more and more to my way of thinking, and unconsciously carried out my reforms, and soon I saw myself seconded by artists whose taste and imagination, rising superior to their art, were far above sentiments of envy and jealousy.

EVEN in the social dance France had lost its leadership to Germany and the waltz. With the Revolution in France more than feudalism had come to an end. It was as if culture, after a long and most beautiful thought, wanted to put a period where it had flowered more extravagantly than anywhere else. True, French was still *the* language of diplomats and of every educated person in the many principalities and dukedoms of Germany. Frederick the Great had his intellectual love affair with Voltaire *en français,* and when Napoleon, raging through German lands, met Goethe in Erfurt he called out, *"Voilà un homme!"*

Central Europe was far from being politically unified or properly divided between the two strong powers, Prussia and Austria. Everything was still in a state of fermentation everywhere; a new world beyond the Rhine and the Alps was in a stage of becoming. It was a matter of course that Romanticism should find its strongest foothold in Germany first. It was not before 1810 that the French became better acquainted with it. The French-Swiss writer Mme de Staël had made a serious study of German Romanticism in her work *De l'Allemagne* and tried to familiarize the French with the contradictory and violent forces she found in the Sturm und Drang movement. Napoleon thought she was romanticizing the Germans in an anti-French attitude and had the French edition seized and destroyed.

The sole Romantic figure of interest that France gave the world at the turn of the century was François René de Chateaubriand (1768–1848). Early in his youth, overcome by melancholy and boredom, he became an idle wanderer. At the age of twenty-three he went to the United States on what seems to have been an aimless sightseeing trip. (He pretended afterward to have searched for the Northwest Passage—but got only as far as Niagara Falls.) America of the 1790s must have been the most alien country to his sensibilities. While visiting Cayuga Indians he noticed, surprised and amused, that a wandering Frenchman he met there was giving dancing lessons to Indians. Certainly a remarkable incident, which, however, might have occurred quite frequently. Chateaubriand met other Indian tribes in a yet romantic and unspoiled landscape. The impressions he gathered there resulted in an epic poem extolling the life of the "savages." The "noble savage" played a great part in Romantic thought and literature at that time, similar to the interest in the child and peasant.

Chateaubriand designed the setting of an ancient castle in the depths of the woods—a scene of many ballet plots to come—and the character of a hero doomed to languish in his defeat. This was in the most admired section, entitled *René,* of a more far-reaching work, *The Genius of Christianity,* published in 1802, dealing with the problems of a sister's passionate love for her brother—the incestuous theme often appearing in life and fiction at that time. His hero René was overcome by a notion of futility and disillusionment, characteristic of all Romantic heroes of the century,† a feeling for which the Germans coined the best word: *Weltschmerz.*

LONG before the French came to understand the mood of the times, England had brought forth two of the most opposite types of the Romantic era: William Blake, the visionary poet and symbolic draftsman; George Gordon, Lord Byron, the satiric poet and "gloomy egoist." Blake was almost unknown to his contemporaries, while Byron made such a deep and lasting impression on them that history refers to the "Byronic hero" whenever it means the generic type of the Romantic at variance with reality.

If it did nothing else to him, Lord Byron's clubfoot certainly magnified his sensitivity and forced him to wear his most brilliant mask; as a constant reminder of human frailty and the imperfection of nature, it made him prove himself time and again. He could not help burning the candle of his life at both ends. What a man, living all his life with the images of lost loves and ideals! Disillusioned by premature sexual experiences, haunted by the failure of an ill-fated marriage, by guilt over his love for his half-sister, Augusta, by memories of countless affairs with contessas and whores, he roamed Europe, restlessly seeking *the* ideal. And in the process he wrote the most imaginative poetry reflective of his mobile moods. He was a man of as many faces as he wished to display, yet whose only real face revealed the shambles of a shattered soul, a face very few people ever saw.

The Byronic hero plays a double role. On the one hand, he radiates glamour; on the other, he is a self-styled outcast, a professional seeker of idealized notions. But essentially—like Rousseau—he is a wanderer searching for the meaning of life. The Byronic hero has not yet overcome young Werther's readiness to throw away his life at the least emotional provocation. There is a streak of the mysterious criminal in him who may not know what really drives him to act against the social laws of society; his actions, his strong beliefs in having to fight in order to right wrongs, are wrapped in mysterious clouds. The national and political fanatics of the Romantic era were a special breed of Byronic hero.

Often the Byronic hero is the man who has survived his own hubris and goes on flirting with the flaws in his makeup. The mistakes he made, the sins and errors lying behind him, remain a well-kept secret. In the early nineteenth century he had a flair for personal drama. He acted with an astounding flamboyance. Byron himself, a witty conversationalist, play-acted in the European salons or wherever he happened to be, down to the tragic moment

† With no hope for any fulfillment in life, *René* is the precursor of Sartre's and the Existentialists' despair after World War II. It is as if Albert Camus echoed Chateaubriand's thoughts when he wrote: "If the only significant history of human thought were to be written, it would have to be the history of its successive regrets and its impotence."

of his death fighting for Greek freedom, a death truly but unnecessarily he-roic. It proved nothing and helped no one. It was a grand gesture fitting the profile of the Romantic hero. It was—as we would say today—a publicity stunt that backfired.

The visionary artist, whose most exemplary figure is William Blake, is not consumed by the Byronic death wish, nor does he flaunt a Byronic flam-boyance in the world's face. With the tongue of a prophetic poet, he shouts his Cassandra verses and epigrams at a world's deaf ears. No one cared to listen to Blake, no one heard his voice, so he turned more and more inward, listening to the hidden voices in his self. This poet-visionary was one of the great mystics, who conversed with God and the dead as the average person does with his milkman or superintendent. Some computerized minds in our time may disparage such excesses, but those desiring to counteract an overly technical society may feel very much akin to Blake. In one of his visions Blake reports having seen John Milton, who, as Blake writes, "came to ask a favor of me. He said he had committed an error in his 'Paradise Lost' which he wanted me to correct . . . he wished to expose the falsehood of his doc-trine that sexual intercourse arose out of the Fall. Now that cannot be, for no good can spring out of Evil."

Blake was light-years away from Lord Byron in his licentiousness, yet he saw in "the improvement of sexual enjoyment" one way for people to throw off "the mind-forg'd manacles" and become their better selves. Blake's pro-phetic eye envisioned the danger of the "dark Satanic mills" of indus-trialism; he attacked the rapacious instincts of human beings. He was also out to burn down the graceless edifice of eighteenth-century rationalism. But what interests us here is Blake in contrast to Byron. While Byron was adored and idealized by a society that wished it could be as brilliantly de-praved as he, Blake belonged, to use Kenneth Rexroth's words, "to the very small group of founders of the subculture of secession which has accom-panied industrial, commercialized civilization since its beginnings." Blake sees in the suppression of man through economics and a growing industri-alization a symbolic parallel to sensual suppression. "Those," he said, "who restrain desire do so because theirs is weak enough to be restrained." This is almost a Nietzschean thought.

What is important in Blake's stress on sensuality and sexual freedom is the notion of purity and regeneration through the freedom and experience of the body. It is one of the major themes of the Romantic movement, which, of necessity, had to lead to the idealization of the ballerina. In *Visions of the Daughters of Albion,* probably written in 1793, Blake introduced the image of the golden flower of sexual delight, plucked by the central figure, Oothoon. Does the flower that she holds against her breast make her happy? First she succumbs to the fear of sin, but then as if suddenly enlightened she feels overcome by the spiritual purity in the power of sexual experience.

Blake turns the blue flower of German phantasmagoria into a golden flower of physical ecstasy. In his "Proverbs of Hell" we find Blake's exclamation: "Exuberance is beauty."

IN the shadow of these two opposite extremes, Byron and Blake, a few generic types of Romantic hero crystallized over the years. But in whatever shape they entered the stage, we cannot help noticing their need for self-revelation while asserting the self. Devoured by the desire for uniqueness, for being unsurpassed by anyone else, with a flourish of extravaganza, came the virtuoso. (Of course, Lord Byron also was a virtuoso in his style of life.) The virtuoso was alienated from his world as all Romantic heroes were, but his alienation was abetted by the magic of perfection with which he mastered whatever he set out to do.

Niccolò Paganini (1782–1840) is considered *the* virtuoso of that time. Fear as much as awe lies in our admiration of the virtuoso. People went so far as to believe that Paganini had made a pact with the devil (a duplication of the Faust-Mephistopheles motif that was then popular). Beyond the novel features of his technique and the mastery of his artistry, the man in Paganini radiated a spell-binding aura of otherness that went from the unimaginable splendor and beauty of what he did to the mysterious power of what he represented. It was in keeping with the Romantic mood that, despite his huge success, Paganini was plagued by melancholy and depression. The exaltation without which no one can reach the ultimate had to be followed by a state of anguish.

Nowadays virtuosity is considered the highest professional accomplishment, but during the Romantic age an aura of the supernatural surrounded it. However, it was not a pact with the devil. It was a pact with the artist's self. This was the secret of Paganini's violin—and this was the secret of the ballerina's body.

The virtuoso's counterpart was the dandy, with his twin brother the bohemian. The anti-role of the Romantic hero is best expressed through them. The dandy also offers perfection, but the perfection of a great elegance without content. Dandies are most often found among the followers of virtuosi. This helps them find some justification and a social function. The balletomane is a dandy par excellence. It is difficult to define precisely a dandy or a bohemian because in their shades and nuances they differ from country to country, even from decade to decade. One thing, however, unites both: they are the decadent side of the Romantic hero. Moreover, being a part of bourgeois life, they are a living protest against its trivialities. In England they have always played the role of the loyal opposition to their peers in literature and the other arts. Oscar Wilde, Aubrey Beardsley, and James Whistler were prototypes of the intellectual always at odds with their fellow-men or the law in one way or another. They are English-style dandies.

Wilde's notion of himself and a dandy is close to how Baudelaire characterized this species in his "Peintre de la vie moderne": as the living indictment of a standardizing democracy, the ideal of an utterly useless, aimless, unmotivated person; as the last revelation of heroism in an age of decadence; a sunset, a last radiant beam of human pride.

Boredom, lack of interest in life, contempt for anything bordering on averageness and vulgarity, endow the dandy with an inner superiority and a feeling of independence. Elegance of dress, fastidiousness of manners, a certain arrogance, and a kind of snobbish attitude are only the dandy's external accoutrements to make him look distinguished and distinguish him from the bohemian.

The dandy can afford to sneer at mediocrity because he feels superior to other contemporary artists—Whistler proved this point to the dot on the *i* with his arrogant attitude and his book *The Gentle Art of Making Enemies;* the other variety of the dandy would even find it beneath his dignity to test himself as an artist. On the other hand, most bohemians have "art" written all over their slovenly appearance. We like to associate them with the starving artist in a Parisian garret or with the pale-looking poet in Viennese coffeehouses.

The realization that life has lost its meaning in a world of shifting values without real changes has probably been more common through the centuries than we may think. Writers invented characters typifying the antihero, such as Don Quixote, Don Juan, and Hamlet. They all live on the fringe of existence, fighting windmills, trying to come to terms with themselves, seeking their identity. However legendary they may have been, they are very much alive in our minds. Every period gave birth to its antiheroes in many guises and disguises.

If the saying is true that every century has its Napoleon but not every Napoleon his century, then the Romantic hero certainly found his period, which, as no other era, recognized him as a vital force in the life of all strata of society.

THROUGHOUT history, certain people have always been at odds with the world, but most of these people overcome their difficulties; they are either silently absorbed by the mainstream or, being in no way heroic, live out their destinies in a state of resignation with minor psychological abrasions. They do not angrily hold, as it were, the mirror of their miseries up to the nature of history, which, always having kept its records in callous disorder, has never taken notice of them. They are the unsung Romantic heroes, fulfilling their task and destiny. These people stand in their own shadow, dreaming of the limelight and grateful for the smallest spotlight that may fall upon them. A case in point is the male ballet dancer in the nineteenth century, degraded to the role of *premier porteur.*

The main interest of the balletomanes and patrons of the art was in the ballerina. The male dancer was overlooked. There he stood as the fading vestige of a knight-errant, forced by the course of history to serve and support the ballerina, to play-act the courting prince, waiting in the wings of her glory to catch and carry her from one grand jeté to the next, to remain the attentive and adoring partner of her pirouettes. Mainly to give her an opportunity to calm her breathing, he was given time to fill with the artistry at his disposal. But soon indeed she would return in the flame of flesh, in all her grace, to light up the scene.

How incidental his position was can best be proved by its contrary.‡ In 1830 a young dancer, Jules Perrot, made his debut at the Opéra. It was possibly the worst moment for any male dancer to start his career, with the woman as the heroine of the show. Théophile Gautier (1811–72), spokesman for the Romantic ballet and its principal critic, appreciated only "physical pleasure and feminine beauty." At best he tolerated men in ballet. "For us," he said, "a male dancer is something monstrous and indecent which we cannot conceive. . . . Strength is the only grace permissible to men." This attitude was emphasized when Gautier could not help praising Jules Perrot, one of the few great male dancers of the time: "This praise is all the less suspect from us because we do not in the least care for male dancing. Perrot has made us lose our prejudice." We can add to it another voice, that of Charles de Boigne, who wrote in his *Petits mémoires de l'Opéra* in 1857: "Perrot was the last male dancer who was forgiven that he danced."

THE first quarter of the nineteenth century experienced new and more daring methods of teaching that also favored the ballerina. With greater experience and certain accomplishments, an ambition to improve standards grew, but mainly to enlarge technique. There were teachers and theoreticians who tried to strike a happy medium between the nobility of the old and the daring of the new. One of them was Carlo Blasis (1797–1878), whose two treatises, above all his *Code of Terpsichore,* written in the 1820s, set down the guidelines for many decades of ballet teaching. The critic and historian André Levinson in his *Masters of the Ballet* described Blasis' role as the mediator between the old and new forces struggling for supremacy: "Blasis viewed the antithesis between routine and novelty exclusively from a literary viewpoint and comes to a rather reconciling decision. His main task consists of directing the boat of the classical dance toward the shores of the Romantic ballet. He succeeded in becoming a new link in the uninterrupted chain of tradition."

Blasis introduced the code for what have become the pantomimic gestures

---

‡ The only choreographer of this era to give the male dancer an even chance and opportunities equal to those the ballerina enjoyed was August Bournonville (1805–79), the prime mover of the Royal Danish Ballet in Copenhagen.

that were to him "the very soul and support of ballet." This highly stylized mimetic expression is classical rather than Romantic, since it limits any freedom of expression, the unrestrained dynamic will, so characteristic of the Romantics in all disciplines. Blasis' method facilitated the floating lightness, the aerial quality of dancing. He could not deny his time its virtuosic demands. On the other hand, he envisioned excess as the great danger for the balletic art. He strove for elegance and the nobility of inner grace, even when he approved the pirouette.

Blasis wrote that pirouettes were "unknown to Noverre and our old masters, who thought it impossible to go beyond the three turns on the instep." Multiple pirouettes in a cruder form may already have been executed in the eighteenth century, but from an academic point of view he was justified in assuming that his famous contemporary dancers, Vestris and Pierre Gardel, invented and perfected the pirouette in the early 1820s. Both were often enough rebuked by critics "for overlooking the dangers of pandering to the public's desire to be dazzled by virtuosity." Blasis described the pirouette in great detail as a multiple twirl executed as high as possible on the half-toe and praises the beauty of its plasticity. However, he blasts technique as a mere trick to dazzle the eye and solicit applause.

While trying to keep technique for the sake of technique under control, he widened the dancer's range of expression. In those days ballet moved further in its defiance of the laws of gravity and balance. Blasis—always finding spiritual sustenance in the sculpture and painting of antiquity and the Renaissance—introduced the *attitude,* one of the basic poses. The inspiration for it came from Giovanni da Bologna's statue "Mercury," with the dancer standing on one leg and bringing the other leg, with the knee bent, behind him at a ninety-degree angle. What delight in virtuosity this pose showed, next to the many variations of the pas jetés! What ideal delight in ever greater deftness of the ballerina's ability to gyrate toward the ultimate approximation of denying reality!

Much had been made of Carlo Blasis the theoretician in all history books, regarding his guiding spirit in ballet classes and onstage. However, little has been said about the creative and intellectual man, unique in his conservative position in a world of romantic excesses. It is fascinating to think that these momentous decades in the history of the dance created and were spiritually dominated by two such different personalities as Carlo Blasis and Théophile Gautier.

Although Blasis believed that our thoughts should take wing and that the human spirit is on its way to novel roads, he still lived in the century of the

Carlo Blasis based the attitude on the work by Giovanni da Bologna (1529–1608) known as "Mercury." (Courtesy Alinari—Scala/Editorial Photocolor Archives)

Great social significance was connected with the loges in the early theaters.
Moreau-le-Jeune: "La petite loge." (Courtesy Giraudon)

Encyclopedists, whom he recalled into his daily existence time and again. He was an erudite man who loved to polemicize with the German philosophers of the early days of Romanticism. In his stand against excesses of any kind—against intellectual ones in the world or aesthetic-artistic movements onstage—he remained the moderate Romanticist who thought that the course of any movement, even when it has reached a certain momentum, can still be stopped. In his essay *Man as Physical, Intellectual, and Moral Being* he envisioned genius as an independently working element of our psyche, but also as the ultimate expression of our intellect, as source and aim of the life-producing powers of progress.

He was an excellent teacher and had an admirable mind. All the more must we regret that of his many choreographic works nothing is left but a few titles. He choreographed at La Scala in Milan after Viganò's death, also in Warsaw and other European cities. His topics were very much those of his time: *Faust, or The Spirit of Evil;* Byron's *Manfred*—he used excerpts and choreographed a ballet in seven sections plus a prologue whose subtitle was typical of the time's mentality: *Illusion and Disillusionment,* based on fantastic contrasts from the worlds of spirits or in the mood of ghosts. How more Romantic can one get?

The conservative in him held on to the concept of the three genres at a time when, from deep within, this notion was losing ground and its raison d'être. These genres were the *danseur noble,* the hero type, the serious dancer and master of the adagio, the slow sustained movement; the *demi-caractère,* a man usually of middle height and mostly seen in a mixture of all styles; and the *genre comique,* danced by small and vigorous men of short and stocky nature. The ever-increasing number of theatergoers now frequenting the Opéra neither understood nor cared much for the danse noble, unless it was mingled with the virtuoso feats of the demi-caractère dancer. The classic distinctions between the genres became blurred. With only the tours de force being applauded, the genre noble in its pure form disappeared, and with it the predominant position of the male dancer.

THE rapid progress that the Industrial Revolution made at the beginning of the nineteenth century also contributed a great deal to the rise of the ballerina and her unique position. Above all, the introduction of gaslight, first in the streets and then in the theater, was an important innovation. The scenic designers for the melodrama were the first to take advantage of the multiple possibilities of gas-lighting onstage, with a gradual variation of illumination, making use of the eerie bluish effect of its radiation. Gaslight achieved surprising stage images for the melodrama with its many Gothic castles or ruins in mysterious forests and wild lake landscapes. When the Opéra—and with it the Romantic ballet—began to use gaslight, then all that was still unimaginable a generation before became the reality of the widest range of illusions. The chandeliers in the auditorium could be extinguished and, at last, from the darkened house, the spectators' eyes could be surprised and stunned by a moonlit scene simulated by gas jets suspended in the flies. First realized in *The Ballet of the Nuns,* gas-lighting illumining the extra lightness of the ballerina in an eerie setting created the sensation of having put reality into its romantic place.

Another important change helped the female dancer into the position of *prima ballerina assoluta.* It was the new costume, the *tutu,* "the many-layered tarlatan skirt," as Lincoln Kirstein referred to it, that gradually replaced the court costume and has ever since been the symbol of the ballerina. Eugène Lami designed it for Taglioni's *Sylphide,* but the argot tutu was coined only in the post-Romantic era. (It matters little that the tutu may be reminiscent of earlier costumes, probably of haute couture ideas that came up during the era of the French Revolution, very likely around 1790.) The ballerina in her flesh-colored tights and that cloud of fluttery gauze came at just the right moment to capture everyone's imagination, and that is all history has ever cared for. The costume created that airy sensation of a seraphic, ethereal being, an impression that was heightened by the use of the toe shoe.

It is generally assumed that Marie Taglioni was *sur les pointes* in *La Sylphide* for the first time. We are not certain that she did dance the sylph on *pointes,* but certainly such attempts had been made for quite some time. There is a print of a dancer on point dated 1821. A watercolor going back to 1790 is in the Stockholm library, showing an unidentified dancer standing on her toes. Reflecting on the "amazing exertions" of Carolina Pitrot Angiolini, who danced in London in 1784, Walter Terry wondered whether she wasn't already somehow on her toes; and when, in the 1770s, Anna Heinel's entrance was described "on stilt-like tip-toe" by a contemporary critic, Lillian Moore suggested that this phrase could easily have meant that the ballerina was on her toes. No one, of course, speaks of how long these dancers *remained* in this position. In 1827 Marie Taglioni appeared at the Paris Opéra and was then compared to a famed dancer, Mlle Geneviève Adélaïde Gosselin, who died in 1818:

> Mlle Taglioni holds herself on the point of the foot with truly remarkable balance. Not since Mlle Gosselin has any nymph of Terpsichore been able to hold such a position so long.

Since it must have been the ballerina's dream for a long time to rise in her soft satin slippers, creating the sensation of utter lightness and grace, the gradual development of the toe shoe was inevitable. By the 1830s the image of the prima ballerina was established as we know her: hardly touching the floor, delicately balanced, or soaring through the air, a creature from another world.

"The Eternal Feminine Draws Us On"

IT WAS NOT BY MERE ACCIDENT THAT GOETHE WROTE THESE WORDS AS THE final line in his philosophical play *Faust*. It was 1832, the same year that *La Sylphide* was presented in Paris. In this ballet an imagined sylph, an airborne creature, entices a young man to follow her. In his dream-fulfilling wish he is lured away from reality, ready to follow the symbolic image of love and beauty.

Goethe had more in mind. The feminine was for him the incarnation of the creative principle that would draw Faust up to the Absolute, to total fulfillment. There is a great aspiration in the human being to act creatively. Faust's struggle was a cosmic symbol, and, while thinking of the power of the eternal feminine, he feels how "all things transitory are little more than a simile."

The Romantic ballet has made the concept of the transitoriness of all things its point of departure. It theatricalized the Romantic agony, its passion for love suffering. A similar trend prevailed in literature, with introspective speculations and self-revelations becoming an intoxicating game. It led to the writing of diaries, replacing the letter-form habit of the previous century. With the growing sense of self and an excessive stress on individualism, the Romantic turned *le journal intime* into the couch for the writer's self-analysis. It started—to mention a few names only—with Chateaubriand, Benjamin Constant, and Stendhal, followed by Tolstoi and Dostoevski.

Such an assault on the central mystery of the self, either in fictionalized form or in a diary, shows the dominant role of the Romantic man's sexual problems. The male was ready to lay down his life for the unattainable dream figure, but not quite so ready to do so for the woman he could go to bed with. Much of his desire for the unattainable was little more than a narcissistic dream that attempted to spiritualize his phallic pride. Ballets from *La Sylphide* to *Giselle* to *Swan Lake* mirrored romantic ambivalences. Some of the great writers of the era described the ballerina by the metaphor of a self-devouring flame. It was an apt symbol of the Romantic's inner state. The first of the many self-revelations in fiction was Benjamin Constant's *Adolphe*, followed by Henri Frédéric Amiel's diary, *Journal intime*. Both Constant and Amiel opened their heavy hearts, the former in the role of a Don Juan, the latter as a man defeated in his sexual desires. Both, in the parts they played in life, characterize the ambience in which the ballerina became the image of the Absolute.

The importance of Constant's novel *Adolphe* lies in the fact that it was the first brutal attack on a writer's own psyche. It was published in 1816. From Constant's self-analysis it became obvious that he did not try to white-wash any of his weaknesses. The picture he draws of himself is that of an intelligent but highly unsympathetic person. Adolphe's loves are passionate yet full of empty gestures. He seems to love his loving more than the beloved.

He was one of the strangest but most fascinating Don Juan types: he suffered incredibly from being able to inflict pain on others or, rather, from being unable not to act out of sheer vanity and weakness. He suffered because his gift of self-observation and detachment from his own actions was remarkable. As the actor of his own life he watched himself playing the character he thought he was. Constant admitted in his diary: "I possess excellent qualities such as pride, generosity, and devotion, but I am not quite a real person." Exactly. He does not accept himself. This is the Romantic's dilemma: What is real?

Henri Frédéric Amiel was born in 1821, when Constant's *Adolphe* was a best seller. He is an anti–Don Juan type, but he never has the courage to find out about himself and his homosexual leanings. Sex, or rather the fear of it, interfered with his giving himself a chance to be himself. Amiel was distinguished-looking and attracted many women. But he indulged in the passionless pursuit of women while, as he confessed in his *Journal intime,* he was tormented physically:

> Sexuality has been my nemesis, my torture ever since childhood. My extraordinary timidity, my violent desires, my ardent imagination, my pernicious readings in adolescence . . . the fatal attraction which I exerted later on delicate and tender women: all this proceeds from a false notion of sexuality. This error has poisoned my life.

The bent toward playing a part while watching oneself was quite common among the intellectual elite at that time. It was just as difficult for many to call themselves back from the region of illusion to reality. Amiel played his roles in full consciousness of playing a fantastic, weird, macabre, romantic game with himself, escaping from his well-ordered, rather uneventful reality into a world of relentless metamorphoses. He exclaimed that he was "no longer his own self" and felt he might surprise himself the following day by being a Japanese, a woman, a madman, a child, a camel, the man from the moon or from Jupiter. He sensed total "sympathy with the universe" and tried to submerge in the mystery of being until he broke out into an anarchic cry, into the negation of his self, asking his friends who he was. This professor at the University of Geneva lived his life as though walking by himself as a stranger.

Leo Tolstoi found a kindred soul in Amiel. He was deeply impressed by the *Journal intime* of the Swiss recluse. Tolstoi kept a diary throughout his life, and in *A Confession* he tells us of his incessant probing into the purpose and meaning of life. The fear that one can lose one's identity began in the early nineteenth century.* The systematic probing of our psyche, which we conveniently date back to Freud in 1895, was long in preparation.

The conscious probing of an inner center soon began with the Romantic rage. In the painful process of looking inward the need to cope with and to transcend the outside world became an ever-growing necessity and at times a compulsive obsession. As a consequence, man fled into the ecstasy of spiritual escape. For this, a focal point was needed; it was found in the idealized image of woman.

One manifestation of this was the romanticizing of adventurous love, which created the notion of the *femme fatale*. It had started in France with the salon of Catherine de Rambouillet, who was extremely influential in high society and among the intelligentsia of seventeenth-century Paris, free from the official reign of Richelieu's newly founded Académie Française. As we have described, these literary salons, social gatherings of creative spirits, became ever more important in the eighteenth century with such remarkable hostesses as Mmes Geoffrin, du Deffand, and Suzanne Necker and Mlle de Lespinasse, and remained a focal point of the cultural elite in the era of Romanticism, when some of the fascinating women were Mme de Staël, Marie d'Agoult (Franz Liszt's mistress and Cosima Wagner's mother), and George Sand, one of the most unconventional of all Romantics, who in her life demonstrated her belief in the equality of women. Some of her relationships, particularly those with Musset and Chopin, have become history. Her novels are remarkable for their frankness, love of nature, and, strangely enough, moral idealism. In retrospect, it almost seems that every woman with a sense of her own greatness as a woman and spiritual force kept a literary salon in the nineteenth century.

No chronicler of history will ever be able to tell how many ideas, deeds, and works of art were born in these salons. The interchangeable effects of these ladies' spirit of grace or grace of spirit must remain a marvel and secret of time. The nineteenth century added to the role of these ladies the Romantic piquancy of woman's fatal attraction and man's readiness to die for her, as some indeed did, thus exalting and glorifying her status with a halo of the macabre. It is characteristic of Romanticism that the term *femme fatale* then came into being.

* In his *Social History of Art*, Arnold Hauser points out: "The disintegration of the personality, in which the emotional conflict goes so far that the individual is no longer clear about his own motives and becomes a problem to himself, does not take place until the beginning of the last century. The concomitants of modern capitalism, romanticism and the estrangement of the individual from society, first create the consciousness of spiritual dissension and hence the modern problematic character."

Her poor relation is the less fortunate type, the unknown seamstress, the shopgirl, the laundress, lacemaker, milliner. If she, too, wanted to escape reality, she often found her way into the corps de ballet. The Romantics—and here the dandies and bohemians acted and play-acted prominently—had a weakness for sickly and helpless women and desired to protect and patronize them. They loved the pale, anemic girls, those doomed to die in their youth. Their pallor, as a symbol of nature's injustice, excited the men of that time. The excitement waxed when, moreover, the female could be cast in the role of a loose woman. (However, men's imagination seemed most challenged when facing a female demon, as in *Carmen*.) It is characteristic of the era that Abbé Prévost's novel *Manon Lescaut*—written a century previously (1731)—about a woman who made her lover a helpless victim of his passion, had a romantic comeback. Massenet, Auber, and Puccini put his story on the operatic stage. Alexandre Dumas fils immortalized the figure of a high-class courtesan, Marguerite Gautier, whose sincere love was dramatized as much as her fatal disease. His *Dame aux Camélias* became the most typical play of the late Romantic era. Its heroine found her way onto the operatic stage as Violetta in Verdi's *La Traviata,* as did a similar heroine as Mimi in Puccini's *La Bohème.*

Marguerite Gautier died of consumption, the major disease of the nineteenth century. Common among young women, it was characterized by paleness and weakness. Another disease, chlorosis (iron-deficiency anemia), overcame mainly poor young women in the cities. This disease was characterized by a greenish-pale or grayish-yellow hue of the skin, weakness, and menstrual disorders. Pallor might be equated with purity in love by a Romantic mind, and even Ovid refers to it as a symbol of sexual passion in his *Ars amatoria.* Both consumption and chlorosis also struck the peasantry, and one of the many symptoms was a severe heart condition. The immortal figure of *Giselle* belongs with these doomed girls.

If we can speak of a near-epidemic disease as fashionable, then consumption was high fashion in the nineteenth century. It was certainly a contagious disease, physically and mentally. It was chic and up-to-date to have a sickly, pale complexion and to pine away in the most languorous fashion. It was easy to identify the self-consuming process of this disease with the unfulfilled longing of the Romantic, with flight from reality and the self. It was a disease that fitted Romanticism in all its colorful ramifications. The dance equated with a self-devouring flame and the ballerina envisioned in flight from the ground where she was only a fleeting moment ago were part of the very same image. The inexplicable desire to seek the realization of one's dreams in the stars derived from a sensation which a witty aesthete of that period, Rahel Levin, described as "the endless depth of emptiness."

THÉOPHILE Gautier, the creator of *Giselle,* thought that "one should not forcibly demand common sense of the ballet" and that "the more chimeral the characters, the less will verisimilitude be insulted." Yet he must have been aware of the fact that anything happening onstage is subject to certain plausibilities and that no one can die within five minutes however grave the fit of madness may be. When Gautier looked for a proper dramatic story to precede Act II of *Giselle,* chlorosis must have been on his mind. Only a weak heart condition can lead to heart failure when Giselle has to endure the shock of a frightful disillusion.

Gautier found the idea for the second act of *Giselle* in Heinrich Heine's book *De L'Allemagne.* The Wilis, those nocturnal dancers, wait for their male victims and dance them to death. In Gautier's version, a man named Albrecht comes to visit the grave of his beloved Giselle when the Wilis appear, and among them is Giselle. She wants to protect him, but the fatal madness takes hold of him and he pirouettes, bounds, follows Giselle in her most hazardous leaps; the frenzy to which he gives way reveals a secret desire to die with his love. (Another example of passion causing man's readiness to die for the beloved.) But four o'clock strikes, and the dawn brings delivery: the Wilis disappear, and with them Giselle.

This second act—close in its conception to *La Sylphide,* with its phantom that has an overpowering fascination for the male—needed a realistic dramatic counterpoint in Act I. Gautier first thought of a beautiful ballroom belonging to some prince as the setting. But the final result was the simple story of a naïve country girl who falls in love with a prince disguised as a hunter. On discovering his deceit—he is betrothed to an aristocratic lady—she works herself into a raving excitement. Her weak heart fails to stand this test of life, and she dies. Such a clinical version did not seem stageworthy and had to be changed to the dramatic fury of madness.

It is a long way from *La Sylphide* to *Giselle* and from *Giselle* to *Swan Lake.* It cannot be measured in years only, although about three generations of Romantics lie in between. The ballerina had become more "absolute" at the end of the last century, as she was in the late 1820s, at the very outset of her supremacy. There was no letup in the needed exaltation of Romantic feelings on the part of the balletomanes. The dancer in the woman was extolled as much as the woman in the dancer. The dancer in the woman was the Romantic's guide on his flight from his self. The woman in the dancer was deified by him. Art as a means of helping us survive the truth of life, to paraphrase Nietzsche, has little to do with any "sacred" act. But the nineteenth-century romanticist needed a goddess, an idolized woman; he needed, in fact, something real but sufficiently removed from his everyday reality in order to keep up the dream of the spiritually pure and unattainable ideal.

Since the advent of Christianity the woman had been spiritualized and glorified. From the image of the madonna figure to an idealized Platonic being in the chivalrous days of knighthood, she was finally moved into the ethereal realms of the Romantic where his tormented soul and body could gratify both through her. Above all and far from all carnal mystery, she is first extolled for the purity of her presence, for the beauty of her spirit. When man awakens in the late Middle Ages, woman becomes the privileged judge at the courts of love and the muse of the minnesinger. Man endows her so often, and for different reasons, with intuitive power. He envisions her in situations that demand his protective role, for which he has demands on her, if only to put her on a pedestal. As the knight he serves her and fights for her. From the troubadours to the many minor poets in our time, he extols her in verbal ecstasies. He has hanging gardens built in her name. In Balzac's and Stendhal's novels he grew and shaped his own image in her reflection as the chosen sun. But all this myth and fiction mirrored the Romantic's mind in real life.

Romanticism has always carried with it the seed of revolution. It is impossible to think that there would be no social repercussions when man puts woman on a pedestal, casting himself in the part of the protector. The exploitation of woman in the name of industrial progress created that pallor on her face and soul which animated and compelled the male to reach out for her with his protective hand and love.

The dominant role of the woman as an object of man's needs strongly helped form the ferment in the struggle of woman's emancipation. In spite of Queen Victoria's thundering no to the movement of the suffragettes, the importance of this movement grew noticeably in the second half of the nineteenth century.

The female dancer contributed, however indirectly, to the movement of emancipation. The ballerina most associated with feminine spirituality and everything ephemeral, Marie Taglioni, appeared in a number of Romantic ballets that show her in martial disguise and militant attitudes. These ballets following *La Sylphide* were less noticeable for the choreographic skill of her father, Filippo Taglioni, than as a reflection of the time. Traditionally an art form obliged to please, ballet could, of course, never go as far as litera-

This "prosecuted picture" shows to what extent the feuds between rival ballerinas were carried in the days of Romanticism. The then famous ballerina Eugénie LeCompte, who appeared as the Abbess Helena in RO-BERT LE DIABLE *at the Park Theater in New York in the late 1830s, was caricatured by Henry R. Robinson in a topless costume. The caricature, circulated among balletomanes, was probably instigated by her rival Mlle Céleste. (From the George Chaffee Collection. Courtesy New York Public Library Dance Collection)*

MADAME LECOMPTE.

Principal Danseuse at the Theatres Royal Paris, London, St Petersburgh &c.
In the Character of the Abbess, in Robert le Diable.

ture in its militant spirit. But it showed that it was with the time and its progressive spirit.

George Sand published her then startling novel *Lélia* in 1833, and her passionate plea for the equal rights of women was heard. Sand's protest against many social conventions was climaxed by her apologia for a heroine who "sets up against the interests of society, raised to the level of principles, the straightforward ideas and simple laws of common sense and humanity." Sand wore men's clothing and showed sentimental feelings for poetic, effeminate men. Her fight for woman's cause was personal and yet typical for the period, with just the right tinge of socialist doctrines borrowed from Saint-Simon, the social philosopher whose writings, early in the century, foreshadowed socialism. When the critic Jules Janin wrote of the ballet *Brézilia, ou la Tribu des Femmes (Brézilia, or the Tribe of Women)*, "The doctrines of Saint-Simon are elevated to a performance of pirouettes and entrechats," he tried to ridicule all progressive trends as much as the idea of the ballet, in which members of a female tribe became sworn enemies of the male sex. This evokes again the image of Giselle's Wilis. Is not the female, in whatever shape, who fights the male or takes revenge upon him a natural reversion of Romanticism in extremis?

It took women a long time before they received some equal rights with men as performing artists. But in the nineteenth century the ballerina reversed the status of the female performer. Of course, moving into the limelight of public attention, the ballerina could not prevent her private life from becoming publicized, and with it the image of the unconventional that hung about her. Patrons have always played their parts in the theater, and more often than not the patrons were male admirers who could not help blending the artist with the object of their desires. There were notable exceptions in dance history, such as Marie Sallé, who was known for her intellectual interests and admired for them; among her friends were Voltaire, Noverre, and David Garrick, who apparently respected her lesbian tendencies.

Some ballerinas, however, nourished the image of notoriety. For instance, the "divine" Émilie Bigottini, who danced at the Paris Opéra, spied for her friend Talleyrand, who combined his well-known immorality with the position of a deputy, representing the clergy, and later of French Foreign Minister. Talleyrand and Bigottini's combined efforts saved the Congress of Vienna (1814–15) from collapse. A year later, Bigottini married a millionaire for protection. While Fanny Elssler kept her relationships with Friedrich von Gentz, the counterpart to Talleyrand on Metternich's side, and with the duc de Reichstadt from public attention as best as she could, the Irish dancer Lola Montez made history with her adventures rather than with her dancing. Somewhat as the Byzantine dancing mime Theodora had been crowned Empress by Emperor Justinian, Lola Montez became the mistress of Ludwig I of Bavaria. She lived in a sumptuous palace in Munich's Barerstrasse, from where, as countess of Landsfeld, she helped Ludwig rule until the March revolution of 1848. The King was then forced to abdicate, and Lola Montez fled to the United States, where she died in poverty. Such a fascinating personality—as a dancer she won some fame imitating Fanny Elssler's Cachucha—naturally found a glorified treatment in the cinematic world and in ballet, the latter demonstrated by Léonide Massine's *Bacchanale* (1939) and Edward Caton's *Lola Montez* (1946).

There *she* is, by the grace of God and Terpsichore, a dream image which, in its ephemeral existence, must always be renewed and never fulfilled. She was manipulated by the eyes of daydreamers and by male choreographers and critics. However, there was still one role waiting for her: her fulfillment as a creative artist at the turn of the century. It was then that she could break the mirror of her own image in order to move into a new artistic freedom.

DANCE CRITICISM AND THE ERA OF GAUTIER

THE NINETEENTH CENTURY, IN ITS TRUE FULFILLMENT OF ROMANTI-
cism, lasted only from the late 1820s until the 1880s. The bourgeoisie was
coming to grips with the reality of power, accepting the heritage of the aristocracy partly by denying the gesture of its nobility, partly by imitating it.
While the aristocracy seemingly enjoyed life without any grave responsibility, the mortal enemy of the bourgeoisie, the working class, became restless. Fighting at the barricades for its own benefits and aspirations, the
workers and students soon began to realize that they had only helped the
bourgeoisie to greater security, that the struggle between these two classes
had then just begun.

Many intellectuals and artists were, between the two revolutions of 1830
and 1848, actively occupied with the political problems of the time. They
were convinced that some form of social adjustment ought to have kept
pace with the machines, whether it was called socialism or was one of the
various idealistic and utilitarian trends of the time. The arts could not help
but reflect the seesaw struggle between the bourgeois in power and the
unprivileged who could not participate in the newly accumulated fortunes.

After the July Revolution of 1830 the French upper and middle classes
were gripped by a buoyant spirit of "bourgeois" life. In 1837, the year
Marie Taglioni started her four-year engagement at the Imperial Theater in
St. Petersburg, Queen Victoria began her reign over the age identified with
her name, which was to last until 1901. It was a period of prosperity for
Britain, which continued to rule the commercial world, but it was a prosperity muted by the misfortune and insecurities of many. The *Principles* of the
English utilitarian philosopher and economist Jeremy Bentham, who died in
1832, shed light on these social contrasts. The bourgeois world paid only lip
service to his ideas that the object of legislation must be "the greatest happiness of the greatest number."

A state of unease prevailed in most parts of Europe after the Congress of
Vienna (1814–15). The early nineteenth century lived in the shadow of
prince von Metternich, who with an iron fist ruled over Central Europe,
where he kept a perfect police state intact. The revolutionary movement of
Young Germany was suppressed, and its Italian counterpart, the secret organization Young Italy, battled against the suppression of the poor.

Fanny Elssler in her famous Cachucha: lithograph by E. Brown, Jr., New York, executed on the occasion of her appearances in America between 1840 and 1842. (Courtesy New York Public Library Dance Collection)

Since Lord Byron died for the freedom of the Greek people from Turkish domination, Romanticism had nourished feelings for strong national identities. This rekindled the interest in national customs and folklore, which was soon to find its reflection in literature as well as in ballet. All through the Romantic era, national dances played an impressive part on the balletic stage, and certain dancers were more closely identified with this trend than others. This interest in national identities enhanced the success of Fanny Elssler in her Spanish, Polish, Hungarian, and Russian dances. She made these *character dances*—as they were called—famous, and they made her famous in the mid-1830s. She realized that these dances were best suited for her body and temperament, for the "pagan dancer" she was, as Gautier described her. She preferred ballets in her repertory in which she could stun her audiences with such dances, as in Jean Coralli's *Le Diable Boiteux* (1836) with its Cachucha, or Joseph Mazilier's *La Gypsy* (1839) with its Cracovienne. Critics and spectators alike began to be aware of the charm and seductive spell exerted by these folkloristic dances, and the choreographers were partial to balletic material that included a tarantella, smolenska, polka, waltz, or bolero.

This stress on nationalism mirrored the growing discontentment of politically conscious people, while, on the surface, Europe lived in a middle-class euphoria. The year 1848 was to be a decisive turning point. Marx and Engels issued their *Communist Manifesto,* and a succession of revolutions tested the stability of bourgeois power: February and June in France, March and October in Germany and Austria. True, Metternich's reign came to an end, but basically the revolutions were lost, the forces of "order" regaining power with reactionary vengeance. A part of it was a severe press legislation. Radical newspapers were eliminated; a climate of unspoken fear made itself felt in literature, in the theater, and in the arts.

THE most significant sociocultural development between the two revolutions was the development of journalism. A surprisingly great number of newspapers and periodicals were published in the 1830s and, with the decades, became more and more an essential part of the sociocultural aspect of French life. These publications could not have flourished had not there been a great demand for them. On the other hand, this demand could have been so great only because the general politicization of life stimulated people's interest in political events and because a sufficient number of fascinating writers began to contribute to papers and magazines. *La Presse,* founded in 1836—Gautier wrote for this paper for almost two decades—made history by cutting its subscription rate in half, making up for the loss through advertisements. Every other paper had to follow suit. *La Presse* originally appeared in an edition of 70,000, a figure that it was able to raise to 200,000 by ten years later. In competing with each other the editors tried to secure contributions from name writers or from promising literary people who realized the advantage of being published in the daily papers or weekly magazines.

Three phenomena were then finally established: the *feuilleton,* the section at the bottom of a page reserved for light literature and criticism; the serialization of novels; and the ghost writer. Serialization was then an accepted practice on a worldwide scale. Tolstoi's *Anna Karenina,* for example, was serialized in a magazine before it came out in book form. Balzac's novels were written for serialization in *La Presse,* with each installment coming to a dramatic or exciting point, titillating the reader into waiting anxiously for the next edition.

Eugène Sue received 100,000 francs from *Le Constitutionnel* for his novel *The Wandering Jew,* an amount that Alexandre Dumas père easily topped. A court action proved that Dumas, working day and night, could— from a purely physical viewpoint—never have turned out as many novels as he did. Seventy-three ghost writers collaborated with him. The heyday began of the literary hacks, whose signature appeared next to those of literary eminence in the feuilletons. Young people with political ambitions tried to call attention to themselves by writing in the papers. Ever since, writing for newspapers has been the beginning of many a literary career.

A gradual process of democratization changed the standards in the arts. In the years from 1830 to 1848 Gautier's *l'art pour l'art* was still respected as the unorthodox movement within the larger Romantic trend. Although after the lost revolution of 1848 Romanticism still remained very much alive, it continued on a new course. The mystical, weird, and mystifying was being transformed. Stendhal, who died in 1842, was a true Romantic who disavowed the lush Romantic style. Flaubert, early associated with the *l'art pour l'art* movement, soon recognized the neurotic self-deception and falsification of reality to which its followers were inclined. He tried to accomplish a style "as rhythmical as verse and as precise as the language of science." Gautier, however, held on to his early ideals, continuing his dislike for the middle-class mentality and anything utilitarian. Only grudgingly did he recognize the many changes in the cultural climate after the lost revolution of 1848. By then the middle class was in the saddle. It demanded light entertainment and showed little understanding for and patience with the poetic, with the shock and wonder of art for art's sake.

The artificially well made plays of Eugène Scribe and Victorien Sardou dominated the stage and prepared the way for the farcical plays of Labiche and Feydeau, those amusing bedroom farces for the tired bourgeois. Melodrama and vaudeville were still great favorites, burlesque being added as a new attraction. It developed into an important innovation in the popular theater of the nineteenth century. Some historians claim that, together with its offshoot the extravaganza, burlesque was the direct, even though early, ancestor of musical comedy. Burlesque began as pure parody, as John Poole's *Hamlet,* staged in London in 1828, proves, but additions and improvements were constantly made. It went through phases in which "gross and vulgar dances," particularly in the Anglo-Saxon countries, gave it a bad name. When, however, more polished dancing was added in the 1830s, one of its successful concoctions, for instance, was the burlesque production of *La Mosquita* in 1838 in which Fanny Elssler was lampooned. From then on, dancing remained a main feature of this type of popular entertainment.

About 1848 another new genre became popular with middle-class theatergoers: the operetta, which included a good deal of dancing. Although the inserted dance numbers were limited in their developmental scope, they gave the composer a chance to light up the sky melodically. The plot was always romantic and sentimental, unbelievable and nostalgic, ready-made for carefree hours in the theater. Each of the two cultural centers at the time, Paris and Vienna, had its great operetta composers: Jacques Offenbach (1819–80) and Johann Strauss, father (1804–49) and son (1825–99). Offenbach was well aware that the Parisians expected lively dance numbers, a tradition that opera lovers perpetuated since the days of Lully and Rameau. All the more surprising is the accomplishment of Offenbach's librettists, Henri Meilhac and Ludovic Halévy: that both plot and witty lines in their songs contained satiric comments on contemporary life without giving up an inch of the entertainment value the audience demanded from an operetta.

Offenbach's Viennese counterpart was Johann Strauss, Jr., whose work goes back to the *Singspiel* as much as Offenbach shows traces of the *opéra bouffe.* Strauss composed his most famous operetta, *Die Fledermaus.* Its success was immediate and lasting; its music and plot hit the taste of the average theatergoer then, as they do to this very day. Srauss's librettists borrowed the basic idea from Offenbach's *Parisian Life,* transposed into the Viennese atmosphere of *Waltzer Gemütlichkeit.* The plot was taken from *Le Réveillon* by Meilhac and Halévy and seasoned with details from Roderich Bendix's comedy *Das Gefängnis (The Prison).* The gaiety in 3/4 time that Strauss brought to the plot and the superiority of his musical lilt turned Vienna into the leading light-opera city, until the American musical began to take its place in the 1930s.

The Victorian era also brought forth operatic masters of the English tongue and taste. The parody portraits of contemporary British life in the ingratiating, easygoing, entertaining style of William S. Gilbert and Sir Arthur Sullivan have become masterpieces of the operatic genre in their fashion. The operetta as light theatrical fare harmonized with the middle-brow needs of an entertainment-hungry people in the second half of the nineteenth century.

YET the artists and critics of this period helped bring about the gradual decline of ballet. (The thirst of the public, its clamor for bravura dancing, had an equal share in the deterioration of balletic art.) When journalism came into being, or rather into its first full bloom, its difficulties as a source of critical information became immediately obvious. Was the critic to guide or please the public? Was he not aware of the producer's aim for financial success and the commercial interdependence of producer and press? Was not the critic's task to stimulate public taste, to inform a potential audience about the story of a play or ballet, to describe the acting and dancing? The skillful journalist would antagonize neither producers, actors, and dancers nor his editors and readers. Each night he had to attend, more often than not, mediocre productions in order to have enough material for his columns that were his livelihood. He was bound to serve a taste often at variance with his own. He had to learn to write between the lines. "A critic is, after all, a man, especially when he has been a poet," Gautier sighed in his feuilleton in *Le Moniteur universel* on August 20, 1855, and he told the brothers Goncourt "that the newspaper does not permit him to expound the aesthetic side of the matter."

The Art of Criticism

WE LIKE TO THINK THAT NO ART CAN PROPERLY DEVELOP WITHOUT A critical echo. The classical Greek dramatists from Aeschylus to Aristophanes had to submit to contests of various kinds. The ten judges of the playwrights, chosen by lot from a large list of candidates, acted as critics, and the selections for first, second, and third prizes were written on tablets, of which five were chosen by a magistrate at random.

While in our age of journalism we may complain that the public depends too much on the judgment of the critics as pronounced in various newspapers and on television, Plato had reason for a complaint in reverse. He blamed the judges for being too easily influenced by the applause of the crowd instead of daring to confront the vulgar multitude with their personal critical appraisal. As an aristocrat, Plato was afraid the arts could suffer from the taste of the crowd and referred contemptuously to this condition as "theatrocracy." But are today's critics able to isolate themselves totally from the will of the audience?

The artisan in the Middle Ages who worked on an altar for ten years knew but one judge: God. His work was done to praise him as well as please the community that acted as his patron. His pride in his work hid behind anonymity. Only the regained self-assurance of the Renaissance with the emphasis on ego invited public critical debate about a work of art. The invention of the printing press between about 1436 and 1445 made it possible to put one's critique into print.

Giorgio Vasari was the premier Renaissance critic. He was also a painter, muralist, portraitist, and architect. But he is best known for his writings on the *Lives of the Artists* (*Vite de' più eccellenti architetti, pittori e scultori italiani*), the earliest prototype of modern art criticism. When he asked himself why Florence gave birth to the most perfect creators in the arts, his immediate answer was: "The spirit of criticism: the air of Florence making minds naturally free, and not content with mediocrity."

According to his own testimony it was due to chance that Vasari became a writer and took upon himself the tremendous task of writing essays on about two hundred artists from the fourteenth to the mid-sixteenth century. In 1546 Vasari dined with Cardinal Farnese and a few humanists. The scholar Paolo Giovio described his plans to write a history of the artists. Vasari found fault with his ideas, whereupon the cardinal and other scholars persuaded him to write such a book himself, since they seemed to agree with Vasari's argument that only a creative artist is best equipped to write about his fellow artists.*

His book became the first best seller of its kind a hundred years after Gutenberg invented the printing press. There seems to have been a need for such a book, as a similar, but less successful, publication about the artists' lives by a certain Ascanio Condivi was issued about the same time. Vasari's work went into a second and enlarged edition. The printing and publishing of books was then a novelty, coming into the world of humanism when its first flowering was almost over. There was a great demand for reading material about both the readers' own time and the past. Between 1445 and 1500 somewhat more than a thousand printing presses were at work in Europe, producing 35,000 titles totaling about 10 million copies. Vasari's *Lives of the Artists* was for decades a leading best seller, and since there were no newspapers or periodicals yet in existence, his writings were of similar significance, stimulating and forming opinions, breaking or making artists.

When we consider nineteenth-century journalism in its initial stage as a profession exposed to many temptations and outside pressures through growing commercialism and a competitive life, and as a way of overcompensating

---

* This argument has, ever since, been supported as much as attacked. Vasari, in the second or third rank of the Renaissance artists, ran the risk of believing he was the best judge of a work of art that he himself was unable to create. Would not frustration render him more biased than Paolo Giovio, who loved the arts and would have brought the broad understanding of a humanist to his task? By the same token, was Nijinsky justified in reproaching the Russian critic Valerian Svetlov for never having made a dance step and therefore having no justifiable right to criticize him?

for one's personal frustrations or of trying to find a career, then Vasari is archetypical for journalism per se. He leaned heavily on adjectives and, since there was no opposing or neutralizing power counterbalancing his statements, some of his epithetics became and remained the descriptive stigma of an artist. Thus, Fra Filippo Lippi was unscrupulous, Perugino irreligious, Raphael eclectic, and Michelangelo divine. Michelangelo, who was once Vasari's master, felt induced to write his former disciple a flattering sonnet after receipt of his essays, which raises the question whether an artist should ever thank his reviewer for having been understood and praised or protest being criticized and castigated. It is doubtful that an ideal relationship between artist and critic can ever be assumed, but if it is, it would have to be one without any personal contact in order to guarantee integrity.

Vasari's example also proves the danger of accumulating extraneous power through power as a critic. Eleven years after the publication of the *Lives,* Vasari was able to induce Grand Duke Cosimo I to found the Accademia del Disegno (the Academy of Design). No one could become a member of Vasari's academy easily; one had to be chosen, as has later been the case with the Académie Française. To become a member was an honor conferred on renowned artists, limited to thirty-six members.

Vasari set himself up as a critic, and soon he was considered *the* authority to pass judgment and make far-reaching decisions on a variety of questions that reached beyond the province of criticism. "Vasari," wrote Egon Friedell in his *Cultural History,* "practiced a dictatorship in the realm of artistic taste of such uncontradicted sovereignty as no other reviewer ever enjoyed again. He himself was a creative artist, but a rather minor one, and thus offers the so often repeated spectacle of the birth of criticism out of creative impotence; moreover, he combined his activity as a critic with the business of an agent which also found many imitators since." However harsh this judgment may sound, Friedell does not doubt the significance of Vasari's book, which now in retrospect looks like a dashing finale to an era of superhuman accomplishments.

But there are certain incidents and facts that show Vasari's quick and superficial judgment, as if pressured by an eleven o'clock deadline. He also seemed to have indulged in pet hates, as in the case of Andrea del Castagno. It may have been a combination of personal dislike and easy acceptance of local rumors as facts that made Vasari refer to Castagno's character as brutal and ill-tempered, an allusion to tales of homicide that were later proved untrue.

Vasari's life and work foreshadowed the art of criticism as the era of journalism necessitated it. His background and personality predestined him to become the archetype of a journalist practicing art criticism. Often when ambition is stronger than ability, reasoning than creative imagination, articulation than frustration, chance than destiny, a reviewer may be born.

Above all, he has always needed an opportunity to have his words put into print. Vasari took advantage of the first euphoria of the printing press. His time was as ready for him as it was, in different external conditions, ripe for Gautier, the first important dance critic, or Baudelaire, who is considered by many the first modern art critic. Since Vasari's appearance in the world of letters, books and treatises in the form of pamphlets were published, even newssheets and gazettes were issued at irregular intervals in France and England, in German cities, and in Venice during the 1600s. But it was not before the eighteenth century that criticism of any art form could make itself felt.

The periodicals that made history were Jonathan Swift's *Examiner* (1710–11), Richard Steele and Joseph Addison's *Tatler* and *Spectator* (1709–12), and Samuel Johnson's *Rambler* (1750–52). These periodicals mainly devoted their pages to literary questions, events of the day, and some experiences related to the arts. The dance scene, in a rather poor state in early-eighteenth-century England, was occasionally discussed. John Weaver, whose work was an island amid an ocean of "amusing trifles," on March 29, 1712, in a letter to *The Spectator,* blamed the theatergoers for applauding and demanding "Capering and Tumbling" instead of "just and regular Dancing in our theatres." And Steele would write on August 25 of the same year:

> For you must know, as trivial as this art is thought to be, no one ever was a good Dancer that had not a good Understanding. If this be a Truth, I shall leave the Reader to judge . . . such impertinents as fly, hop, caper, tumble, twirl, . . . and, in a word, play a thousand pranks which many Animals can do better than a Man. . . .

In Number 88 of *The Tatler,* Addison speaks of a strange experience he had when, one morning, he was awakened "by a sudden shake of the house . . . followed by two or three repetitions of the same convulsion." To make his long story short, he went upstairs and found there an agreeable young man trying to dance according to the early dance notations of Feuillet. Addison was not a critic of the arts but a critic of manners, as this example proves. However, he was very much interested in the opera and even concocted an opera libretto.

We must be reminded here of the tremendous vogue that Italian opera then enjoyed, with the tenor dominating the scene. Addison's reflections on this art form, appearing in *The Spectator* in 1711, had great influence on the German theorist Johann Mattheson, considered one of the early modern music critics. He founded the first periodical totally devoted to music, *Critica Musica* (1722–25). This journal dealt with topics of historical and aesthetic interest and, to a great extent, with contemporary trends in music.

There was frequent discussion of the controversy between the old polyphony of Johann Sebastian Bach and the new melodic style of Handel and Telemann. Mattheson's periodical was such a success that soon other magazines keyed to current musical problems were issued, such as *Der getreue Musikmeister* and *Der critische Musikus,* to mention only two of many.

With music publicly debated so much in Germany during the first half of the eighteenth century, we might expect to encounter similar interest in France about ballet. But nothing of such scope was then happening for the ballet, which, at best, had some literary echo in the latter part of the century. Whatever was written on the dance scene was a report with little aesthetic evaluation. An example is the report about the historic event in London in 1734 when Marie Sallé appeared in her ballet *Pygmalion,* which in almost every respect defied the current balletic spirit. The London correspondent of the *Mercure de France* informs his readers about it in describing the plot in detail, almost accounting for each little event onstage:

> The statue . . . emerges from its insensibility; she expresses astonishment at her new existence and at all the objects surrounding her. . . . Pygmalion holds out his hand . . . she tests the ground . . . and gradually steps into the most elegant poses that a sculptor could desire. . . .

The writer did not know how to assess a totally new motivation for movement, or how to evaluate the entire presentation, which anticipated the future ballet d'action. He could only register his surprise about Marie Sallé's costume:

> You can imagine, Sir, what the different stages of such an action can become when mimed and danced with the refined and delicate grace of Mlle Sallé. She has dared to appear in this entrée without pannier, skirt, or bodice, and with her hair down; she did not wear a single ornament on her head. Apart from her corset and petticoat she wore only a simple dress of muslin draped about her in the manner of a Greek statue.

Such reporting is a far cry from the serious analyses and discussions in the German musical periodicals. The German-speaking people became the incontestable leaders in the musical field from the early 1760s on, with Haydn, Gluck, and Mozart opening the doors for the musical geniuses of the nineteenth century. The question arises whether the critical interest in music during two generations did not engender musical sensibility in a people and prepare its receptivity. Or could its susceptibility to music provoke and necessitate a critical discussion, to further the emergence of so many geniuses? The fact is that the musical genius of the Germans and Austrians coincided with their national rebirth and the emergence of Romanticism and the waltz.

The Germans apparently took to music at the very beginning of their rise to power, much as the Italians did to humanism and the visual arts in the fifteenth century, or as the French embraced the Baroque and ballet. But however strongly external forces and the cyclic phases of history may have cooperated, it was owing to an intensified intellectual preparation that musical genius took hold of the Germans and Austrians in the classical period and carried them—with Mendelssohn, Schubert, Brahms, and Wagner, with Richard Strauss and Gustav Mahler—into our time, in which Schoenberg and Alban Berg, Hindemith and Webern wrote the epitaph to a musical triumph lasting about two hundred years.

When ballet passed through its period of classicism, dance criticism was not yet born. The deterioration of a unified concept of balletic productions after Lully's death and the new craze for the danse haute prompted some aestheticians to refer to the dance. These were general remarks, in the main stressing the need for pantomimic expression and the dancer's task of making gestures and steps meaningful. The only book devoted to the dance in its entirety was Louis de Cahusac's *La danse ancienne et moderne, ou traité historique sur la danse* (*Ancient and Modern Dance, or Historic Treatise on the Dance*), published in 1754. In it the significance of single gestures is emphasized: they are the bearers of the soul's emotions. Cahusac thought that Marie Sallé pointed the way into the future, demonstrating, as she did, that expressiveness is essential for the art. He envisioned a *danse en action,* with which to express all human passions, about six years before Noverre took up his fight for the ballet d'action.

But neither this book nor an occasional mentioning of the need for meaningful pantomime, at a time when current ballet productions were badly in need of a more frequent analysis, could be in any way compared to the profoundly critical annotations on music in regularly issued periodicals dealing with musical and operatic problems. Nor did the second half of the eighteenth century essentially change with regard to ballet criticism. In the gazettes and magazines it continued on a rather perfunctory level.

Since Charles Batteux gave the dance full credit as an art form in his often quoted work *Les Beaux Arts reduits à un même principe,* published in 1746, more and more philosophes tried to define ballet, which, after two hundred years of existence, had to wait for the Encyclopedists to find formal recognition as an art, equal to all the other art forms. Though it was still a far cry from any critical evaluation, the eighteenth-century record was, in this respect, not all bleak.

There was one exceptional case among the chroniclers of the eighteenth century, a nondancer who almost wrote about the art like an expert dance critic. But neither the Parisian public nor the contemporary dancers ever learned about his critical appraisals. Baron Friedrich Melchior von Grimm (1723–1807), a German strongly attracted by French culture, went to Paris at the age of twenty-five and befriended Rousseau and Diderot, with whom he formed a lifelong friendship. Grimm had a brilliant mind, combining emotionalism with German thoroughness. In 1753 he established a private news service for foreign princes and well-to-do people interested in what was going on in the cultural center of Paris. Grimm wrote literary letters, which he dispatched every fortnight, usually through diplomatic channels. In this letter-writing century Grimm's *Correspondance littéraire* chronicled all kinds of events, reviewing books, discussing writers and musicians as often as painters and sculptors, shedding light on the social scene and theatrical experiences of the day. There was hardly anything he did not write about, but whatever he wrote was well founded and well written, with tact and verve, with sensitivity and forcefulness. When his *Literary Correspondence* was collected and published in several volumes from 1812 to 1814, with a final edition issued by 1830, the importance of this writer became obvious; his magnificent work has been described as the first attempt at modern criticism.

He was able to formulate whatever he experienced with clarity, precision, and integrity. It is interesting to see how Grimm reacted to Noverre's method of composition, in which mime scenes linked the various pas seuls, pas de deux, de trois, and de quatre, and in which soliloquies, duets, or trios expressed love, jealousy, or despair in the manner of the ballet d'action, never being devoid of meaning:

> . . . in the ballets of Noverre, dancing and rhythmical walking are quite distinct. There is dancing, but in the great movements of the passions, in the decisive moments, in the scenes, there is walking, in time it is true but without dancing. The transition from rhythmic walking to dancing, and from the dance to the rhythmic walk, is as necessary in this spectacle as is the transition from recitative to song and song to recitative in opera, but dancing for the sake of dancing cannot occur until the danced play is over. . . .

Noverre restaged his *Caprices de Galathée* in November 1776, and Baron von Grimm saw this performance at the Paris Opéra, when the dancer Le Picq made his first appearance. He wrote to Frederick of Prussia about this production:

> . . . Simple though the idea of this pantomime may be, hackneyed though the tableaux may seem, it is in its execution most pleasing and effective. One cannot imagine anything more fresh, it is a bouquet of flowers, a thought of Anacreon such as Boucher might have given it expression on canvas.
>
> The role of Galathea was supremely rendered by Mlle Guimard; it would be impossible to seize with greater finesse the various gradations of the same caprice, it would be impossible to marry its various shades with greater artistry or more grace.

Le Picq, as the shepherd, left nothing to be desired. A charming face, the slenderest of waists, the easiest and lightest of movements, the purest and most vivacious and yet most natural style, such are the qualities which mark the talent of this new mime. . . . If he has not all the nobility, all the expression of Vestris, all the strength and balance of Gardel, he has perhaps in his execution something softer and yet more brilliant. His grace and lightness triumph above all in demi-caractère dancing and that is the genre of the new ballet. . . .

Baron von Grimm made us know about Noverre's work and the dancers of his time more than anyone else. What a pity that Grimm did not live and write for the papers and periodicals during the heyday of the Romantic ballet! Dance criticism and the ballet might have profited from it.

Noverre's *Letters* were also, of course, criticism of the status of ballet at the end of the 1750s. It was the criticism of a creative dance mind setting forth principles of imaginative awareness, but it was criticism of a very special kind, that of a visionary teacher who sensed the spirit of his time and desired to see it expressed through the dance. An expert dancer and choreographer spoke to the world about the problems of his craft; in fact, he was addressing an imaginary class of his, attended by his colleagues, most of them not kindly disposed toward him. His writings on the dance were therefore an achievement very much apart, having their own private niche in ballet history.

Dance criticism, in the true sense of the word, begins with the Romantic ballet, which coincides with the commercial development of the press and the first flowering of journalism. The man who symbolizes the beginning of dance criticism is Théophile Gautier.

Between Two Revolutions

. . . To be just, that is, to justify its existence, criticism should be partial, passionate, and political, that is to say, written from an exclusive point of view that opens up the widest horizons. . . .

CHARLES BAUDELAIRE CLEARLY CIRCUMSCRIBED THE SCOPE OF THÉOPHILE Gautier's approach to criticism with these words. As Gautier is considered the first dance critic, then the first modern art critic was his contemporary Baudelaire (1821–67), whose aesthetic principles were rooted in the tremendous storehouse of the artist's imagination and in his concept of beauty. Realism was anathema to Baudelaire and a denial of the creative imagination. He had only contempt for the current naturalistic trends—mainly the landscape painters, Courbet and those of the Barbizon school. In "L'Art philosophique," an essay Baudelaire never finished, he tried to explain pure art: "It is to create a suggestive magic containing at one and the same time the object and the subject, the external world and the artist himself." The key words in this definition are "suggestive magic," in which Gautier believed as well.

One could claim that Baudelaire transcended Romanticism. If he stood above it, he certainly took its accoutrements with him. Romanticism, of course, is difficult to define, because it "is precisely situated neither in choice of subjects nor in exact truth, but in a mode of feeling," as Baudelaire said, in the same essay. "For me, Romanticism is the most recent, the latest expression of the beautiful. To say the word Romanticism is to say modern art —that is, intimacy, spirituality, color, aspiration towards the infinite, expressed by every means available to the arts."

A spiritual kinship existed between Baudelaire and Gautier. In writing about *L'Art romantique,* Baudelaire devoted a chapter to him. In 1861—after three decades of Gautier's literary activities—Baudelaire was able to envision much of his work and its underlying concepts. He recognized the poetry inherent in whatever Gautier wrote and, though he himself did not belong to the *l'art pour l'art* school of which Gautier was the most articulate exponent, he said by virtue of his own poetic insight that "poetry, however little one descends into oneself, interrogates one's soul, recalls one's memories of enthusiasm, has no object but itself." Baudelaire's concept of the poetic coincided with Gautier's in its essentials. Poetry has nothing in common with morality or truth, and its only object is being itself and being as unique as possible, reflecting the diamonds and flowers of the poet's dream. The poetic temper will brook no intrusion of verisimilitude. Its first and last principle is the human aspiration toward a superior beauty re-created with an enthusiasm that can transport the soul.

Baudelaire was not interested in ballet per se, but as an art critic writing in similes of visual power and being immersed in the process of creation he recognized the classical ballet as a foremost example of an art emerging from hard work and physical effort. He was all the more impressed by the final product of grace and lightness as total denial of the perspiration that went into it. This made him see in the dance poetry come alive, "composed with arms and legs," with the ideal and sensual being equally potent for him. From this perspective one can evaluate Baudelaire's admiration for Gautier: "Théophile Gautier is the writer par excellence because he is the slave of his duty, because he constantly obeys the necessities of his function, because a feeling for beauty is his destiny, because he has turned his duty into obsession."

This statement sketches with four bold strokes the way Gautier functioned. Only a kindred soul could perceive it so vividly. Even one of Gautier's most vociferous contemporary critics, M. Cuvillier-Fleury, finding fault with many aspects of his work, had to admit some positive features, though with tongue in cheek:

> One must do justice to M. Théophile Gautier: He never seeks originality. . . . He has Romanticism in his blood. . . . He was born a keen, first-rate jumper, a daredevil rather than an inventor, a painter before being a writer, a lover of form, impassioned by color, grasping no other expression of thought than the one hitting his eyes, no other interpretation of ideals but through the picturesque. . . . Find fault with him, and he will save himself through a singular turn, through his inoffensive originality and the amusing exaggerations of his mercurialities.

This biting laudation conveys some of Gautier's weaknesses, but more of his fortes. No doubt he made mistakes, but through his mistakes, his likes and dislikes, pursued with passion, he influenced the course of ballet. To express preference is, however, the prerogative of the critic. Gautier's counterpart in the field of the visual arts exerted little, if any, influence on the current art scene. The significance of Baudelaire's critical writings was recognized only later, and this in spite of the fact that he also blundered sometimes in his evaluations. Baudelaire's blind belief in Delacroix's genius and his rejection of Ingres, Courbet, and Millet made him also overlook the greatness of Manet and the dawn of Impressionism. However, Baudelaire's importance lies in having established aesthetic principles, the art of modern art criticism, as much as Gautier's bulk of critical writings made him the father of modern dance criticism.

BEFORE Gautier entered the scene, Romanticism was waiting in the wings, ready to rush forward into the limelight of events. The painters and poets preceded the dancers. By 1832, when *La Sylphide* intoxicated the hero James and the balletomanes, the spiritual preparations for a romantic euphoria were made. Of the painters, Eugène Delacroix (1798–1863) and Joseph Mallord William Turner (1775–1851) were setting the mood, though with different colors and accents. Delacroix triumphed with virtuoso excesses of line and color, with powerful Byronic themes, while Turner excelled with dream-lost touches in space lit up by a most sensitive color scheme.

Delacroix startled the art world when he exhibited "Dante and Vergil in Hell" in 1822. The subject he chose was romantic, but his Romanticism was checked by the eyes of a cool observer and seemed closest to that of Stendhal, who, in Julien Sorel, created the first modern hero of fiction in an analytic fashion. As with Stendhal and many Romantic artists, Delacroix's dualistic quality was best perceived by Baudelaire, who likened him to "the crater of a volcano artistically concealed by bouquets of flowers." Apollinaire echoed this statement, broadening it when he said that Delacroix "was passionately in love with passion and coldly determined to search for means to express passion in the most visible terms." And Delacroix, who proved himself to be very articulate in his *Journal,* which comes close to Leonardo's *Notebooks* in profundity, revealed his dualism: "The foremost merit of a painting is to be a feast for the eye." As if his cerebral alter ego had immediately to strain itself, he added, "That is not to say that reason should not find its place in it." The idea of creating a feast for the eye was first on his

"Four Studies of Arabs" by Eugène Delacroix, who was one of the first painters to have been attracted by the faraway and oriental. His journey to Morocco ended, however, in some disappointment. (Courtesy The Art Institute of Chicago. Gift of Mrs. Francis H. Hardy in memory of her husband)

mind, and this was exactly what Gautier desired to see on the balletic stage. This painter who loathed bourgeois complacency (as much as Gautier did), and the reliance on materialism and the so-called progress of his contemporaries, would never have denied the power of passion as one of the major forces in the creative process. But he was not willing to credit great passions as the source of genius. Since there are no rules for great souls, Delacroix thought that the source of genius is "imagination only . . . or better still, what amounts to the same thing, that delicacy of the organs which makes one see what others do not see, and which makes one see in a different way."

Though he questioned being a Romantic, he was a child of his time, not only because of the delirious and drunken intensity with which he experienced life and colors, past and present, but also because he was conscious of his heritage—Dante and Shakespeare, Michelangelo and Rubens, appear and reappear in his *Journal* as living mementos. At the same time, however, he could not help escaping Europe and its civilization, whose doom he felt as acutely as Gauguin did some time later. In spite of his closeness to the past masters, he bypassed Italy—which, since Winckelmann, was the Lourdes of sick artistic souls—and traveled via Spain and Algeria to Morocco. He sought dignity, nobility, and timelessness there. But he did not find what he was looking for. The crudities of reality shook up many of those romantic escapists. What those wearisome journeys mostly produced was—besides renunciation and disillusionment—a renewed insight into oneself. Delacroix gained a new intensified sense of color and went so far as to say that "painting has not always need of subjects." Thus he envisioned, beyond the Impressionist experiments, the era of nonobjective art.

Delacroix, however, never attempted what Turner accomplished, which was typically Romantic and yet characteristic of our own time. Solid objects are, in general, here to be captured on canvas, from an apple to trees, from a landscape to the human form. Turner recorded what he perceived, yet while he recorded, the colors transformed the solidity of the objects he painted. Movement and fluidity are his characteristic achievements. It seems as if his cloud formations could make themselves independent from the sky. This translucent flow—which we also see in his flames and waves and certainly in the mist hovering over the mountains—is reminiscent of the gauzy and diaphanous tutus of the ballerinas soaring through the air. Turner reified a longing for the pictorial realization of a radiant, iridescent dream, for lightness of movement, for freedom from any material object. Phenomena like rain and smoke, steam and speed, until then beyond the painter's brush, found their way onto Turner's canvases. Dusk over Venice became not only the reality of Venice in the late evening hours, but its poeticized reality. As in ballet, there is no longer the question of verisimilitude, but the poetry of truth, the dream reality.

One could, of course, easily claim that the sky and with it the clouds were, so to speak, essential features of Romanticism. The moon also began to play a great part in the mentality of the nineteenth century. The critic John Ruskin (1819–1900) equated good art with natural truth, believing in Nature (always capitalized) as being subject to Moral Law. It was the time—starting in the early days of the century—in which the nature worshipers focused their interest on the sky and hitched their dreams onto the clouds. Kenneth Clark tells us in his *Civilisation* that "in 1802 a Quaker named Luke Howard read a paper on the 'Modification of Clouds,' which tried to do for the sky what Linnaeus had done for plants." John Constable, who exerted great influence on the landscape painters of the Romantic Age, did innumerable cloud studies, and, Clark says, Ruskin admitted that he "bottled clouds as carefully as his father [a wine merchant] had bottled sherries." Clouds are wonderful metaphors, and skyscapes may evoke sensuous feelings, but also feelings of the ephemeral or eternal flight from reality. Clouds and Turner's skill of capturing the mystery in cloud formations are part and parcel of the romantic image. It corresponds beautifully with the atmosphere of *The Ballet of the Nuns* in *Robert le Diable*, finding its climax in the spiritualized character of the Wilis act of *Giselle*. In his imaginative use of light and pure color, Turner reflected the aspirations of the Romantic ballet while anticipating French Impressionism in at least equal measure as Delacroix.

In the first three decades of the nineteenth century, Romanticism moved to the fore on a broad front. All the arts became involved. Yet the battle decisive for its general recognition was fought on February 25, 1830, five months before the July Revolution, at the Théâtre Français over Victor Hugo's play *Hernani*. Although the battle was won by Hugo's followers at the opening night, skirmishes continued with the rear guard of the classicists. Out of convenience we consider this day the beginning of modern drama, though Lessing had already propounded the same ideals in his *Hamburgische Dramaturgie* about sixty years previously, and Hugo himself in 1827 wrote a preface to his play *Cromwell* that must be taken as a major document, the Romantic Manifesto. When it was published Gautier exclaimed in the most characteristic exaggeration of Romanticism that "it shines before our eyes like the Ten Commandments with which Moses came down from Mount Sinai."

In this preface, Victor Hugo celebrated Romanticism as the liberalism of literature. A new era began, which Delacroix defined succinctly when he said: "He who speaks of Romanticism, speaks of modern art." The strongest towers of tradition may finally have been destroyed during that battle. But all revolutions—won or lost—have lasting repercussions. Malraux pointed out that "in the nineteenth century, for the first time, the artists and the ruling class ceased to have the same values." With Romanticism victorious in

Joseph Turner, Romantic master at evoking a spiritual atmosphere in his landscapes and cloud formations: "Study of Sea and Sky." (Courtesy the trustees of the Tate Gallery, London)

1830, a continuous warfare between creative minds and an ever more consuming society ensued. The victory over *Hernani* coincided with impressive advances of the Industrial Revolution and progress in the sciences. Romanticism was one of the immediate consequences. The relationship between the artist and the ruling class was compelled to become more and more tenuous, leading, by stages, to the artist's alienation and isolation from society and from himself. The *l'art pour l'art* movement to which Romanticism immediately gave birth was only the first of many phases of isolation in which the artist created a select minority.

Hugo wrote in his preface to *Cromwell:* "Let us throw down the old plastering that conceals the façade of art. There are neither rules nor models; or, rather, there are no rules other than the general laws of nature." Already Lessing had escaped the straitjacket of the classical unities to destroy the domination of French culture in Germany. Hugo repeated Lessing's actions in his home country, against a different background. Liberalism meant to him nature never submitting to a rationalist or classical order. Romanticism meant freedom from tradition. Art must be free from all formalism, to stir us with strangeness and wonder, with the paradoxical and grotesque in nature. This world of contrasts was best perceived by the medieval civilization, Hugo believed, and it expressed the mixed character of reality. All art must be open to all phases of reality, that is, to truth. "It will realize," he wrote, that

> everything in creation is not human and beautiful, that the ugly exists beside the beautiful . . . the grotesque on the reverse of the sublime . . . it will set about doing as nature does, mingling in its creation . . . the body and the soul, the beast and the intellect; for the starting point of religion is always the starting point of poetry. All things are connected.

Existence is full of contrasts, full of the lovely and the hateful on each side of the very same coin, and so are appearance and reality, which both played a major part in the Romantic ballet.

Auguste Rodin: "Victor Hugo." Rodin caught the spirit of Hugo proclaiming the message of Romanticism. (Courtesy French Cultural Services)

GAUTIER began as an art student; a chance meeting with Victor Hugo, who was quite an accomplished draftsman and painter, was decisive for him. Hugo persuaded him to take up writing. While Hugo left a museumful of drawings and paintings, there is little left of Gautier's artwork. It seems that his visual instinct and sensibility were much stronger than his technical ability to translate his visions onto a canvas. But he never stopped seeing with the eyes of a painter: "If ever I had the honor of being Director of the Opéra, I should have the ballets composed by painters." How much visual impressions meant to him can be deduced from the fact that, whatever senses were addressed, in him the stimuli were caught by or translated into visual reactions. So he remarked in one of his feuilletons in *La Presse* in 1843, about the impact of hashish, "My sense of hearing became particularly strong. I could hear the sound of colors. The green, red, blue, yellow reached me perfectly clear as if coming to me on waves."

Gautier, the frustrated human being! Everything in him was keyed to painting, but destiny turned him into a writer. He soon trumpeted to the world that he "was struggling for the ideal of poetry and for the liberty of art." But the issue of his first volume of poems was eclipsed by the turbulent events of 1830. The public of the successful July Monarchy was money-minded and superficial in its taste. It was interested only in newsy events and the name writers about whom people talked because they could read their feuilletons in the papers. Pecuniary needs drove Gautier into the arms of journalism. Now people could read and quote him, but, alas, as a critic and not as a poet. He was filled "with a sentiment of defeat and powerless hate." This young man who hailed the liberalism of the arts and limitless freedom of expression heaped scorn on those who had unleashed the revolution. The feelings and attitudes of this rebel soon acquired a veneer of conservatism. On the other hand, how he loathed the soulless and lifeless life of the bourgeoisie, whom he called "fluid nonentities," as we can read in the *Journal* of the brothers Goncourt.

Although Gautier was of middle-class background, he hated the bourgeoisie with articulate fury. Flaubert and Delacroix disliked not only the bourgeoisie, but also bohemianism and Romanticism; yet they remained associated with both in the eyes of their contemporaries. They felt that Romanticism had an early-nineteenth-century stigma and was something one had to outgrow. They were allergic to the excesses of this movement as displayed by the bohemian attitudes of a Gautier, whose belligerent anticonventionalism was a struggle from below and had something plebeian about it. The confusion was great since, for the first time in history, writers of aristocratic background were mingling with those of the middle class in the general campaign for romantic ideals and against bourgeois complacency.

How must Gautier the reviewer have felt as the slave of a bourgeois public whose growing hunger for information forced him to turn out column after column, which became a badly needed activity for his livelihood. All his life he loathed being known as a critic and not as a poet. On some occasions he lost his temper and protested the stupidity and tyranny of the people for whose pleasure he was engaged to write. One such occasion was his column on Berlioz, who, like Gautier, was forced to become a journalist. In this feuilleton Gautier deplored the waste of talent forced upon an artist compelled to serve an unenlightened public that must be told what it sees and hears. However, as he was often under attack as a critic, he could not help defending journalism and his role as a reviewer in public. Thus he wrote that journalism also has its positive aspects; it makes one mingle with the crowd, it humanizes one, it lets one constantly realize one's own measure and keeps one from being infected with the disease of solitary pride.

Despite so much disgust for his own activities, so much contempt for the readers of his thoughts, he managed to deliver himself fairly, if not extremely, well. And yet all his life he was a frustrated man, suffering severely from the discrepancies between his own aspirations and the yoke of daily realities. He dreamed of having been born to do nothing but creative work, to prove himself the great poet he felt he was. Considering the incredible amount of words he had to write week in, week out, based on what he read and viewed, this Sisyphean work as a reporter in the daily journals did not, he claimed, permit him to prove his mettle.

This may of course have been a blessing in disguise. Since he thought of himself primarily as a poet, we propose that a man's being and becoming may be determined by sensibilities finely attuned to beauty and sentiment, to dream and vision, without necessarily making him write poetry. Gautier wrote poems most of his life, but his poetry did not stand the test of time. As a poet he does not rank with Hugo, Lamartine, Musset, and some other contemporary poets. Rightly or wrongly, he blamed his journalistic work for his not having been able to live up to his destiny. Yet sometimes destiny knows why it must play foul. It may do so in kindness to its victims.

Gautier may have scorned and challenged the bourgeoisie from time to time. This was a gesture one expected from a true Romantic. But he himself lived according to bourgeois rules: he cared for his two sisters, for his children, his son Théophile, the result of a long relationship with Eugénie Fort, and his two daughters, whom he had together with his wife, Ernesta Grisi. She was the sister of the dancer Carlotta Grisi, the one woman he really loved and whose name was on his lips when he died. Could there be any more final frustration in life than to be happily married to the sister of one's great love? *Le bon Théo* was his nickname. He was truly liked and admired by his friends for his kindness and wit, for his readiness to help—he did not have the strength to say no—and occasionally to write a glowing review for someone who badly needed it.

We may read Edmond Goncourt's impressions and thoughts of Gautier's funeral: "The cemetery is full of obscure admirers, of little-known colleagues, hack writers of the boulevard press, who all bring back the memory of the journalist, not of the poet and not of the author of *Mademoiselle de Maupin.*"

WHEN Gautier started to write reviews he shared a studio in the rue de Doyonné with Gérard de Nerval, whom he had befriended while studying at the Collège Charlemagne in Paris. Nerval was a tragic figure but a brilliant, though capricious, writer. He was Romanticism incarnate, with a dissolute genius, and he had a tragic love affair with an actress who died two years later, haunting his life and novels as the fugitive image of the Eternal Feminine. Early in the year 1855 he hanged himself on a lamppost in the rue de la Vieille-Lanterne in Paris.

In the years that Nerval referred to as his *bohème galante,* years of gallant unconventionality, his and Gautier's studio became the meeting place of the *l'art pour l'artistes* and the center of bohemianism. Yet life was then not all idleness and discussion of the arts. Nerval would stimulate and prompt Gautier to write columns. Nerval founded and sponsored the periodical *Le Monde dramatique* in 1835, giving Gautier a chance to write his first four columns. The magazine, however, was a short-lived venture. Nerval lost most of his money on it, but continued to work with Gautier on other essays and reviews. Then Gautier was engaged as a reviewer by *Le Figaro* in 1836, for two years; he was also appointed by editor Émile de Girardin as a weekly contributor to *La Presse* in 1837. Through May 1838 some of his contributions carried the byline *GG,* initials referring to Gautier and Gérard de Nerval. Even the most often quoted comparison between Marie Taglioni and Fanny Elssler still carried the signature *GG* in *La Presse,* but those knowing Gautier's spiritual handwriting have no doubt that this imagery and verbal sweep are his alone:

> The dancing of Fanny Elssler could not be further removed from the academic conceptions; it has a character all its own which sets her apart from other ballerinas. Hers is not the aerial, virginal grace of Taglioni, it is something much more human which appeals more sharply to the senses. Mlle Taglioni is a Christian dancer, if one can use such an expression about an art which is proscribed by Catholicism. She floats like a spirit in the midst of a transparent mist of white muslin with which she loves to surround herself, she resembles a happy spirit who scarcely bends the petals of celestial flowers with the tips of her pink feet. Fanny Elssler is a completely pagan dancer. She reminds one of the muse Terpsichore with her tambourine and her dress slit to reveal her thigh and caught up with clasps of gold. When she fearlessly bends back,

throwing her voluptuous arms behind her, one has a vision—one of those beautiful figures from Herculaneum or Pompeii that stand out in white relief against a black background, accompanying their dance with resounding cymbals. . . . Undoubtedly spiritualism is something to be respected, but in the dance some concessions can well be made to materialism. Dancing after all has no other object than to show beautiful bodies in graceful poses and develop lines which are pleasing to the eye. It is silent rhythm, music to be seen. Dancing is ill suited to expressing metaphysical ideas; it expresses only the passions—love, desire with all its coquetries, the aggressive male and the gently resisting woman. . . .

This critique is often quoted—and here at great length—because, in a nutshell, it pinpoints Gautier's aesthetic beliefs. It also reveals the schizophrenic trend of those Romanticists for whom esoteric revelation was their daily bread, which they buttered with down-to-earth experiences, blending sensuous suffering with sensual enjoyment. Gautier desired to lose himself in a beauty alarming all his senses to the point of being able to touch and to smell what his eyes saw. A beauty that does not serve any other purpose than being beautiful is true beauty, he felt. Baudelaire also maintained that all forms of beauty contain an element of the eternal and an element of the transitory—of the absolute and of the particular. Yet absolute and eternal beauty is nonexistent or is, rather, an abstraction of different beauties. "The particular element in each manifestation comes from the emotions: and just as we have our own particular emotions, so we have our own beauty," Baudelaire wrote.

Nothing could be more subjective than beauty for Baudelaire as well as for Gautier, who vociferously denied the existence of a generally valid beauty. The notion of beauty runs like a labyrinthian thread through Gautier's work, which reverberates with euphoric desçriptions of it. As his witness he called Plato, "whose definition must suffice. The beautiful is the splendor of truth." He wanted to believe with the ancient Greeks that the perfect shape of the human body was the paradigm for anything beautiful. To prove the purity of his sensuous excitement, he was ready to concede that the classical hermaphrodite would be closest to his ideal, "an unsexual beauty that is beauty itself."

When, time and again, his similes go back to antiquity it is because he strongly believed that art had not advanced a single step since the ancient Greeks revealed its beauty. If Romanticism in the first half of the nineteenth century may be seen as a reaction to industrial progress, then Gautier's anachronistic attitude, his constant recollection and evocation of antiquity, indicates a desperate attempt to deny the existence of any sociocultural roots of the arts. Of course, one could claim that his way of seeing the arts and the ideal of beauty is that of a frustrated painter and sculptor. Yet there was a general trend and dualistic quality in art criticism at that time, juxtaposing and vacillating between "soul" and "body."

Dichotomizing between Taglioni, the Christian dancer, and Elssler, the pagan dancer, was part of this vacillating tendency. Also, calling Taglioni a Christian dancer was paying her a left-handed compliment. First of all, Gautier was compulsive about ugliness, which he considered an insult to his eye. Physical beauty was "the first condition required in a dancer . . . she has no excuse for not being beautiful, and she can be blamed for her plainness as an actress can be blamed for her bad pronunciation." Taglioni was known for having a rather ugly face, which Gautier was valiantly overlooking. Second, when using the image of a Christian dancer he was well aware of his belief that Christianity was to be blamed for the degradation of the human body—"a prison has been made of what was once a palace," he wrote in *Souvenirs du Théâtre.†* If Gautier referred to Taglioni as the Christian dancer, he also had in front of his eyes a dancer covered, more or less, from her shoulders to her toes.

Gautier was always conscious of the desirability of mystery plus flesh, the esoteric and the realistic. When he saw Carlotta Grisi he was immediately struck by her beauty, which unified and reconciled mystery and flesh. Professional enthusiasm and personal feelings for Carlotta Grisi inspired him to create a ballet for her: *Giselle.* Toward the end of the 1830s Gautier felt there was too much ethereal flight, too much whiteness on stage, too many *ballet blancs,* as he termed the deluge of Taglioni imitations patterned on *La Sylphide.* He tried to create a composite of the images of Taglioni and Elssler. The sylph—the image of Taglioni—was only a creature in the hero's mind, a dreamlike phantom. Why not juxtapose to it a real creature—the image of Elssler—that through dramatic events would become the unreal creature, the romantic idol? And thus *Giselle,* with its realistic first act and *Sylphide*-like second act, emerged from Gautier's maxims: flesh and flight from reality, the sensuousness of passion and the poetic dream of love.

With the prevailing interest in everything exotic, the next ballet scenario Gautier wrote for Grisi was *La Péri.* It was a logical step from Heinrich Heine's Wilis in the Harz Mountains to the peris and the atmosphere of the *Arabian Nights.* In Persian mythology the peris are fallen angels that assume the shape of elfin sprites. Novalis' romantic dream of the blue flower turns into the flower of immortality—again a symbol of the unattainable—the lotus for which Iskender searches and finally finds in the hands of a sleeping peri. He takes the flower from her, but becomes so enchanted by her that he is ready to bring down the heavens for a kiss. Whereupon a touch of *La Sylphide* is added to the story, as if proof were necessary that romantic

† In our time Ruth St. Denis took off from where Gautier stopped, blaming St. Paul's dichotomy of man in a befouled body with a blessed soul for all evil, while advocating and rekindling the concept of the sacred dance.

dreams are the same in all zones and across all times. The peri dances and Iskender returns the flower.

> Then the lotus seemed like snow and gold . . . in the evening sun. The form of the peri appeared to melt into the light. . . . Iskender saw her disappear. And realizing that this signified his approaching end, he felt the shadow encircling him.

Gautier gave the story a more dramatic and far more complex plot. In his version La Péri enters the dead body of the slave Leila, who has been shot as a fugitive from the harem. But essentially, as in *Giselle,* the synthesis of dream and reality is kept alive with metaphysic subtlety, and everything ends with the triumph of spirit over matter. The effectiveness onstage of oriental dream and exotic reality proved one of Gautier's concepts: "The more fabulous the action . . . the less will probability be offended. Legends, fairy stories, hashish- and opium-inspired dreams, all the fantasy beyond the realms of possibility are the true sphere of ballet."

However, the complex stage action of his version is all the more surprising since the simple story line of the original contains all the possibilities of what a ballet should offer, according to his maxims: a succession of artistic poses, expressions of beauty and of passion in plastic terms, pleasing and graceful. In fact, Gautier totally disapproved of any ballet d'action and wrote in a review about Mazilier's ballet *La Fonti* in *La Presse,* January 16, 1855, that this ballet belongs to the genre called ballet d'action and thus stands outside the conditions to which true dancing should be subjected. "Each art form," he thought, "corresponds with certain classifications of subjects which it can best present: sculpture expresses form; painting form and color; poetry form, color, sound and thought; music volume, tone, a feeling that never ends and remains uncertain, the notion of what is not and the memory of what has never been; the dance expresses everything plastic and the rhythm of movement and—why not say it?—physical voluptuousness and feminine beauty."

Gautier helped establish the prominent position of the ballerina. He went to such exaggerated statements as to refer to a male dancer as something inconceivable, in fact, freakish and indecent. He granted him at best the grace of strength, a contradiction in itself. This one-sided viewpoint made the male dancer suffer relegation to the degrading role of a premier porteur and was to have serious consequences. He had eyes only for the beauty and bravura of the ballerina and neglected to see in the corps de ballet the source of future ballerinas.

Gautier never found fault with the mediocre music that so often served as background. He was not particularly attuned to music, and his appreciation of it was limited. He nevertheless could not help reviewing operas, his critiques having little value for the history of musical criticism. Long after his death, in 1890, his daughter Judith wrote in the leading newspaper *Le Temps* about her father and his difficulties in this part of his critical work. She said, "He wrote with surprising competence about subjects with which he was little familiar. . . ." This is at best a tribute to his journalistic skills but plainly concedes his musical inaptitude.

He also had no critical eye for the decors, which are hardly ever discussed in his reviews, even though he started out as a painter. Yet he would describe the costumes of the ballerinas meticulously. This concerned him; the costume was closest to the skin and could be seen as responsible for the beauty of the body line.

Despite all this, Gautier was not primarily a dance critic. His dramatic criticism was published in 1858–59 in six heavy volumes under the title of *History of the Dramatic Art in France During the Last Twenty-five Years;* and these were preceded by another collection of art criticism. He was, more accurately, a feuilletonist who jotted down thoughts and impressions, vignettes of life, literary evaluations, and critical reactions. Apart from these journalistic trifles, written in haste, there is some outstanding criticism of literary significance. To say that Gautier was a diligent writer is a gross understatement. He worked on a critical assembly line in order to make both ends meet.

It is obvious that under these circumstances he could not be selective about what to cover. The arts and literature filled quite a few of his columns, but the theater was a playground for his feuilletons: he wrote on drama, comedy, opera, fairy plays, circus, pantomime, burlesque, and ballet. It took him two years of writing these critiques before he turned to ballet. By then he was an established writer and respected leader in the Romantic movement. But when he began to write on dance he had little technical knowledge. In the beginning he did not understand the need for the turned-out feet, which he referred to as "one of the most abominable positions ever invented by the pedantry of the past," and made fun of basic positions and figures. At first he undoubtedly approached the ballet from a literary viewpoint, with predetermined aesthetic tenets. But he soon realized that the ballet was the one art form coming closest to his artistic ideals. He rather quickly grew on ballet while it grew on him.

Perhaps Gautier could not help loving the ballet because, irrational art form that it is, the theater dance fulfilled his expectations: it can never re-create life. At best it is an image of life projected onto the stage by the power of our imagination and by the vision of our dreams. In *Le Moniteur universel* (November 21, 1859) Gautier made it quite clear that if art succeeds in reproducing reality the way it is, art disappears.

By contrast, Balzac's novels were then best sellers. They portrayed characters in the midst of societal conflict. Balzac, like Dickens, realized that "the individual exists only in relation to society," and both writers dared to penetrate the social surface, depicting the discrepancies and cruelties of existence.

Gautier was part of this complicated social web, although, as the leading Romantic escapist, he was far removed from it. In a symbolic way, the ballet was an aesthetic refuge to him.

As one reads Gautier's critical annotations during the heydays of Romanticism as much as through the declining days, Oscar Wilde's saying comes to mind that the highest, as well as the lowest, form of criticism is a mode of autobiography. In Gautier's case it goes beyond it, becoming a biography of its time. There was something of Hamlet in Gautier, who, in explaining Romanticism to the world to come, could say in the mood of Hamlet's "What a piece of work is a man!" speech: "It was a movement akin to the Renaissance. A sap of new life circulated impetuously. Everything sprouted, blossomed, burst out all at once. The air was intoxicating. We were mad with lyricism and art."

Between 1848 and 1872 Gautier began to think there was something foul in the state of Romanticism. Had he not been preoccupied with his own frustrated life and had he not died with the name of the unattainable woman on his lips, his last words might have been an afterthought to his eulogy of Romanticism. Hamlet ended his glorification of man in the Renaissance with the resigned sigh: "And yet, to me, what is this quintessence of dust?" Gautier ought to have realized that history might blame him for having neglected to see that even the ideal of beauty for the mere sake of being beautiful is doomed to pale, and that the most enchanting flesh must still go the way of all flesh.

And yet, to us, what glory was this quintessence of Romanticism!

So Ended the Romantic Dream

BALLET, THE APOTHEOSIS OF ROMANTICISM, REIGNED SUPREME FROM 1832 to 1843, the period in which Gautier exerted his greatest influence. But the political and artistic climate changed drastically after 1848. The general liberal views turned more and more toward the right. Most people were becoming weary of experiments and new approaches, and the intellectual climate began to harden to pronounced contrasting positions.

On the surface it was an era of wealth and material progress, with the gold rush in California luring many Europeans into adventure. Tunnels and bridges were being built; miles of railroad tracks covered the lands like spider webs. In the 1860s Walt Whitman wrote in *The Shapes Arise* of "shapes of factories, arsenals, foundries, markets . . . two-threaded tracks of railroads . . . sleepers of bridges, vast frameworks, girders, arches." Depending on one's personal lot, one might have thought one was living in a glorious age of gaiety or a corrupt and sordid one. The contrasts of life were everywhere. It was as if history wanted to prepare a foretaste of the Gay Nineties.

Under the dazzling reign of Napoleon III, who kept himself upon his precarious throne with the help of the police and censor, Paris became an international luxury and pleasure mart. The French fashion designers rose to prominence. The age-old hoop skirt came back under the new name of crinoline. The new sewing machine, patented by the American inventor Isaac Merrit Singer in 1851, brought forth an orgy of puffing and pleating, of braiding and tucking, a fashion that corresponded to the mentality of the time.

The populace was sporadically caught by a compulsive need to give its life stronger accents of gaiety. Ballroom dancing was then in full swing. About 1815 the quadrille had assumed the form popular since. The dignified ceremonial polonaise was never quite forgotten, but throughout the century the waltz dominated social dancing. Its only rival was the polka, which emerged from Bohemia in the early 1830s, followed by the mazurka from Poland. A best-selling book in those years was *La Polka Enseigneé sans Maître* (*Polka Taught Without a Teacher*) by J. J. Perrot and Adrien Robert, offering this introductory advice: "To dance the polka men and women must have hearts that beat high and strong. Tell me how you do the polka, and I will tell you how you love." The polka usually ended with a fast galop, which Offenbach immortalized with his operetta *Orpheus in the Underworld,* and which became the standard musical fare of the bands in all European spas.

Social dancing was not limited to festivities and ballrooms; it was practiced in all bourgeois homes. This was made possible by the popularization of the piano, which became the favorite instrument of the nineteenth century. It was a status symbol to have a piano in one's home. Franz Liszt and Frédéric Chopin made serious piano music known everywhere. The piano was the ideal accompaniment for the German *Lied,* which flourished during the century with Schubert and Schumann, Brahms, Hugo Wolf, and Richard Strauss. It has often been claimed that the nineteenth century was the century of music, just as we could name it the age of painting or of the Romantic ballet. It certainly brought forth many musical giants in the symphonic and operatic field, composers most characteristic of the era such as Mendelssohn and Tchaikovsky, Verdi and Wagner.

Paris was still the cultural center of Europe, with the greatest interest no longer focused on the theater but on the artists' studios and exhibitions. During and after the 1860s the visual arts, with Impressionism and post-Impressionism, eclipsed everything else in their singular significance. Many more names than even in the field of music made history, not only creating a

Honoré Daumier caricatured the sociocultural and political life of his time. Here he caught a glimpse of mid-nineteenth-century balletomania in the wings, as he lampooned the ambition and the protective eye of the "ballet mother." (From Le Charivari, January 24, 1857)

new world of colors and imagery but also reorienting our visual perceptions: Whistler and Daumier, Millet and Courbet, Manet, Monet, Seurat, Renoir, Degas, Cézanne, and Rodin.

When Gustave Courbet, an avowed realist and opponent of vested authority on the aesthetic as well as the political level, exhibited his "Burial at Ornans" in 1850, a staunch defender of the new trends, Jules Champfleury, wrote: "From now on the critics must decide for or against realism." And the fight was on. In the latter part of the century scandals and lawsuits became the rule in an atmosphere in which mediocrity and censorship triumphed. But some of the scandals and lawsuits helped establish the new movements. The brothers Goncourt were cited as offenders against morality. So was Flaubert for certain passages in *Madame Bovary* in 1857; in the same year a court condemned as obscene six poems of Baudelaire's *Fleurs du mal*. Two years later, Gautier still rejected any attempt at artistic expression through realistic or naturalistic means. Nevertheless, as time passed he had to modify his *l'art pour l'art* concept. However, these modifications were minor, forced upon him by the changing style of life.

Gautier, opposing this new world of artistic expression, remained the spokesman for most of his contemporaries. They may have been frightened by the Romantic excesses of the beginning of the movement, but after 1848 Romanticism was fully absorbed and accepted by them. The general public loved the noncontroversial ballet and operetta. Gautier had no ideological or aesthetic difficulties in reviewing them. He had a far more troublesome time with plays, especially in the days when censorship was strict.

In 1867 the brothers Goncourt recounted an event characteristic of those days but even more so of Gautier. He was telling them of his encounter with Count Walewski, then Foreign Minister of Napoleon III:

> . . . someone asked Gautier why he did not write the things he had just said. "Let me tell you a little story," Gautier replied with perfect self-possession. "One day, Monsieur Walewski told me that I was to stop being indulgent to writers, I had his authority to write exactly what I thought of all the plays produced. "But," said I, "it is So-and-so's play that is opening this week." "Indeed?" said he. "In that case, suppose you begin the week following." Well, I am still waiting for the week following.

Gautier knew how to keep himself out of trouble at the expense of his conscience as a critic and of his integrity as a man.

Honoré Daumier (1808–79), suffered a similar fate to that of his contemporary Gautier. He, too, had to put his artistic genius to the grindstone from the 1830s into the late '70s. He was a painter and a journalist who exposed the unjust and tragicomic in life. Balzac was one of the first to recognize that this biting lithographer‡ was a genius: in his daily cartoons for *La Caricature* and *Le Charivari*—and even more so in his few paintings, which, in

‡ There is one more important parallel between Daumier and Gautier as the spokesman for the Romantic ballet, which is closely associated with the toe shoe. George Balanchine protested that without the toe shoe he would not have become a choreographer. In its constant development and refinement, the toe shoe was a by-product of the Industrial Revolution. And so was the lithograph, which was to the growth of the press and journalism exactly what the toe shoe was to the ballet. For both it was a triumph of technique helping the one to suggest an escape from reality and the other to visualize reality in its naked truth by blowing it up to a caricature.

concept and brushwork, were far ahead of his time—Daumier revealed a sculptural power often likened to Michelangelo. Daumier did not permit himself the luxury of escaping reality as Gautier had done. Daumier risked imprisonment and was out of work because of censorship from time to time, while Gautier advanced to the position of official critic for *Le Journal officiel* and *Le Moniteur universel*.

As one of the foremost combatants for Romantic principles, Gautier was caught between the era's spiritual persuasions and its social contradictions. Since he could not come to terms with reality, he also could not perceive that naturalism and Impressionism were merely setting scientific accents on the dream of humankind, replacing an escapist spirit with an objective spirit of idealism.

Yet, ironically, Gautier anticipated naturalism long before it came into being when he juxtaposed a scene of the Wilis with a scene of utter realism. Giselle was no longer a dreamlike creature, an unattainable sylph, pure and ephemeral. She was a simple country girl facing human problems: deceived love, the unbridgeable chasm between the aristocrat and the peasant. The moonlight scene that had started this trend in *The Ballet of the Nuns* was there; but so was the tragic fate, set in a bucolic background, of a lovable girl with whom one could identify, something rather inconceivable with a sylphide or the daydreaming, duped James. If one wishes to classify art ad nauseam, then Gautier created the first naturalistic-Romantic ballet with *Giselle*.

IN the last decades of his life Gautier traveled a great deal, hoping that his journeys would yield material for a series of books. A patroness gave him a sinecure as a librarian to make life financially easier for him. He still functioned as a critic, but a noticeable feeling of nostalgia prompted by fatigue, or of fatigue caused by nostalgia, crept into his ballet reviews, as if he were no longer able to believe in its importance as an art.

Taglioni had retired from the stage in 1847; Elssler, four years later. Grisi had left Paris in 1849, still dancing in various opera houses, and in St. Petersburg and London, before finally withdrawing in 1853. Other ballerinas took their places. The aging Gautier—with most of the other critics and the public—could not help comparing these ballerinas, who mainly came from Italy, with his former idols. They were to him, brilliant imitations at best. He could not even help comparing Fanny Cerrito, Emma Livry, Carlotta Vecchi, or the German-born ballerina Adele Grantzow with the shadows of his memory.

Where were the days when he wrote in praise of Elssler's "voluptuous arms" and found that "true voluptuousness is always chaste"? Then, seeing Elssler dance, he broke out in ecstatic exclamations: "How she twists, how she bends! What fire! What voluptuousness!" Almost thirty years lay between enthusiasm and resignation. On March 20, 1868, Gautier reviewed *Le Corsaire,* which Joseph Mazilier had choreographed in 1856. Was the restaging of this ballet so poorly done, or was Gautier so weary that night, that he could write: ". . . these modern ballets are nothing but a sequence of steps, disconnected and without any life to them"?

The public no longer appreciated anything but technical bravura in the dancer. This was something Gautier should not have disliked, but there was an undertone of disappointment in his words, letting us feel his disgust with the state of the ballet and blaming it on the audience. On the occasion of the opening night of *Coppélia,* when Giuseppina Bozacchi danced the role of Swanilda, press and public alike were enchanted.* On May 10, 1870, Gautier wrote in *Le Journal officiel:* "La Bozacchi . . . is a charming girl of sixteen. . . . There is a grand neatness in her *pointes,* and she has a beautiful line, as one says in the choreographic lingo. One must praise her graceful attitudes. . . . She was received with an enthusiasm that one rarely finds nowadays at a ballet performance." This was written two years before he died. His phraseology was threadbare. Gautier no doubt projected his own waning enthusiasm onto the public, whose passion for bravura dancing never waned.

Did Gautier, at the end of his life, recognize cause and effect, the *mene tekel* on the wall as his own handwriting? One could claim that he only articulated what was in the air. But his *l'art pour l'art* concept had driven the theater dance into an aesthetic isolation, a position on exquisite heights where it no longer breathed the same air as the other arts.

Gautier took refuge in the Paris Opéra as a literary man in search of an ideal. On January 1, 1840, he wrote in *La Presse:*

> The Opéra is the only refuge for poetry and fantasy. It is the unique place where the verse is still perceived, the last sanctuary of the gods, sylphides, nymphs, princes and tragic princesses; where uncouth reality is not admitted; it is a little world blazing in its gold and light . . . there is nothing of the actual, nothing of the real; one is in an enchanted world. The word is sung, the steps are pirouettes . . . an evening at the Opéra rests you from real life and consoles you for the number of frightful bourgeois in overcoats you are obliged to see during the day.

Gautier took the ballet with him to the glory of its romantic flight. The ballet gave wings to his feelings and his ecstatic words gave wings to the ballet. That all this one day had to turn into an atrophied gesture was inescapable and recorded in history.

* Her death from a virulent fever on her seventeenth birthday during the German siege of Paris in 1870 was one of the most tragic events in balletic history.

HISTORY gave credit for it to Marius Petipa (1822–1910), but not without a good deal of admiration and gratitude for some great works. Petipa was destined to transplant the triumph of the Romantic ballet from France to Russia and, giving it the touch of his genius, to guide it to its turning point at the dawn of a new era. With the ballet's emphasis shifting from Paris to St. Petersburg and Moscow after mid-century, Gautier could from then on no longer influence its course of development.

At the time that Gautier journeyed through Russia (*Voyage en Russie,* 1866) Petipa had not yet quite established his reputation. He still tried to profit from the experiences of his predecessors Jules Perrot and Arthur Saint-Léon. Four years before Gautier's book on his trip to the East was published, Petipa scored some success with a five-act ballet, *La Fille du Pharaon* (*The Daughter of Pharaoh*), based on a short story by Gautier, "Roman d'une momie" ("The Novel of a Mummy"). This theme was cleverly chosen since the entire Western world was then in a state of excitement about the Egyptian excavations. Gautier capitalized on it, and so did Petipa. (Furthermore, over many decades choreographers repeatedly used themes from Gautier.)

What pleasantly surprised the audiences of *The Daughter of Pharaoh* was the dimension of the crowd scenes and the orderly skill with which the corps de ballet mastered the big stage. This was to become Petipa's forte. But failures followed this initial success, with the exception of a divertissement number, *The Little Moujik,* which appealed to the nationalist feelings of the Russians. The year Gautier published *Voyage en Russie,* Petipa had another failure, called *Florida.* Petipa's international fame came after Gautier's death. Therefore, Gautier never knew how the Romantic ballet changed in the hands of the greatest choreographer of the latter part of the century, how he gave it its classicist face, clipping the romantic exuberance from its wings.

Serving under four czars in the course of almost sixty years, Petipa made Russia the leading country of ballet. He raised the standard of dance technique and choreography with the help of Lev Ivanov, the Swedish dancer Christian Johansson, and the Italian Enrico Cecchetti. His aesthetic concepts were those of a formalist thoroughly grounded in tradition. He strove for order and symmetry, but however conventional his stage effects were, they were theatrically convincing. He perfected the pas de deux, believing in dancing for the sake of dancing and in virtuosity heightened to a spectacle. He could never choreograph satisfactorily for the male dancer, who appeared in his ballets mainly as the cavalier supporting the lady in her adagios. In neglecting the danseur and giving a stellar position to the ballerina, he even outprejudiced Gautier.

Petipa's work, seen in its totality, was flawed by his idolization of the ballerina and his meticulous formalism, his "limited circle of choreographic methods within which he had enclosed himself," as Yuri Slonimsky said. And yet how stupendous is the repertory of the classic-Romantic ballet he left behind! Generations of ballet lovers have enjoyed such works as *The Sleeping Beauty, La Bayadère, Don Quixote, Raymonda,* and *Swan Lake* (the latter together with Lev Ivanov). His work had all the earmarks of the earlier Romantic ballet, with themes in which the exotic is mixed with the weird, in which the escape from reality is depicted through fairy tale and legend. Undoubtedly destiny charged Marius Petipa to summarize the accomplishments of the nineteenth-century theater dance in a few strokes of genius and, at the same time, to bury it in its own greatness.

The Growing Awareness of Movement

TWO INVENTIONS COINCIDED WITH THE BIRTH OF THE ROMANTIC BALLET: lithography and photography. Both have become inextricably connected with the dance. They may have a life of their own, but, time and again, they have served the dance well.

It is an often-heard complaint of contemporary writers on the dance that a picture book on this art is more in demand than any treatise, historic or otherwise, and that the question of illustrations is of paramount importance for any dance book. A historic counterpart can be found in the 1840s. This was the time when the publication of albums on dancers, full of pictures, with the text kept to a few words, became the rage. Gift books on the dance, illuminated like a medieval Book of Hours, were everywhere in demand.

French and British printers asked for a close collaboration between artist and writer. This was the heyday of the vignette. Souvenir programs and albums—as they are published in our day for any major dance company—were then brought out quite profusely, particularly in France. These pictorial *cahiers* were issued in serial form and bound by their collectors. The publishers cashed in on this vogue and saw to it that such cahiers, each a unit in itself, would be assembled and then offered as bound volumes, often containing 100 or 200 sections of portraits, complemented by "literary portraits" of a few pages.

Is it a by-product of Romanticism to indulge in looking at pictures? Or did the early Romantic age of the ballet already anticipate the visual-mindedness of our own time? Undoubtedly balletomania contributed to the pictorial mania. And also the mere technical accomplishments of the daguerreotype photographic process had reached their first stages of perfection when the Romantic ballet rose to its culmination. Although attempts at photography had been made from the early nineteenth century on, it was not before 1837 that photography became an astounding reality. Professional photography dates back to the beginning of the 1840s, and, with it, the era of the ballet souvenir program.

Printers in London and Paris collaborated to make these elaborate keepsakes possible. Compared with later ballet souvenirs, *Les Beautés de l'Opéra,* issued in Paris and London in 1844–45 and edited by Théophile Gautier, Jules Janin, and Philarète Chasles, may have been a small undertaking. Yet already it was extravagantly illustrated and one of the finest examples of ballet souvenirs. To please the opera fans, too, ballets and operas received equal treatment. These were the great favorites of that year: *La Giselle* (issued April); *Le Barbier de Séville* (June); *Le Diable Boiteux* (August); *La Juive* and *Les Huguenots* (both October); *Ondine* (November); *Norma, Don Juan,* and *La Sylphide* (all December), to judge by the dates on their frontispieces.

From the very beginning these souvenirs contained everything they do today. They told the plot and action of each ballet or opera in condensed form and briefly depicted the composer, librettist, scenic designer, and major interpreters. Special care was taken to make the frontispiece as attractive as possible. Most of the time the likeness of the heroine in action adorned the title page. Also, original paintings were commissioned by patrons or the Opéra, and their steel-engraved images, enclosed in an ornamental border, were used on the cover.

The picturesqueness of the souvenir programs was characteristic of those flamboyant days of the Victorian Age. Its eclectic architectural fashion was based on revivals of older styles, glorifying some elements of the Gothic while watering down others with an overuse of towers and turrets, of bays and other excrescences. Between the 1820s and '60s architecture became more and more confused. What was once Rococo extravagance turned into romantic overindulgence. The souvenir programs of the mid-nineteenth century are some of the finest proofs of the era's artistic flourish. And *Les Beautés de l'Opéra* are as good an example as anything that followed.

These were not the first attempts to record visualization of dances and dancers. The process of engraving and etching reaches back to the fifteenth and sixteenth centuries respectively; but lithography, invented circa 1796, had made printing easier. The first souvenir program coincided with the production of the *Balet Comique de la Royne* in 1581. It was nicely illustrated, although without an engraving on the title page. Yet ballet souvenir programs could not be issued more frequently until lithography and photography came of age.

Photography came as a surprise to the Romantic Age. It was one of the first "toys" of the mechanical revolution. This toy developed into a device of

CARLOTTA GRISI.
LA GISELLE.

A.E.Chalon R.A.   H.Robinson

Carlotta Grisi in Giselle: *frontispiece from* Les Beautés de l'Opéra,
1845. (Courtesy New York Public Library Dance Collection)

manifold possibilities. The rapid development of ever better photographic techniques and their popularity furthered abstract art forms. Photography freed painting from likeness, then the moving picture freed sculpture from its static existence and also led to the kinetic mobile.

The first notable change in the aesthetic approach to reality occurred with the emergence of Impressionism at a time when photography grew out of its stage of infancy. We could say that this was merely coincidental, without any logical or causal interrelation between painting and photography. But no event of historic importance has ever occurred without emerging from a deep-seated need in correspondence to other phenomena of the period. The Impressionist school of painting and the development of less legible imagery in the visual arts were reactions to the progress of technology.

This etching of Charles Baudelaire by Édouard Manet was made after a Nadar photograph. (Courtesy the Author)

It is, of course, idle conjecture how much the existence of photography has contributed to Fauvism, cubism, futurism, expressionism, Dadaism, and particularly surrealism, as much as to the powerful reign of the various forms of abstract art. There can be no doubt, however, that photography has forced artists more and more to think in terms of anti-photographic images. When photography itself ventured into the realm of artistry, discovering its own symbolic and expressive potentials, the arts turned to the extremes of nonliteralness.

The photographer has learned to see with the camera's eye, acquiring and displaying sensibilities formerly reserved for the visual artist. "Painting is dead!" the French painter Paul Delaroche cried out when the approval of the patent for Joseph Nicéphore Niépce and Louis Jacques Mandé Daguerre, inventors of photography, was announced. The day: August 19, 1839. Delaroche's shock was understandable and, for a historical and portrait painter, certainly justifiable, even though time proved him wrong. Painting was not doomed, it was forced to make the best of a new situation, to withdraw from established concepts and to find new ways of expressive freedom.

A painter needed a great deal of self-confidence in order to overcome a queasy feeling about a new mechanism that could shake his existence or undermine his pride.† Painters such as Ingres, who protested against this device with idealistic and aesthetic arguments, did not, however, look askance at the possibility of utilizing the very same mechanical contrivance for their work. In 1845 Delacroix wrote to a younger painter:

> How do I regret that such a wonderful invention has come so late—I say this in thinking of myself! The possibility of making sketches based on photographic prints would have had great influence on me. . . . Photography is an ostentatious proof of drawing after nature, a fact of which, so far, we have had the most imperfect concepts. . . .

Manet's famous etching of Baudelaire in 1865 was done from a photo portrait taken seven years earlier by Nadar, one of the finest photographers then in France.

Truth may have many images, but to convey the truth of a momentary scene and the essence of action itself is a photographic notion, which at that time was best realized by Edgar Degas. Degas's vision of his dancers and dance scenes have a photographic quality, which may have helped ensure their popularity. Degas did not share the Impressionists' love of the effects of color and light, which had to create shape and space for them.

For the public—in its quick and free association exercises—ballet and

† The computer with its awe-inspiring potentialities would be an analogy in our own time, even more so because of its all-embracing power.

Degas have become synonymous. But Degas and ballet got together at a time when he became tired of painting jockeys on horses and when the face of ballet began to show a stereotyped and tired expression, badly in need of regaining its lost enchantment. Dance and dancers were a pretext for Degas to paint "pretty materials" and to delineate movement. Paul Valéry clarified the painter's attitude: "No matter how great his interest in dancers, he captures rather than seduces them. He defines them." Nameless and faceless as his dancers were, they represented the image by which he was haunted—the truth behind action, the one fleeting moment of the many telescoping the essence of movement. What makes Degas interesting in this context is the dispassionate eye with which he looked at models and the stage atmosphere. Dispassionate and detached was his approach to the ordinary movements of a human being in motion. There was an affinity between his perception and that of a high-speed camera.

Naturalists have had no qualms in facilitating their work through photography.‡ But painters such as Cézanne and Gauguin, Munch and Picasso also took advantage of the camera, which furnished them with inspiration now and then. Nature has always been the primary source for the visual artist. Its replica on the photographic print enjoyed the durability of the captured image. Yet the development of the aesthetic aspect of photography is also indebted to the artistic statements of the visual artists. Their eyes had the advantage of painterly training. Degas's exploration of new types of composition was, in particular, of singular consequence for photography.

His preferred use of dance as subject matter should not be a surprise. In the 1860s dance images were seen everywhere. The Romantic ballet had become the accepted artistic commodity of the middle class, and to use the dancer as a motif in the visual arts was not new. A host of minor painters and photographers resorted to this motif as their *carte de visite*.

Degas was a symbol for the great new impulses that set imaginations afire in the latter part of the nineteenth century. He and other artists of the period were at the dawn of an era in which motion began to capture the popular imagination. Movement per se seemed to have been the final and basic answer to everything human beings ever dreamed of: to be faster than sound, to track down and subjugate the cosmos, to snatch the secret of creation from God. Among the many who tried to prove that motion was the

‡ The same trend was noticeable in French literature. Its most fervent spokesman was Émile Zola, a vociferous advocate of the early Impressionists, particularly Cézanne and Manet. He hailed their readiness and ability to break with a pontifical past and the escapist world of Romantic notions. He felt they did with their brush what he did with his pen: to clear the sky and canvas of rusty myths and to use art as a means of discovering the truth of reality, life seen in its nakedness. He became fascinated by the camera and its undistorted replica of the physical world, and he himself turned into an ardent photographer. He took up the threads of Enlightenment of a hundred years before his time and, with poetic fury, envisioned a future world destroying itself with corrupted needs and false hopes.

essence of life was the English-American Eadweard Muybridge, who a year before his death—he was then seventy-four years old—experienced the gratifying feeling that man had finally moved a flying machine successfully from the ground. Muybridge left his mark on history as an experimental cameraman who, with his consecutive-series photographs of humans and animals in motion, made an important step into cinematography. Through his device of taking sequential photographs of rapidly moving objects he established that in a certain phase of the gallop a horse had all four feet simultaneously off the ground. Degas was very much influenced by Muybridge's snapshots in the years he painted racing horses. Muybridge's influence on Marcel Duchamp and the Futurists was especially significant. The human eye became attuned to the problems and possibilities of movement in photography, a fact of singular importance in the visual world of which the dancer is a vital part.

In any culture, the sum total of little symbols anticipates the great events to come. Without visionary obsessions as the propelling force in life, our civilization would still be in a state of unfulfilled dreams. If the daring of the Renaissance had run its course in the seventeenth century instead of accepting and wrestling with ever-new challenges, European history would have taken the route of Eastern civilizations. Action-driven Renaissance man had to fulfill his destiny and reached the point in the nineteenth century where nothing could keep him from final fulfillment. Civilization moved from the categorical to the exploratory to the explosive.

FIN DE SIECLE:
A NEW BEGINNING

No one who was living at the end of the nineteenth century—between the years 1895 and 1905—could foresee the scope of the cataclysmic events that were to come. Yet these were to follow one another with such technological ferocity that the face of the world would be changed forever. No one believed—or wanted to believe—that civilization had by then reached a turning point. Not until 1918 did Oswald Spengler warn of the dangers of a final decline of the Western world in *Der Untergang des Abendlandes* (*The Decline of the West*). He envisioned how the machine would take the place of God and make man wield omniscient power, which would turn against him. Who could imagine that so many precious things that the Renaissance had come to cherish could so painfully disintegrate?

Politically the whole world seemed at peace, having been divided up between the so-called civilized nations before the century came to an end. The United States and the disunited European states had arrived at a stalemate in their power game. On the surface, a portentous calm prevailed. But the uneven distribution of colonial wealth foreshadowed trouble.

By contrast, other spheres of human activity moved at a feverish pace. The most astonishing intellectual feats, inventions, and discoveries took place within this fateful decade. They revolutionized our existence, reconditioning the impulse and creative process of many artists. The Wright Brothers made their historic flight in 1903. Internal-combustion engines, already tried out in Germany in 1885 by Karl Benz and Gottlieb Daimler, led to the manufacture of new models in the United States in the 1890s. In 1903 Detroit became the automotive center of the world and, shortly afterward, Henry Ford put the horseless car on the map.

In 1879 Thomas Edison constructed an incandescent electric lamp that could be commercially exploited. Two years later he developed a central electric-light power plant. By the time Marconi was ready to send wireless signals over a distance of more than a mile, Edison had invented the Kinetoscope. Everything seemed prepared for radio, film, and television.

Other discoveries of great consequence were made. Marie Curie suspected a radioactive element besides uranium in pitchblende. Her husband, Pierre, joined her in the research, and in 1898 they were able to announce their discovery of two elements, polonium and radium. In 1895 the German physician Wilhelm Conrad Roentgen discovered X rays; in the same year Sigmund Freud published his first paper (*Studies on Hysteria,* together with Josef Breuer), which, about two years later, led to the reinforced concepts of Freudian psychoanalysis. Einstein's first paper on relativity in 1905 brought us closer to the splitting of the atom. Einstein began to rebuild the image of the world. Thus in those early days of the century a new beginning was made, a beginning of traumatic consequences.

THE artists tried to keep pace with the scientific and technological innovations. The rebels among them began to recondition our senses, to reconstruct the visual and aural world of imagination and make-believe. They must have had great conviction and daring when turning against the trend of their time, so strongly characterized by the Art Nouveau style that had given the lost struggle of the Pre-Raphaelites a heavily decorative and commercially exploitable image. The last days of a predominantly Romantic century presented a richly ornamented world, the *Jugendstil*—as Art Nouveau was called in Central Europe—with its characteristic whiplash linearity and its heavily symbolized, exotic, and decadent figurations. But bold architects such as the Viennese Adolf Loos and the American Frank Lloyd Wright began to build the first unornamented cubic houses and advocated a pure, functional form, a new aesthetics of structure.

These ten years were the beginning of a long period of fermentation, of escape and rebellion. It was a creative ferment, an ingenious escape, a potent rebellion. It was a time in which artists lost their feeling for any form of continuity, something even the wildest Romantics never felt. For the first time in history an artist like Braque could say that "art is made to disturb." And Malraux's dictum that art is a revolt against man's fate was proved true in those years. Artists began to disbelieve in their environment, to feel confined, lost on a dead-end street. To save their own imaginative world and artistic sanity, they had to break out and leave the past to history.

A fascination with the East, Africa, and remote islands provoked a series of far-reaching experiments and enriched the lives of some artists. They discovered that there were other ways of being and sought avenues leading to them. Paul Gauguin escaped to Tahiti: "I am no longer conscious of days and hours, of good and evil. I only know that all is good, because all is beautiful." Ruth St. Denis embraced the spirit of the East: "The highest function of the dance is to ennoble man's concept of himself." Was it destiny presenting one of its more important chances when Pablo Picasso's eyes saw through Congo masks a world of geometrical shapes? "When we invented cubism, we had no intention whatever of inventing cubism. We wanted to express what was in us."

The growing uncertainty about established artistic patterns brought about an awareness that artists had to give way to novel ideas, to more violent forms, in order to be of their time. The search for identity was on. The path on which this search took place became more and more chaotic, but just as irresistible. At the height of Romantic protest against all bourgeois values the artist could still renounce "belonging" and deny reality in a *l'art pour l'art* gesture. After the turn of the century the notion of art for art's sake was translated into a more desperate and defiant "art for my sake," as D. H. Lawrence expressed it. The century to come was a ready-made period for all varieties of the iconoclast in the artist.

In the Name of Light and Drapery

ESCAPE AND EXPERIMENT WERE THE KEY WORDS OF THE GAY NINETIES. Under the tremor of the eerie gaslight, people tried to snatch some joy from life in the dancing halls, while Loie Fuller (1862–1928) and Isadora Duncan (1878–1927) experimented, one with electricity, the other with the expression of her soul. And drapery was common to all of them.

The Gay Nineties started in kaleidoscopic contrasts. In 1892, when Loie Fuller arrived in Paris to dance at the Folies-Bergère, the fortress from where she conquered all of Europe, Gerhart Hauptmann's *Die Weber* (*The Weavers*) received its production at the Freie Bühne (Free Stage), which had opened three years previously with Ibsen's *Ghosts*. Hauptmann's revolutionary play about the misery of Silesian workers losing their fight against the machines is often called the first socialist drama. Bernard Shaw's *Mrs. Warren's Profession* was then written, certainly revolutionary in theme and resolution during the *fin de siècle,* dealing with the circumstances surrounding professional prostitution. As a counterpoint to these plays, Maurice Maeterlinck's *Pelléas et Mélisande,* a highly symbolistic and mystical play, was finished in the same year. Claude Debussy—who ushered in musical Impressionism—immediately began to compose an opera based on this play, though it took him about ten years. But in the early 1890s he also composed the symphonic prelude *L'Après-midi d'un faune* (based on Mallarmé's poem *Afternoon of a Faun*), which was destined to play a decisive part in the development of the dance.

These were the years in which Auguste Rodin found himself. He breathed the inner face into the expression of stone and marble, he showed man's deep, underlying drives, his fury and joy, longing and resignation. It was at the same time that Rainer Maria Rilke emerged as a major poet, a magician of visionary power who turned the visible world into images of transcending beauty and often veiled meaning. It is characteristic of the time, those years of Rilke's becoming, that his work, a peculiar blending of Impressionism and mysticism, reflected a frightful struggle between body and soul, between a spiritual visualization of life and a haunting fear of death.

The Gay Nineties were a period of confusing trends. This was a society seething with new ideas, beset by a multiplicity of attempts to find a new way of articulation. The first major battles caused by the Industrial Revolution created a deep cleavage between people. But it was overshadowed by so much sham glitter, uneasy laughter, and an escape into a meaningless "after us the deluge" attitude. No one wanted to admit that he was frightened, and everyone cushioned his fear with plush. The playing of the piano, the singing of *Lieder* by Brahms and Hugo Wolf, and the reciting of poetry belonged among the pastime of any good bourgeois household. The corps de ballet was a haven for girls dreaming of fame. Glamour, however meretricious, mattered. It was a generation that loved to flirt with the Muses.

The fashion, too, betrayed people. Even though Ibsen's Nora had frightened the philistines and the echo of the suffragettes' first outcries still reverberated in the air, women still forced their bodies into the prison of a most absurd, unbecoming, and unhygienic exterior. In high-heeled shoes they waddled around with corseted wasplike waists, sweeping the city streets with froufrou ruffles. The sleeves of their dresses were the size of balloons, each sleeve containing enough material for a whole dress. The last vestige of the struggle for emancipation was the bloomer suit, badly needed for bicycle riding. Yes, women on bicycles were then in high fashion. To add more irony to the ridiculous, everyone wanted to be athletic: played tennis and golf and mild croquet and went swimming. But even when bathing, people were ludicrous to watch: they went fully dressed into the water. The pretentiousness and preciousness of the ladies in the age of Louis XIV were topped by the *fin de siècle* and its Victorian prudery. Décolletés were anathema, ankles or arms were never shown. Egon Friedell tells us in his *Cultural History* "that to stay alone with a gentleman in a room or to go out without a chaperone was under no circumstances permitted; words like 'sex' or 'panties' were erased from the woman's vocabulary."

DURING the 1890s ballet history was still being made in Russia under Petipa's reign, with the cooperation of Peter Tchaikovsky and Lev Ivanov. It was as if the Romantic ballet once more remembered its past greatness and lived up to the greatness of its memory. In 1890 Petipa's *Sleeping Beauty* was premiered, and two years later Ivanov's *Nutcracker;* in 1895 *Swan Lake* was resuscitated by Petipa and Ivanov. Russia was still the scene of ballet action.

Toulouse-Lautrec's lithograph of La Goulue and Valentin le Désossé, 1894.
(Courtesy German Information Center)

After Gautier's death in October 1872 the emphasis on important balletic events had decidedly shifted from Paris to St. Petersburg and Moscow. This date has no factual but a highly symbolic significance, since in March of the same year Serge Diaghilev was born. For the sake of convenience we may envision one curtain being called down—*Coppélia* was the last important ballet of the era to have its premiere in Paris, in 1870—while another curtain was being prepared to go up on a new era. The countermovement was located in Russia, symbolized by Michel Fokine's rebellious spirit and Diaghilev's fortuitous exodus from St. Petersburg, through which gradually ballet was again given back to Paris and, by the same token, received a new lease on life.

However enfeebled the Paris Opéra ballet happened to be toward the end of the century, many dancers still felt the need to be seen there before appearing in Russia. Thus Paris managed to hold on to some magic of its former reputation. But the *creative* impetus that the ballet world had received from this city for so long was lost. There was a vacuum to be filled. The spotlights moved from the Opéra to the music halls, the Folies-Bergère and the Moulin Rouge. The cancanization of the decade was on and it became indicative of its spirit, of a magnificent vulgarity, of wanton despair, of the extravagance of a decadent age.

Montmartre had been a household word since the mid-eighties. It was a city within a city; it signified a carefree, sometimes daring, enjoyment of life —especially night life. The dance halls were the centers of events. First people frequented the Élysée-Montmartre, then the Moulin Rouge. A bourgeois leisure class participated beside those people of the working class who had to take care of their businesses during the day to become great dancers in the evening. They were not professionals, but they made an art of music hall dancing.

The cancan in all its variations, whether the *chahut* or the *quadrille réaliste,* was one of the symbolic—as well as flamboyant—symptoms of the social malaise of the time. It was not the Moulin Rouge alone, it was the Alhambra in London or smaller dance halls in Vienna where the bourgeoisie found escape and where the intellectual elite could find the fascination and vibrations of life that the commercial theater did not offer. Poets and painters were caught by this music hall life as if it were a world apart, which in many ways it was. Their vital interest in and association with it gave the dancing at these places, as well as the dancers and the places themselves, the unspoken status of being avant-garde. Their reputation was also enhanced by the fact that what they did had become fashionable and many socialites mingled with the lower layer of society on the dance floor. Here the contrasts between people seemed to be wiped out, though in reality they were accentuated. There was a prevailing feeling that the music halls were one of the last bastions where life was still worth living. And everyone wanted to be part of it.

Some dancers achieved stardom, and most of them achieved it overnight since all one needed there for recognition as a major artist was a natural talent. La Goulue was one such talent, a sixteen-year-old laundress who was discovered by Valentin le Désossé one night and from then on lit up the artificial cyclorama of this very real world. Imitated from Montmartre to the Bowery in New York was "La Goulue's chignon, piled high on top of her head like a helmet." Challenging the world, it "sprang from a single strand tightly twisted at the nape of her neck, so that it would not fall down when she danced," as Yvette Guilbert said in *La Chanson de ma vie*. When she danced it was with unstudied and unconstrained virtuosity. Valentin, who ran a little coffeehouse near the former Halles Centrales, was one of the most agile dancers, the Fred Astaire of the 1890s, nicknamed "the Boneless." His body control was as admirable as that of any great ballet dancer. He could turn and twist and jump without any visible effort and seemingly without training. And what was even more remarkable was his choreographic inventiveness. His quadrille and waltzes were known for his on-the-spot creation of most complex steps and intricate figures. The particularly difficult steps increasingly added to the quadrille were a handicap for many an amateur. But La Goulue and Valentin danced not only for the enjoyment of the other visitors to the Moulin Rouge, as if onstage, but also with the public. Both were at best nonprofessional professionals, dancers who, due to their native gift, accomplished virtuoso feats. And so to a great extent were Loie Fuller, Isadora Duncan, and Ruth St. Denis, who had a system rather than a technique.

Jane Avril, another dancer and star of the Moulin Rouge, never received any formal training as a dancer or an actress, but she succeeded as both. Avril was atypical of the music hall milieu, but not of the period. Where La Goulue was known for her bewitching coarseness, Avril was utter gentleness, literate, lost to her dreams, a living poem. She danced as if in a trance, preferring whirling movements. If Botticelli's Three Graces could have come alive, one of them might easily have appeared in the shape of Jane Avril. By mere chance she found out one night that she was a dancer, and the admiration she harvested was the diploma of her professionalism.

The ladies of the Moulin Rouge, whose raison d'être was to kick the highest and show the most, were also aware of the theatricality of drapery when they appeared with many ruffles on their petticoats. In fact, they often wore several layers of petticoats to create the impression of a sea of billowing laces. It was drapery with visceral spontaneity and the gutsy vulgarity triumphant over fear of life.

The nineteenth century, which gave birth to the concept of the virtuoso, has made it clear that, in all artistic expressions, the artist depends on a craft, on formal training. It was left to the twentieth century to change this conception and to accept any articulation of the Self as a work of art. The trend was started by that handful of dancers at the turn of the century. Since then we have learned to recognize and judge craftsmanship separate from artistry.*

LOIE Fuller, one of the most flamboyant and admired dancers of the Gay Nineties, was at the height of her fame when the Curies made their discovery of radium in 1898. She had experimented with light for several years. About forty engineers worked for her, switching on the electric current and inundating the stage with light. *La Belle Américaine,* as Fuller was named, wrote to Madame Curie to help her make butterfly wings of radium, as she had learned about the pale ethereal light that radium emitted. A few years later, in 1904, Loie Fuller was able to extract phosphorescent paint from the residue of pitchblende. She painted one of her drapery-like costumes with it and moved in a sea of electric light in her *Radium Dance.*

The Curies belonged to the many intellectuals who admired Fuller's genius, not only the artist onstage, but probably even more the indomitable spirit of the researching amateur scientist in her. Fuller, in turn, dedicated her *Radium Dance* to the Curies in gratitude for their inspiration, whereby this dance was a variation of an earlier work called *The Butterfly.* This, of course, matters little, since most of her dancing was impromptu, with interchangeable steps and movements. Fuller started her public career as a temperance lecturer in the States and later became a not very successful actress. Even though she was an admired dance figure of the Gay Nineties, she was not really a great dancer. She was a cultural phenomenon of her time, a spectacle defying definition.

Loie Fuller was certainly one of the fascinating figures of the 1890s, as an artist—I do not say dancer—utterly representative of the period and its spirit. She did not from the very beginning set out to become a dancer, as Isadora Duncan did. Fuller stumbled upon her greatness. She turned a moment of chance into destiny. There exist at least two versions of this fortuitous moment, but since there is always more than one truth, we may simply assume that, wrapped in billowy folds of drapery, she was gliding about the stage and suddenly realized the stupendous theatrical effect that her gauzy skirt achieved in the light through motion.

She tells us in her autobiography, *Fifteen Years of a Dancer's Life,* that she stood in front of a mirror and noticed how the sunlight made the material she wore translucent. "Golden reflections played in the folds of the spar-

---

* The reader should be reminded of the Middle Ages when the notion of the artist was still unknown and art meant craftsmanship. It was not before the early Renaissance, with its stress on the individual, that the concept of the artist in the craftsman began to emerge.

kling silk, and in this light my body was revealed in a shadowy contour." This was the beginning of her famous *Serpentine* and *Skirt* dances with which she enthralled Paris and half the world. This idol of Paris, who was able to transform the Folies-Bergère into an artistic shrine, was totally ignorant of classical technique or of any other dance form. She moved as spontaneously and naturally as a gifted child would do.

Loie Fuller believed that a human emotion is best expressed when unburdened by the technical knowledge of how it should or could be done. "The moment you attempt to give dancing a trained element, naturalness disappears. Nature is truth, and art is artificial." She also said that "motion and not language is truthful," a statement resembling Martha Graham's notion that movement never lies. But Graham meant the movement of the body and Fuller the manipulation of drapery and light. She never really cared about the line of her body onstage, but was interested only in creating optical illusions and resemblances to such natural objects as an orchid, a butterfly, and clouds.

Loie Fuller was a part of the great scientific and artistic revolution of the time. The dancer's body always remained of secondary importance to her since it practically vanished in the magic of light effects, in the seductive images of iridescent silk and whirling drapes. Light—i.e., electricity—was then *le dernier cri* onstage. Its marvels and complexities had caught the fancy of stage directors and scenic designers. There would have been no Loie Fuller without electricity. Where other artists were merely intrigued by the use of electric light, she made of it a lifelong experiment. Indeed, she became an expert electrician and ran a laboratory in Paris where she experimented in great secrecy with six assistants. She was right in saying that she knew no other dancer who would have been so intensely interested in science. She worked with carbon arc lights, colored gelatins, and large magic-lantern projectors with slides that she painted in a wildly imaginative way, as for instance in her *Radium Dance,* using a multicolored slide first, then superimposing another while withdrawing the first. In her famous *Fire Dance,* which she created in 1895, the dancer was lit from below by red light emerging from a glass-covered trap.

Her *Fire Dance* was very likely the one with which she was and still is most closely identified. In his lithograph of this dance Toulouse-Lautrec helped our memory to retain the sensuous surprise that must have overwhelmed the spectators. A sensation of transfiguring fascination emanated from this artificial flame in whose midst a female figure moved wearing an enigmatic smile. Yeats must have thought of it when he wrote these three lines in *Byzantium:*

> Dying into a dance,
> An agony of trance,
> An agony of flame that cannot singe a sleeve.

Loie Fuller: FIRE DANCE. *Lithograph by Toulouse-Lautrec, published by Marty. (Courtesy New York Public Library Dance Collection)*

Auguste Rodin, who later fell in love with Isadora Duncan, said that Loie Fuller was "a woman of genius, with all the resources of talent," and that she painted nature in the colors of Turner. And yet Turner is artistically far removed from the Art Nouveau style whose sensibilities Loie Fuller most vividly reflected and which made her coast along the edges of kitsch so often.

Obsessed with the idea of creating a dance theater of illusion with electricity and projections, she became one of the more important pioneers of stage lighting and scenic design. In this context one can trace her work to the Bauhaus and from there to Alwin Nikolais' dance theater. Her experimental work was paralleled by two most important pioneers who established new concepts of stage design. They were Adolphe Appia and his apostle Gordon Craig.

Both turned against the schools of naturalism and realism in the theater that followed the ecstasies of Romanticism. Their concepts were mainly poetic. They advocated a complete stylization of setting, lighting, and costuming. They wanted to create fluidity and suggestiveness, an elusive and allusive feeling onstage. Appia was the first to use color and mobility of light, with which he established the mood and atmosphere of a play or an opera. He sought the "loftiest expression of the eternal in art," as he said in *Die Musik und die Inscenierung* (1899). First Appia thought he could find this expression fulfilled through music. But then he felt that light had the same emotionally suggestive power as music onstage, that it can create a unifying mood and help convey the inner magic that is the deeply imbedded, hidden, but very essential aspect of a play. Only light, he stressed, can express "the inner nature of all appearance," with its "infinite capacity for varying nuance."

Adolphe Appia was not brilliant in articulating his ideas, nor could he deliver an impressive drawing of his stage ideas; in both of these Gordon Craig excelled. What is fascinating about Appia and many pioneering artists of the time and of the coming century was the strength of their convictions, which so often made them grope in the dark until they reached an artistic breakthrough. Appia said, "I began to practice a completely unknown art for which all the elements had yet to be discovered and organized. Still I was convinced that, following my own vision, I would find the truth," as he expressed in *L'Oeuvre d'art vivant* (*The Living Work of Art*).

Gordon Craig, so much more vocal than Appia, was a visionary fighter for a new theater as a mystically conceived reality. He saw the theater in visual and architectural terms. All his life Gordon Craig searched for a "magnificent overpowering unity of impression," for an oversized stage image coming closest to a total work of theater art, of which Richard Wagner also dreamed. Craig envisioned poetically abstract designs on "a platform of heroic size on which figures of a heroic mould shall move. . . . The movements on these scenes shall be noble and great: all shall be illumined by a light such as the spheres give us, not such as the footlights give us, but such as we dream of, . . ." as he delineated in his quarterly *The Mask*.

There was a very distinct coordination in the diversified attempts of these artists to change the visual aspect of the stage, with lighting playing a predominant role. It is also characteristic of the entire period that the rejuvenation of the theater came about not through the drama but through the visual and physical image of the stage, through scenic design, lighting, and new concepts of production, as in the early seventeenth century. It is here that Loie Fuller's importance can be seen.

If anyone still doubted the aesthetic proximity between the visual arts and the dance, drapery must dispel such doubts. In both it is charged with similar, if not the same, functions. Drapery accentuates the mysterious and has been used for emphasis of the landscape of the human body. The Greeks were so much in love with the beauty of their nakedness that their expression of physical joy eclipsed all thoughts of sin. The sculptural evidence shows that, on many occasions, Greek dancers were depicted either in the nude or heavily cloaked, in which case the drapery became an important part of the dancing. From the very beginning, artists have been aware of how much stronger the suggestiveness of nudity is when a light, clinging garment covers the body or some drapery falls upon parts of the body. This was the case in antiquity as in its revival during the Renaissance.

How much poetry can lie in the revelation through concealment is best proved by Botticelli's Three Graces in his "Primavera." How meaningful are the garments there, giving us a feeling of seductive beauty, but a chaste seduction. This sensation is enhanced by the dancing gesture of these Graces in which the drapery accentuates a rhythmic notion. The obviously lyric beauty of the entire scene is underlined by the sylvan and somber background, reminiscent of a Gothic tapestry. Botticelli was a master in the conception of drapery, which he also used in a most imaginative way in "The Birth of Venus." The floating, undulating movement of the hair falling like drapery along the body conveys the suggestion of motion through its rhythmic structure.

Isadora Duncan was carried away when seeing Botticelli's "Primavera" and described her enthusiasm in her book, *My Life:* "I will dance this picture and give to others this message of love, spring, procreation of life which has been given to me with such anguish. I will give to them, through the dance, such ecstasy." Whereas drapery was for Fuller an end in itself, an ac-

Sandro Botticelli (c. 1444–1510) caught the draped dream of Romanticism in his painting "Primavera," of which this is the detail of the Three Graces. (Courtesy Scala/Editorial Photocolor Archives)

complice of her artistic deed, it was for Isadora only an accessory, mere trimming. She must have loved the sensuous feeling of velvety material and the sight of anything that would fall in elusive folds, hinting at an endless flow. Her tunics were draped around her as if on a Greek marble statue. When she was photographed, drapery was nearby. In her autobiography she described her studio, which "was like a chapel, and hung round for about fifteen metres high with my blue curtains." *Her* blue curtains! In a smaller room she saw "sable black velvet curtains . . . reflected on the walls in golden mirrors." She probably felt she moved more lightly when her rapturous being was set off against such drapery, even though all that mattered to her was the articulation of her inwardness.

Neither Duncan nor Fuller was the first to incorporate drapery as a dynamic accessory in her dance creations. The scarf has always played a significant part with dancers, ever since it came into fashion in the eighteenth century. In those days, scarves were long and exquisite Indian shawls, favorites in high society. Scarves were often worn instead of coats and particularly suited the temperament and mood of Mediterranean ladies. Then one did not speak of a lady as well dressed but of being beautifully draped. The Parisian danseuse Mlle Marie Miller, who became Pierre Gardel's wife, gave private lessons in draping and scarf dancing. In her novel *Corinne,* Mme de Staël immortalized the scarf dance of one of the most renowned women of the Parisian salons of the eighteenth century, Juliette Récamier. Records show that the scarf dance was even then taught in schools for girls.

During his Italian journey in 1787 Goethe was a guest of Sir William Hamilton, British ambassador to the Kingdom of Naples. Emma Hart, who later became Lady Hamilton, was in love with pantomime, movement, and scarves. She imitated the poses of Greek sculpture. This was not unusual in the days of Winckelmann: on the contrary, anything that had to do with antiquity was in fashion and a part of intellectual diversion. Lady Hamilton never became a famous dancer, but she was unique in her plastic attitudes borrowed from antiquity. She charmed her guests when she appeared as a Greek statue or relief into which she slowly breathed rhythmic life. At one point Sir William Hamilton held candles behind her to magnify the theatrical effect. Goethe described this pantomimic experience in his journal in great detail:

Émile-Antoine Bourdelle used Isadora Duncan as a model for his friezes on the façade of the Théâtre des Champs-Élysées and for statues representing dance. He wrote in 1913: "When the great Isadora Duncan danced before me, thirty years of my life looking at all the great human masterpieces became suddenly animated in these planes ordained from within by the spirit's aspiration." (Courtesy French Cultural Services)

[Sir William Hamilton] has had a Grecian robe made for her which becomes her extremely well. She puts it on, lets her hair down, drapes a pair of shawls around her and then assumes such a variety of attitudes, postures, and expressions that you think you are dreaming. . . .

Lady Hamilton had many imitators, the best known being a German dancer, Henriette Hendel-Schütz, who anticipated a great deal of what Isadora Duncan was to find more than a century later.

Floating drapery had a vital life in itself, creating the illusion of a rhythmic line, the allusion of embodied energy in movement. It is a Baroque notion and can be seen in a variety of paintings, as in Poussin's and Boucher's canvases depicting "The Triumph of Galatea." At that time, the early eighteenth century, Marie Sallé impersonated Galatea (or rather Venus) in her famous choreography of *Pygmalion*. As the statue of Venus she was wrapped in a simple muslin robe modeled upon Greek draperies, and her hair fell down her shoulders à la Botticelli when Pygmalion fell in love with his own creation.

Toward the end of the nineteenth century, in the wake of an unmitigated enthusiasm for everything oriental, particularly Japanese, drapery came into its own again, more often in a vulgarized form and with less stylistic conviction. Drapery easily lends itself to both the sublime and the banal. Fuller and Duncan, however unconsciously, tried to achieve the spiritualization of drapery, to give it a soul of its own. The ornamental style of Art Nouveau, still quite beautiful in the drawings of Aubrey Beardsley or the paintings of Gustav Klimt, contained drapery-like features bordering on triviality; they became a point of departure for fashionable illustrators and commercial designers as well as architects and were beloved by the well-to-do bourgeoisie of the early 1900s. In its most negative usage, drapery was reduced to mere commercial decoration to mitigate the *horror vacui,* to fill the empty spaces in theaters and restaurants, in subways and homes. Drapery was very much related to the demands of the time for overstuffed rooms full of bric-a-brac from the Orient (or its cheap imitation), and cozy Turkish corners with the divan hidden behind a bead portiere.

Duncan, Decadence, and Rebirth

TO BE ONESELF IS A DEFIANT GESTURE AT ANY TIME IN VIEW OF THE complex social structure of society, and it was most manifest on the threshold of the coming century. Those were the years when the first breakthroughs against conventional notions occurred, particularly against the standard notions of beauty, when artists became aware of the challenges of the time and tried to break ground for new concepts. Artists felt the need to be reborn. In order to be reborn, they had to find their way back to nature again, to the primitive, and, above all, to the self. The human desire to look into the intricate mechanism of the psyche turned into a scientific trend that was to characterize and overshadow the age to come. The curtain went up on the drama of self-recognition and man's conscious struggle to master his unconscious Self.

This trend of self-reflection took various forms and a variety of different expressions. But they are all interrelated and throw light on the difficulty of the era and its society. Some artists, reflecting certain trends, gave color to a complex picture. August Strindberg, for instance, was drawn to introspection all his life, and in the 1890s he embraced symbolism wholeheartedly. His work was, according to Thornton Wilder, "the fountainhead of virtually all of modernism in the drama."

Strindberg's life was a series of anguished experiences that found expression in most of his works. His favorite drama, the child of his greatest suffering, he called *A Dream Play,* written in 1902. This play has particular significance for this study because Strindberg did not dramatize a "whole character" but the fragmentation of departmentalization of his symbolized self. The characterization of the hero falls into three components: he appears as an officer, a lawyer, and a poet. This has been a favorite device of Martha Graham in many of her roles. The threefold images or phases of one and the same person—as in her story of St. Joan, *Seraphic Dialogue*—are one such striking example of an analytic approach to the complexities of a human being.

To the trend of self-analysis among writers belongs Anton Chekhov, who wrote most of his plays in the 1890s. They were translated into stage realities in Moscow's Art Theater by Konstantin Stanislavsky. His staging—now familiar as Lee Strasberg's Method—intended to do away with the hollow pathos of classical acting, the declamation, and its counterpart of superficial realism. His was a theater of "inner feeling," and he saw Chekhov's plays as mood pieces with a nostalgic longing for something lovely and beautiful in life that is hard to come by; plays in which people wear their regrets and tragic frustrations like Sunday clothes; plays in which through every phrase and pause the seekers and dreamers are either lost in their hopes and loneliness or turn into fighters for ideals against the terrible realities of their time.

Occasionally images of lost and desperate souls emerged in the art of this period. Edvard Munch's lithograph "The Cry" appeared in 1895. Today it conveys the impression of a primal scream. This incarnation of emotional upheaval appears to be shaken by her emotions suddenly set free. There is a similar anguish in the flaming colors of Van Gogh, who described himself as

"boiling inwardly." His skies reflect the rage of his inmost despair; his writh-
ing olive trees are the visualization of his tortured psyche.

The creations of most artists are autobiographical. But this was not so obvious in earlier centuries. Only at the beginning of the Romantic Age did
the artist indulge in self-revelation, which at the end of the century turned
into frantic introspection. Those journeys within, soul-searching as they
were, mark this period.

Among the writers who objectively investigated and analyzed the mechanism of the human psyche was Arthur Schnitzler. He skillfully dissected his
characters while writing with wit and elegance. He was always interested in
the game of love and life and in the intricacies of human reactions. He is
best known for the play *Reigen,* or *La Ronde.* Schnitzler's entire philosophy
is telescoped in this round dance of flirtation leading to the carnal act, and
promiscuity leading to emptiness and loneliness. The farce in it shows us
that we are sexual animals unable to escape the urge. On another level,
Reigen is a study of human reactions to the life source that is sex, of the
middle-class misunderstanding of it, and of the fascinatingly different ways
in which the various classes of society react to it. But when the light goes out
(indicated in the play by a few asterisks, stars hanging in the dark night of
mankind), it is always the same, all the time—yesterday, today, and tomorrow. The interrelation of psyche and sex, dramatized in *Reigen,* also sheds
light on Isadora's life source and trauma, the result of her constant struggle
with her self and society.

Schnitzler recognized despair as an unrecognized symptom of a disease
that had reached epidemic proportions in the 1890s: the seeking of pleasure.
He encouraged people to go on exploring life—as long as they explored
themselves at the same time. In his tender tone he warns us against the illusion that irresponsible pleasure can make us happy. Knowing the struggle in
men and women, however, he often came back to the thought that we
should leave nothing untried, for at the end we remain alone to face the
past, our backs to the wall, awaiting the embrace of death.

Arthur Schnitzler was a physician who had learned to cure; as a writer he
had learned to weigh and not to judge. He re-created the mysteries of
human existence like a learned psychologist. Sigmund Freud lived around
the corner from Schnitzler. But the two never met. One day the dramatist
received the following note from Freud:

> For many years I have been aware of the far-reaching agreement
> between your and my conceptions existing in many a psychological
> and erotic problem. . . . I have often wondered and asked myself
> from where you could have taken this or that insight which I have
> acquired through such laborious explorations of the subject, and I
> finally came to the point of envying the poet whom otherwise I ad-
> mired. . . .

Aubrey Beardsley's image of Salomé in her STOMACH DANCE. (*Courtesy The Fogg Art Museum, Harvard University. Grenville L. Winthrop Bequest*)

Another writer with uncanny insight into the human mind was Oscar Wilde. In one of his philosophical dialogues, he referred to the madness by which one can suddenly be gripped, which is induced by the poison of unquenchable desires and the pursuit of visions that can never materialize. Wilde was the very product of the *fin de siècle:* a moralist accused of and sentenced for immorality because he was strong enough to remain true to himself and dared to flaunt this truth in the face of the Victorian philistines; a dandy, to Baudelaire's delight, with a flower in his buttonhole, dropping foolproof epigrams on his way to *De Profundis.* Wilde wrote *Salomé* in 1893, a play that reveals the most decadent aestheticism of the period and Wilde's fascination with the macabre and morbid aspects of life. Aubrey Beardsley's drawings gave the work an unmistakable Art Nouveau stamp, and the "Dance of the Seven Veils" in the opera based on Wilde's play has puzzled and frustrated sopranos and stage directors at opera houses ever since.

In denying the vulgarity of naturalism, an artist like Oscar Wilde, holding the mirror up to *l'art pour l'art,* had to reject nature, as also was the trend of the time. He wrote a dialogue-essay, *The Decay of Lying,* the most lucid aesthetic manifesto of the 1890s, in which there are more thoughts characterizing the period than can be noted here. He tries to explain that all perceptions, aesthetic or scientific, are based on and governed by conventions; that art which imitates life—he castigates Zola's school of naturalism—is decadent art since it misses the goal of art, which is to shape the dreams of the past and future; art deals "with what is unreal and nonexistent . . . as a method realism is a complete failure. . . . Art finds its own perfection within, and not outside of, herself. . . . The proper school to learn art is not Life but Art. . . . Nature is so imperfect. . . . Art is our spirited protest, our gallant attempt to teach Nature her proper place. . . ."

We could easily gloss over such remarks if Oscar Wilde had made them at a moment of facetious whim to spite some philistines. But he truly expressed here his own opinion and the spirit of his time's artificiality. To remember this is to see Loie Fuller in a different light and Isadora Duncan's daring in proper perspective. Artificiality belonged with the hedonist of the 1890s. It is only half the truth that he preferred a perfect illusion to imperfect reality. As the hedonist he is, he throws himself into experiences for the sake of experiencing them, and when he realizes their threadbare, monotonous meaninglessness, the very thing he tried to escape, he then undergoes his soul-searching.

In the nineties, people were fully aware of living in a morbid, decadent atmosphere. They spoke and wrote about it as if it were the most normal thing to do so. Around the turn of the century a great number of books were published dealing with the phenomenon of decadence, and one of the more popular ones, considering the surprising number of editions it reached, was

Max Nordau's *Degeneration,* published in 1892–93. Nordau diagnosed the syndrome of the *fin de siècle* as hysteria, hedonism, escapism, prudery, eccentricities, all kinds of morbid and anarchic, i.e., antibourgeois tendencies. We find in Nordau's pantheon of degeneration some of the most luminous names, from Baudelaire to Nietzsche, from Wagner to Wilde. The most interesting artists have never found a place in the matrix of patterns and norms. Their inclination toward experiments and everything lying remote from present reality became in the eyes of their adversaries an *idée fixe* and was for the artists the most obvious point of departure forced upon them by history.

Also at that time the first noticeable antinomy developed between journalism and literature, turning up where literature seemed manifestly isolated from the mainstream of society. Oscar Wilde settled this growing dilemma with one of his famous epigrammatic asides when he had one of his characters say: "Oh, journalism is unreadable, and literature is not read." The satirist Karl Kraus took language to be a symbol of man's conception of himself and identified most journalism as the evil betraying and corrupting the world.

Karl Kraus recognized "the demonic possibilities of mediocrity," as Erich Heller said in *The Disinherited Mind.* Kraus unmasked what was to him the prostitution of the intellect of which he accused journalism. With the historic impasse at the end of the last century he foresaw the deterioration of society and, with Cassandra-like fury and verbal pyrotechnics, predicted *The Last Days of Mankind,* as he called his monumental satire on World War I—last days which, to this very day, have become later and ever later. Kierkegaard declared that "the individual cannot help his age; he can only express that it is doomed." That is exactly what Kraus did. As early as that decade of decadence he predicted what would, from the beacon of his satiric vision, look like slow disintegration and ultimate decay.

But we can easily comfort ourselves with faith in the resurging forces in humanity. Contemporaries of Kraus in the age that delighted in its decadence and listened with fascination to the voices of doom were the French critic and chief apologist for the symbolists Remy de Gourmont, and the British poet and essayist Arthur Symons, mediator between the avant-gardes in London and in Paris. Both accepted decadence as something that went hand in hand with a total reorientation in our mental and intellectual processes and with a search for new ways of expression. In 1893 Symons said about literature and the arts of the time that they have qualities characteristic of all periods destined to be the starting point of a great new epoch: "An intense self-consciousness, a restless curiosity in research, an oversubtilising refinement."

One could easily claim that Loie Fuller, Isadora Duncan, and Ruth St. Denis strongly relate to this decadent era. But at the same time they possessed those necessary qualities of which Arthur Symons spoke. They were in every respect children of their time, charged with the awesome task of pointing the way for those to come.

TODAY we may smile at the notion that bearded men wept when seeing Isadora dance. We can understand it only when we envision the setting in which these artists struggled with themselves and with a world to which they still bore witness, but against which they gave decisive, sometimes violent, evidence. It was no longer a question of how to display one's creative abilities, but of how to disclose the inmost urge to make an artistic statement, how to discover and reveal the mystery of one's self.

Isadora Duncan threw the accessories of ballet with its classical technique out of the window and erased from her face the studied smile that comes with the turning of a pirouette. But, historically, did she destroy the basic concepts of ballet? Of course not. She gave ballet new impulses. It was by mere chance that Isadora found herself dancing without sandals one day. It was different and seemed attractive to her, and the barefoot dancer was born. Her costumes and draperies were Greek in inspiration, but the movement, she correctly felt, was American in the freedom of its expression. As to its deeper reality, it reflected the escape of an imprisoned and tormented soul, an escape into the most natural and the simplest language of the body.

Dance was Duncan's individual response to sensory and emotional stimuli; it was the momentary translation of a mood, of rational and irrational sensations, into movement. It is difficult if not impossible to convey her structural choreographic concept to another person, let alone a group. Since she "worked" with her "soul," seeking a centrifugal force that would reflect a "spiritual vision," she created her own limitations as a choreographer.

She evoked the unknown spirits within her as a vital power and made them respond to the vibrations from without. In her autobiography she made it all sound the simplest thing in the world:

> It would seem as if it were a very difficult thing to explain in words, but when I stood before my class of even the smallest and poorest children and said: "Listen to the music with your soul. Now, while listening, do you not feel an inner self awakening deep within you—that it is by its strength that your head is lifted, that your arms are raised, that you are walking slowly toward the light?" they understood. This awakening is the first step in the dance, as I conceive it.

Oskar Kokoschka: "Portrait of Karl Kraus," 1909. This picture best characterizes Kokoschka's attempt to penetrate the portrayed person's psyche. (Photo: Walter Dräyer. Courtesy Walter Feilchenfeldt, Zürich)

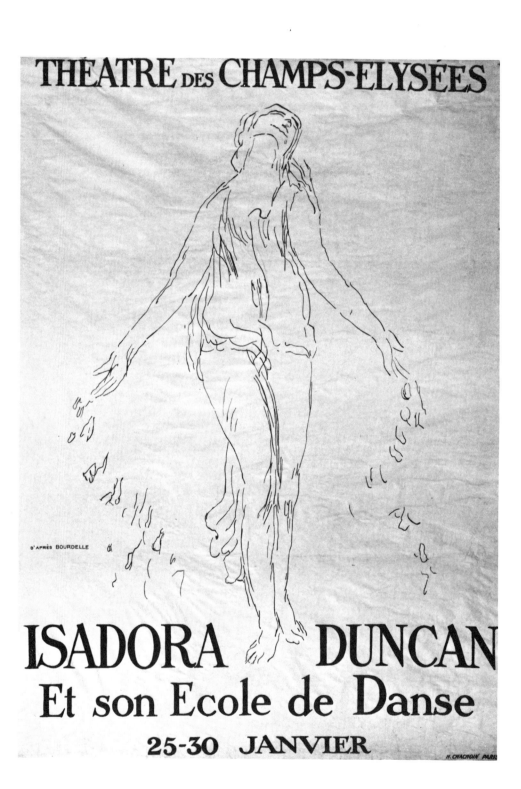

It was self-deception for her to believe that it would be easy for everyone to listen with the soul and, above all, to locate this complex and elusive mechanism of the psyche. She had a natural feeling for how to move with graceful simplicity and how to let one movement flow into the next. Even as a young girl she rebelled against the restrictions of the ballet technique, which, she sensed, would prevent her from being herself. But she only gradually developed her theories, tailored to fit her own abilities: to dance as one feels. She claimed: "I realized that the only dance masters I could ever have were Jean-Jacques Rousseau ('Emile'), Walt Whitman, and Nietzsche." Almost in the same breath she declared that her first dance masters were "wind and wave and the winged flight of bird and bee." Both claims reflected her defiant spirit, the unconventional vision of a life beyond ordinariness, and a rhapsodic lyricism in her artistic articulations.

Perhaps too much has been made of Isadora's discovery of Greece when she came to London and the British Museum, studying the vases and tanagras, enthusiastically reading Winckelmann's *Journey to Athens,* or when, some time later, the whole family made a pilgrimage to Athens, "the very holiest shrine of art," as Isadora wrote. She learned, however, more from the Louvre and, above all, from Botticelli and his "Primavera" in Florence.

She must have been familiar with the Greeks when still a young girl. She made it quite clear in *My Life* that on her first journey to Chicago, trying to see one manager after the other in the hope of an engagement, she had taken along "her little white Greek tunic" to dance in. Her mother, an eccentric but educated woman, must have called her children's attention to Greek antiquity. In the 1880s the newspapers were full of descriptions of the sensational discoveries in Troy and other excavations made by the German businessman turned archaeologist Heinrich Schliemann. Schliemann had in fact settled in California, where he died in 1890. When Isadora turned twelve, ancient Greece was the talk of the town among the intellectual upper class. She frequently visited the Oakland Public Library, whose chief librarian was a minor poet who took a liking to the omnivorous young reader and may have spoken about ancient Greece to her. After Isadora had been to Greece she realized more than ever before that she was an American dancer, that she could sense and borrow the spirit of the past without having to revive its dances, of which so little is known. Lincoln Kirstein best expressed that, long before she was in Greece, Isadora was

Émile-Antoine Bourdelle made innumerable drawings and sculptures of Isadora Duncan after 1909, when he first saw her dance in public at the Théâtre du Châtelet. This is one of his drawings, used for a poster in 1914. (Courtesy French Cultural Services)

possessed by that indefinable spirit of inner greatness which we associate in our imagination with what ancient Greece may or ought to have been.

Duncan stressed the point that, born beside the sea, she was immensely influenced by "wave and wind"—both to be taken allegorically. The embrace of spatial vastness, the remote, seemingly never-ending horizon, the tides, the calm and stormy waters stimulated her imagination to the point of excitement. There was something magnetic and mysterious about the expansive presence of the sea for her. It must have given her a physical feeling of transcendental power, of time being and eternity.

She felt the immediateness of nature expressed in her own body and tried to evolve her movements from the movements of nature, where everything seemed to her to move in undulation and harmony. The nude—as the apotheosis of nature—is the noblest form in art, she felt, and the correct conception of beauty can be gained only from the shape and symmetry of the human body. What is dance, if not beauty awakened in the human body? And it is in this context that we can hear the faint, but very distinct, echo of Gautier and the spirit of Romanticism. This spirit was not dead in Isadora: on the contrary, it was wholly there, reborn on the threshold of a new age.

Oscar Wilde's belief that art must derive from art and not from life must have been anathema to Isadora Duncan, and even more so the thought that nature is imperfect and art must teach it a lesson. It has become a rather popular notion by now that, through the growing interest in African culture at that time, Picasso, fascinated by the geometrization of objects, introduced the concept known as cubism. But much too little has been made of the rediscovery of nature by Isadora Duncan. Her deed was all the more daring since her defiant gesture became symbolic of her entire life. She challenged a strongly entrenched belief in artificiality, a belief that anything reminiscent of nature and naturalness was suspect. After all, it was the tail end of the Victorian Age.

And yet the rejuvenation of dance took place within the larger framework and tremendous vogue for physical culture, gymnastics, and sports at the time. This fad—we have already mentioned the bicycling craze for both sexes—started in Sweden and England and quickly spread to all of Europe. Dance and "rhythmic gymnastics"—as gymnastics was then generally called —were interchangeable notions for most people. The awakened interest in the body took the form of a crusade for the old slogan of *mens sana in corpore sano*.

THE idea of movement was so omnipresent in the last few years of the *fin de siècle* that it influenced human thought in remote as much as related areas. Indicative of this was the revived interest in Delsarte's ideas and the emergence of Émile Jaques-Dalcroze. These two musicians wanted to help students in their field and have unintentionally contributed largely to the dance scene. François Delsarte died in 1871, but the impact of his teachings became noticeable only at the turn of the century, or at the time when Dalcroze began to devote all his time and effort to an intelligent method of making his music students find a better sense of rhythm. One may find differences in their methods, but not in their goals.

After having suddenly lost his voice as an opera singer because of incorrect training, Delsarte devoted his life to the study of the laws that govern expression, becoming a philosopher of gesture and pantomime. He believed that all arts and science have a trinitarian basis. His approach to gesture is minutely worked out and based on the triple division of the human being—the intellectual, emotional, and physical—channeled by the triple conditioning of the natural laws of time, motion, and space. The Delsarte system has nine laws of gesture and posture, on which he based his exercises for freedom and relaxation of each part of the body with the purpose of educating each part to express intelligibly emotions and ideas. "Nothing is more deplorable than a gesture without a motive. Perhaps the best gesture is that which is least apparent," he said.

A great many singers, teachers, orators, and such renowned actors as Rachel and William Charles Macready were Delsarte students. The American actor Steele MacKaye was his favorite pupil and the one designated to succeed him. Immediately after the master died in 1871, he propagated the Delsarte method in the United States. His enthusiasm was so contagious that Delsarte's *System of Oratory* was the most popular method of speech training in the New World until the 1920s.

Following Delsarte's death, his reputation waned in Europe while finding a new life in America. Ruth St. Denis and Ted Shawn were strongly attracted by the man and his method. All three had in common humility, faith in God and in themselves as artists, a near-Messianic feeling as teachers and leaders. Ted Shawn wrote his paean on Delsarte in the book *Every Little Movement*. Ruth St. Denis learned most about him from Genevieve Stebbins, one of the few Delsarte disciples who turned his ideas into imaginative improvisations. She and her student Irene Lewisohn, best known for her work at the Neighborhood Playhouse in New York City, created dances of a symbolic and mystical quality that were close to Isadora's concepts.

A curious but very important phenomenon happened in Delsarte's wake in Europe, one that has never received the attention it merits. Because of the influence of his teachings, elocution was finally given a foundation and philosophy. Declamation, or rather public and private recitations of literary works, mainly poetry, became a drawing-room attraction, and by the 1890s it had established itself as a regular pastime of the artistically minded. Ever since, readings of authors have remained an institution in European cities. At the *fin de siècle* they were daily occurrences. Newspapers reported them, and people discussed the recitations as if they were agons of a new kind. Paul Valéry once said, "To recite poetry is to enter into a verbal dance."

The concept of the recital, of a one-man theater, was quite common when Isadora started out. It was not her innovation, as is often assumed. Also, some actors specialized in the art of the recital, which has always suited the European mentality better than the American temperament. Not only must a recitalist be able to command the attention of an audience for an entire evening or matinee, the audience itself is charged with a far more cooperative participation than when facing the performance of an ensemble.

Solo dances—except within the framework of a ballet—had before then been extremely rare. Whenever we come across such solos in the eighteenth or early nineteenth centuries, we indubitably face a female performer, a society lady and nonprofessional (as in the case of Lady Hamilton). Certainly strong impulses for the development of the recital came from the salons, with performances arranged for the benefit of the guests. The salons gave way to the drawing rooms of the upper classes of the bourgeoisie in the second half of the nineteenth century, and it became routine for the lady of the house or a specially invited guest to entertain with a recital on the piano, of poetry or dance.

The new "liberated" dancer chose the recital to express herself. What better ambience could there have been for the fulfillment and expression of her self? There she danced in the glory of her ego, defying and charming the world of yesterday! Loie Fuller and Jane Avril preceded Isadora Duncan in solo dances. But Isadora's success finally established the recital as possibly the best form of presentation for the "modern" dancer. What a delightful postscript to think of *The Dying Swan* in this context as a historic coincidence, created, as it was, as a recital piece by Michel Fokine for Anna Pavlova at the time when the expressive solo began to be in vogue (1905). No other work of consequence followed in the course of balletic development. The solo field was left to the modern dancers, first to their soulsearching, then to their nonliteral needs of expressionism.

DELSARTE cannot very well be credited with having fathered the recital form, but history took its cue from him and went its own way. Something similar happened to Jaques-Dalcroze, the Viennese-born musician of Swiss parentage who in 1892 was professor of harmony at the Geneva Conservatory. As he was an all-around knowledgeable man, we may rightly assume that he knew about Delsarte and his method. Like his predecessor, he was dissatisfied with the rhythmic sensibilities of his music students and, out of frustration, developed a theory and method that aimed at improving a person's sense of rhythm through the translation of sounds into physical movements. Dalcroze realized that musical rhythm depended on motor consciousness for its fullest expression and, to deepen the awareness of good rhythm, he tried to create "a rapid and regular current of communication between brain and body" with the help of rhythm. Dalcroze also believed in the trinity of body and mind, dividing the body very much as Delsarte did into head and upper chest as the seat of the intellectual and spiritual person, the middle part of the torso as the habitat of the emotions, the abdomen and the hips as the animalistic zone or the physical center. It all seems self-evident, and any similarities in the thoughts of these two musicologists are coincidental logic.

Dalcroze came at the right moment in history when motion was of prime interest; when dancers emerged who wanted to reveal inmost experiences through bodily articulation in a free-flowing style, unhampered by century-old rules; when Pathé created its first moving pictures in Paris. Dalcroze was riding the wave of physical education, and schools of the Dalcroze method sprang up everywhere. His system is known under the name of eurythmics—the good rhythm—and it seemed at first sight to be of an attractive simplicity. It developed in the form of a symphonic work, with each dancer following a specific instrument note for note. But his music visualizations were full of rhythmic subtleties and harmonic structure.

These notions are reminiscent of recurring attempts in dance history at expressive gesturing, exactly cadenced to music. Viganò was striving toward a very similar goal when he tried to give his ballets dramatic substance through a plastic rendering of the music. And even further back, in the early days of the Renaissance, it was Baïf's academy whose humanists attempted to find an ideal balance between the rhythm of the music and its physical realization. These academicians wanted to recapture the unified expression of music, the spoken word, and movement that they believed was all lost with the Golden Age. Apparently, over time and different cultures, mankind has longed to establish rhythmic harmony in the human body.

With Dalcroze, music and rhythmic movement again began to play a central role in educating the whole being, in refining a new sense of self. He never intended to create dances or propagate a new school of dancing; he had a modernized Greek conception of the whole person in harmony with the rhythmic experiences of what he hears and sees and the way he moves. Dalcroze was a man inspired. Although his exercises were to the point of his concepts and beneficial, he had a limited and conservative attitude toward human creative needs. His was a Platonian philosophy. Plato, the patrician, condemned the Bacchic frenzy in the dancer and recommended soothing and calm movements, since they mark the dance of peace, the emmeleia. Also, for Plato the dance was never an exercise for the body only, but an art form that came from the gods and, in turn, pleased the gods. He said in *The Laws:*

He who best blends gymnastics with music and applies them most suitably to the soul is the man whom we should most rightly pronounce to be the most perfect and harmonious musician.

Since for the Greeks a musician was, at the same time, a dancer and the soul stood for the whole man, this pronouncement could also have come from Dalcroze's pen. The importance of Dalcroze and his method can be measured only by the impact he had on some of the greatest names of his time, from Pavlova to Mary Wigman and Hanya Holm, from Nijinsky to Uday Shankar, from Marie Rambert to Kurt Jooss. German Maecenases built an impressive and complete college for Dalcroze in Hellerau near Dresden. Hundreds of students from all over the world came annually to study there; innumerable Dalcroze schools sprang up in many cities, directed by some of his most gifted students.

Two different incidents in the wake of Dalcroze's success may shed light on the simultaneity of ideas at a given time. Adolphe Appia stressed the identity of their aims in a letter to Dalcroze, even though their points of departure and the roads they took were not the same. But physical education through and for music seemed to Appia a major step in the right direction. Dalcroze was delighted to have found a kindred soul in Appia, whose approval of his method and encouragement meant a great deal to him. When Appia became familiar with Dalcroze's ideas, Appia had already written two of his major theoretical works. By chance he was present at a public demonstration of Dalcroze's rhythmic gymnastics in May 1906. What he saw convinced him that an "abnormal subtlety, a pliable and controlled mobility" were the important prerequisites for any performer to meet the needs of the "new staging."

When Appia and Dalcroze met, both reformers knew what they were aiming at, but they were still far from being able to define their methods clearly (both shied away from naming their findings a "method"). Between 1906 and 1909 Appia would often show up at Dalcroze's studio, devising short scenes for the students, who executed them to music. Yet he learned from Dalcroze how to "make music vibrate" in the body. It was Appia's idea to have built "rhythmic spaces," platforms at various levels and of different shapes, thus creating a "living space" for the moving singer/actor/dancer. For some time the two men advanced their ideas in imaginative harmony. In the summer of 1912 the garden city of Hellerau was inaugurated with Dalcroze's dance-drama *Echo and Narcissus,* followed by the scene in Hades from Gluck's *Orfeo ed Euridice.* Appia, who had designed the sets, could proudly state that "for the first time since the Greek era, a perfect fusion of all media of expression and in close mutual subordination has been realized. . . ."

Another incident took place soon afterward. Dance historians like to point to the famous meeting between Vaslav Nijinsky and Dalcroze's assistant Marie Rambert (then still a young Polish girl by the name of Miriam Rambach). At that time Nijinsky was to choreograph Stravinsky's *Sacre du Printemps.* Diaghilev believed in Nijinsky's choreographic gift but was also well aware of the rhythmically complicated score. Thus he took Nijinsky and the entire company to Dalcroze to have their rhythmic sensibilities improved. While the other dancers of the Ballets Russes did not take to Dalcroze's ideas, Nijinsky, as a Pole sharing an idiomatic and emotional language with Miriam Rambach, made the best of it. He was able to transcribe plastically the rhythmic differentiations in the dancing characters and corps. His wife, Romola, described his accomplishments:

> The choreography was the most amazing and correct visualization of the score. Each rhythm was danced, the counterpoints were built up choreographically in the groups. It is through rhythm, and rhythm only, that the dance identified itself with the music. The rhythmical counterpoint is employed in the choral movements. When the orchestra plays a trill on the flutes, movements thin out, and so do the dancers. Then the tune begins on woodwinds two octaves apart, and on the stage two groups of three dancers each detach themselves from the lines and dance, corresponding to the tune. The mouse-like shuffling of the Sorceress, the rapid steps of the young men, correspond to the musical expression of the movement as do the intricate rhythms of the joyful dance of the Chosen Maiden.

Early in this century Dalcroze's discreet handwriting could be detected on several dance works, such as Ruth St. Denis's *Unfinished Symphony,* in which each individual dancer represented a single instrument, and all pictorial images evoked by the rhythm were finally fused into a choreographic entity. She called it a "synchoric orchestra." It carried the stamp of her personality, but was recognizable Dalcroze.

Dalcroze was forgotten after World War II. He had become a fixture of history, and the man so subtly attuned to good rhythm somehow seemed out of tune with his time. But he taught in Geneva until his death in 1950. He became reappreciated with the growing interest in dance therapy in the 1960s, and several European schools began to revive his ideas. Only Rudolf Steiner's Anthroposophic Society has never stopped practicing eurythmy, a word very close to Dalcroze's eurythmics.

The Anthroposophists often produce plays, mainly classics and among these mostly Goethe. They have their own Dalcrozean way of moving to words and music. The motivating forces, however, are different from those of Dalcroze. Eurythmy wishes to visualize "the spiritual law and quality of word and tone through gesture and movement and raise them to the level of an artistic experience." To accomplish the visual language of eurythmy, one needs a "mind awareness," which can help realize artistically what lies hidden behind each vowel or consonant, each syllable and word, each tone and sound. The Anthroposophists' strong belief in ultimate awareness is remotely suggestive of Dalcroze's endeavor to bring us closer to a state of rhythmic harmony within ourselves and with the world.

Dalcroze may have had only tangential importance for the ballet, but he played a significant part in the awakening of movement consciousness at the beginning of this century. He helped prepare the ground for many creative minds and bodies to explore artistic possibilities beyond his method. And he did so without being actually involved in the evolutionary trend in dance history. Isadora Duncan, who was one of the prime movers in this direction, preceded Dalcroze by a few years. But those who came after her and particularly those European dancers profiting from her spiritual guidance, originally emerged from Dalcroze schools.

His contribution may be described as exploration by way of teaching, and he remained a teacher. Isadora may at best have been methodical in her curiosity, but an emotional urgency toward self-realization was the essence of her being. She was out "to express the truth of my being in gestures and movement," as she said in her autobiography, then adding: "It has taken me long years to find even one absolutely true movement." The story of her standing in front of a mirror seeking physical release for all that went on spiritually in her seems to have had more symbolic than practical value. Ignoring the academic past, she was utterly free in directing her strength toward the sources of movement.

It would be wrong to look at her deed as a mere deliverance of the dance from the shackles of the past. She aimed at the deliverance of humanity, and dance was a means to this end. She discovered the roots of that impulse toward movement which is the natural response to an experience. She believed that spontaneous movement of the body to sensory or emotional stimuli leads to ultimate artistic expression. Progressive civilization tends to dull and inhibit this fundamental and universal desire in us. The conscious use of this faculty must be revived in order to deepen and broaden the whole range of life. Through spontaneity we can regain our freedom from established rules and postulates. Only when we have the courage to touch life in the raw will we come closer to the awareness of our inherent power. Only our true being can resist the forces that constantly try to throw us into a conventional existence. These are some basic concepts that belong with Isadora's ideas about life and dance. Her body interpreted her awareness of inner experiences. She did not create modern dance; she made its becoming possible.

Escape, the East, and Ruth St. Denis

SINCE THERE ARE NO ISOLATED PHENOMENA IN HISTORY, IT IS TO BE expected that other dancers would appear at the same time with dance works in a free and antiballetic style. Irma Duncan, one of the six "Isadorables," claimed that Isadora was well aware of having been imitated. "Everyone is running off with my ideas!" she is supposed to have said quite often. Irma Duncan's assertion that Dalcroze and the Russian Ballet belong with Isadora's imitators is bordering on the ridiculous. True, she had impressed Michel Fokine for some time, but this was the only direct influence of importance, of which history has taken notice. There is of course no doubt that, in a very general way, her daring had a stimulating effect on many dancers of her time.

Take the case of Maud Allan, the Canadian-born dancer, Isadora's contemporary, with ideas surprisingly similar to hers. Maud wanted to revive the classic Greek dance and mainly danced barefoot in a loose Greek gown. She was trained as a musician, and she was a self-taught dancer. Imitation or influence? Coincidence or parallelism of concept? Allan used only semiclassic or classic music for her dances, another predilection she shared with Isadora. Some of the dances in her repertory were *Peer Gynt,* to Edvard Grieg's score, Mendelssohn's *Spring Song,* and Chopin's *Funeral March.*

Was Maud Allan not also justified in wishing to revive the ancient Greek dance when, since Schliemann's excavations in Troy and Mycenae, a revival of everything Greek was in vogue? Allan had made her headquarters in Vienna, then the world's musical center. The Parliament in that city, an imposing edifice with a statue of Pallas Athena in front of it, had been built in modified Grecian style in 1883. Not so long ago, a yearning for everything medieval expressed the escapist feeling of the Romantic era. But by the 1880s and '90s the magic of the medieval knight was gone. With growing industrialization and fear of an uncertain new age, the idealization of the Greco-Roman past again became the window display of the neo-Romantic days. Public buildings and banks rested on the solid columns of ancient Greece, as if a Doric, Ionic, or Corinthian column could create a feeling of security. The classics had been revived and studied ever since the Renaissance, but now they became the heart of education and were commercialized, with organized journeys to the ruins of antiquity. The notion of the classical grand tour to Italy was then born. Men like the French historian Maurice

Emmanuel reconstructed movement fragments from Greek vases and reliefs, comparing and blending them with nineteenth-century Greek folk dancing and really believing they had rediscovered the dance of the ancient Greeks. Maud Allan did not necessarily have to imitate Isadora Duncan, she may simply have made use of the fads of her time.

Whatever Maud Allan danced was charged with strong dramatic accents. She made her debut in Vienna in 1903 with *The Vision of Salomé*, to Richard Strauss's music. It was a mimed and rather realistic dance. In its final moments she would press her lips to Jokanaan's severed head in the best of Grand Guignol styles. Her bosom was loosely held by a halter and her flowing skirt seemed transparent. *Salomé* was her most impressive vehicle; with it she stunned her audiences. Allan was a far more accessible dancer than Duncan and successful wherever she appeared, which was almost everywhere in the world, places which *"die göttliche* Isadora,'' as the Germans called her, never reached: China, Australia, New Zealand, South Africa, India, Malaya, South America, and Egypt.

History is not fairer than life, but it has its own laws that rule its decisions. It is not a schoolteacher grading the accomplishments of artists. It records what is happening and then shelves its records for future generations to make use of them as they please or feel fit. Ruth St. Denis, who began to tour Europe in 1906, when Duncan and Allan were already established dancers, writes about the latter in her autobiography, *An Unfinished Life:*

> During the Scala engagement [St. Denis was dancing at the small tucked-away Scala in London at that time] Maud Allan was playing to packed houses at the Palace Theater. She played for months, with lines, blocks long, waiting to see her performance. "And so much for the irony of the world," I thought, when I heard that Isadora Duncan had slipped, practically unheralded, into the small Duke of York Theater where she was giving performances before a sparse audience. In my two years of intensive work I had never had a chance to see her, so I rushed to the theater and bought a ticket. . . . Oh, the irony, the irony, I thought as I went out; Maud Allan might dance before kings and receive a good stipend, but neither she nor any of her successors could be more than a faint echo of this pure spirit of the dance.

Ruth St. Denis had made her decision and, so it seems, did history.

"One's whole career, in retrospect, seems only a great first act to an incompleted drama of the soul," is one of the key sentences in St. Denis' story of her *Unfinished Life.* "Where was I," she asked herself, "the immortal and essential Me, when the Ruthie Dennis, canonized by David Belasco into an undeserved sainthood, was dancing her way around the world?"

She created the legend of her early beginnings by relating her encounter with the image of the Egyptian goddess Isis on a cigarette poster while, as an actress, she toured with David Belasco's company in Buffalo. There is a fairy-tale touch to it. The best fairy tales have an obvious moral, not necessarily articulated but buried in their symbolism and ready to be resurrected at the least provocation. There was the uncertainty of a dream being carried around in her waking hours and holding her "essential Me" up to the mirror of reality until the cigarette poster stopped the aimless flow of her visions. It acted like a challenge thrown at her and made the illuminations of her inner world—to use her phraseology—suddenly break open like a flower. She had realized the emptiness of her acting parts in Belasco's company and, at the same time, a yearning for new experiences. This coincided with her sudden interest in Buddhism. "Undoubtedly," she wrote, "I was preparing myself, unknown to me, for the rapidly approaching moment when all my perplexities would be clarified, all my energies brought into a dazzling focus."

What was apparently unknown to her was the influences from outside that constantly added new colors to the illuminations within. Since Commodore Matthew Calbraith Perry forced the opening of Japan to the Western world in 1853, European and American artists were stunned by the delicacy of the Japanese paintings and prints; toward the end of the last century these exerted more and more influence on Western culture.

Particularly during the first decade of the twentieth century, Europe became sated with a secondhand experience of everything oriental, which was another way of refuge from reality. Seen from a histrionic viewpoint, David Belasco's play *Madame Butterfly,* produced in 1900, triumphed at all opera houses in Giacomo Puccini's version from 1904 on. Ruth St. Denis must have been well aware of it. It was certainly the time of a thousand and one books on oriental themes, which overflooded the bookstores. The attraction of the East was also personified by Eastern poets. The Bengal poet Rabindranath Tagore was one of the great successes early in this century. His major works were translated into all European languages. They are characterized by a subtle lyricism, an extollment of the beauty of life and the universe, by a sincere belief in God and simplicity. His life and work must have fallen on fertile ground with St. Denis. His prose sounded like poetry, and his poetry was like an image of tenderness and reverie woven in a carpet. His words were another beacon of hope, of faraway beauty and peace for those who painfully felt the pressures of a menacing civilization and progress.

Speaking of one of her first major successes at the Scala Theatre in London, Ruth St. Denis mentioned her attempt at a Japanese dance. It was in reality only an episode from a haunting love story by Lafcadio Hearn under whose spell she had just come. It was called *A Shirabyoshi* (dancing girl of ancient Japan). Lafcadio Hearn, who had left the United States for Japan, where he married a high-ranking Japanese lady and where he died in 1904,

Ruth St. Denis in RADHA, *1904.* (*Courtesy the Author*)

was only one of several writers who became infatuated with the Orient. The American Hearn presented an idealized Japan in most of the stories he wrote during the 1890s. A many-sided man, Hearn also had a philosophical bent and tried to trace the link between the doctrine of Karma in Buddhism and the role of heredity according to the then latest scientific advances. He was the translator of several books—among them, those of Pierre Loti, another popular writer of exotic stories.

As a naval officer, Loti enjoyed the personal experience of faraway countries and people. His novels expressed the need of people to escape the realities of their time. But it would be unjust to dismiss him as a skillful writer of exoticism and adventure. His philosophy is somewhat reminiscent of Schnitzler's point of view when Loti envisions love as an escape from the fear of death and when he despairs over the transitoriness of sensual pleasures. A deep compassion for humanity is gently expressed in his stories, but beyond his story-telling dexterity he has touched upon the doubts and obsessions of the twentieth century—the seeking of relief from the perplexities of the psyche, the stress on eroticism, and the rebellion against the past and norms. He anticipated the existentialist feeling of futility and was attracted by the irrational, by the wilderness of the unknown.

In glorifying primitive life and pagan love, Loti was on the same wavelength as Paul Gauguin. In trying to escape the realities of their time, these artists were, above all, discovering the sensation of total aloneness and were losing the sense of belonging in the truest romantic fashion. Gauguin's entire life and work were a protest against the soul-destroying materialism of a wearisome bourgeois civilization. In 1891 he wrote to Strindberg: "You suffer from your civilization. Barbarism is to me a renewal of youth." Gauguin preceded by a few years the Braques and Picassos, the Kokoschkas and Klees, whose art was aimed at disturbing and challenging their contemporaries, who wanted "to be as though newborn," as Klee said, "knowing no pictures, entirely without impulses, almost in an original state."

The need in the artist to go back to the beginning in order to find the expression of the inmost self is the same unconscious process that drove Isadora Duncan and Ruth St. Denis to create the way they did, or rather could not help doing. The writers and painters were prompted by the same momentum that made the various modern dancers find their way of expression. When Gauguin demanded "a reasoned and frank return to the beginning," it sounded like the trumpet call of a new age. Gauguin loathed Europe and its civilization. His escape from it—he died in the Marquesas Islands in 1903—was marked by melancholy and despair as much as by the total fulfillment of a great dream.

Many artists may be in possession of a passport to greatness, but only a few dare to make the journey. Many artists at the turn of the century dared, among them Ruth St. Denis, who never felt that she had a career but that she had a mission. She referred to herself as a self-appointed prophetess. What was her message? The great mission of the dancer, as she saw it, was to better humankind; the highest function of the dance was to enable people to grow beyond their ordinariness. Her thoughts had an oriental feeling. We so easily forget that the Near and Far East gave us our great ethical prophets: Moses, Jesus, Buddha, Mohammed, Confucius. When Ruth St. Denis escaped to the East, she carried the Bible with her. She fused Tao and the Way with the Sermon on the Mount and Gethsemane.

She was as self-taught a dancer as Duncan and Fuller. She admitted that she had taken three ballet classes only and knew three of the basic five positions. But art was alive in her. She was beautiful to boot, and already beautiful to watch in *Radha,* her first dance, delightful in her exotic costume and setting. As the goddess Radha she rose from deep contemplation to express the sensual joys of human existence. But then, realizing how futile are the delights of the flesh, she returned to her mystic stage of contemplation. (It is as if Schnitzler or Loti had written the scenario for her.) There was simple, organic logic in the way her line developed, flowing into a monumental gesture. At times the rhythmic power of a walking step was the driving motivation for her body. Even moments of stillness in her poses must have evoked a strange, if not sensual, pleasure. People were enthralled seeing her without understanding or caring for any otherworldly meaning.

Some, however, did receive her message. Among them was the Austrian poet Hugo von Hofmannsthal (1874–1929), who aimed at the appreciation of the higher values in life, rejecting man's futile concentration on those passions precious to the aesthetes and hedonists of the Nineties.

Poet Philosophers and the Dance

IN THE TWO YEARS RUTH ST. DENIS SPENT DANCING IN GERMANY AND Austria, from late 1906 to 1909, she found a deeper understanding and appreciation on the part of her audiences than anywhere else in Europe. Paris and even London were ballet-minded. In Germany—with the exception of the extravagant interlude in Stuttgart in the 1760s—the ballet never really took root. This is why the Germans were far more open to such totally new dance experiences as those offered by Fuller, Duncan, and St. Denis. Duncan's fame had been established in Germany for two years before Ruth St. Denis came to Berlin, and St. Denis had doubts that the Germans would take to her way of dancing as much as they had to Isadora's. She noted afterward that the spirit of the Germans is philosophical and serious and attuned to the revelations of new artists in a profound and analytical manner, searching for cause and reason where others are satisfied with effect only.

She was justified in making this observation because during the first three decades of this century the culture of the German-speaking people no longer stood in the shadow of French accomplishments and, before the rise of Hitler, was unique in the 1920s. In an experience similar to those of her two American predecessors—three if we add Maud Allan—she was gratified to find a knowledgeable interest and not only the enthusiastic acclaim of entertainment-hungry theatergoers. Count Harry Kessler, an ardent sponsor of the arts, introduced Ruth St. Denis to other Maecenases who made her acquainted with Hugo von Hofmannsthal, by then an esteemed writer in the German language. Not only did his critique of her "temple" dances give her the necessary courage to continue on her way, but his personality also "stirred a strange beauty in my dormant emotional spirit," as she wrote in her autobiography.

She was then twenty-six years old and far more beautiful than Isadora. Hofmannsthal was only six years older, but a very mature man and artist, having achieved great acclaim as a writer of thought-provoking and form-fulfilled poetry when only sixteen years old. He was a typical product of his age, as much the heir of decadence and overrefinement as Ruth St. Denis was the New World edition of Hindu asceticism. They were both, in their fashion, dreamers of the ultimate and beautiful in life.

In Hofmannsthal's diary we find a note, dated January 17, 1907, in which he mentions her particular impressionability, in everyday experiences as much as in questions of artistic taste. Her sensibility and intelligence embodied in his eyes the essential attitude of a person who thought with her feelings. And in her unpublished notes she depicts him as an extraordinary man who, in the radiation of his intellect, emanated the kind of thinking and feeling that is constantly dedicated to the beautiful.

He wrote twice about his impressions of her performances, once a very long essay. He was moved by her mysteriously strange presentation, which neither pretended to be genuinely ethnographic nor worked by sensational means. He underlined the experience of how European imagination could be suffused with Asiatic beauty. "I feel that something here has, like a flame, penetrated the real and sensuous. . . ." The metaphor of the dance as a flame appears and reappears with the writers of that time. Hofmannsthal found that she viewed the eternal things of the East "with eyes which were not at all ordinary" and that the dream of the Orient is beautifully reflected in her "unforgettable gestures."

In the magazine *Die Zeit,* Hofmannsthal wrote a long descriptive essay on Ruth St. Denis' stage visualizations. There was the semidarkness of the interior of an Indian temple onstage, incense rising up, gongs being beaten, priests, hardly visible, practicing their rites. A bluish light was concentrated on the goddess sitting in the attitude of the Buddha:

> Nothing in her stirred; her eyes were open, but her eyelashes did not move. Some untold force held together her entire body. This scene lasted fully one minute but one would have wished to go on viewing this motionless figure. It had no resemblance to a statue as imitated by a human being. There was no forced, artificial stiffness in it, but rather an inner spiritual necessity.

The images retained by his inner eye were immediately associated with previous experiences. He discovered a mysterious smile on this dancer, as if emanating from "her motionless eyes." It made him recall Buddha's smile, "a smile not of this world, an unfeminine smile." It also reminded him of the impenetrable smile on Leonardo's paintings. When Ruth St. Denis began to dance, her slow, measured movements were like those of the Javanese and Cambodian dancers who, in 1889, had come to Europe for the first time:

> It is of course the same that all Oriental dances are aiming for: the dance, the dance as such, the silent music of the human body: the rhythmical flow of unceasing and true movement, as Rodin has put it.

Hofmannsthal's critique was for Ruth St. Denis a diploma with which she could proudly return to the States.†

Next to Eastern motifs, the stories of the Bible were closest to her heart. The figure of a dancing Salome was a recurring theme, befitting the *fin de siècle,* and a most obvious choice for her. Ruth St. Denis' aesthetic feelings must have been revolted by Oscar Wilde's conception of Salome, and Maud Allan's then popular version must also have disgusted her. The theme of Salome has fascinated sculptors and painters, particularly in the Middle Ages when people had a great understanding for everything excessive and freakish in human passions. What St. Denis had in mind was a Salome close to the biblical concept, with none of the decadent reflections of the time. Hofmannsthal worked on such a scenario for her, but the plans did not come to a conclusion. There are remarks about Hofmannsthal's interest in this topic in letters to a fellow writer in Vienna and to St. Denis; some letters, however, addressed to her with detailed ideas about the dance were lost. The motif of intense narcissism was undoubtedly a guiding line for his concept. "Her condition," he wrote, "of the most subtle, self-sufficient egoism means that she is intent on making use of all things, that the entire sense

---

† These were still the days when American artists had to be approved by European audiences and critics in order to be recognized in their home country.

of existence becomes focused in her." A posthumous sketch from those days indicates how he envisioned this dance for her:

SALOMÉ

Every limb being tested, vain self-enjoyment of the limbs' own harmonies. Everything is here to serve, each sphere and form of nature used up by this servitude. The gesture perceived as the acme of existence.

In front of an idol under whose deadly eyes the gratified elation becomes torture. The idol is forcefully spiraled upward in order to become humble. Specter of fear, the whole world converged in the idol. Touch of nocturnal air. The flame of a torch dying down, a shadow on the ground.

Count Kessler and other admirers of Ruth St. Denis in Germany offered to have a theater built for her in Weimar, which at the same time would be a home for music, sculpture, and painting besides the new dance. However, the dancer was plagued by homesickness for America and could not see herself signing a contract for five years. Had her decision been in the affirmative, Denishawn might not have been, but Hugo von Hofmannsthal would have had a place for his theatrical activities as he and his friends desired for him.

What a collaboration between St. Denis and Hofmannsthal would have meant for dance and literature at that point in the careers of both artists would be idle speculation. But we know how much Hofmannsthal was intrigued by the dance, which to him was a lyric-dramatic experience that could never find a substitute in the word. He felt that every gesture held the nucleus of a dance, and in his essay "On Pantomime" he stressed the importance of the gesture onstage. He also put his belief into practice. For instance, in his opera scenario *Elektra* for Richard Strauss, he has Elektra circling around Aegisthus in a sinister dance. "Why do you stagger around with your light?" Aegisthus asks her. "What do you dance?" Hofmannsthal believed that, at certain climactic moments, expressive movement is the only means of conveying a dramatic experience. When Agamemnon's death is avenged, the poet has Elektra descend the steps, and his stage direction reads: "She holds her head thrown back like a maenad. She raises her knees, her arms are stretched out, it is an indescribable dance in which she moves forward." The dance is indescribable because the feelings of human triumph are inexpressible. Hofmannsthal felt that all one can do when one is happy is to be silent and dance.

HOFMANNSTHAL sought to unravel the mystery of life and to re-create the beauty of being through symbolism. In spiritual proximity moved another German poet, Rainer Maria Rilke (1875–1926), whose fame came with the turn of the century and for whom art and life were interchangeable experiences. In a letter to the princess of Thurn and Taxis he wrote: ". . . I must do something for Nijinsky, the Russian dancer . . . a poem which so to speak must be absorbed first and then danced." He did not think of a poem to be spoken to the dance, but of one to be turned into a dance.

Rilke was also impressed by Alexander Sakharoff and his wife, Clothilde, a dancing team whose recitals in Europe and South America enjoyed a great vogue early this century but are nearly forgotten today. In their concert dances they developed an individual style that they called by a confusing term: *Abstract mime.* The critics maintained that their dance works were highly emotional about stylized themes, with those of the Renaissance particularly acclaimed. Sakharoff began to be known in 1911, two years before the German *Ausdruckstanz* (expressionistic dance) was born. Rilke called Sakharoff *"poète de la danse,"* defining his dancing as "music of free movement." With music having achieved such a vital presence in those days, Rilke also chimed in with the intellectual chorus and saw in the dance the realization of music in visual form.

Rilke's portrayal of the Cambodian dancing girls is of descriptive and vivid power. What fascinated him most about these "gracile little dancers," which impressed him like "metamorphosed gazelles," was their hands, reminding him of Buddha hands, for only Buddha hands know "how to sleep . . . to rest for centuries on laps." He wrote a lyrically inspired study of the human hand while secretary to Rodin. Ever since, the expressiveness of the human hand, whether chiseled in stone or fully awake as the articulation of inmost emotions—and particularly the moving hands of dancers—set his imagination on fire.

Even when the theme did not involve dancing, we find a recognizable rhythmic pattern in Rilke's poetic language, modulated by the repetition of images. The verbal sound often imitates a circle or a march, and one can easily detect an intentional cadence in his poetry or prose. Certain of his word sequences convey the feeling of phrases moving through contraction and release. Movement and metamorphosis are key concepts of his entire poetic output. Rilke said in *Dialogue* that "dancers visualize but do not explain themselves," and in reading most of his poems I have often been impressed by the verbal power of this poet, who visualizes without explaining himself.

Poets like Hofmannsthal and Rilke were prone to be attracted and inspired by the "otherness" of the dancers from the East and by dance per se, since for them the essence and surprise of art were wrapped in wonder, in the elusive gesture of something enchanting and remote.

AFTER the Romantic rage had spent its creative power, many writers tried to give the ballet some literate substance and literary sustenance, em-

bracing the art form with a new aesthetic awareness. It was as if these profound poets felt the need for a philosophic afterthought or a poetic postscript to the dance. Because of its ephemeral character among the arts and
never having had the mindful support of the intelligentsia to a sufficient
measure, dance had been condemned to a Cinderella-like existence. Is it really feasible that the inseparability of the dancer from the artist's corporeality, of mind from body, gave the intellectual an excuse for expressing
or suppressing a feeling of disdain for the dance as an art form?

At the time when theater dance suffered a serious low, social dancing experienced a euphoria. It was joined by the first wave of imports from the
New World in ragtime, with its strange syncopations and shifted accents.
The enthusiastic reception of ragtime indicated another act of liberation, a
freedom from the yoke of harmonic music. With the ragtime craze, Europe
joyfully accepted the constant influx of American social dances: the
Brazilian maxixe as early as 1890; the one-step and turkey trot around the
turn of the century, and the cakewalk in 1903. This, too, was part of
Europe's fascination with the faraway, the need to escape its own surround-
ings.

As an antidote to the rhapsodic music hall and ballroom dancing we find
the heightened interest of the poet philosophers in the dance, which coincided with a novel and wholesome reorientation in this, as in all other arts.
These dancers used the dance as a means by which to explore new poetic
scopes, since both dance and poetry share something basic in their mode and
mood of expression. Their strongest momentum lies in their suggestiveness
through which the mysterious world of our emotions is more easily penetrated than with the help of any directed statement or factual description.

One might be inclined to hear Gautier's voice when Stéphane Mallarmé
said, as though coming out of a trance or meditation, "Beauty alone exists,
and it has only one perfect expression, poetry." In a commemoration of
Gautier in *Toast funèbre* in 1873, poetry was extolled by Mallarmé as the
symbolic means of re-creating Eden. Mallarmé wanted poetry to recapture
the magic of evocation and suggestiveness from music without yielding a
verbal inch of the intelligible word. He intended to write a book in which
innocence and experience would reflect his vision of the evolution of beauty.
This he wanted to do when he settled down in Paris and became acquainted
with the ballet. He wrote in a letter (November 10, 1885) to Paul Verlaine
that his two passions in the arts were to see a ballet and to hear the organ
played.

Gautier and Jules Lemaître (1853–1914) were writing in the daily press
and for a living. As a consequence they could not muse about a subject as
Mallarmé or Paul Valéry did. Gautier's and Lemaître's philosophic and poetic attitudes toward dance were subjected to utilitarian influences (something Gautier would loathe to hear), to the commercial interests of the

paper, the political situation, and public opinion. Mallarmé was in a different position. He made his living as an English teacher, not as a journalist. If journalism was not anathema to him, it certainly was incompatible with his way of thinking and writing.

In contrast to Gautier, he rarely went to the theater—even though he thought that the theater was of the highest importance—and only on occasion was he seen at a ballet performance. He mistrusted the contemporary stage and its ability to create a memorable production. Sometimes Mallarmé wrote critiques: that is, he developed his poetic-philosophical thoughts, taking the performance of a dancer as his point of departure, as he did with Loïe Fuller or the ballerina La Cornalba.

For Mallarmé the dance was never reality but "only the mysterious and sacred interpretation" of something real. He saw the ballet as a symbolic art and wished to replace the notion of the ballerina by "some nameless, impersonal, glittering glance of absoluteness." He envisioned the dancer as a phenomenon that denies the body, that lets us forget that there is a body at all, and yet with one metamorphosis linked to another the dancer is able to renew herself—as a dancing image, not as a dancing woman. Even though the legs become visible, they are, for Mallarmé, never the legs of a certain dancer, they are essential tools with which the dancer evokes an idea, and the dancing itself becomes an idealized process in the dehumanization of the dancer from woman to a metaphor.

Mallarmé also demanded the "absolute" vision of the theatergoer as a precondition to seeing in any work of art the essence of its being, not only its meaning and certainly more than mere visual or emotional pleasure in viewing the dance, as Gautier and Lemaître prescribed and practiced. But this precludes a process of growing into an impersonal spectator who must learn to look through and beyond the dance in order to absorb and reflect on what the dancer creates, which, in the final analysis, becomes an "ideal wedding of thoughts." Mallarmé identified the ballet with "the plastic rendering of poetry," of poetry that speaks to us in symbols and whose aim is the purity of expression. Ballet is the transposition of reality into a dream world. The dancer is a being apart, "the prodigious being withdrawn beyond all possible life," only half human since she is a mute symbol only. If the dancer is a symbol, she is an idealized symbol of Mallarmé's imagination, and he attached little importance to her physical being. His was a powerful plea for the abolishment of the human and emotional factors, which he felt only blurred the vision.

Paul Valéry also realized the plastic beauty of the art and at least partly denied seeing the woman in the dancer. When he says that "there is nothing of her," that she is "a bodiless thing," and that only when she ceases to dance does she return to her feminine nature, he sounds like Mallarmé's echo. Valéry admitted to having been Mallarmé's disciple. Although Valéry's poetry and prose are interspersed with similes of the dance and dancer, he hesitated to write his profound symposium *L'Âme et la danse* (*The Soul and the Dance*) because, he admitted, Mallarmé had already exhausted the subject. But while following the traces of Mallarmé, he ventured beyond his master's speculations. Valéry did not see the sculptured beauty of the female body as an apotheosis of flesh-become-art, as Gautier did, nor did he see a totally dehumanized figure and spiritualized metaphor in the dancer, like Mallarmé. Valéry goes back to the beginning and questions with Plato the justification of the arts and grants them the status of a refuge, suggesting that it be declared as such.

He could not help comparing poetry with dancing and found that both are "action without an end." The same ephemeral feeling, the fading into meaningful nothingness, is common to both. Movement and life can never be separated from one another because complete rest is death, as Pascal said. Movement and rhythm are the "most real in reality" and dance is a climactic moment of existence achieved in joyous intoxication. Time and again Valéry returns to such similes as "Life is a dancing woman who would divinely cease to be a woman if she could pursue her leap up to the skies."

Valéry sees the dance as intoxication and the dancer as the intoxicated who is able to involve others in her intoxication. He lets Socrates, the focal character in his symposium, say that "amongst all intoxications, the noblest, the inimical to ennui, is the intoxication due to action. Our acts and particularly those of our acts that set our bodies in motion may throw us into a strange and admirable state." Valéry may also have remembered Loie Fuller when he had Socrates rhapsodize about the dancer:

> Does she not look as though she were living quite at her ease in an element comparable to fire, in a highly subtle essence of music and motion, while she inhales inexhaustible energy. . . . O flame! Living and divine! But what is a flame, if not the moment itself?

Valéry juxtaposes to all metaphysical speculation the dictum "One must dare to live," and, after having given due credit to Mallarmé's purely spiritualized image of the dancer, he recognizes the human being in the dancer again. She is no longer a symbol only, but also a dancing reality. He does not minimize the fact that this flesh-turned-flame accomplishes its feats, the conquest of gravity, the flight into oblivion, through many hours of hard and precise work.

Because in his eyes the dancer is a wave "celebrating the mysteries of absence and presence" and because the dance is movement and action in its most pure, it is many different things and yet the very same to the poet philosophers. They may try to capture its meaning and essence with the slings of their imagination, but, in the last analysis, the enigma of its beauty and the secrecy of its being seem to defy verbalization. For you cannot know dance only by the mind, you must see it with your heart.

SINCE movement is basic to men and women, its artistic expression is a ready-made vehicle for the poetic mind, and particularly for the mind escaping into a world of imaginary reality, the most private province of the self. The poet philosophers rang in the new century with their thoughts in flight. They found some intuitive truths while divesting the ballerina of her lived reality.

There were great similarities in the personal attitudes of these poet philosophers. What they had in common was their reference to the dancer as a female as if she were the sole person dancing. They accepted it as a fact that they did not question nor doubt. Surely they were the heirs of a period in which the image of the female dancer reigned supreme and absolute. In the perverted mind of the Romantic the woman, earth mother, image of constancy in contrast to the hunting, fighting, and dreaming male, became a phantom and the essence of the ephemeral. But in dehumanizing her a few decades later, in divesting her of her reality, she became more real again because eternal, the vessel of life's wonder, the intuitive origin of all things.

The Romantics of the 1830s needed the ideal figure of the unattainable to bolster their dream of the blue flower or of Goethe's vision of the eternal feminine, the creative principle drawing Faust up to the realm of the Absolute, to man's fulfillment. In completely unsexing the woman in the dancer the neoromanticists surrendered their dream and closed the last century with the admission of man's failure in the face of man-made reality. To borrow a phrase from Kierkegaard, they have become the knights of infinite resignation. They made the spirit of the *fin de siècle* perfect, and in many ways perpetuated it into the 1920s.

Neither Friedrich Nietzsche nor Martin Buber was preoccupied with the ballerina as the instrument and representative of the dance. Nietzsche tried to overcome the earthbound heaviness in man through a Dionysian "promise of life." His was an impassioned call to overcome gravity, since "the devil is the spirit of gravity," and to reach out for a higher type of man whom he called superman. He projected the dancer and God outside man, a thought that culminated in his famous sentence "I should only believe in a God that would know how to dance."

Martin Buber sought the dancer in man. He thought that the dance of primitive people, with its playful and expressive gestures, was resuscitated in the new "liberated" spirit of Nijinsky. Buber appreciated the playfulness and expressiveness in the bodies of primitive people. Recalling the movement of Nijinsky, Buber writes:

. . . the playing and the expressing gestures become a part of human existence, the body's enjoyment of itself and its spirituality. . . . His dancing body is at once wholly its own and wholly interpenetrated by the spirit. His attitude comprehends playing gestures and expressing gestures, but both thoroughly transformed.

Play is the exultation of the possible.

Buber had read about Nijinsky's sickness and, in total philosophical recall, saw the dancer move in front of him again. He could not have known of Nijinsky's *Diary* at that time, he could not have envisioned Nijinsky walking through the woods and over the mountains of the Engadine, holding on to trees, speaking with the tongue of a mad mind to these trees and through these trees to God. Buber could not have known that, during some semilucid moments before eternal night embraced the dancer, he signed his *Diary:* God and Nijinsky.

Earlier another genius walked through the woods and valleys of the Engadine, denying God and admonishing man to rise above himself in order to become superman, a notion willfully misunderstood and maliciously misinterpreted by Hitler. Friedrich Nietzsche thought that to grow beyond his ordinariness, man needed that inner lightness which is the lightness of the dancer. Since even "the worst thing hath two good dancing legs," Nietzsche's *Zarathustra* says:

. . . praised be this wild, good, free spirit of the storm, which danceth upon fears and afflictions as upon meadows! Ye higher men, the worst thing in you is that none of you have learned to dance as ye ought to dance—to dance beyond yourselves! What doth it matter that ye have failed!

When Nietzsche died in 1900, a century was coming to an end and, with it, an age that had lasted four hundred years. Strange, that one of the more significant philosophers at the end of the last century should, symbolically, have envisioned the dance as the liberator of humankind. His *Zarathustra* said: "Better, however, to be foolish with happiness than foolish with misfortune, better to dance awkwardly than walk lamely."

Nietzsche was well aware that his life bridged two ages. In *Ecce Homo* we read: "Besides being a *décadent,* I am also its counterpart."

A world had by then come to an end. But there is no death without another renascence.

ON THE CULTURAL CRISIS OF OUR TIME

ALL ART IS A PRODUCT OF ITS TIME AND CONSEQUENTLY REFLECTS THE continuous changes of history. In the nineteenth century, art was still popular with most of society. The artists' "communication" was legible. Even those who felt ill at ease with romantic outbursts and later with the attacks of the naturalists and realists could still accept them as part of the inescapable game of life which they, too, knew how to play.

But as the changes in twentieth-century society became more dramatic and perplexing, the artist became divorced from the mainstream of life. Reacting to the bewildering events of the time, as if cornered, artists were forced to break out into sallies of nihilistic and destructive fury. They frantically searched for "identity," embracing a host of "isms." This artistic tantrum anticipated the cataclysmic events to come. Since World War I, society has gone from despair to hope to indifference to despair. Never before has the artist so acutely felt the profundity of life's emptiness than in our century, progressively growing worse after Hiroshima.

With the world out of joint, artists could not help feeling spiritually isolated. While trying to stem the avalanche of crumbling values, they escaped into a variety of outcries and protests: stammering Dada; howling expressionistically; embracing the non sequitur and the archaic; floating with an incongruous grin and a bleeding subconscious into a surrealistic dream; finally calling existence absurd and life futile.

"We are living at a time," Stravinsky wrote, "when the status of man is undergoing profound upheavals. Modern man is progressively losing his understanding of values and his sense of proportions. This failure to understand essential realities is extremely serious. It leads us infallibly to the violation of the fundamental laws of human equilibrium." Stravinsky himself went through several phases of experimentation, but his apprehension kept him from extremism.

However, the Dadaists and Surrealists were another matter. They claimed as their ancestor Alfred Jarry (1873–1907), whose fame as a writer goes back to a dramatic prank written as a schoolboy with which he lampooned an incompetent professor at the lycée at Rennes whom he called Ubu. The play, later somewhat enlarged and known as *Ubu Roi,* set the dramaturgically anarchic tone for all future avant-garde dramatists, from Apollinaire to Ionesco. It was grotesque and absurd in its exaggeration, full of painful laughter, simplistic in its social satire.

This satire had its basis in the political reality of the day. Kaiser Wilhelm II and his bungling ministers were creating a fear of Pan-German fury. They conducted war-blustering, heavy-handed diplomacy, full of threats and bullying. The sociopolitical scene in Europe at the beginning of the century became as frightening as it was ludicrous. Germany was reaching out for its place in the sun, meaning its rights to colonies in Africa and for recognition as a world power. It was a mercantile struggle for access to raw materials, a life-and-death struggle over world markets. With nationalism whipped up to a frantic point in Germany and Russia (where it was called Russification), war was inevitable. In response to this German saber-rattling, Britain, France, and Russia formed a Triple Entente, which facilitated cultural exchange between these countries.

DURING the first decade of the century two cultural centers vied with each other for world attention: Paris and Vienna. Zürich, Munich, and Berlin soon also became rallying points for the experimental artist. Each of these cities left a different imprint on art history. Paris remained the Eldorado of the visual arts, but its bohemian climate had a strong competitor in Freud's Vienna. Before Zürich became the birthplace of the Dada movement, it was a foothold for Jung's analytical psychology. One of Zürich's then most important figures, Albert Einstein, was a student and teacher in this city before he moved to Bern, where he wrote the first epochal essays about the theory on relativity in 1905.

The social and artistic atmosphere in all these cities was specifically their own. Yet, when the century was still very young, Art Nouveau or Jugendstil had a strong hold on Europeans everywhere; it was a movement which, of necessity, had to lead to styles of a new and greater immediacy, expressive of the twentieth century. The geographic and artistic frontiers were fluid, particularly among the painters who moved from city to city. At this point of history, it is important to look more closely at those who broke away from tradition.

Vienna, the capital of the Hapsburg empire of many nations, was then a cultural crucible giving birth to many new thoughts. The man who made music history was the Viennese Arnold Schoenberg (1874–1951). Followed by his Viennese pupils, Alban Berg and Anton von Webern, he introduced the concept of atonal music. It was in 1909—an important year in our study —that he began to write in this new form, to which he later added the technique of serialism. Strange that such pioneering ideas could emerge from an atmosphere full of romanticized life, of the aesthetically appealing and superficially beautiful.

The mood of perfumed eroticism then prevailed in Vienna, where Oskar Kokoschka (1886–1980) attended the Arts and Crafts School in 1904. Though he would not fall in with any demands of convention, at the beginning of his career he was very much under the influence of the fashionable Art Nouveau, then dominated by the Viennese Gustav Klimt and the Swiss Ferdinand Hodler. But Kokoschka, whose poetic writings have remained remarkable to this very day, wrote and illustrated a book, *The Dreaming Boys,* which at that early date (1908) showed unmistakably surrealistic features. The exploration of the inner man became his forte. In his portraits—long before he became a leading expressionist—he achieved a penetrating psychological image of the model, even at the expense of expected likeness. In those years Vienna was bristling with geniuses. But also a young would-be

Wassily Kandinsky called his abstract expressionism "concrete painting" and referred to many of his pictures as musically inspired. One could just as well see in them the choreographic designs of a contemporary dancer. (Courtesy French Cultural Services)

painter then roamed the streets of the old Kaiserstadt, twice trying to be accepted as a student at the Kunstakademie and unfortunately for humankind, twice rejected. His name was Adolf Hitler.

Wassily Kandinsky (1866–1944), Russian by birth, had his headquarters in Munich, where he studied Art Nouveau. In 1910 he painted the first nonobjective watercolor. He liked to call his abstract expressionism *concrete painting*. He was one of the heralds of a new concept of being and seeing, founder of the famed *Der blaue Reiter* (*The Blue Rider*), an articulate poet essayist: ". . . we are fast approaching a time of reasoned and conscious composition, in which the painter will be proud to declare his work constructional. . . ." Kandinsky's expressionistic abstractions bore names of musical compositions. Another painter, whose studio was not far from Kandinsky's, associated music with color, form, and poetry. It was the Swiss Paul Klee (1879–1940), whose pictures were pure poetry turned into graphic images of musical rhythms. People were stunned and perplexed by the paintings of Kandinsky, Klee, and Kokoschka. Art had become a means of self-expression.

A group of young painters who exhibited in Paris in 1905 became known as *Les Fauves,* "the wild beasts." But there was nothing wild or beastly about them. All they wanted was to express themselves beyond the forms of nature, with all the intensity and enjoyment of seeing in colors, of being free in their designs. Henri Matisse (1869–1954) was the best known among them. "What I am after above all is expression," Matisse explained.

It was the year in which Isadora was in Moscow. Michel Fokine (1880–1942) was strongly impressed by her. As early as 1904, at the age of twenty-four, he dared to write to the director of the Imperial Theaters what his ideas about ballet were: "Dancing should be interpretive. It should not degenerate into mere gymnastics. . . . Ballet must no longer be made up of numbers, entries and so on, it must show artistic unity of conception . . . a unity of a harmonious blending of the three elements—music, painting, and movement." He used to embarrass his teachers and choreographers with such impertinent questions as: "Why is the style of a dance seldom in harmony with its theme, costumes and period? Why does a dancer execute difficult steps if they do not express anything? Why is ballet technique limited to the movements of the lower limbs and a few conventional positions of the arms, when the whole body should be expressive?" There were no answers to his questions, since tradition must remain undisturbed. And his letter was filed for posterity.

The encounter with Isadora made him feel certain that he was on the right track. In April of that year his first choreography, *Acis and Galatea,* was mainly done with movements and poses suggested by Greek art. Shortly afterward he staged the pas seul *The Dying Swan,* for Anna Pavlova, a brief work that was proof to him that "the dance could not and should not satisfy only the eye, but through the medium of the eye should penetrate into the soul." In *Eunice,* created in 1907, the Duncan influence could be seen in the undulating arm movements of the barefoot dancers.

When Serge Diaghilev (1872–1929) saw Fokine's *Chopiniana*—later renamed *Les Sylphides*—he realized that Fokine was artistically daring and competent enough to become the chief choreographer for his Ballets Russes. Diaghilev's instinct was uncanny, and he relied on it. When he heard Igor Stravinsky's *Scherzo Fantastique* and *Fireworks* at a concert he was so strongly impressed that soon afterward he asked Stravinsky to compose a ballet for him. This became *The Firebird,* performed during the second season of the Ballets Russes in Paris. The first Diaghilev production was really *The Firebird,* one that he initiated from the very beginning, with the music specially commissioned and with close collaboration among composer, choreographer, and scenic designer under Diaghilev's supervision.

Diaghilev's reign over the Ballets Russes from 1909 to 1929 is credited with achievements of staggering proportion. What were the conditions that made his coming possible? Russian culture was at that time relatively unknown or misrepresented in the West, while everything French had always been highly appreciated in Russia. With Russia and France moving closer politically, in their encircling maneuver of Germany, interest in the other's artistic activities were nurtured and supported by both governments.

The artistic trend in the entire West was oriented toward the new and unexpected; it was in a revolutionary state of ferment. The public was waiting for the man with the message to fill the vacuum. When Diaghilev came to Paris with his ballet as the driving motor of a total theater concept, he polarized the diverse art lovers. Total theater had already been the dream of Richard Wagner, who tried to achieve such synthesis in music drama. Mallarmé rightly criticized Wagner for not having gone the whole way and particularly for having minimized the role of poetry and dancing, which he considered as the nucleus of any total theater. Adolphe Appia and Gordon Craig had envisioned such a theatrical *Gesamtkunstwerk* (total work of art), but from the viewpoint of the scenic designer. Diaghilev's ideas were not new, but the Zeitgeist was with him, or rather he was with it.

Diaghilev's often intolerant and overbearing reactions created difficulties for him, particularly with Vladimir Telyakovsky, the director of the Imperial Theaters. He also realized that, having for several years successfully stirred the artistic conscience of his compatriots, there was little left for him to do in Russia. He decided to show the world the treasures of his country— which went very well with the general nationalistic current of the time and his personal ambitions.

Diaghilev was an aristocrat of mind and soul with an innate arrogance that gave him the assuredness and strength to overcome his enemies and the monetary difficulties facing any impresario. When he described himself in a letter to his stepmother in 1895, it was tongue in cheek, since he knew only too well that although he might not have any special craft, he had enough talent to make his voice heard in the world of the arts:

> I am, firstly, a charlatan, though rather a brilliant one; secondly, a great charmer; thirdly, frightened of nobody; fourthly, a man with plenty of logic and very few scruples; fifthly, I seem to have no real talent. None the less, I believe that I have found my true vocation—to be a Maecenas, I have everything necessary except money—but that will come!

Portrait of Diaghilev by Jean Cocteau. (Courtesy French Cultural Services)

His stepmother told him once, "When one wants to, one always can do it," a sentence he took as his life's motto along with him in his mental rucksack.

His physical appearance carried much weight, with the heavy bulk of his body, the big head, the monocled face, and its observing and penetrating eyes. He was an impressive man, never seen without his cane and always with gestures revealing a sensual hedonist in the mantle of a Stoic philosopher. Certainly not a man to be overlooked. But Diaghilev could just as well be very human and passionate, ludicrously superstitious, constantly afraid of infections, such as a cold, and of finding death through drowning.

He came from the provincial town of Perm to St. Petersburg, pretending to study the law while trying to become a composer. Rimsky-Korsakov liberated him from this illusion, but Diaghilev's music understanding would be of great help to him later. At that time he had scant knowledge of and only a superficial liking for ballet. He went to see it because it was the thing to do. In the home of Alexandre Benois he met Léon Bakst, and Diaghilev's interest in painting and art criticism was awakened. Overnight he found himself the spokesman of a new movement that turned against everything then in the limelight: the Slavophiles that fought the Westerners, the academy that looked down on the Peredvizhniki, the Society of Traveling Exhibitions. In 1899 Diaghilev founded the magazine *Mir Iskusstva* (*The World of Art*). It was a new voice attacking the academy for its deadening influence and the Peredvizhniki for its incompetence. It proclaimed an art-for-art's-sake attitude in keeping with the *fin de siècle*'s and Diaghilev's own spirit. In his magazine and through his personal activities he made the Russians aware of their old culture and the new trends in the West. Some of the best Russian artists worked for the magazine: Alexandre Benois, Léon Bakst, Nikolas Roerich among them.

Diaghilev then received a special assignment from the Imperial Theaters to edit a yearbook, which turned out as stunning as most of the issues of *Mir Iskusstva*. However, his "gentle art of making enemies"—to use Whistler's phrase—forced him to turn his attention toward the West; but not before making a prophetic speech on the occasion of the opening of an historic Portrait Exhibition, which Diaghilev had put together at the Tauride Palace:

> . . . we live in a terrible period of transition. . . . We are doomed to die to pave the way for the resurrection of a new culture. . . . I cannot be reproached as an artistic radical, but I can say boldly and with conviction that . . . we are witnesses of the great summing-up in history, in the name of a new and unknown culture, which will be created by us and also will sweep us away. . . . I raise my glass to the ruined walls of the beautiful palaces as well as to the new commandments of a new aesthetic. The only wish I . . . can express is that the forthcoming struggle should not

damage the amenities of life, and that the death should be as beautiful and so illuminating as the resurrection.

The year was 1905. The bullets of the Russian soldiers had just silenced the people's first dramatic uprising. Certainly Diaghilev cannot be pictured as a man of leftist leanings. He was, in fact, the last dandy, a passionate individualist, with a loathing of the masses. "One of the greatest merits of our times is to recognize individuality under every guise and at every epoch," he had written in *Mir Iskusstva*. I suspect he even had nothing but contempt for his audiences, but for the sake of art he needed them. He abhorred, however, the idea of boring them. When the years became more and more tumultuous—1912, 1913, 1917—he did not mind shocking his audiences; indeed, he liked a theater scandal for the sake of the scandal and the theater arts. In spite of the fact that he had written in his magazine, "The sole function of art is pleasure, its only instrument beauty. . . . It is blasphemous to force ideas," he loved to force ideas.

First he established Russian paintings in Paris; then he came with music and opera. Feodor Chaliapin was a resounding success in the title role of *Boris Godunov*. "From opera to ballet was but a step. Ballet contained in itself all these other activities," he once said. He opened the first season on May 19, 1909, at the Théâtre du Châtelet with *Les Sylphides, Cléopâtre, Le Pavillon d'Armide, Prince Igor, Le Festin*. Although the echoes of the past could still be heard in these ballets, the first season not only changed ballet history, it galvanized the artistic scene, its reverberations being felt in all human activities.

Probably Diaghilev was more in love with theater than with ballet, but he saw in ballet the best vehicle to further his aims. He was very much at home with music and acquired a fine understanding and liking for the visual arts. To exploit both theatrically, he could have chosen the opera or the ballet. That he opted for the latter must have had more than the one tangible reason that the French agent Gabriel Astruc tried to convince him that his best bet would be the ballet, which was in such a sordid state in Paris.* Anna Pavlova, with six other colleagues, had been seen dancing in a few northern cities the previous year, and she was so much admired that rumors

---

* Inspiration through personal relationships has often been decisive in the development of an art form. That Diaghilev—having been creative in his way—may have wished to indulge his feelings for Vaslav Nijinsky, later for Léonide Massine, and again for Serge Lifar is probably more than coincidental. Diaghilev was rightly reproached for having neglected to found a school, with the result that after his death the Ballets Russes immediately disintegrated. But it has been overlooked that during Diaghilev's reign the male dancer achieved a stellar position again, which he had yielded to the ballerinas during the nineteenth century. Male reemergence in the dance field was then accentuated in the thirties and forties; it was also espoused by the modern dancer, as the examples of Ted Shawn and his all-male company as well as José Limón show, a trend only minimized by George Balanchine, who has continued to see the focus on the ballerina as ballet's raison d'être.

of her greatness became the apéritif conversation in Paris. Or it may have been a chance remark or glance from Vaslav Nijinsky. No one can tell what finally made Diaghilev decide on the Ballets Russes. It may have been any one of these incidents, or all of them. Great historic events have a habit of communicating in a mysterious language with those who are destined to play a great part in them. During the second decade of the century, a decade of cataclysmic upheavals, it was the dance and the visual arts that became the most articulate of human expressions.

The Escape from Destiny

NO SINGLE PERSONALITY, HOWEVER INNOVATIVE AND CREATIVE, CAN CHARacterize an epoch. But through making a decisive contribution and having an aura of magnetism, one person can be transformed into a symbol. People latch on to a name as an abbreviated image. Their thoughts need to write in shorthand the symbol of a genius and its consequences. Four such symbols emerged in the first decade of this century.

We are often inclined to speak of our Freudian age and mean the totality of psychic awareness that has penetrated our entire existence. Einstein is still associated with his theory on relativity, but his name was elevated to the point of a simplified metaphor embracing the whole scientific and technological achievements of our era, as if he alone could be praised or blamed for its wonders and miseries.

A galaxy of rebels have scribbled their names in the history books of art. Two of them whose innovations, eclecticism, and productiveness have come to signify modernism with all its positive and negative connotations were Igor Stravinsky (1882–1971) and even more so Pablo Picasso (1881–1973). They have become household words in our intellectualized vocabulary. In the course of the decades many more figures have become legendary— Nijinsky or Martha Graham, for instance. Others, artists of no minor abilities, have sanctified themselves through their publicity-prone glamour as has Salvador Dali.

I have chosen Stravinsky because, as a new force, he never reached the point of calling himself in question as so many other innovating artists did. He imposed on the cacophony of our time the order of a mathematical mind working with austere simplicity. "Music creates a common order between man and time," he said. His work was never far from classical principles, without losing sight of ever-new rhythmic formulas. He designed with the precision of an architect, creating blueprints without ornaments, with an inner relatedness in their structure, always fascinating and often witty. From his revolutionary *Le Sacre du Printemps* (*The Rite of Spring*), written in 1913, with its displaced accent and polytonal chord, to his later formal-structural peculiarities, he has cast an inimitable spell, influencing several generations of composers, painters, and choreographers. (His collaborative efforts with George Balanchine have become dance history.) With our growing perspective, it will become even more obvious what a dominant force Stravinsky has been.

Picasso raged through this century, changing his face whenever he felt ready and creating with untiring energy one work after another. He created trends only to throw them overboard again. When, early in this century, the old notion of beauty was not yet outworn, Picasso was the prime mover toward a reoriented response to art, toward the new criterion of "interest."

"I do not search, I find," Picasso liked to say, as if destiny would have to play the part of the muse. Apparently it did in his case when, in the spring of 1907, he had dinner at Matisse's home. That evening Picasso saw an African Negro mask for the first time, and the entire evening he sat staring at it as though hypnotized. The result was soon to be a painting, "Les Demoiselles d' Avignon" ("The Young Ladies of Avignon"), considered to be the beginning of cubism. Picasso explained:

> The masks weren't just like any other pieces of sculpture. Not at all. They were magic things. They were against everything—against unknown, threatening spirits. . . . I understood; I too am against everything. I too believe that everything is unknown, that everything is an enemy!

His friends and the world were shocked when seeing his painting. Malraux tells us about a visit to Picasso's studio: "You have to drag the people out of their sleep," he told me; "one must force them to see the things they identify with in a different way. One must create unacceptable pictures so that the people fume with fury. One must make them realize they live in a crazy world without security, a world that isn't the way they think it is."

In Picasso's eyes, Cézanne was the embodied symbol of the past. Cézanne was still the master who saw his world as a totality, well constructed. "A picture used to be a sum of additions," Picasso said. "For me, a picture is a sum of destruction." The word *destruction* was soon to become a key word in the artist's conceptual notions. In this respect the first radical voice to be heard was that of Isadora Duncan. When she was in Moscow in 1905, at Anna Pavlova's house, she told Diaghilev defiantly, "I am the enemy of ballet, which I look upon as false, absurd, and outside the domain of art. . . . I thank God that a cruel destiny did not inflict upon me the career of a ballet dancer."

Igor Stravinsky went through several phases of experimentation. Caricature by Jean Cocteau. (Courtesy French Cultural Services)

By the end of the first decade there were many artists defying the past. There was tumultuous violence or silent despair in them. The paintings of Giorgio de Chirico (1888–1978), for instance, have a dreamlike quality of a metaphysical stillness. Life seems deserted on his canvases, caught in the naked fear of shadows and loneliness. There is already a touch of surrealism in his way of painting, with the alogical made credible. "What shall I love if not the enigma?" was the inscription on one of his self-portraits in 1911. He kept to himself like a mystic, frightened of the world lost to its despair. He did not join those who cheered the madness of the future, nor those who attacked it.

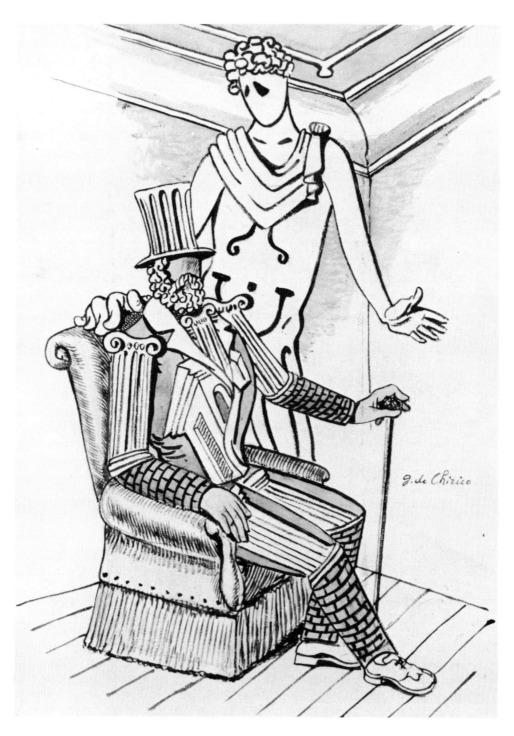

On rare occasions Giorgio de Chirico worked for the ballet. This is the cover for a playbill; the ballet was LE BAL. *(Courtesy Wadsworth Atheneum, Hartford)*

His compatriot Filippo Marinetti (1876–1944) was the founder of futurism, whose manifesto appeared in the Paris *Figaro* on February 20, 1909, two and a half months before Diaghilev startled the art world. Marinetti called himself a "mystic of action," worshiping all kinds of action made possible by the machine. He sang the glory of technology, and the only thing right about his concepts was the idea that the machine and technology were the future. He tried to prove the painter Ingres wrong—Ingres had once said that "locomotives have absolutely nothing to do with art." Speed-mad Marinetti hailed those early puffing and fuming automobiles that began to invade the landscapes like raging cockroaches demanding more and better roads, and he thought of them as being "more beautiful than the Nike of Samothrace. . . ."

Futurism is a misnomer and "means the Present, with the Past rigidly excluded," according to Wyndham Lewis, the British writer, polemicist, and painter whose vorticism was a near-relative of futurism, which Lewis tagged "automobilism." Futurism, an outgrowth of cubism, played a most important sociocultural role; it was the first movement to sever radically all links with past art aesthetics. What mattered to the futurists was no longer an involvement in an art process—its inner value still of importance to the cubists—but art as an expression of history and as its instrument. Briefly, they became agitators, propagandists of ideas.

Marinetti, poet-antipoet, maintained that art could stay alive only if it found ways and means of bringing itself to an end. Vacillating between inherently nihilistic precepts and rhapsodies over power, motion, and machines, the futurists created, willy-nilly, a new attitude toward the arts that no longer wanted to give us poetic truth in order to help us over the lie of life. "From Futurism on," Harold Rosenberg said, "the aesthetics of each new advanced art movement—from Dada, Surrealism, Constructivism, and Social Realism to Action painting, anti-Formal art, and Conceptual art—has included a conception of the historical situation and a strategy for dealing with it."

Futurism did not bring forth any remarkable works, simply because propagandists may produce memorable manifestos and posters relating art to action, to the reality of a political Now or technological phenomena, but it rarely leads to artistically essential statements. The historical significance of futurism lies in the fact that it forced excellence in art into the background and legitimized any decoy with which an artist could triumph over society. As a side effect, Marinetti's message of the machine inspired several artists from Duchamp to Tinguely. Above all, Fernand Léger (1881–1955) comes to mind, an architect turned painter who specialized in the mechanization of the human being and also glorified technological advances. He wrote: "For me the human figure . . . has no more importance than keys or bicycles." He differed from the pure futurists in seeing in mechanical forms an architectural, geometric abstraction. What the futurists achieved was a first attempt at dismantling modern aesthetic feelings and an incipient step toward dehumanization, which was to have a serious impact on future dance generations.

An offshoot of futurism was constructivism, which found its home in Russia immediately after the war and its most artistic expression in scenic design. The demand for social realism was then not yet formulated, but intuitively recognized and acclaimed. In ejecting poetic illusion from the theater, constructivism advocated the straight line of iron constructions and streamlined shapes, of everything reflecting the mechanical civilization surrounding us.

The Russians recognized the propagandist potentials of these new stage ideas. The stage director took over: Alexander Taïrov wrote, "The stage is a keyboard," and Vsevolod Meyerhold, "No more bourgeois staging!" The stage was bare, though full of iron poles, runways, stairs, and steps, of concentric and smaller platforms. Cubic planes suggested a landscape of mountains. Adolphe Appia had already suggested that space had to be something alive as a cubic volume, a single plastic unit within which a continuous functioning of light takes place. Appia's stage was full of symbolist suggestiveness.† But after the war, futurism, combined with cubism, transposed Appia's ideas into a cubistic atmosphere of abstract prisms.

Germany became infected by this trend in staging plays between 1919 and 1925. The new space concept got out of hand. Entire plays were acted on stairways. Actors were made to run up and down, to swing back and forth. to do all kinds of acrobatics. Movement began to play a major part onstage. As Meyerhold said, "Words are the design upon the outline of movement. We must put the body back." Futurism helped advance movement consciousness. It consequently created a new awareness of space, which was to play a major part in the early years of Mary Wigman's experimentations. Stylization and functional suggestiveness became a long-lasting *dernier cri*.

With the actor, the playwright also became a puppet in the hands of the stage director, whose dictatorial powers became incontestable in the 1920s. (There is a parallel to the rising importance of the film, in which the director has always been power incarnate.) Meyerhold abolished the front curtain. Later imitated by Bertolt Brecht, Meyerhold's idea was to keep the audience constantly aware of the fact that they were in a theater and that the theater is no longer a world of illusion. The lights in the auditorium were kept on, and Meyerhold dared the audience to face the naked brick walls of

---

† In 1913, at the Dalcroze School, Appia brought to the stage his version of Claudel's *Tidings Brought to Mary,* as Mordecai Gorelik tells it. The settings followed the sketches he had made for *The Valkyrie* in 1895. It had become possible, in the interim, to create on the stage that cubic volume of illumination which must have seemed only a fantastic notion eighteen years before.

the stage for the first time. These were revolutionary breakthroughs. His actors' costumes were overalls, then most fashionable; dancers appeared in practice clothes, and they all ran and jumped over skeleton settings constructed of wood, glass, and metal. The mechanical age had obviously conquered stage illusion.

Marinetti began an irreversible trend. But it needed the scurrilous, light-headed mind of an *enfant terrible* like Jean Cocteau (1889–1963) to conceive a ballet, *Le Train Bleu,* for Diaghilev's company in 1924. Cocteau explained: "The first point about *Le Train Bleu* is that there is no blue train in it.‡ This being the age of speed, the train had already reached its destination and disembarked its passengers. . . ."

For whatever caprices history will credit Cocteau, it will not be able to dispute his innovating sallies, which brought forth some astounding results. When the Ballets Russes were young, so was Cocteau. He took to the exuberant youthfulness he sensed in this company, which electrified so many brilliant minds: the writers Paul Claudel, Marcel Proust, Jules Lemaître, Marcel Prévost, Henri Ghéon; the critics Camille Mauclair, Anna de Noailles, Jean Louis Vaudoyer; the composers Igor Stravinsky and Erik Satie; the painters Henri Matisse, Pablo Picasso, Georges Rouault, José María Sert—to name a few.

Cocteau with his enthusiasm for the Ballets Russes was in good company. Most poets, composers, and painters were then ready to support Diaghilev; however, he was chided by conservative critics such as André Levinson for betraying the ideals of ballet when using a dramatic emotion instead of letting considerations of pure form serve as the raison d'être of each step. "Diaghilev consistently seeks his inspiration outside the dance itself," he wrote. Progressive critics like Camille Mauclair, on the other hand, were impressed by the high standards of Diaghilev's theatrical spectacles. Almost all critics thought highly of the Bakst decors and found that they gave them a "feeling of escape into the realms of dream and fantasy. Everything is true, but nothing is real. An aesthetic truth of four arts combined in one."

The literati were not concerned with the ballet as an art form; they realized that Diaghilev reawakened creative powers in all the other arts while giving the theater renewed greatness. "He splashed Paris with colors," Cocteau said. He joined the company, designing posters and writing and illustrating booklets. In the first three seasons Diaghilev was still in his *Scheherazade* mood. Cocteau was then only twenty, an age when a writer should rebel. His aesthetic values were still, however, those of yesterday, with Oscar Wilde his favorite author. He had not yet paid attention to the

‡ A generation later, Eugène Ionesco called his first play *The Bald Soprano* because no soprano, bald or not bald, appears in the play or is ever referred to.

BAKST
1911

fact that the arts were in a growing state of agitation. Diaghilev's dreamlike, colorful, exotic ballets fascinated this facile poet, who roamed through life with wide-open eyes, adoring and being adored.

The vogue of exoticism was not yet over, and in May 1912 Cocteau's scenario for the ballet *Le Dieu Bleu* was in the program of the Ballets Russes. It was one of those cliché stories of Eastern romance in which a young girl tried to stop her lover from becoming a priest. Unfortunately Reynaldo Hahn's music was so flat in all keys that it only helped to underline the threadbare conventionalism of the undramatic events in a Hindu temple. Neither Nijinsky and Karsavina in the main roles nor Léon Bakst's gorgeous designs for costume and set could save the ballet. Fokine modeled Nijinsky's poses on temple sculptures, but everything remained papery and pedestrian.

It was more than just another theater flop, it was a turning point in ballet history, like a curtain coming down on the past. Sixteen days later the curtain went up on a new era, on a changed Diaghilev and a changing Cocteau, on the birth of a new choreographer. Vaslav Nijinsky (1890–1950) seems to have played the role of a catalyst in Diaghilev's life at that time. For two seasons Diaghilev was able to present the dancers of the Ballets Russes in Paris under his management, though they were still employed by and attached to the Imperial Theaters, dancing there also for a number of months each season. In one of his sulky moods, Nijinsky provoked an internal scandal at the Maryinsky Theater when he omitted wearing the customary shorts over his tights. He was dismissed. Yet Diaghilev felt it was his responsibility to engage Nijinsky for the entire year, and this necessitated the engagement of the entire company. Thus it was not until 1911 that his own company was born as a permanent institution.

A trip to Greece with Léon Bakst, chief designer for the Ballets Russes, produced the idea of a ballet that was to be a moving bas-relief, based on Mallarmé's *L'Après-midi d'un Faune,* with Claude Debussy's music. The rehearsals were conducted behind closed doors with Nijinsky as the choreographer and in the title role. Bakst is rarely credited with having been Nijinsky's main inspiration for this choreography, which resulted in Diaghilev's first *succès de scandale.* Nijinsky danced barefoot, and his movements were accentuated by rigid and angular poses.

This choreographic tableau was the first step in the process of liberating the theater arts from nineteenth-century conventions. It achieved unusual images and a new expressiveness of the dancer's body. The body was Nijinsky's, but the minds behind his movements were those of Bakst and Diaghilev. After the first storm of disapproval subsided, Diaghilev had the

One of Bakst's costume sketches for LA PÉRI, *1911. (Courtesy French Cultural Services)*

courage to ask the audience at the Théâtre du Châtelet to sit through the ballet once more (it lasted twelve minutes only). The anti-Faunists were silenced by this unexpected turn of events, which proved Diaghilev as an extraordinary theatrical strategist. The first battle was won by Nijinsky, who, due to this success, became the new choreographer of the Ballets Russes.

Diaghilev sensed he could not rely on Fokine forever and that a change attuned to the new trends in the arts was needed. From then on, a little theater scandal became a sure sign for him that ballet was alive and au courant. Fokine was annoyed about the secrecy with which Nijinsky was elevated to the position of a second choreographer. His own works were eclipsed by the attention Nijinsky received from press and public, and he left the company. There was no doubt in Diaghilev's mind that, with *Afternoon of a Faun,* a new era had begun for the Ballets Russes. He had discovered a new, exciting choreographer and the way into twentieth-century ballet. Fokine had left, and such ballets as Cocteau's *Le Dieu Bleu* belonged to the past, so he ignored Cocteau for some time. The poet tells of that night some time after his defeat and Nijinsky's success when they were walking home from supper after the performance:

> Nijinsky was sulking as usual. He was walking ahead of us. Diaghilev was amused at my behavior. When I questioned him on his reserve (I was used to praise), he stopped, adjusted his monocle, and said to me: "Surprise me!"

"Surprise me!" became the catchword of the age; it best expressed the furor with which artists searched for an ever-new expression of the time. This was the hour of conception of a long period of experimentation in all the arts. Diaghilev correctly read the signs of that moment in history when he charged Cocteau with the slogan "Étonne-moi!" Often enough this was translated into "newness for the sake of newness," or *"shock pour l'art."* Cocteau went into hiding. Five years later, in 1917, he surprised Diaghilev and the world with *Parade,* expressing the notion of newness in balletic terms.

From then on, Cocteau followed many artistic ways. He was a dazzling dramatist, a surrealistic film experimenter, a novelist, and a draftsman. But whatever he did was done with the touch of one who always looked upon the poetic as antipoetic. He explained himself best when he wrote:

> A wave of the wand and books are written, the camera grinds, the pen draws, the actors play. It is very simple. Magician. That word facilitates everything. It is useless to analyze our own work. It was put together without effort.

However much we wish to admire him, or try to point to his weaknesses, he symbolizes the speed with which people in this century try to pass them-

Nijinsky in Afternoon of a Faun: *painting by Valentine Gross-Hugo.*
(*Courtesy French Cultural Services*)

selves. *Parade* was the first modern ballet. It experimented with the baffling elements of surprise; it heightened the commonplace to poetic reality; it extolled the non sequitur; and it enjoyed the naïveté of the obvious. The opening night in May 1917 at the Théâtre du Châtelet was another scandal in which Diaghilev delighted and which—for the sake of all future experiments—was one of the more important events on the way to our fulfillment.

Parade introduced Pablo Picasso to the theater. "I'm responsible for his becoming a stage designer," Cocteau proudly claimed, and Gertrude Stein noted: "That was really the beginning of the general recognition of Picasso's work. . . ." The program bill contained an explanatory note on *Parade et l'Esprit Nouveau* by the poet-essayist-dramatist and champion of the avant-garde Guillaume Apollinaire (1880–1918), in which he said:

Picasso's curtain for PARADE. (*Courtesy French Cultural Services*)

Poster for PARADE *featuring a costume design by Pablo Picasso. (Courtesy French Cultural Services)*

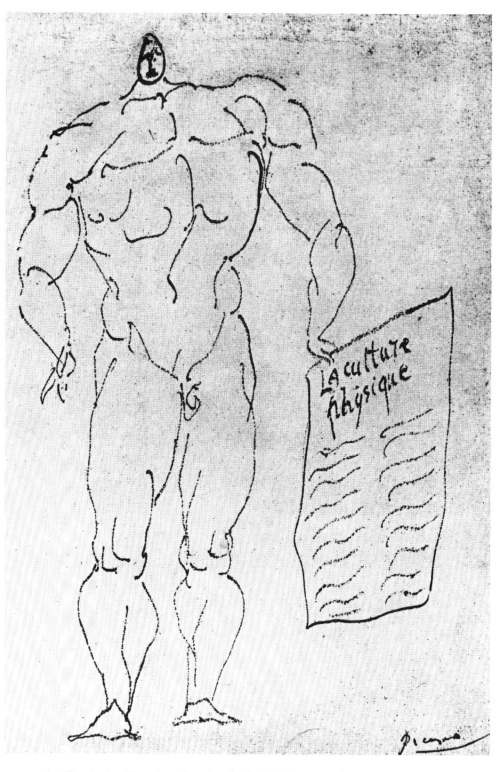

Apollinaire as Hercules: drawing by Pablo Picasso. (Courtesy French Cultural Services)

From this new alliance—for until now costume and décor on the one hand, choreography on the other, have been linked only artificially—there has resulted in *Parade* a kind of *surrealism* which I see as the point of departure for a series of manifestations of the New Spirit that today finds an opportunity to show itself. It will not fail to captivate the elite and promises to transform arts and manners into universal joy, for common sense wants them to be at least on a level with scientific and industrial progress.

It was the first time that the word *surrealism* was used. Apollinaire also took it as his subtitle, *A Surrealist Drama,* when a month later his play *Les Mamelles de Tirésias (The Breasts of Tiresias)* was produced in Paris. It was entirely unrealistic and illogical, and Apollinaire explained "surrealism" in his preface as a return to nature without imitating her photographically: "When man wished to imitate walking, he created the wheel which does not resemble a leg. He was engaging in surrealism without knowing it." Apollinaire saw something joyous in infusing the theater with a new spirit, and what is modern to him is the blending of all the arts without creating any logic links between

> *Sounds gestures colors cries noises*
> *Music dance acrobatics poetry painting*
> *Choruses actions and multiple decors*

This was exactly what *Parade* was about or wanted to achieve. Cocteau thought it was all in "the spirit of cubism," as Léonide Massine, *Parade*'s choreographer, reported in his autobiography. In fact, it was far more Dada than anything else.

Parade could probably not have been, had it not been preceded by another theater scandal of milestone proportions in 1913. Nijinsky had to choreograph the new piece chosen for the season, Stravinsky's *Rite of Spring.* With *The Afternoon of a Faun* Nijinsky proved that his choreographic strength was not cerebral, it was far more the volcanic expression of someone whose tortured soul was haunted by strange images. "Diaghilev made up his mind," Stravinsky tells us in *An Autobiography,* "that he would spare no effort to make a choreographer of Nijinsky. I do not know whether he really believed in his choreographic gifts, or whether he thought that his talented dancing . . . indicated that he would show equal talent as a ballet master. . . . To be perfectly frank, . . . the idea of working with Nijinsky filled me with misgiving, notwithstanding our friendliness and my great admiration for his talent as dancer and mime. His ignorance of the most elementary notions of music was flagrant."

Diaghilev must also have been uncertain about Nijinsky's musical susceptibilities, and he took the whole company to Dalcroze in Hellerau, where he received the needed understanding and assistance. Stravinsky's music was radically different in rhythm and color from anything composed before. It cries out for movement and yet its complexity, its stark primitivism, easily perplexes and tricks the choreographer. The story from which the score emerged had its roots in human credulity and raw passion. "I saw in my imagination a solemn pagan rite: sage elders, seated in a circle, watched a young girl dance herself to death," Stravinsky said. "They were sacrificing her to propitiate the god of spring." Nijinsky envisioned a circular dance in unbroken motion accentuated by archaic movements, steps and gestures turned in, simple in their imitative drive.

The opening night on May 29, 1913, turned into a chaotic scandal. In the ensuing tumult the dancers could not even hear the music. The audience was outraged; it felt fooled and insulted by what it took to be bewildering, dissonant sounds and a monotonous repetition of movements. It could not yet sense the wild pathos of death and birth in it, the convulsion of sophisticated naïveté.

These sounds and the tumult in which they were drowned foretold something of the coming war years. Diaghilev must have had a triumphant feeling of a new battle won in this defeat, when (as Cocteau tells us, eyewitness of the scene) they all drove to the Bois de Boulogne that night—Stravinsky, Nijinsky, and Diaghilev, who ecstatically recited Pushkin in Russian, with tears running down his cheeks. These men were full of pain-stricken nostalgia, as if they alone could know that the old world was about to be wrecked in order to be rebuilt, and that they were the wreckers and builders.

In many respects the year 1913 was a turning point in the history of the arts on two continents. The scene in the Bois de Boulogne was matched by an incident in Switzerland's Ascona, on the Monte Verità. There a twenty-six-year-old girl met a man whose eyes were afire with a vision. Rudolf von Laban (1879–1958) taught rhythmic movement or dancing there, and one of his students that summer was Mary Wigman (1886–1973), who had been sent there by the painter Emil Nolde. He thought she wanted to dance the kind of free-rhythm dance that Laban did. The terminology in the nascent thing which was to become *Ausdruckstanz* was still poor in those days and borrowed descriptive words from gymnastic schools or from the ballet.

Mary Wigman had a contract in her hands for a teaching position in one of the important Dalcroze schools in Berlin. At the end of the summer she showed the contract to Laban, who smilingly congratulated her on having a good job for her lifetime. Then he added, "But you are an artist, you should be dancing on a stage." These words made her tear up the contract and gave birth to the German *Ausdruckstanz*.

Before World War I, American art consciousness was still behind the exciting artistic developments in Europe. Not until 1908 did a group of painters calling themselves the Eight—later better known as the Ashcan School—scandalize New Yorkers with their realistic, "undignified" canvases. Later, during the 1920s and 1930s, such painters as George Bellows and Edward Hopper were belligerent in their way of depicting saloons, cheap rooming houses, ugly street scenes—briefly, the ordinariness of life. They defied the National Academy and dared to deny "beauty" its academic politeness.

Also in that year Alfred Stieglitz (1864–1946) began to show the work of Matisse at his "291" gallery, followed by exhibits of Picasso, Cézanne, Toulouse-Lautrec, and others. Stieglitz was the first to fight for photography as an art, gaining for himself an international reputation as photographer. He strongly believed in the artistic potentialities of America and in the need to expose the public to the new trends of art.

But all these attempts were eclipsed by the greatest event in the history of American art, which had far-reaching repercussions: the Armory Show, as it is referred to, the exhibition of paintings and sculptures at the 69th Regiment Armory on Lexington Avenue at 25th Street. It was like a great battle won, since it won a whole new continent for the arts.

The Association of American Painters and Sculptors, the sponsors of the International Exhibition of Modern Art, as its official title was, had no revolutionary notions in putting this show together. They intended to assemble a bigger exhibition of the independent artists working in the United States but also of those in European cities, since at the beginning of this century a great many American artists went to live in Europe. On the other hand, the implication was that Americans had reached a point of artistry where they could measure up to their European counterparts. The word *international* was stressed, and the intention was to prove the value judgments of the academy insignificant in the face of such a giant show of the international vanguard.

One third of those exhibited were the daring Europeans, with Duchamp's "Nude Descending a Staircase" and Matisse's "Blue Nude," and this one third turned the show into a riot. The people were just as infuriated and enraged about being fooled and insulted as the first-night audience was at *Le Sacre du Printemps*. The controversies did not stop for years to come. The public may have felt scandalized, but also the artists, the members of the Association of American Painters and Sculptors, did not know what had happened to them. They were just as baffled about their own deed when they began to realize what they had exhibited to spite academic routine and the concept of past prettiness. The artistic influence of the Armory Show on the artists themselves was not immediate. But their shock was of lasting intensity.

The war cry was against institutionalism. The principle of newness for the sake of newness had triumphed in New York, Chicago, and Boston, and the whole art world was surprised about its own daring. The era of "surprise me" set in, or, as the art critic Harold Rosenberg expressed it: "The tradi-

Martha Graham was still dancing with the Denishawn company in 1920. This shows her in XOCHITL, *one of the Aztec stories in the Denishawn repertory. (Courtesy the Author)*

tion of the new has reduced all other traditions to triviality." What was immediately established was the awareness of art per se. The original small vanguard of the intelligentsia that was determined to keep "modern art" alive began to swell. Gertrude Stein, who had exiled herself to Paris, was strongly associated with the Armory Show. She was not only an outrageously daring writer, she also was behind the latest cry for art expression; Stieglitz had published her long monographs on Matisse and Picasso in his famed New York magazine *Camera Work*. A new audience and collectors were created for the "new." In looking back at the Armory Show in 1964 Harold Rosenberg noted:

> Today, the vanguard audience is open to anything. Its eager representatives—curators, museum directors, art educators, dealers —rush to organize exhibitions and provide explanatory labels before the paint has dried on the canvas or the plastic has hardened. Coöperating critics comb the studios like big-league scouts, prepared to spot the art of the future and to take the lead in establishing reputations. Art historians stand ready with cameras and notebooks to make sure that every novel detail is safe for the record.

Who is to blame or praise for it? The dealers who sensed that a new wind was blowing and that the new art consciousness would be big business one day? The curators and educators who were not sure of themselves and confused about what the criteria of art were or were to be tomorrow? Or the critics, afraid to be left behind the bandwagon? Or the artists who became so sure of their own insecurity and—in the words of Harold Rosenberg— found out that "art can meaningfully assert its own nonsensicality"? The greatest evolution was on, destined to change the world. The artist sensed intuitively the coming cries of death and the pangs of rebirth, the irony of existence and the triumph of the human spirit.

The dance had made its own confusing and contradictory statements. Diaghilev's *Rite of Spring* and *Parade* tried to render the anxieties of the future meaningful. Anna Pavlova pirouetted all over the world, awakening a dream of beauty that was not to die. Michel Fokine, returning to the Diaghilev company for a brief stay in 1914 before settling for good in New York, formulated once more the fundamental ideas of his reform in a letter to the London *Times*. There he reiterated that one must "create in each case a new form of movement corresponding to the subject matter" and abandon "combinations of ready-made and established steps"; that "dancing and mimetic gesture have no meaning in ballet unless they serve as an expression of dramatic action; that "man can and should be expressive from head to foot"; that "the new ballet, refusing to be slave either of music or of scenic decoration, and recognizing the alliance of arts only on the condition of complete equality, allows perfect freedom both to the scenic artist and to the musician."

It was the same year, 1914, that Ruth St. Denis happened to meet a former divinity student, Ted Shawn, who shared her belief in the religious message of dancing. Together they founded a school and company that became known as Denishawn. However eclectic they were in their creative choices, reminding the audiences of the metaphoric beauty of Hindu and Aztec stories, of Spanish and American Indian material, Denishawn was called upon by providence to play its providential part for the modern dance, that expressionistic American version of what Laban and Wigman's meeting was all about on Monte Verità in 1913.

The Denishawn School practiced a simplified ballet technique on bare feet and half-toes, making use of some Dalcroze ideas. Soon after its most prominent dancers, Martha Graham, Doris Humphrey, and Charles Weidman, left in the 1920s, the Denishawn company disbanded and the partnership of St. Denis and Ted Shawn broke up. In 1933 Shawn founded the Jacob's Pillow Dance Festival, held annually in summer. He was also instrumental in helping the male dancer gain recognition. Ruth St. Denis continued her crusade for the dignity of the dancer as a total being.

Years of Hope

THE SCENE WAS ZÜRICH, 1916. WORLD WAR I WAS TWO YEARS OLD. SWITZerland, one of the few neutral countries, attracted many creative and revolutionary minds who practiced the arts and the art of surviving. Romain Rolland and Hermann Hesse met there, both abhorring the senseless slaughter of the war. Both men tried to establish a *"union sacrée de l'esprit européen,"* calling upon intellectuals in Germany and France to help stop the brutality and stupidity of the war. But by then the German intelligentsia had already published a belligerent manifesto with the refrain of "God punish England." There was no hope for peace.

The emigrants living in Zürich were a motley crew. There were the Germans Hugo Ball and Richard Huelsenbeck; the Romanians Marcel Janco and Tristan Tzara; the Viennese Walter Serner; Jean Arp, the Alsatian; James Joyce from Dublin, Vladimir Ilich Ulyanov Lenin from Russia. They and many more lived there, frequented the public library, and met at the Café Odeon, then the coffeehouse of the literati. Another attractive meeting place for them seems to have been Rudolf Laban's dance studio. Mary Wigman was there, Suzanne Perrottet and Sophie Taeuber, who later became

Sophie Taeuber-Arp, better known as a painter than a dancer-choreographer of the Dada movement.

Dada was born in Zürich in 1916, in a beer parlor converted into the Cabaret Voltaire. It became the focal point of exhibitions, lectures, poetry readings and dancing. Once they rented a bigger hall, and the whole Laban school got involved with a Dada show. It was a storyless dance. Arp designed a set of abstract forms and Janco's masks did not pretend to be facelike. And so was Sophie Taeuber's dance abstract. It was probably the first modern dance of this kind.

Isadora's dances issued from emotional experiences; the works of Ruth St. Denis were inspired by Eastern metaphors; Mary Wigman had by then done her first *Witch Dance*. But Taeuber's movements were done for the sake of movement. Jean Arp, in remembering her, said: "She drew radiant, geometric messages." Looking at them, we can more easily translate them into what may have been her dance movements: geometric designs simplified to the utmost. Jean Arp tells us about her way of expressing herself:

> Sophie Taeuber and I painted, embroidered, and did collages; all these works were drawn from the simplest forms and were probably the first examples of "concrete art." These works are realities, pure and independent, with no meaning or cerebral intention. We rejected all mimesis and description, giving free reign to the elementary and the spontaneous.

There were as many different Dadaists as there were artists professing Dadaism. In principle, Dada was the most important reaction to, and reflection of, the twentieth-century trauma. Although it was absorbed by surrealism in the mid-twenties, it reappeared in the fifties and sixties and is still with us, whatever disguise it may choose. In 1916 Dada was a glorified invective spat into the face of a world that asked for it. Its frightening appearance has only become more frightening and its challenging questions have remained unanswered to this day.

The entire Dada movement is a collective expression of artistic hostility. "The Dadaist considers it necessary to come out against art because he has seen through its fraud as a moral safety valve," Richard Huelsenbeck said. The Dadaists saw human salvation in political and artistic anarchy, in total destruction, and, at best, in a defiant detachment.

Ball played the piano, Tzara read his poetry, and Huelsenbeck, a medical student and militant pacifist, blackened his face and performed pseudo-African dances. Ball maintained, "What we are celebrating is at once a buffoonery and a requiem mass." He introduced his *Verses Without Words,* phonetic poems or sound paintings, the literary equivalent to the Dada collages by Arp. They all felt like God's clowns.

Kurt Schwitters—of whom Tzara said he would have been Dadaistic even

Sophie Taeuber-Arp was among the artists who introduced Dadaism. Her sparse abstractions were the first of their kind. This oil painting, "Peinture en Commun," was done in 1939, yet it still enables us to envision a possible pattern of her abstract dances between 1916 and 1918, of which there are no traces left. (Courtesy Sidney Janis Gallery)

if Dada had never been invented—continued to play with these sound paintings for many years after the war, culminating in his *Ursonate,* which began with the line:

Fümms bö wö tää zää Uu . . .

He became known for his *Merz* pictures, collages, and sculptures. Why *Merz?* It rhymes with *Schmerz* (pain) and *Herz* (heart) and is the root of the verb *ausmerzen* (eradicate). True, Dada wanted to destroy the hoaxes of reason and to discover an unreasoned order, as Arp thought; in spite of his Dadaistic prestidigitations he believed in man and his return "to nature as a part of nature." Schwitters' antics also expressed hope: ". . . the whole fraud people call war came to an end. . . . One can also shout with garbage, and that's what I did, glued and nailed refuse together. I called it Merz . . . everything was kaputt, and now we had to rebuild something out of bits and broken pieces. . . ."

What made the twenties such an important decade was its will to rebuild, to seek new ways in a dangerous world. The past was wrecked, and some artists, Tzara among them, felt that the work of destruction was not yet fully done; they were willing to drive the garbage van with all the wreckage into nowhere. But most of them saw a new spiritual reality ahead of them.

Immediately after the war Huelsenbeck returned to Berlin, joining the revolutionary forces. The great disillusionment of the war created a revolutionary effervescence whose strongest artistic expression was found in Berlin. Compared to the tranquillity in Zürich, the moral and physical crisis in Berlin cried out for action. A series of propaganda meetings were organized, short-lived magazines issued, a Dada Club founded. Huelsenbeck was supported by George Grosz and Walter Mehring, and later by Otto Dix. A propaganda meeting for May 1918 announced the reading of "simultaneous poems, noise music, and cubist dances by 10 ladies." It was in Germany that Dada systematically used art as a political weapon against the vestiges of the past.*

---

* Hugo Ball withdrew to the Ticino, the southern part of Switzerland, where he would meet Arp, and became a mystic. Huelsenbeck emigrated to the United States before World War II and turned into a prosperous psychoanalyst on New York's Central Park South before he also decided to spend his last years in the Ticino. George Grosz came as a refugee to New York, where he was very successful changing his style and approach to the arts and life. In his book *A Little Yes and a Big No* he wrote: "If Dada made no sense to the masses, it at least served as an outlet for the rich playboys who financed our movement. We simply mocked everything. . . . Nothing was holy to us. . . . We spat upon everything, including ourselves. Our symbol was nothingness, a vacuum, a void. . . . We travel along strange paths. I did some thorough thinking and discarded many former ideas as illusions. Now I sharply rejected my previous work.. . . . I found new worlds were available. Nature came closer to me in its greater simplicity, unity, beauty and inexorable permanence. Yes, the second phase of my life began in America, but with it came an inner conflict over the break with my past. . . ."

Victorious France did not have the same serious problems as defeated Germany. A more sober attitude toward Dada began to prevail in France. People began to tire of the many editorials, news stories, and gossip items. The Dadaists always had a flair for making headlines. In March 1920 the *Journal du Peuple* voiced what most people thought:

> It must be admitted that it is the work which counts, that the work alone must be judged. The author can be what he likes, mad, two-headed, notary public, fourfooted, a Bolshevik, chimney-sweep or paralytic, a fortuneteller or a paranoic. The work is capable of stirring up our mental menagerie. Dada is not a mystification; it is the entire human mystery.

In France, Dada appeared at the end of its revolution and a reorientation seemed necessary. André Breton (1896–1966) was interested in many things despised by the diehard Dadaists. He was deeply interested in Freud's theories; he visited Freud in 1922. The Dadaists were either opposed to or ignored Freud. In 1920 Breton had written in an essay about the poetic realization in a surrealistic approach in which the images beyond our conscious control could become the artistic creation of dreamlike realities. Eros and the automatic release of subconscious imagery became the pillars of surrealism. It systematized much that was contained in Dada. In his *Manifeste du surréalisme,* issued in 1924, André Breton could say: "I believe in the future resolution of the states of dream and reality, in appearance so contradictory, in a sort of absolute reality, or *surréalité,* if I may so call it."

Because more disciplined, surrealism had a wider creative range than Dadaism, including Joan Miró's playful fantasies and Max Ernst's nightmarish imagery. Salvador Dali could prove that even academic illusionism might lead to a work of anti-art. The trinity of Freudianism, Dada, and surrealism became a potent force in the arts. Dance, although more slowly developing than the other arts, was also nourished by it.

DURING the 1920s the most feverish artistic activities took place in Germany. The Bauhaus in Weimar and later in Dessau became an institution of international importance in its revolutionary teaching of and experimenting in the visual arts, architecture, industrial design, and dance. It was a rallying point for *Neue Sachlichkeit (New Functionalism)*. Founded and directed by Walter Gropius, it tried to combine art and modern technology. In the twenties the modern style of architecture became consolidated. Architecture, city planning, the building of highways, bridges, and tunnels will, for future

This satire by George Grosz was made in 1926. He called "Pillars of Society" one of his mordant indictments of society in Germany after World War I. (Courtesy German Information Center)

generations, best characterize our century. The strongest architectural impulses came from the Bauhaus.

Yet the visual arts were not neglected. For instance, Oskar Schlemmer, a teacher of scenic design at the Bauhaus, was interested in humans in space. His dancers were creations of his imagination, sexless figures or eternal types of humans moving like mechanical puppets in a variety of moods through space. He metamorphosed the *Tänzermensch* (man as dancer) into the mechanical human figure he called *Kunstfigur*. He saw with the eyes of a painter, and his dance theater was a nondancer's attempt to eliminate all literary and emotional aspects of stage movement and to rely on plastic images within geometric patterns. His *Triadic Ballet* was his strongest statement of fascinating shapes in motion. Inspired by geometric logic, he tested the scientist in the artist, and vice versa.

The twenties were a period of unease everywhere, but particularly in Central Europe. It was the time when Franz Kafka created the nightmares and obsessions of lostness. Life demanded intensified activity. There was violence in the streets and theaters. Bertolt Brecht fought for a new reality in cold stage light to shock his audiences into awareness through alienation. Erwin Piscator went beyond Brecht's epic theater, creating his political stage, shaking his fist against the complacencies of the bourgeois world that bought the best seats to applaud him. Most loved by them was the figure of the highway robber Mackie Messer in *The Threepenny Opera*. Expressionism was the rage, with its explosive cries, its intense distortions, and its outpouring of passionate feelings.

These were the years when the English discovered that there was dance in them. Marie Rambert, who was briefly with Diaghilev, opened a ballet school of her own in London in 1920; this later became the Ballet Rambert. She can hardly be called a dancer or choreographer. But her genius at spotting and developing some of the outstanding dance talents in England was of momentous importance. If she had done nothing else but nurture Antony Tudor and Frederick Ashton, her merits would be indisputable. Ninette de Valois was the other, more practical, power in laying the foundation of a British ballet tradition. The Royal Ballet took less than two decades before becoming one of the world's great companies.

Marie Rambert was always more interested in experimental work, free from outward pressures, which secured for her school and company a unique position. In contrast to their German counterparts, the British artists of the era between the wars were not caught by any experimental fever. The

This is a characteristic picture of how Oskar Schlemmer, of the Bauhaus, envisioned the abstract image of a dancer. In his experiments he worked with live dancers. This picture is now in the Neue Pinakothek in Munich. (IN-Bild Foto Inter Nationes. Courtesy German Information Center)

Irish Abbey Theatre, with its lyric realism, soared to enviable heights. In general, however, an intellectual aristocracy then ruled the British waves, from Virginia Woolf to H. G. Wells, from John Galsworthy to Stephen Spender. Some of the most creative British minds preferred to live as self-styled exiles in America: D. H. Lawrence, Aldous Huxley, Christopher Isherwood, W. H. Auden. In the twenties, even more so the following decade, some of the greatest European minds veered toward the New World.

In the decade after World War I the expressionistic dance flourished in Central Europe. Mary Wigman was the most articulate dancer of this circle. We can understand her dances only when we envision her pitted against the tumultuous background of the postwar era. She saw herself as the product of her time. She drew strength from her daily experiences. Whatever she danced was an ecstatic manifestation of existence. To say yes to life was a necessity in order to survive. She heard many calls, the calls of death. To her, it was a voice calling life back into the deep darkness from where it came. The carnage of war was for the Germans an ever-present specter. No other nation produced in the latter part of the twenties so many antiwar books as the Germans, with Erich Maria Remarque's *All Quiet on the Western Front* the best known. In the year 1930 Wigman was in Munich choreographing and dancing in *Das Totenmal,* a monumental show in memory of war and death.

She was always aware of the ultimate questions and, above all, of overcoming the averageness in herself, a truly Nietzschean thought. Sacrifice was another notion constantly on her mind, and it also found expression in several of her dances, which even in their lightest mood were never lightweight. All her dance creations emerged from her awareness that her body was the visible manifestation of a being that exists only as the truthful mirror of humanity. Although her dances were rooted in the passion of her mind, they were not cerebral. Like her American counterpart Martha Graham, she drew from rich sources of symbolic-primitive origins, and her work showed a strong leaning toward a mystical belief whose depth remains as elusive as it is unfathomable.

Out of the same milieu and experiences came two diametrically opposed figures. Harald Kreutzberg (1902–68) is a symbol of contrast to both Mary Wigman and Kurt Jooss (1901–79). The twenties were full of eccentrics,

"WITCH DANCE *belonged to one of the 'great' solo dances of my career,"* Mary Wigman *said. "What it reflected was the image of one possessed, wild and dissolute, repelling the fascinating . . . the mask possessed its own personal life . . . the body something of the animal-like quality in the image of the enigmatic Sphinx. . . ." (Courtesy the Author)*

among them ivory-tower artists, as the example of Rainer Maria Rilke proved; up to his death in 1926, he tried to hold on to the idea of living in a protected vacuum of an isolated world. Kreutzberg was not of this sort. However, an artist can create in the isolation of a dream world.

Kreutzberg best explained himself by saying:

> I am not a leader nor a creator of any school of dancing. I dance to express myself. I dance from my heart, blood and imagination. . . . I do not believe that dancing should tell a story or have a meaning; nor do I feel that a dancer must draw upon his experiences to express fully dances of great joy or great sorrow.

If modern dance is self-expression per se, then Kreutzberg was its epitome. Today it may no longer be important what he danced, and the memory of his theatricalized lyricism may die with the few who have seen him and remain a small footnote to the history of dance. He is not mentioned here because he was profound—he was not—but because here is an early and

Kurt Jooss's GREEN TABLE, *as produced by the Robert Joffrey Ballet. (Photo by Herbert Migdoll. Courtesy The Robert Joffrey Ballet)*

perhaps warning example, like that of Isadora, how far you may dare to take your ego on an artistic trip.

One more reason for mentioning him is the manner of his "free adaptation of the ballet," as John Martin termed it. This relates him more closely to Kurt Jooss, who can claim Laban as his teacher and who makes good use of Laban's space and movement concepts. Jooss is far more of a theater man than Laban ever was. As a child of the twenties, he believed that expressionism was the form of art best fitted for the dance, that dance must be theater dramatizing a story with natural, not stylized, gestures underlining plot and characterization. He liked to employ a minimum of decor and pure, streamlined movements eschewing pirouettes, entrechats, and toe dancing as anachronisms. He was a new Noverre who wanted to give the ballet d'action a twentieth-century face. He surprised an international dance congress held in Germany in 1928 by advocating a new approach for both schools of technique. Jooss pointed out the need for the classical ballet to come to terms with the modern dance as the true representative of its time. He visualized that the modern dancer, in order to succeed, would have to accept and absorb a great deal of the classic technique. Jooss's vision was a few decades ahead of his time.

He was a committed artist, committed to his time, deeply involved in and disturbed by the frightening interlude between the two wars. He saw *Mein Kampf* as the mene tekel it was and created in 1932—a year before Hitler came to power—the antiwar dance drama *The Green Table,* whose simple conception and allegorical power has become a most unique Dance of Death. Significantly, it was shown in Paris first and has been in the repertory of many companies ever since.

Another great event of the twenties in Germany was the final establishment of a notation system, known as *Labanotation* or *Kinetographie,* first published in 1928 and put to the test eight years later when, for a mammoth presentation on the occasion of a dance congress, notated dance scores were sent to forty different cities, where the dance was rehearsed. When the dancers gathered, the parts fitted together very well and, after one dress rehearsal, the show was presented. It was the first major step toward the elimination of the illiteracy of the dance. As early as 1700, Raoul Auger Feuillet created the first workable method, which was used until the French Revolution. Despite its obvious limitations it would have helped us to know more about Noverre's dance works, had he not rejected the Feuillet notation altogether.

The need to write down the dance movements, as music is being written, has always led to new attempts in this direction. The Benesh notation, mainly used in Britain, was one of the more successful endeavors. Film and video have turned out to be mere helpful crutches. Of course, dance exists in the dancer's body, but it also fades away the minute it is done if not notated.

Louis Horst, the grand old man of modern dance, tutored three generations of American dancers. He was an indefatigable fighter for American modern dance and instrumental in charting its spiritual direction. (Courtesy the Author)

Labanotation has proved the most comprehensive tool toward preservation. Together with its expanded "Effort-Shape" development and the recent experiments to program Labanotation onto a computer, it may give dance a literate basis.

The center of Labanotation is in New York, which, after World War II, became the Mecca of dance. As early as the days of the Armory Show and the coincidental foundation of Denishawn, the notion of art took on greater meaning for a wider spectrum of the American population.

One of the extreme experimenters exhibited at the Armory Show was Marcel Duchamp (1887–1968), who settled in New York in 1915. He found in New York (which he loosely took for America) the nervous drive and scintillating excitement that Europe no longer offered him. As he proved by his provocative painting "Nude Descending a Staircase," he was fascinated by movement, which in this case he solved by cinematic implication. His "Readymades," such as "Bottlerack" or "Urinal," are creations to negate creation. His "Large Glass" was described by Breton as "a mechanistic and cynical interpretation of the phenomenon of love," and it could just as well be interpreted as the transparent triumph of indifference. "Irony," Duchamp said, "is a playful way of accepting something. Mine is the irony of indifference. It is a 'meta-irony.'" Duchamp's ideas were as important as Cocteau's in *Parade*. Their real influence, however, was felt only in the early fifties, with Rauschenberg, Cage, and Cunningham. What Duchamp and the circle around Stieglitz's magazine *291* immediately achieved, was to provoke new thinking.

Louis Horst (1884–1964), accompanist and conductor of Denishawn, was one of those who wanted to see the dance find a new meaning in a changing world, with all the other arts undergoing decisive transformations. A short stay in Europe made him realize that the dance must break with the eclectic prettiness of the past. He recognized the potential genius of Martha Graham. He also encouraged Doris Humphrey (1895–1958) and Charles Weidman (1901–75), the most promising members of Denishawn, to find a new way to their artistic self-fulfillment. He wanted the dance to gain the same freedom and originality that the other arts enjoyed, but he was also determined to give it structure and discipline (which most of the other experimental arts did not have). After Martha Graham's first recital in 1926 the American version of the modern dance was born.

Historians oversold the idea of the second coming of the modern dancers in the twenties as a rebellion against Denishawn. Denishawn had simply outlived its raison d'être by then. The reevaluation of all old values that changed Europe after 1917 also had its repercussions in the United States. The theater renaissance in America began at the same time with Eugene O'Neill and Elmer Rice. New powerful writers appeared: Fitzgerald, Hemingway, Dos Passos, Wilder. Edmund Wilson, reviewing T. S. Eliot's *The Waste Land,* wrote: ". . . sometimes we feel that he is speaking not only for a personal distress but for the starvation of a whole civilization. . . ." This was written in 1923. Someone coined the phrase "the Lost Generation." Many American intellectuals sought self-styled exile on the Left Bank of Paris from a Prohibition-drunk society which tried to deny the birthright of our primates in a monkey trial and which made Sacco and Vanzetti heroes and martyrs. The eternal prejudice of humanity was seasoned by the giddy mentality of a new cashocracy rushing toward an earthshaking stock market crash.

Yet America woke up culturally. The flight of Graham and Horst, Humphrey and Weidman from the artificialities of Denishawn at that time has to be seen in this context. Perhaps without Isadora there would never have flowered a Mary Wigman, giving body and direction to modern dance. "I see America dancing," Isadora said prophetically, and the new wave of American dancers at the end of the twenties were expressionistic in substance and romantic in spirit. Their work showed the conscious influence of Isadora and the unconscious influence of Mary Wigman, who was seen in the United States in 1930 and 1931. The modern dancer in America went beyond Wigman, giving more body and direction to the modern dance and giving modern dance its technique, second only to ballet. The work of these dancers remained, however, mainly representational, dramatizing the psyche in a literal and narrative style. It was revolutionary in appearance, not in essence. In fact, it intercepted the real dance revolution begun by *Parade* with the help of Diaghilev's Ballets Russes, which in the twenties were far less daring than in the teens.

Modern dance is not so much a system as a state of mind, flexing its individual muscles, stressing its personal artistic dream. What seemed to be a weakness of the new movement was, at the same time, its natural forte: the excess of individual expression. Helen Tamiris (1905–66), who came from the ballet to join the other pioneers, set forth their principles in 1928 in a program note sounding like a manifesto. Indicative of the revolutionary spirit of this period was her thought that there were no general rules and that each work had to create its own code, that each age created its own art carrying the stamp of its environment. She felt that the modern dance was "a genuine expression of America."

Martha Graham (born in 1894), the most unique personality in this field, is deeply rooted in her environment. There could be no better proof of the awareness of American culture than Martha Graham's growing work. "The dance reveals the spirit of the country in which it takes root." Some of her earlier dances stress the self-consciousness of belonging. In *Frontier* (1935) she evoked the image of the vast American plains and the indomitable will of the people to conquer them. *Appalachian Spring* (1944) is full of almost sentimental love for the pioneers of this country who have built it. This work breathes the exuberance of hope and is carried by a characteristic dramatic lyricism.

From the very beginning Graham had to strike out into new directions, for which she needed new means: ". . . the old forms could not give voice to the more fully awakened man," she said. From a sociocultural viewpoint her phrase "fully awakened man" characterizes the American mentality of the time. It is also significant for the self-assuredness of her personality that, in retrospect, she could say, "I never wanted to destroy the ballet, I only went my own way." This was no doubt said in reference to Isadora and her anti-balletic crusades thirty years previously. We must not forget that Isadora had to flee her country, then in the last phase of America's Gilded Age and dragged into McKinley's imperialistic adventures. Yet Graham found self-fulfillment in the Roosevelt era, which had "nothing to fear but fear itself." It seems whatever Graham danced, whether St. Joan or Clytemnestra, she tried to penetrate the complexities of motive and deed embedded in the character's psyche, but more from an emotional than cerebral

In her earlier period, Martha Graham was fascinated by Americana, and EL
PENITENTE, *produced in 1940, belonged with her interest in American Indian material. At that time—as the photograph shows—her male partners
were still Erick Hawkins and Merce Cunningham. Louis Horst composed the score. (Photo by Barbara Morgan. Courtesy the Photographer)*

approach. As little as Wigman could ever deny Germanic introspection,
Graham could not help betraying the American vigor of an outward-going
drive.

Her repertory is rich in scope and colorful variety. Most often prolificness
is one of the signs of genius, and undoubtedly genius is in her, especially in
her personal vocabulary of tensions and percussive movements, which would
take hold of the entire body in the form of a beat, of contraction and
release. The concepts of the Graham technique are now accepted and practiced from New York to San Francisco, from Stockholm to Tel Aviv. They
are movements expressive of our age, symbolizing our anxieties in the con-
tractions and our aggressiveness in the emotional release into freedom and
action.

Not only is Martha Graham famous for her emotionally complex situations and conflicts and the probing of her characters' psyches, she can also enchant with lyric lightness, as in DIVERSION OF ANGELS, *as now danced by her company. Peggy Lyman and George White, Jr., are in this picture. (Photo by Martha Swope. Courtesy Martha Graham Center of Contemporary Dance)*

José Limón's MOOR'S PAVANE *is one of the masterpieces of American modern dance. It has also been incorporated in the repertory of several ballet companies. The picture shows José Limón as the Moor and Betty Jones as Desdemona. (Photo by Walter Strate. Courtesy the Author)*

Martha Graham was not alone in her search for a new way of expressing the modern dancer's freedom. Doris Humphrey, with her partner Charles Weidman, was destined to become another vital force of this trend. Early in her career she stated:

> I wish my dance to be based on reality illumined by imagination; to be organic rather than synthetic; to call forth a definite reaction from the audience; and to make its contribution toward the drama of life.

The drama of life and the relationships between people were the central issues of her creations, beginning with her *New Dance* trilogy, which John Martin said "marked the coming of age of the American dance." Doris Humphrey began to observe her body in its struggle with gravity, and the experiment resulted in her theory of "fall and recovery," of the dramatic realization of giving in and resisting, of maintaining equilibrium.

She also began to experiment with choreography, of which *Water Study* is still performed, as is *The Shakers*. She could translate the architectural beauty and the spirit of religious ecstasy into movement as pure and simple as Bach's music in her *Passacaglia* in C Minor (1938). Crippled by arthritis, she continued her career as choreographer of her company. She recognized the choreographic genius of José Limón (1908–72); supported and guided by her, it brought forth some of the classics in this field, of which his *Moor's Pavane* has taken its place in the repertory of many ballet companies. This work is a feat of contained magnitude in which the stately rhythms of a pavane embody the tragedy of Othello. Many of Limón's other dances, such as *Missa Brevis* or *There Is a Time,* celebrate the dignity of human beings and the nobility of spirit that marked their thinking and being.

Already in the thirties many young people were attracted to modern dance with its limitless ways of self-expression. In a generation Isadora's dream came true, and it seemed as if all of America were about to dance. The youthfulness of the country and the restlessness and mobility of Americans were essential assets. But what really made it happen was a few teachers, Doris Humphrey, Louis Horst, and Hanya Holm (born in 1898), who created the receptivity for a yet unknown challenge. The young were caught as if by a fever of having to express themselves through movement. Everywhere professional groups were formed, whose members felt the need to go out on their own, forming new groups. By the end of the thirties America's dance consciousness was a remarkable phenomenon, and by the end of the forties, when modern dance began to suffer from its first crisis of excessive self-expression, it was recognized as an authentic American art—as American as jazz.

The classical ballet, too, was a part of the American renaissance in the dance. Before George Balanchine (born in 1904) arrived on the scene there

Hanya Holm is one of the more important forces in the development of American dance. Originally an assistant of Mary Wigman, she directed the Mary Wigman School in New York, later the Hanya Holm School. She is best known for her choreography of American musicals (KISS ME, KATE; MY FAIR LADY), but her contribution to the modern dance helped to establish this dance form in the 1930s and '40s. One of her early works was TREND (1937). (Photo by Barbara Morgan. Courtesy Hanya Holm)

was already quite a lot of ballet activity in the larger cities. A similar restlessness prevailed among the ballet dancers as among their barefoot brethren, except that their pioneering potentials were limited by their traditional vocabulary. And yet they also tried to find a new formula for an American-oriented ballet, true to the new spirit of national awareness. In the mid-thirties Catherine Littlefield created such genre works as *Barn Dance* with her Philadelphian company. In Chicago, Ruth Page choreographed some of the first ballets of American folklore with such ballets as *Frankie and Johnny.*

Lincoln Kirstein (born in 1907), then a young aesthete, brilliant writer, and dance enthusiast, was destined to play a royal part in the growing prominence of American dance. He was a nondancer playing a role similar to that of Diaghilev. In the thirties he sponsored many great talents, and the titles of their ballets, such as *Filling Station* (Lew Christensen) or *Billy the Kid* (Eugene Loring), mirrored the momentum with which American folklore found its way onto the ballet stage. The name most often associated with it is that of Agnes de Mille, whose *Rodeo, Fall River Legend,* and choreography for *Oklahoma!* have set the highlights of Americana in balletic terms.

Although Kirstein was fully aware of the nationalistic trend of the time and supported it, he nevertheless decided to bring Balanchine to New York as the one choreographer who could make his dream of creating *the* great American ballet company come true. He had seen Balanchine's *La Chatte* in 1927 and *Apollon Musagète* a year later, both done for the Diaghilev company. Reminiscing about his decision, Kirstein wrote in *Theatre Arts* in 1958: ". . . I knew that what Balanchine made meant ballet to me, because ballet was about dancing to music, not about painting to pantomime."

It was a calculated risk to bring a choreographer with him who was alien to the American scene and artistic expectations. They went through rough times, but there had never before existed such a sincere and lasting rela-

George Balanchine, restaging his early work SERENADE *(1934) for the Balanchine-inspired company at the Zürich Opera in September 1978. (Photo Dave Brüllmann. Courtesy Zürich Opera Ballet)*

tionship between a patron and artist. In the beginning there were the disruptions caused by the Second World War and the obvious difficulties of keeping a big company alive. Moreover, there was adverse criticism from all sides, particularly from John Martin, powerful critic of the New York *Times,* who found fault with every work Balanchine presented: "While every region is entitled to whatever decadences it pleases, there is nothing to be gained by importing them." Or ". . . while gifted American artists were starving . . . there is money available for the production of European importations of this caliber." But more than a decade later, in 1952, the same critic wrote in his book *Modern Ballet:* "The bringing of Balanchine to America in 1933 was an event of considerably greater moment than anybody realized at the time except perhaps Lincoln Kirstein, who brought it about."

When, in the beginning, he had to brave the worst criticism, Balanchine rejected the idea of using folkloric material. It was only after he was generally recognized in the fifties that he proved he could do it too. In quick succession after 1954 came ballets such as *Western Symphony, Square Dance,* and *Stars and Stripes.* Balanchine's recognition reached its climax when in 1963 the Ford Foundation announced that the New York City Ballet would receive a grant of nearly $8 million, unprecedented in the history of ballet and the arts in general. It was further proof that dance had received the stamp of full recognition by the arbiters and administrators of the country's fortune. Balanchine and his associated ballet enterprises were chosen as a symbol for having reached an institutional status, with school and performing company.

He is probably the last genuine representative of the classical ballet tradition, considering himself as the heir to Petipa's legacy. But in such ballets as *Agon, Four Temperaments, Episodes,* and *Ivesiana* he has proved to be attuned to the angularity and dissonance of our time. Balanchine felt that America was "the land of lovely bodies" and that the dancers had a "kind of angelic unconcern toward emotion." With his first ballet choreographed in this country, *Serenade,* he already tried to give this "American young look," as Edwin Denby said, the look of grandeur and nobility without making the dancers feel embarrassed.

His dancers are best equipped for his approach to pure ballet, in which the moving body alone is artistically expressive, evoking images of fantasy and human relationships. The story he tells is locked in the body of the dancers. Balanchine's movements are akin to Stravinsky's music in the control of line, calculated precision, visual sparseness, analytically designed poses marked by surprising wit and invention.

In the upsurge of American dance consciousness the New York City Ballet was not alone. As an offshoot of the Mikhail Mordkin group—Mordkin, Michel Fokine, and Adolph Bolm had settled in the States between the wars —American Ballet Theatre came into being in 1939. This company has revised classic works, but its merit—giving to the American ballet scene some of the strongest impulses over the years—lay in the creation of ballets with American subjects and the discovery of new choreographic talents: Herbert Ross and Eliot Feld, and, above all, Jerome Robbins.

Robbins (born in 1918) is a protean talent. He has a very acute feeling for the American scene, having carefully listened to its pace, accent, and jazzy idiom. To have come out during the war with that triumphant snapshot of three sailors on shore leave, *Fancy Free,* proved that he could catch the tune of his time. He found in Leonard Bernstein a composer with a kindred soul. Both enlarged the idea of *Fancy Free* to a musical, *On the Town.* How more American and timely could anyone have been, creating, as Robbins did in 1957, the musical *West Side Story,* the *Romeo and Juliet* theme translated into terms of New York street gangs? He looked for challenges everywhere and found them on Broadway as much as on the ballet stage, sometimes amusing himself as, for instance, in turning the second act of *Giselle* into the Kafkaesque idea of having devouring female insects dance the male to death. Only he would dare to rechoreograph an *Afternoon of a Faun,* giving the wistful, romantic encounter between two dancers and their mirror images in a studio a narcissistic touch. Robbins can be bold in his abstractions, as in *Moves,* a ballet in silence, or lyrical, as in his *Dances at a Gathering,* or mystical in the penetration of life, as in *Watermill.* He is the embodiment of American showmanship, with insight and depth.

Most characteristic of the Freudian age is the work of Antony Tudor, who, as a young, almost unknown English choreographer, was launched by American Ballet Theatre. Tudor was close to the spirit of the modern dance. Such ballets as *Lilac Garden, Dim Lustre,* and *Pillar of Fire* proved that his choreography was getting beneath the skin of the characters, that he was not only interested in the motivations behind a character's reaction expressed through movement, but also created a mood, lyrical or dramatic, which held his dancers together like the setting of a jewel. He gave different styles of movement to the various dancers in *Pillar of Fire* simply because they expressed the emotional experience of the character. He even introduced, as Edwin Denby said, ballet movements "set against the non-ballet dancing of the exciting low-life crowd—they dance and whirl in a sort of wild rumba style . . . while the calm hero, in contrast to everyone, comes on not as any kind of dancer, but walking across the stage as modestly as a Fuller-brush man. Tudor fuses these heterogeneous elements brilliantly."

It is the revelation of the emotional experience and struggle that gives his characters and ballets a new and wider dimension. Unspoken memories or inexpressible thought feelings suddenly come to life. Tudor is a master teller of stories, unfolding them with the sensitivity of a poet who has learned to read the secrets of human beings. In the early forties the psychological ballet, as Antony Tudor made it happen, became firmly established.

Peter Martins as one of the three sailors on shore leave in Jerome Robbins's FANCY FREE. (*Photo by Costas. Courtesy the Photographer*)

It is interesting to contemplate that the great upsurge of dancing should occur in a nation that has achieved the highest degree of mechanization. As one of the ways of holding on to himself, man has desperately tried to return to his soil, his roots. Newly inflamed nationalistic tendencies were one of the consequences, and the sudden appearance of many national folk ballets, from the Ballet Folklorico de México to the Moiseyev Dance Company to Inbal, the dance theater of Israel, showed the unconscious need of people to protest the dangers of mechanization with the convincing simplicity of their native symbolism.

This trend had begun at the dawn of the Industrial Revolution in the Romantic Age, with its growing interest in foreign folklore, finally leading to the escape into Orientalism at the turn of the century. This flight from self became accentuated after the two cataclysmic events in our time. Yeats,

Pound, and Brecht embraced No; Wigman danced in Japanese masks; Cage, Cunningham, and the Beatnik generation became devotees of Zen. The twenties and thirties, moreover, elevated the gypsy dance to an aesthetically valid and emotionally rousing art form: the neo-Spanish dance. In a different way and out of different reasons we can hear the faint echo of the slogan "back to nature." Some think that civilization moves in cycles; others envision a huge spiral. Whichever it may be, people face similar problems on different levels, which recur at the most unexpected turns of history.

The Mass Media

THE IMPACT OF THE MASS MEDIA ON OUR CIVILIZATION HAS BEEN STUPENDOUS. First, photography has liberated us from the bondage of any locally restricted experience. We are no longer limited to the scope of our imagination while reading about art treasures remote in distance and time. Photography and film can bring them to us. Some processes of reproduction have been improved to such perfection as to give us, for instance, a more impressive color feeling of a painting than the original could—like a translation betraying the original by improving it stylistically.

When photography exploded on the art scene in the mid-nineteenth century, some men of letters were concerned about its inherent power of temptation, possibly leading to the destruction of the arts themselves. In 1859 Charles Baudelaire wrote about *The Modern Public and Photography,* saying that he was "convinced that the ill-applied developments of photography, like all other purely material developments of progress, have contributed much to the impoverishment of the French artistic genius. . . ." He continued:

> Poetry and progress are like two ambitious men who hate one another with an instinctive hatred, and when they meet upon the same road, one of them has to give place. If photography is allowed to supplement art in some of its functions, it will soon have supplanted or corrupted it altogether, thanks to the stupidity of the multitude which is its natural ally.

Baudelaire has been proved both right and wrong as to the way photography had its influence on the visual arts and established itself as an independent art; and undoubtedly the cinematic art has become a characteristic phenomenon of our time, a part of the democratization that has embraced the mass media. Both photography and film have traumatically changed our habits and attitudes. However much we desire to view the mechanical development from all its positive aspects, some serious thoughts ought to cause us sleepless nights. Our concerns are no longer those of Baudelaire; they have deviated and risen in proportion to the role that film and television have come to play in our daily life.

We have learned to accept the technical accomplishments mythologized through a variety of apparatuses and gadgets as something that has taken an inalienable place in our present world. These gadgets are accepted as something self-evident, and their real function is often illusionary. Mechanization is a frightening process, as it endangers our aesthetic sensibilities; it heightens the lingering danger of our growing apathy toward values. It gradually turns us into passive nonbeings pushing buttons and turning knobs for no real purpose. It cannot help but become a mechanical reflex, setting in motion a mechanical gadget in a highly mechanized world.

Television demonstrates its overt blessings—as all technological miracles do—for the old, the sick, and lonely persons, trying to justify thereby its attention-consuming existence and the danger of creating an easily malleable society. This is the price we must pay for an apparently unlimited profusion of ready-made music, words, and pictures.

Yet some theater and concert productions transmitted by the camera and relayed all over the world are a cultural boon. Where only a few might have had access to a stunning artistic experience, its recording and transmission to millions everywhere is and remains a triumph of technology; that such rare experiences can remain recorded for future generations is an immeasurable advantage our time has over the past.

THE mass media ask for a new approach in creating the material to be viewed and in viewing itself. Film, at home in a technological civilization, is much closer to a materialistic interpretation of the universe than ballet, born in a world of elitism. Dance and cinema are both concerned with the creation of moving images, but in a competitive manner: man-made against machine-made art. The essence of theater dance is its miracle of make-believe, the poetry of its suggestiveness, its physical and allusive distance. Theater dance is defined within its architectural frame. The spectators' eyes are actively engaged in following the events onstage from a distance. We are emotionally and intellectually involved, but, even more important, the dancing onstage induces our kinesthetic rapport.

These are essential facts. Dance on film demands another quality of poetic revelation. Film creates an intimate, kinetic relation to the viewers, who, deprived of the poetry of distance, are denied traditional involvement. They no longer see the dancer, they see the camera seeing the dancer. They may feel the emotional and intellectual impact, but their kinesthetic rapport will remain passive because it becomes a secondhand event.

In the theater we experience the movement as the dancer experiences it;

in filmed dance, ours is the camera's experience. The camera is the sole interpreter and manipulator. Reality is rebuilt, reorganized, and our eyes are forced to see the world in our way, but with a different logic. The eye of the camera makes it clearer to us that our inner world is only seemingly cohesive: in fact it consists of many fragments and offers, as a substitute for the lost poetry of distance, at its best a poetry of fragmented reality.

It was inevitable that, with the beginning of cinematography, dances and dancers would be recorded on film. This has been done by filmmakers, photographers, and the dancers themselves as a documentation of their works. While the filmmakers have often been trying to interpret the dance through the varied means and tricks of the camera, the dancer-choreographer has been more interested in the straight filming of studio performances or of those onstage for cataloging and preserving dance creations. This has become a customary act.

Cultural history is also reflected by the hobbies of the multitude and the activities in which the dilettante indulges. The camera and the jet plane have changed the habits of life in the second half of the century. Our ability to use the jet to see the world has brought about the industrialized plague of our time: tourism. At best, it establishes the threshold of tolerance toward other humans, alien to one's own background, who take advantage of being looked at on a commercial level. Most travelers are not mentally equipped to absorb the beauties of the world. The camera has become their indispensable crutch. It also gives the dilettante the feeling of sham creativity. Susan Sontag rightly claimed:

> Needing to have reality confirmed and experience enhanced by photographs is an esthetic consumerism to which everyone is now addicted. Industrial societies turn their citizens into image-junkies; it is the most irresistible form of mental pollution.

To realize how fully mechanized our era is, we only have to compare our hobbies of photography and amateur filming with those of former periods. Drawing, for instance, was a desirable romantic pastime activity in the days of Goethe and Mendelssohn (both excellent draftsmen); playing of the piano was simply *the* thing one did in every well-to-do bourgeois home from the mid-nineteenth century to the dawn of the phonograph.

We cannot silence science or stop progress, and the modern human dilemma is our inability to replace the old tradition we are in the process of losing. Technology gives us too little time to absorb and assimilate artistically the possible advantages progress may offer. Television is a self-devouring hydra, and the mass media have particularly reflected the feeling of a glittering façade behind which the dance is seduced and violated. The sugar-coated attractiveness of the mass media lies above all in their promise of success and financial rewards. No doubt, film and video have millions of viewers. Without being able to foresee their technical applications, Baudelaire was rightly concerned about the irreconcilability of progress and poetry.

So mechanized is our era that dances created for the stage are transplanted to film without hesitation. No one would transpose a ballet choreographed for film or video onto the stage. *Coppélia* or *Swan Lake* or any other classical ballet transposed in its stage version onto film or television can only be an incongruous, because enfeebled, replica of its true being. Faced with the choice between photographing the stage version of a ballet and subjecting it to cinematic devices that must leave the balletomane with an utterly frustrated feeling, we could only do some justice to tradition and this new medium by forgetting the known stage version and creating a new *Coppélia* or *Swan Lake* in the ideological terms of a mechanized world. Such a cinematic, newly conceived version may startle balletomanes but hurt their aesthetic feelings far less.

From generation to generation we have felt the need to tamper with classical material in order to give it an up-to-date meaning. Desecration of a work of art stops being desecration at the point where a new version proves its artistic validity. But why try at all to impose the past on our own time? Reinterpreting *Hamlet* to bring it closer to the prevailing ideas of the time or making any play of the past more acceptable to the world we live in may be justified because it still happens within the framework of the traditional stage. But the conceptual philosophy of the cinematic media is alien to any stage image. The new media and their artistic potentialities must be considered a perfect synthesis of technology and art, and they therefore demand a new generation of artists.

The camera is inventive and imaginative in its own way. When the film came of age toward the end of the thirties there was a great deal of dancing in the movies, but, with very few exceptions, it was theatricalized studio dance. In those early days the great debate was between Fred Astaire—by many, including George Balanchine, considered the greatest American dancer—who opposed all camera tricks that would make the audience more aware of the photography than his dancing, and Gene Kelly, who, on a commercial level, experimented with all the tricks the camera could offer.

Some time after World War II, film reached a certain intellectual and psychological freedom. The Italians were the first to produce extraordinary movies praised for their realism and imagination. Television gained a favorite place at the home front. Dance films became a rarity.† With dancing having reached an unprecedented height of popularity, an uneasy liaison began between the dancer and television producer.

† Enjoyable exceptions were the rather skillful transpositions of such outstanding musicals as *West Side Story* and *My Fair Lady* onto the screen.

In the same period the literary products most in demand were books probing and revealing the human being, biographies, and, above all, autobiographies. In a parallel trend the documentary entrenched itself on television, a form best suited for this medium. Even dance has sometimes benefited from the documentary approach. An interview superimposed on dance sections can create the biographical intimacy of a personality and offer insight into a dance work. It is television journalism feeding and perhaps gratifying the multitude hungry for a closeup of the dancer's world.

It is far more complex with an attempt at pure fantasy. George Balanchine wrote:

> The importance of ballet for motion pictures is the element of pure fantasy. The average picture seldom deals with free fantasy but is tied up closely with real life. . . . It is mainly because of its purely imaginative—I would say artificial—quality that ballet is important for motion pictures. It introduces a completely imaginative world whose form is of a plastic nature—a visual perfection of an imaginative life.

It cannot be said which facet of the dance—folk, ballroom, ballet, or modern dance—will prove to be most akin to this new medium. As a choreographer of ballets, Balanchine felt induced to equate the artificiality of ballet with the mechanical artificiality of the celluloid medium. But Astaire and Kelly proved their point through tapping themselves into the limelight. A number of modern dance creators could be called as witnesses for having contributed to television what seemed to have been successful in some eyes. A free style of dancing may most easily and logically adjust itself to video: that is, a modern dance style to which any other technique may be added when the work to be created asks for it.

A desperate romance exists between dance and television; in this nascent video dance, the dialogue between medium and art will remain polemical and uncreative as long as both have not found a lingual exchange in which they understand what they are talking about. A total redefinition of time, space, and motion will be needed. The work of the experimenting rebels has always influenced and pushed forward the productive potentialities of the mainstream. What is needed is a new species: the choreographer as filmmaker or the filmmaker as a choreographer whose work will no longer be a bastard but the legitimate child of progress and poetry.

Pauline Koner with Martha Curtis during a rehearsal. Koner, who has been a soloist and was also a member of the Doris Humphrey and José Limón companies for many years, now has her own group presenting her choreography, in which she reaches out for timely statements of universal significance. (Photo by Jack Mitchell. Courtesy Pauline Koner)

With the emergence of the film, Proust and Joyce opened new avenues in literature; they envisioned a new space-time relationship, broke up and merged events and experiences of past and present, unraveled the simultaneity of inner happenings, and showed the interchangeability of things within the flow of our memory, our unconsciousness. Have their novels, in structure and content, such great similarities to the sensibility and quality of cinematic techniques, or is the film the technological translation of the symphonic stream of spiritual interrelationships? In this process of simultaneity of the human soul—it was Henri Bergson who discovered the *simultanéité des états d'âmes*—lie the roots of a new aesthetic experience. I can foresee a new dance form, a synthesis of two divergent concepts, which may one day emerge from this notion of mistaken identity. It will presume not only a novel artistic approach but also a knowledgeable audience that has learned to accept the triumph of the lens over the human eye.

The Age of Anxiety

THE WAR HAD COME TO A VICTORIOUS CONCLUSION AND, WITH THE BOMB in their hands, the Americans had reached a saturation point of world power. They saw their major task as containing communism and began to build up the defeated nations as bulwarks against the East. Germany and Japan were slowly getting back on their feet. During this time of peace, the arts flourished.

Early after the war, the radio play was surprisingly creative, as television was soon to be. Some shows were stupendous; it seemed as if the television play would become a new serious genre. But due to pressures from within and without, this medium could neither fulfill its promise nor sustain its achievement, and soon returned to trivia.

Broadway had moments of fascination, especially with the musical. Choreographers found a fertile field in this American light-opera medium. Its impact on the theatrical scene is comparable only to the perfection of the *opera buffa* by the Italians in the eighteenth century. Because of its unlimited range of subjects, the musical permits the use of all types of dance techniques. In the 1930s, George Balanchine adjusted his classical ballet style to

Pearl Lang has become known for the warmth and intensity of her lyricism and the dramatic sweep with which she conjures up images of mythology, the Bible, or legends of Jewish folklore. This picture shows her in SONG OF DEBORAH. (Photo by Walter Strate. Courtesy Pearl Lang)

the musical when he choreographed *The Ziegfeld Follies* in 1935 and, a year later, *On Your Toes,* in which the main dance number, *Slaughter on Tenth Avenue,* set the standards and helped shape the taste for this new art form. Other choreographers following him have employed tap, jazz, ethnic, and modern dance. A dance form unique to American musicals evolved, making use of any idiom fitting the theme and of the vitality and adaptability of the dancers. Some of the choreographers whose contributions marked the developmental stages of the musical were Agnes de Mille (*Oklahoma!* and *Carousel*), Helen Tamiris (*Annie Get Your Gun* and *Inside U.S.A.*), Hanya Holm (*Kiss Me, Kate* and *My Fair Lady*), and Jerome Robbins (*The King and I* and *West Side Story*). This theatrical form, eclipsing the old operetta, coincided with the rise of modern dance. Both emerged from the grass roots of America.

In the 1940s the early pioneers of the modern dance were bringing in a rich harvest; in the wake of it, some younger dancer-choreographers, who believed in unraveling the beauty hidden in expressive dance, have given it a few works of substantial merit. At that time such a mesmerizing performer as Pauline Koner was noticed for the first time, creating solos of sculpted imagery, monumental in their sweep; or there was Valerie Bettis in *The Desperate Heart,* which was inspired and inspiring. Modern dance had just then reached its final stage of recognition when a number of young dancers tried to test themselves.

"The technique I employ is Graham modern as I have personalized it and expanded upon it for my creative purposes. I look to my own interior for the 'material in turmoil,' so to speak." This is what Pearl Lang, one of several dancers emerging from the fold of Martha Graham, had to say about herself. These dancers were heirs to an only recently formalized and consolidated art expression and the seekers of a new and very individual way of giving meaning to their inner "turmoil." Among the many who over the years proved the durability of their choreographic talent are Sophie Maslow (distinguished by her strong feeling for the poetic image, folklore, and her own past) and Anna Sokolow (her *Rooms,* one of the masterpieces of the American modern dance, is testimony to her rebellious spirit that wants to right wrongs in dramatizing human fears and forlornness). A spectacular personality was Lester Horton, with headquarters in Los Angeles. He was inspired by such divergent sources as Garcia Lorca, Duke Ellington, and Paul Klee, by the American Indians and an orientalized Dalcroze version. His seventeen dance compositions were all dramatically motivated, bold, and colorful. A near-genius, he was cut off from becoming a vital force in the American dance when he died in 1953. From the Midwest came a lone fighter for new forms, Sybil Shearer, an uncompromising dancer and extraordinary example for those in the 1940s and '50s searching for their identity.

Sophie Maslow with William Bales in one of her earlier works, FOLKSAY, *which shows the exuberant and earthbound quality so very much her own. (Photo by David Linton. Courtesy Sophie Maslow)*

Jeff Duncan in "Panic," a section of Anna Sokolow's ROOMS, *which has become a modern classic. In all her works, Sokolow is strongly interested in the
plight of human beings, and her social compassion finds expression in highly
charged dramatic scenes. (Photo by Edward Effron. Courtesy the Photographer)*

Shearer knew how to break away from the narrow concepts of self-expression, being eloquent with a minimum of movements. But those were the days when self-expression was taken too literally by a host of minor dancers. In the late 1940s self-expression without reaching universal validity in its statement turned out to be artistically fatal to too many dancers.

However, the preoccupation with self-expression brought about a new branch of modern dance. The idea of utilizing dance—that is, rhythmic movement—to help mentally disturbed or sick people could have been born only in that period when the soul-searching phase in modern dance reached a climactic point. The realization that people could open their hearts through movement of their bodies made the way free for a possibly therapeutic application. Ever since 1946, when Marian Chase began to experiment with mentally handicapped people in hospitals in the East and Trudy Schoop on the West Coast, dance therapy has drawn an ever-growing following. With human loneliness so rampant in the decades following these early investigations, therapeutic help through movement became more and more recognized, even by medical people. Today we know that movement can create a valuable link between body and mind, and that the touch of the hand can reach a person's psyche when the scientific word often cannot.

In the early 1950s, a new word entered the vocabulary—*noncommunicativeness*. It was not that people did not want to speak about their anxieties; they only lacked the means of communication. Words were suddenly without meaning; it was a linguistic problem. It was the time in which we rediscovered Nietzsche's saying about God's being dead. We simply no longer heard the articulation of his silence. Some artists refused to accept this dictum. They answered with a flood of religious dramas. T. S. Eliot and Graham Greene were militant knights, lyric dramatists like Christopher Fry drowned while praising God in the beauty of their verbal waves. When the religious drama had run its course, dead wordage was lying around on the shores next morning.

At the same time, some dancers attempted to save the spirituality of God through movement. Ruth St. Denis had always tried to bring the dance back to the Church. In those days her dream of a rhythmic choir, a "Cathedral of the Future," came true by way of a movement that called itself "sacred dance."

In danced ecstasy, people may often have felt the silence locked within them become the articulated silence of God. In its spontaneity, the movement seemed pure and justified as a sudden release of deep-seated emotions. This would have been "it," had not the artistic ego wished to play its part and be noticed dancing. What was the all-too-conscious verbal reality in the religious play was the physical aspect of dance. Through movement the dancer may find the shortest distance from his soul to his Redeemer—but then it is a lone, private, and uncommunicative experience. Some Shakers or Hasidim may have chanced such ecstasy sometimes. Most often the aesthetically phony would replace the experienced holy, and the sacred dance movement withered away in the big nothingness of life's progress.

People discovered the "tragedy of language" of mind and body, and the phrase "language of movement" was anathema to the experimental dancer. In his first play, *The Bald Soprano,* Ionesco made a parody of the tragedy of language, playing havoc with cliché-saddened statements that have become the daily manna of our talks:

> Words had become empty, noisy shells without meaning; the characters . . . empty. Everything appeared to me . . . moving in a timeless time, in a spaceless space . . . once I had finished . . . I fancied myself having written something like the tragedy of language! . . .

As early as the end of the last century, Hugo von Hofmannsthal feared that the poetry of the word was lost. He wrote: "People are rather tired of having to listen to talk. Words deeply nauseate them: Because the words have stopped in front of the things. . . ." In 1928, when the most vehement attacks on language came from James Joyce and Gertrude Stein, he wrote: "I shy away from words. They deprive us of the best." From the very first days of this century, Karl Kraus—as we may remember—voiced his conviction that language was expressive of human living, thinking, and feeling. Kraus sensed that language, fingered, raped, and vandalized as it has been, symbolizes man's moral bankruptcy. The philosopher Ludwig Wittgenstein confirmed the Krausian dictum: "Ethics and aesthetics are one."

Some dancers still believed in the word and gave the dance drama a last big chance. The works of the poetic dramatists—Lorca, Tennessee Williams, Yeats, Synge, and many others—were used by literary-minded choreographers in the 1950s, among them Valerie Bettis and Mary Anthony, as subject matter, often with the spoken word to orchestrate their movement patterns. They also wanted to deviate from the introspective trend of modern dance that began to lose itself in self-analytical paroxysms. But the times were obviously against them.

THE year 1952 was a pivotal point, in the wake of existentialism and the theater of the absurd, in which man, in his semifutile struggle with himself, tried to catch his Being in the very act of existing. Samuel Beckett (born 1906) came out with his play *Waiting for Godot.* For him the task of the artist was "to find a form that accommodates the mess." He became the most accomplished form-smasher of the time. His plays became progressively more cryptic, finally reduced to a mouth speaking onstage. But he was constantly searching for the ultimate Self. *Waiting for Godot* is the story of human exile in existence. Beckett's tramps are the last individuals crying out from underneath the electronic world of the masses, desperately imploring Godot's messenger:

> Tell him . . . tell him you saw me and that . . . that you saw me. . . . You're sure you saw me, you won't come and tell me tomorrow that you never saw me.

Beckett was concerned about the lie tying language to reality and, again and again, about the enigma of human beings in a sea of nothingness. He borrowed his favorite motto from Democritus: "Nothing is more real than nothingness."

This was all very close to the heart of John Cage (born 1912). In 1952 he presented a work at Black Mountain College consisting of dance, poetry and prose readings, motion pictures, and recorded music. It was a "happening" in which Cage's genius triumphed. He refused to accept any limits to music because for him there were no limits to sounds and the manner in which they were produced. Neither the traditional means of structuring a composition nor the traditional instruments sufficed.

At Black Mountain College the traditional aspects of performing were gone; the environment—later to become an important feature in performing dances—was a part of Cage's production. His sounds, often at a terrific volume and high pitch, came from different angles and distances. The audience, seated in the center, was bombarded with happenings from all sides. Suddenly a performer would rise among the people to recite; other readings came from ladders on both sides. While films were thrown onto ceiling and walls, Merce Cunningham danced around the outer space.

A companion piece to "newness" became the "bombardment of the senses" through multiple experiences. If John Cage became the father of a new dance movement, of the revolution against classical modern dance, then Marcel Duchamp was its godfather, blessing their rebellion from a past distance:

> It was my intention not to make a painting for *the eyes but* a painting in which the tubes of color were a means and not an end in themselves. . . . There is a difference between a painting which is only directed toward the retina and a painting which goes beyond the retinal impression—a painting which uses the tubes of color as a springboard to go further . . . pure painting doesn't interest me either in itself or as a goal to pursue.

Merce Cunningham translated the movement of the dance into his private, ready-made imagery. The continuity of Cunningham's dances no longer relied on a narrative or psychological motivation. Neither did it need music for support, whereby both arts could function at a common place and

Merce Cunningham's Travelogue *(1977) has Robert Rauschenberg decors and costumes. The dancers manipulate fanlike shapes, and the set has a touch of Orientalism. (Photo by Charles Atlas. Courtesy Merce Cunningham and Dance Company)*

time while independently expressing their own concern with space and time. The clarity of the movements without disguising costumes eliminated any psychologizing; they did not attempt to say something, they simply *were*. They were derived from both modern dance and ballet, but they were discovered through methods of chance‡ or, later, of indeterminacy, with movements changing from one performance to another. Cunningham said in his book *Changes: Notes on Choreography:*

> Movement is an intrinsic part of the "total theater" concept. The logic of one event coming as responsive to another seems inadequate now. We look at and listen to several at once. For dance it was all those words about meaning that got in the way. Right now they are broken up; they do not quite fit, we have to shuffle and deal them out again.

‡ Jean Arp: "From 1915 to 1920 I wrote my *Wolkenpumpe (Cloud Pump)* poems. In these poems I tore apart sentences, words, syllables. I tried to break down the language into atoms, in order to approach the creative. At length I rejected art, because it distracts us from the depths and disturbs the pure dream. . . . Chance opened up perceptions to me, immediate spiritual insights. Intuition led me to revere the laws of chance as the highest and deepest of laws, the law that rises from the fundament. An insignificant word might become a deadly thunderbolt. One little sound might destroy the earth. One little sound might create a new universe."

‡ 412 ‡

If there is a meaningful world without conventional meaning, then Cunningham provokes it. A contemporary of Ionesco, he can be as absurd as in *Antic Meet,* with a dry, wry humor. He can be tender in a detached way in his love lullaby *Night Wandering.* Or his *Summer Space* becomes an abstract painting of moving colors in a late August landscape as seen through half-closed eyes. With the years, Cunningham has proved his many-faceted

Jackson Pollock's "Composition No. 12": with his work exhibited at Peggy Guggenheim's "Art of This Century" gallery in 1943, the rage of abstractionism was unleashed. (Courtesy French Cultural Services)

skill in being different from the expected, in contradicting the established and himself by making an artistic entity of the fragmentary, by creating a heightened awareness with his "mere-movement-collages," or by giving a clear contour to his aesthetics of discontinuity. He can create such a delightful work as *Duets,* making us see the pretentiousness of a pas de deux and adding to the ironic touch a beauty all its own. What still seemed to be a put-on in the 1950s has gradually been put on the dance map as a unique accomplishment.

Robert Rauschenberg was a student at Black Mountain College in North Carolina and soon joined the Cunningham company as stage and costume designer. Rauschenberg—like Jasper Johns—became famous for painting objects and images until then considered unsuitable for painting since they

TENT *is one of Alwin Nikolais' works most expressive of his abstract metaphoric imagery. (Chimera Photo. Courtesy Nikolais Dance Theatre)*

were materials of our too-familiar environment. A link leads from Duchamp to Rauschenberg, who, in his "combine paintings," consciously explores what separates art from life by adding to the paintings modern gadgets like fans, radios, electric light bulbs, and other mechanical or engineering devices. For *Antic Meet* he used chair and umbrella, objects constantly recurring in his art.

Cage, Cunningham, and Rauschenberg were phenomena of the post-existentialist era. They presented life as it was. The no-exit solution in life with its incongruities gave them the freedom to choose without obligation or justification what they were doing. They continued and developed what Cocteau had started in *Parade*. This was the point in the early fifties when art and nonart became interchangeable. After the "bomb" was dropped, the destruction of all form in the arts was the artist's answer to the triumph of technology.

Even before this trio suggested that what we have thought of as civilization is undergoing traumatic changes, abstract expressionism, or "action" painting, created a new tradition by abolishing the old ones, by revolting against all tired shibboleths of the past. In 1943, with Jackson Pollock's work exhibited at Peggy Guggenheim's "Art of This Century" gallery, the rage of abstractionism was unleashed. Pollock was only one of many significant figures of the abstract-surrealist trend in which the American artist—Mark Toby, Willem de Kooning, Hans Hoffmann, Robert Motherwell—became the tastemaker all over the world.

These trends in painting had their counterparts in the variety of electronic music that became firmly established in the 1950s following the development of highly sophisticated electronic instruments and of such studios for electronic music as those in Princeton and Cologne. If the action painter was no longer interested in creating a picture but an event, using the canvas as an area in which to act, then the composer used the music synthesizer to produce tones—of any frequency, duration, timbre, and intensity—the way he desired them by feeding them into the machine through programming input. Also, Alwin Nikolais put together his own sound collages and painted some of his projections for his theater of movement, sound, color, and light. "One of the major characteristics of our current dynamics," he said, "is our capacity to transcend the literal and to replace it with an abstract metaphoric language." Looking back, he reminisced:

> Although I am sure that I used devices of Theater of the Absurd as far back as 1953, I did not do so consciously. Abstract Expressionism, Theater of the Absurd, Dada, Pop and Op art were all tools to my theater—but never consciously. I used them as they served me. I never served them.

Nikolais created movement effects like triumphant flights from reality. On the rainbow of his imagination he takes us into lands of inanimate fairy tales where the atmosphere is permeated with the playful wonders of tomorrow's technology. Waving his choreographic wand with half-closed eyes, but with all windows of his subliminal mind open, he lets things happen. Most often, depersonalized bodies move in harmony with personalized props and costumes. He found his very own nonliteral expression.

Zen had left a strong imprint on Cage and Cunningham, but oriental philosophy also became a way of being and dancing for Erick Hawkins. His work lies outside all confines of theatricality and beyond all traditional concepts of pacing and phrasing. Based on the philosophy of the Tao Te-ching, which says, "By nonaction everything can be done," Hawkins and his company move with utter tranquillity, seeking an expression of purity, the feeling of movement rather than the movement itself. His technique produces a quality of almost meditative effortlessness and poetic sensuousness. Hawkins has made orientalism central to his choreography, thus giving it a ritualistic feeling.

These major trends in the experimental dance pointed the way into the sixties. The Beatniks disgustedly turned their backs on an ever-growing consumer spirit of society and took, like the poet Jack Kerouac, the road of no return:

> "What are you trying to do, Kerouac?" I'd ask myself in my sleepingbag at night, "trying to deny reality with all this Buddha stuff, ya jerk?" . . . "Poor detailed immaculate incarnate fool, and you call yourself Self. . . . Take off your coat and crash wits." And I realized that all this Buddhism was a STRAIN at telling the untellable emptiness yet that nothing was truer, a perfect paradox. . . .

These years leading into the 1960s were a time of spiritual slogans—Pablo Picasso: "Art is a lie that makes us realize truth"; Jean Paul Sartre: "Hell is other people"; Ezra Pound: "Make it new." W. H. Auden, who thought that "Aloneness is man's real condition," called this period "the Age of Anxiety" in 1946. Four years later, Jerome Robbins choreographed a dramatic ballet based on Auden's poem and Leonard Bernstein's Second Symphony, bearing the title of *Age of Anxiety*. Robbins depicted four people trying to find themselves. He pointed out that his ballet is different from both the poem and the score: "It is a ritual in which four people exercise their illu-

Erick Hawkins in "Discovery of the Minotaur" from OPENINGS OF THE (EYE): *Hawkins has always been interested in probing the prime sources of myth as much as in the wonders of Eastern thought. Whatever he dances becomes a revealing of the hidden forces in the human being. Designs by Ralph Dorazio. (Photo A. John Geraci. Courtesy Erick Hawkins)*

sions in their search for security. It is an attempt to see what life is about." It seems that people took their age of anxiety seriously. For many, however, it had started much earlier than 1946 and for some it has not yet ceased to be.

The Roaring Twenties in Their Sixties

THE SIXTIES BEGAN TO LOOK THEIR AGE, THE AGE OF ANXIETY EDGING EVER closer to explosion. It acted in excesses on all levels of existence. If art, as Malraux once said, "expresses a defense against fatality," then the artist's defense mechanism worked overtime. Everything that was touched upon in the twenties was blown up to grotesque, militant, anticlimactic forms, to the bathos of nonsense, to the travesty of existence. The Dadaists once called for a *tabula rasa;* the neo-Dadaists in the sixties went to the point of no return.

When in 1919 Duchamp—with his most famous antiart gesture—wanted to ridicule the enigmatic smile of the Mona Lisa with a moustache and beard, he aimed at destroying the prestige of the past through caricature. It was an act of defilement of a public idol. Duchamp maintained he intended to call attention with it to Leonardo's dualism—his homosexuality. Perhaps there was some purpose behind it. But in the 1960s Rauschenberg presented a painting he called, "A de Kooning erased by Rauschenberg." Was it a boyish prank to call attention to destruction and violence? It was certainly a sophisticated graffito, and soon graffiti were elevated to "art" in the sixties.

It was all there again, the Dadaists' dream: the non sequitur, the irrational focus, fragmentation instead of any concept of composition. When in the sixties James Waring was asked what motivated him to create, he replied that the dances in those days had no philosophy, no point of view behind them. It all looked like an extension of what the twenties had dared as the ultimate bluff against art and its superstructure.

In 1964—at the beginning of the Vietnam War—Cunningham choreographed his *Winterbranch,* full of frightening and oppressing images, to high-pitched sounds produced by Cage. Was there no point of view behind it? he was asked in an interview, and he replied:

> *Winterbranch:* a) bombed cities—New York; b) concentration camps—Germany; c) nuclear war—Japan; d) shipwreck (my favorite. From a sea-captain's wife). Right you are if you think you are. I prefer directness, but that's not always possible in a society so indirect. The facts I dealt with were: people falling; light at night in our time as it strikes objects; and the formal shape of entering

(walking into) an arena, a space; beginning and completing a figure, done by one or more persons; and walking out of the arena.

The lights of which he spoke were turned against the audience, blinding them, similar in effect to Francis Picabia's ballet *Relâche,* which he conceived in 1924. He interpreted it by saying that it was everything you could see in it or think of:

> . . . perpetual motion, life, love free from the conventions of shame . . . without a moral for the stupid. . . .

When Picabia's second curtain was raised, bearing insulting texts, the audience was blinded by 370 spotlights. The blinding light was punctuated by Erik Satie's music. Perhaps there was something new to the lights the way Cunningham employed them.

The artists of the sixties denied art as a conceptual notion. To this very day some artists, echoing the daring of those times, still claim that they do not recognize art as "art." It all goes back to Rauschenberg's Dada-inspired remark that he functions "in that gap between" art and life. Cage made us believe that his music is purposeless play, and James Waring declared: "Dance is any aimless movement—any movement without an object in mind. Art is anything you point your finger at and say, 'This is Art.'" Andy Warhol, who skillfully popped art into our faces with Campbell soup cans to lampoon our consumer society, topped Waring by running an ad saying, "You can bring me any old or new material in your possession, and when I sign it, it will be art."

Any action or performance blurred the borderline between art and life. Cunningham, in one of his collages, rode a bicycle around the stage, appeared with a chair tied to his back, even had dancers perform gestures of daily life like combing their hair, washing their hands, filing their nails. In her earlier years, Meredith Monk brought an older lady onstage, saying, "This is my mother," who smiled and then exited. When fully dressed, Monk stepped into a basin of water and then, dripping wet, left it shortly afterward. Here life became the artistic act of the neo-Dadaists who, like Ann Halprin, felt that "the process is the purpose . . . and what happens generates its own purpose." The artist abdicated by no longer pretending that the essence of creation lies in the final product, but rather in the moment of doing it. The spectator was reduced to the status of a voyeur permitted to watch as if through a keyhole.

IN the mid-1960s many changes took place on all levels of life. These were fundamental changes under the smoke screen of great affluence. The Vietnam War damaged the prestige of America. The disenchantment with and fear of the nuclear world widened the escape routes into drugged illusions. Other addictions were those of meditation as prescribed by Tibetan and Indian gurus. Simultaneously, they were years rich in money and little gestures, more flamboyant than innovating. In spite of and possibly because of all the riches accumulated by middle-class society, anxieties and anger, disillusion and lost hopes erupted in riots of fury.

It also happened with blacks in the United States. Their artistically vital potential had been bypassed for too long. It was not before mid-century that blacks could assert themselves as mature artists, and it was not before the 1960s that their militant stance for recognition on an equal level with whites established their viable contribution to theater dance.

During the many decades of suppression, blacks held on to their spirituals and improvised dances with tapping feet. These improvisations were a link between the music of the slaves and jazz. The blues song lamenting their suppression came into being when blacks began to compose by mixing the African with acquired American musical styles. Syncopation, the spirit of jazz, a basically African idiom, broadened scope and dynamics of dance in our time. But black performers remained identified with "minstrel shows" and nightclub revues for almost a century. The names of Josephine Baker and Bill Robinson became symbols of the black entertainer.

In the 1940s, the image of black performers began to change. With the rise of the modern dance, they found an artistic means for free expression without betraying their ethnic past. The earliest contributions came with Katherine Dunham's theatricalizations and Pearl Primus's dramatic visualizations of spirituals. A host of dancer-choreographers followed whose kinesthetic intensity is of astonishing power. From Donald McKayle to Alvin Ailey, they have poetically dramatized the plight of black people, having added a flavor to the American dance theater without which it would be the poorer. The Dance Theatre of Harlem, the first all-black ballet company, led by Arthur Mitchell, is one of our nation's most accomplished classical groups. Blacks may not yet have achieved all their desired goals on a social level, but they certainly secured for themselves an adequate place on the dance stage.

Other social eruptions during the 1960s have not fared that well. Those who believe in cyclic recurrences may have expected a third world war toward the end of the 1960s, but with the superpowers holding the trump card of mutual annihilation in their hands, the mass slaughter was postponed, with no date set. Instead the battlefield shifted to the universities, and a restless middle-class youth rebelled against their affluent fate and its hollow

Judith Jamison in Alvin Ailey's THE MOOCHE, *which shows this powerful dancer as the extraordinary actress she is. Jamison, internationally known, is one of many black performers unique in their individual talent as dancers. Miss Jamison is a stellar performer with the Alvin Ailey Dance Theater. (Photo by Costas. Courtesy the Photographer)*

grimace. Since the working class looked at these desperate young people with disdain, their revolution of 1968 broke down. They were thrown back into disillusionment; some joined the establishment, others wasted away in the drug scene.

While history was taking this sidestep, New York reached its position as the world center of visual arts and dance. All these years the cornucopia remained tilted, an abundance of foundation grants and collectors' fortunes overflooding the artistic fields. Dance companies and individual dancers began to profit as never before. Curators and dealers were following the ratings established by leading critics, who became professional starmakers. One could hear the big splash in the art business in all capitals of the world. Artists were made. But was it art *they* made?

The visual artists had a strong impact on the modern dance, often referred to as New Dance or Performance Art. The avant-garde dancers, mainly those close to the Judson Dance Theater, took their cues from the minimal, environmental, conceptual, and Pop forms, with movements reduced to a minimum, eyeing the theatrical without its dramatic structure and using everyday movements. Some fled into multimedia. It was all indicative of the close dancer/painter relationship that such artists as Rauschenberg, Morris, and Robert Whitman participated in dance events and even tested themselves as choreographers. (Cocteau had preceded them in such adventures.) The musical influence still came from John Cage and especially Robert Dunn, who worked with Cage ideas, with methods of chance, indeterminacy, and time durations.

Anna Kisselgoff suggested in a New York *Times* article:

> The close relationship between the music/art avant-garde and the 1960s dance experiments has never been overlooked. But it has not been turned around to suggest that once the original inspiration from music and art faded, the impetus for fundamental alterations of our notion of dance faded too. In other words, is it possible that dancers in the 1960s were really innovative with forms not intrinsic to their own medium? Transposing ideas that were applied to music and the visual arts is not the same as changing dance itself through dance.

This is one of the reasons for the lull in dance experiments in the 1970s. Cunningham could oppose the psychological trend of modern dance. The members of the Judson Dance Theater could not rebel against Cunningham, they could only take the path suggested and try a few detours. The fundamental challenge was gone. All that was left of challenge was the one to their own self. They were not concerned with the process of creation or with an artistic statement. There was no attempt at characterization. They presented themselves in their mental and physical nakedness without pretending to create any mood. They might play games, call numbers, play love, but everything was done in a most casual manner as when one scratches an itch or says hello. Movements were repeated ad nauseam to equate boredom with existence. It was called new dance or new theater because it was neither.

The notion of experiment was stretched to the point of indeterminate irrelevancy. In "celebrating unfixity," to speak with John Cage, and in letting life "act of its own accord," the dancers had to take their "actions" out of the theater and studios, gyms and lofts, and they moved—in imitation of environmental art—into railway stations, gardens, and museums. There they were doing their thing, which was a form of heightened nonart. Some of it showed that too much of the waste products of our civilization has become subject matter in the arts.

This extreme wing of the modern dance has been an in group with its own audience and home in Manhattan. There are also some small experimental groups in various European countries, but the only one whose dance essays merit attention is that of American-trained Pina Bausch in Wuppertal, Germany. For despite their way-out material and their defiant and often militant attitude toward established norms and accepted rules, these works present ideas in some structured form.

In the destructive course of our society, the artist's fear often escapes into fury which in turn may lead to mental self-flagellation. It also shows how far the modern, expressive dancer can go in demonstrating his self and remonstrating for topical issues. In the corset of formal technique, ballet prevents the dancer from pirouetting into belligerent outcries against the injustices of life and pretenses of society. It is as if the etiquette of formal speech must leave it to the vernacular idiom to talk of things that matter. We may criticize the modern dancer for not doing it, or for not doing it the way we see it. But we must defend his freedom to misuse it as an artist if he wishes to deny the world and himself.

Many of the excesses in the theater during the 1960s can be traced back to Antonin Artaud, whose revolutionary ideas about the theater were inspired by seeing Balinese dancers. This iconoclast was rejecting the narrative style, or any social message, in a play in the 1930s. He wanted to go back to myth and magic, expressing through movement and gestures what is inexpressible through words in order to expose the deepest layers of human feelings. He envisioned a mass communal rite, a theater that would inundate the audience, attack the spectators' sensibility on all sides. With movement considering a primary force, Artaud exerted his greatest influence on the many experimental theater and dance workshops in the 1960s. He was responsible for the vogue of audience participation, which intended to take the concept of the theater back to where it started.

Most characteristic of the decade was the Living Theater, which took

many cues from Artaud. It began in a loft in Manhattan and rose to international notoriety. It was a radical theater of improvisation, whose prime aim was to change the world, or at least capitalist society. Physical movement as expressive of an idea was emphasized in all its productions. For many years in the 1960s, the Living Theater—radicalizing Erwin Piscator's political-theater concept of the late 1920s—was best known for its show *Paradise Now*. It became the rage with the hippies and could be best characterized as a theater group fighting with violence for nonviolence. It was most indicative of the new generation in revolt. With Artaud and Piscator in mind, it wanted to purge civilization of its evils, accusing and shocking a society whose pillars constitute producing, selling, and buying. They considered nudity one of their strongest weapons for shock effect.

NUDITY is not a new phenomenon. For the ancient Greeks, nudity never was a matter of much consideration. Restoration comedy is another case in point. There was a swing from the extreme of Puritanism to an extreme of bawdiness. Love was crudely converted into sex and the sharpest wit was directed below the belt. At the end of the Victorian Age, some writers again fought against hypocrisy and the double standard applied to sex, among them and above all Frank Wedekind, Arthur Schnitzler, and, later, D. H. Lawrence.

It was left to our century to use nudity as a means of social protest. Wars with their physical and moral devastations bring about a breakdown of all ethical—but also aesthetical—codes and values. Revolutions and their insecurities have always caused a misunderstanding of the limits and meaning of personal freedom. In times of hardship, people throw themselves indiscriminately into pleasure; the difference between an orgasmic wilderness and the freedom of taking delight in oneself as the being one is seems quickly wiped out.

A mingling of the first major attack of anxiety with a newly experienced sensation of freedom led to a general trend toward nudity in the 1920s. Sometimes it can be a romantic gesture to show oneself in one's native beauty with emphasis on the body's movement, as Doris Humphrey's picture proves. In 1929, in her revolutionary spirit, Helen Tamiris strongly believed in dance as the purest art form and experimented with the aesthetically valid notion that the dancer's body should communicate without the aid of costumes. Isadora Duncan impressed and shocked her audiences with the simplicity of her tunic, which reflected her spirit of freedom. In the Germany of the twenties, where moral and monetary inflation was high, nudity

Doris Humphrey in a movement study, 1926, Denishawn Company. (Photo by Muray. Courtesy Charles H. Woodford)

was en vogue on- and offstage. The best example was a minor dancer, Anita Berber, who was in the habit of attending theater performances in a fur coat covering her skin.

The undeniable physicality of the dance may carry with it an erotic potentiality. Even though the flesh is accidental, our sensuous experience may coincide with our sensual instincts. Everyone has his own ways of sublimating primary impulses. We cannot deny the devil his due. Everything in life, from architecture to the smallest utilitarian object, carries sexual connotations.

George Balanchine knows why he prefers the dancers without costume because, in leotards, the dancer comes closest to being nude, presenting the most natural and ideal shape for our experience of utter union with the object. No doubt Romanticism and the introduction of the tutu and toe shoe stressed the legs and the dream caught in the flesh. And modern dance has never shunned dealing with the most emotional human experiences in physical terms.

A certain fascination with nudity in the twenties reappeared in the sixties as the very disease it wanted to fight. It broke all records with its bluntness in the film industry to the point of nausea. It became an habitual sight onstage in plays and modern dance works. It was the decade in which the pill and promiscuity began to "facilitate" life, with the arts aping life and adding titillating incentives. We may see in it a breakthrough to new frontiers of living, or regret that our behavior degraded sex to an activity as mechanized as the button-pushing conveniences in life.

Kenneth Tynan's dramatic venture in nudity, *Oh! Calcutta!,* tested the outposts of our voyeuristic mind; yet the pas de deux of the dancing couple in the nude turned surprisingly into a great aesthetic experience. You can rage with nakedness against "the disguised sexual exhibition of most dancing," as Yvonne Rainer said and did. Tynan, however, succeeded in proving that danced nudity can be an artistic statement, reminding us of the ideal costume baring the classic line of the dancing body.

A similar case in point is Ann Halprin's *Parades and Changes,* in which the dancers undressed onstage, putting their clothes on again only to take them off. So far the act of disrobing would have had little meaning, but then masses of paper were brought onstage, and the stark-naked dancers started romping in the paper. Beautiful shapes of moving bodies and paper emerged as if from nowhere, growing into sculptural forms, flesh-colored and paper-hued, ever changing into a variety of fascinating shapes. There were no longer naked bodies, but nude images in joyful unconcern about their bare skin, wading through the mounds of paper, conveying a feeling of innocent ecstasy.

There is a legitimate place for nudity in all art forms. Nudity onstage must serve a choreographic purpose, for it is monotonous and boring if not

Yvonne Rainer was one of the important avant-garde dancers of the 1960s. This picture shows her jumping mattresses, one of her many casual pieces. (Photo by Al Giese. Courtesy the Photographer)

Paul Taylor, who started to dance with Martha Graham, has for quite some time established himself as one of the most inventive and witty choreographers, who, over the years, has created an impressive repertory for his company and has become famous for the fluency of his ingenious imagery. This picture shows his Polaris. *(Photo by Costas. Courtesy the Photographer)*

justified by any dramatic urgency. It must be there to enhance our feeling of being human, to heighten our awareness of our inner strength and outer beauty, or, in other words, to create a feeling of humility as much as pride in the humanity which we all share.

Many infuriating and fulminating artistic gestures in the arts dazzled our eyes during the 1960s. Although they were, no doubt, most characteristic of the decade, we must not lose sight of the mainstream of the art that continued to function in a "business as usual" manner. The Western world, in its euphoric state of affluence, supported an apparently ceaseless flow of ballets and modern dance works, mainly originating in New York City with its leading ballet companies, while a number of choreographers belonging to the heirs of the classic modern dance defended the accomplishments of the past.

It was as though the immense impetus issuing from New York was relayed to other art centers and capitals in the West, where the feverish excitement over all forms of the dance began to show a flowering abundance. Even Germany, a latecomer to ballet, was among those which profited from this increased interest in dance: John Cranko stepped out of Noverre's historic shadow in Stuttgart and John Neumeier gave Hamburg a new balletic profile. Masses of young people were attracted by Maurice Béjart's group, with its headquarters in Brussels. His fascination did not emanate from his

Wisconsin-born John Neumeier—who has for several years been director of the Hamburg State Opera Ballet—has triumphed in Europe by giving classic and semiclassic ballets a new look. He is one of many American dancer-choreographers to have found a new field of activity in the Old World. The picture shows his Gustav Mahler's THIRD SYMPHONY. *(Photo by Gert von Bassewitz. Courtesy Hamburgische Staatsoper)*

choreographic skill, but from an overextended theatricality, from the different and unexpected, from such large themes as Faust, Nijinsky, and God, mingling with the magic of meditation and Indian incense. It was the accentuated formula for a desperately needed escape from reality for which the young yearned in the 1960s.

Postscript

HISTORY HAS A WAY OF WRITING ITS OWN POSTSCRIPTS. THE ONE IN THE 1970s could be as brief as "Nothing new on the artistic front." A lull set in, but it was a lull of some significance. It was as if time wished to stop and ask progress for time to reconsider. The prevalent mood indicated caution or insecurity about the road leading into the future. Perhaps it was only a feeling of exhaustion after having gone the way of all "isms" for so many decades and the need for consolidating one's forces in the hope of strengthening the rear guard, in order to advance as soon as the new and unexpected should emerge.

More books were written in the last decade than ever before and were published in the name of a consumer spirit that invested high sums in best sellers while the cemeteries of the remainder houses bought up more plots. The visual arts still followed the slogans of the past, with figure painting hesitantly showing its head according to the new mood of a tentative neoromanticism. Film broadened its mass appeal. No new opera was heard of, composers did not have the necessary breath for a symphony, while the recording industry flourished. In the great lull of this decade, mass culture entrenched itself and decided the criteria of success.

The expansion of dancing to a final scope of undreamed-of proportion may have taken the inherently creative forces by surprise. Either they were paralyzed or they tried the quick road to success. The expansion was horizontally, not vertically, oriented; the haste of the time did not permit ideas to ripen and take root. Suddenly there were so many dancers—and rather good ones—who stepped on each other's mental toes. They were vociferous, but not articulate. There was no real urge to create, only to act, to use opportunities and facilities. The ballet had its regional branches spread out

The work of Maurice Béjart, the guiding spirit of the Ballet of the 20th Century, is greatly appreciated in Europe. He is a facile choreographer of crowd scenes and displays a particular sense of the theatricality of movement. This photo shows Jorge Donn and Shonach Mirk in CE QUE L'AMOUR ME DIT. *(Photo by Beverley Gallegos. Courtesy the Photographer)*

over the whole country, living in a euphoric state with its delusive jetés of grandeur.

We produced so much talent that our cups were full and spilled over. America exported its dancing talent to Europe. Dancing became a world-wide enjoyable affliction, with American dancing applauded and cheered ev-erywhere. About half of each continental company is American-born or American-dance-bred. Finally, American dancing found itself famous for being famous, the reason being that no other dancers—perhaps the Russians excluded—are technically so well equipped as the Americans. And in their perfect technique they have remained freer in development than the Rus-sians. There is no lack of basic talent. All the more surprising must be the small radius of creativity in the 1970s.

The modern dance played its historic role to perfection, but also to the point of self-exhaustion. Isadora Duncan inspired Fokine and Nijinsky to new ways of balletic expression. The impact of the classical modern dance led the ballet to a total reorientation; in fact, it gave ballet its twentieth-cen-tury face—psychological awareness, heightened expressiveness, a wider range in its subject matter, and a loosening of its strict technique. In this sense we must understand George Balanchine's answer to the question of what he, Pe-tipa's heir, thought of the modern dance: "I see no difference between ballet and modern. I only know good or bad dancing."

Of course, there was quite a difference. The modern dancer's raison d'être was total freedom of self-expression. There was something urgent and vital in what the dancer had to say. There was incontestable weight in the intel-

Left: Asian-born dancers have frequently been members of American modern dance groups since World War II, and American modern dance has taken root in Asian cities, mainly in Japan. Kei Takei was trained in Japan and since 1967 has headed her American dance company. Her choreographic no-tions combine Eastern philosophy with Western expressionism, rhythmic rit-ual with highly charged action. Her work is exemplary for the artistic ac-complishments due to a fusion of East and West. This photograph by Hiiki shows Kei Takei and Carmen Beuchat in LUNCH. *(Courtesy Kei Takei)*

Far left, top: Nancy Meehan in PTARMIGAN WALL: *her movements are generated by nature images, which correspond to states of mind and being. In her works she tries to enter new areas of content, form, and structure. (Photo by Johan Elbers. Courtesy Nancy Meehan)*

Far left, bottom: This is one of many attempts at multimedia in the dance field. In this work, in which dance is juxtaposed to film, Frances Alenikoff choreographed for one dancer (herself), using slides, tape collages, music, and the spoken word. (Photo by Edward Effron. Courtesy Frances Aleni-koff)

lectual power of what he or she wished to express. In the great exchange between ballet and the modern dance, something curious happened. The classic school of dancing gained by having been influenced by the modern dancer into reshaping its aesthetic values. Most modern dancers have accepted ballet training, and by becoming richer and more accomplished dancers they are ending up poorer, losing their basic motivations and intellectual bite, thus paring down the profile of the expressive dance. Kurt Jooss's dream—which he voiced in the late 1920s—about the merging of the two came true. But the 1970s proved that one of them may be the loser. It seems to be the one Jooss would not have liked to see hurt. Even though the classic dance profited from this exchange, it has not yet produced any new outstanding choreographers. If there was any logic to historic developments, ballet would have to strike the next rejuvenating chords.

The modern dance has remained strong over so many decades because its renewal has always come out of the midst of what was accomplished. The pioneers of the classical modern dance emerged from Denishawn as Cunningham came from Martha Graham. He continued what Cocteau and *Parade* began. Because he is a great artist and the mood of the 1950s was with him, Cunningham succeeded. Those who followed him did not rebel against him. They took him by his word, not by his creative gesture, and went all the way into an artistic dead-end street, shouting their belligerent "noes" at all past cultural achievements until their echoes faded, along with their efforts, into NOwhere. Self-destructive despair hovered over the sixties with their blown-up riches. The emptiness of the seventies made this clear.

We have learned to look back with nostalgic eyes to the 1930s. And so did Twyla Tharp, the one new name catapulted into the limelight of the seventies. There was a huge vacuum into which she stepped, impressing all with the unconventional looking improvised, believing in movement for its own sake, giving it an atmosphere of cool intricacy. What is remarkable about her style—and symptomatic for much of the dancing during the last decade —is the glamour of superficiality and of a vitality going nowhere. It seems as if she were the living proof for the deadness of this past era.

Of course, there are at least as many choreographers in the United States and in Europe as there are companies. In fact, their number is stupendous. Some of them are, no doubt, talented. There is also no dearth of writers, composers, and painters. On the contrary. But at this point in history, we finally seem to encounter the complexities of our technical and technological ingenuity, which is as overwhelming as the hunger of the masses for a certain level of entertainment. We are facing the temptation of having everything facile in life. We feel compelled to struggle with so many things lying outside of ourselves that we do not find the time and need to struggle with ourselves. Creativity has always been based on an inner struggle, on trial and error. Also, creativity can only properly unfold when nourished by a

SUE'S LEG *was Twyla Tharp's first most incisive statement of her choreo-graphic concept (1975). Ever since, she has known how to cast a spell on her audiences with her seemingly improvised and yet tightly structured works, which appear either as variations on a theme or as the daring search for the new. (Photo by Herbert Migdoll. Courtesy the Photographer)*

background of knowing and of the fertile sources of past experiences. The haste of our computerized age has made us lose the sense of past and continuity, the feeling for who we really are.

ALL artistic expressions should be characterized as human products of the *joy of being,* even if the means employed and the target chosen are novel and different from the established norms. Sophocles, standing at the majestic graves of the past, shouted at the memory of Egyptian priest-kings: "When men have slain joy, I do not think they are alive!" Every masterpiece, as Malraux thought, "implicitly or openly, tells of a human victory over the blind face of destiny." But the fact that the change in quality of the world in our century was more drastic than ever before also changed our being. Dostoevski was certain that men and women cannot be without art. Is it still human dreams translated into art that makes life worth living? If we can believe Buckminster Fuller's vision, the artist of the future will be a scientifically molded, complex, artistic creature:

> Only the free-wheeling artist-explorer, non-academic, scientist-philosopher, mechanic, economy-poet . . . holds the prime initiative today. If man is to continue as a successful pattern-complex function in universal evolution, it will be because the next decades will have witnessed the artist-scientist's spontaneous seizure of the prime design responsibility and his successful conversion of the total capability of tool-augmented man from killingry to advanced livingry—adequate for all humanity.

Probably any age through which human beings have lived must sometimes have appeared puzzling, questionable, or disturbing; but hardly any time so far has had so many odds against it and so much greatness going for it as the one we are now experiencing. This may easily be one of the most decisive periods of transition.

At the very end, we must ask again what explains the importance of the dance at this point in history. Is it the eternal liberation of our self that dancing may suggest? Do we unknowingly remember it as the primary source for self-recognition and self-revelation, exploring the intuitive truth of being, our "mythic consciousness," as Suzanne Langer referred to it? In former times we could omit the prose of nature in our creative efforts and concentrate on its spirit and splendor. But, tomorrow, with science totally dominating nature, our way of thinking will be forced into other grooves of routine. Do we then, with this unexpected upsurge of dancing in our time, anticipate the nihilistic trend of technology and try to protest against this mechanization of our existence? Or is this phenomenon merely the concomitant of our visual-mindedness and motion madness? It is probably all this and the erosion of human inwardness which makes us hold on to this extroverted art with its built-in physical excitement of motion and speed.

‡ DANCE IN ITS TIME ‡

The artists of the 1970s were holding their breath, as if exhausted from these long Ages of Anxiety, watching the human drama being enacted on all continents, waiting for history to make the next moves in a power game that, time and again, has had the look of finality. Piet Mondrian (1872–1944) wrote in a letter to James Johnson Sweeney: "I think the destructive element is too much neglected in art." Looking back, I think the destructive element in the arts kept faithful step with the destructive trends in nature and human life, as if preparing for a new holocaust.

Yet if tomorrow the world were no longer to be, and we had a last chance to see what the creative genius and ingenuity, the faith and daring of mankind at all times and places over the last five thousand years have achieved, we would have to admit that it was a worthwhile experiment of the Creator to have us thrown out of Paradise. True, we may never regain it. Too much wrong and evil have been done. We built and destroyed what we did in order to rebuild it. But when it is all added up, the miracle of humankind—created in the image of God—has been honored by humanity with its own acts of creative magic.

BIBLIOGRAPHY OF SOURCE MATERIAL

Alighieri, Dante. *La Divina Commedia.* Translated by J. A. Carlyle, Thomas Okey, and P. H. Wickstead. New York: Dutton, 1933.

Andersen, Hans Christian. *The Complete Andersen.* Translated by Jean Hersholt. New York: Limited Editions Club/Heritage Press, 1949.

Angiolini, Gasparo. *Lettere di Gasparo Angiolini a Monsieur Noverre sopra i balli pantomimi.* Milan: G. B. Bianchi, 1773.

Arbeau, Thoinot. *See* Tabourot, Jehan.

Arp, Jean (Hans). *Arp on Arp.* Edited by Marcel Jean. Translated by Joachim Neugröschel. New York: Viking Press, 1969.

———. *On My Way: Poetry and Essays 1912–1947.* New York: Wittenborn, Schultz, 1948.

Artaud, Antonin. *The Theatre and Its Double.* Translated by Mary Caroline Richards. New York: Grove Press, 1958.

Balanchine, George. *Balanchine's Complete Stories of the Great Ballets.* Edited by Francis Mason. Garden City, N.Y.: Doubleday & Company, 1954, 1968, 1977.

Ball, Hugo. *Die Flucht aus der Zeit.* Munich and Leipzig: Duncker & Humblot, 1927.

Barrett, William. *The Illusion of Technique.* A Search for Meaning in a Technological Civilization. Garden City, N.Y.: Anchor Press/Doubleday, 1978.

———. *Irrational Man: Existentialism and the Crisis of Our Time.* Garden City, N.Y.: Anchor Press/Doubleday, 1958.

Baudelaire, Charles Pierre. *The Mirror of Art: Critical Studies.* Translated and edited by Jonathan Mayne. New York: Phaidon Publishing, 1955.

Beckett, Samuel. *Waiting for Godot.* New York: Grove Press, 1954.

Berenson, Bernhard. *Italian Painters of the Renaissance.* rev. ed. New York: Oxford University Press, 1930.

Bishop, Morris. Letters of Petrarch. *Horizon,* Vol. IX, No. 1, Winter 1967.

Blake, William. *Complete Writings.* Edited by Geoffrey Keynes. New York: Random House, 1957.

Boccaccio, Giovanni. *Decameron.* Florence: Per il Magheri, 1827–34.

‡ BIBLIOGRAPHY ‡

Borgese, Leonardo. *Daumier.* Translated by Cesare Foligno. Novara. Uffici Press, 1954.

Brecht, Bertolt. *Brecht on Theatre: The Development of an Aesthetic.* Edited and translated by John Willett. London: Methuen; New York: Hill and Wang, 1964.

Breicha, Otto, and Fritsch, Gerhard, eds. *Finale und Auftakt Wien 1898–1914.* Salzburg: Otto Müller Verlag, 1964.

Buchheim, Lothar Günther. *Die Künstlergemeinschaft die Brücke.* Buchheim Verlag Feldafing, 1956.

Burckhardt, Jacob. *The Civilization of the Renaissance in Italy.* Translated by S. G. C. Middlemore. New York: A. and C. Boni, 1935.

Cage, John. *Silence: Lectures and Writings.* Middletown, Conn.: Wesleyan University Press, 1961.

Casanova de Seingalt, Giacomo Girolamo. *History of My Life.* Translated by Willard R. Trask. New York: Harcourt, Brace & World, 1966.

Cellini, Benvenuto. *Memoirs of Benvenuto Cellini.* Translated by Anne Macdonell. New York: E. P. Dutton & Co.; London: J. M. Dent & Sons, 1952.

Chaffee, George. The Romantic Ballet in London: 1821–1858. *Dance Index,* Vol. II, Nos. 9–12, 1943.

Chujoy, Anatole, and Manchester, P. W. *Dance Encyclopedia.* rev. ed.: New York: Simon & Schuster, 1967.

———. Russian Balletomania. *Dance Index,* Vol. I, No. 4, 1948.

Clark, Kenneth. *Civilisation: A Personal View.* New York: Harper & Row, 1969.

Cocteau, Jean. *The Journals of Jean Cocteau.* Translated by Wallace Fowlie. New York: Criterion Books, 1958; London: Museum Press, 1957.

Craig, Edward Gordon. *The Art of the Theatre.* Introduction by Edward Gordon Craig and preface by R. Graham Robertson. Edinburgh and London: T. N. Goulid, 1905.

Cunningham, Merce. *Changes: Notes on Choreography.* New York: Something Else Press, 1968.

———. An Interview with Merce Cunningham. *Ballet Review.* Vol. I, No. 4, 1966.

Delacroix, Eugène. *The Journal of Eugène Delacroix.* Translated by Lucy Norton. London: Phaidon Press, 1951.

Dormer, Lore Muerdel. Berührung der Sphären. *Neue Zürcher Zeitung.* April 15–16, 1978.

Duchartre, Pierre Louis. *Italian Comedy.* Translated by Randolph T. Weaver. New York: John Day; London: Harrap, 1929.

Duncan, Isadora. *Art of the Dance*. New York: Theatre Arts, 1928.

Durant, Will. *The Story of Civilization. Vol. II: The Life of Greece*. New York: Simon & Schuster, 1939.

Dürer, Albrecht. *Dürer: Schriftlicher Nachlass*. Herausgegeben von Hans Rupprich. Berlin: Deutscher Verein für Kunstwissenschaft, 1956.

Ellis, Havelock. *Dance of Life*. Boston: Houghton Mifflin, 1923.

Erdman, David V. *Blake: Prophet Against Empire*. Princeton: Princeton University Press, 1954.

Esslin, Martin. *The Theatre of the Absurd*. rev. ed. Garden City, N.Y.: Anchor Press/Doubleday, 1969.

Evans, Herbert Arthur. *Introduction to English Masques*. London: Blackie & Son, Ltd. n.d.

Ferguson, Wallace K. *The Renaissance in Historical Thought: Five Centuries of Interpretation*. Boston: Houghton Mifflin, 1948.

Fletcher, Ifan Kyrle; Cohen, Selma Jeanne; and Lonsdale, Roger. *Famed for Dance: Essays on the Theory and Practice of Theatrical Dancing in England, 1660–1740*. New York: New York Public Library, 1960.

Fokine, Michel. *Fokine: Memoirs of a Ballet Master*. Translated by Vitale Fokine. Boston: Little, Brown, 1961.

Frazer, Sir James. *The Golden Bough*. New York: Macmillan, 1947.

Friedell, Egon. *Kulturgeschichte der Neuzeit*. 3 vols. Munich: C. H. Beck'sche Verlagsbuchhandlung, 1930.

Fuller, Buckminster. *Ideas and Integrities: A Spontaneous Autobiographical Disclosure*. Edited by Robert W. Marks. Englewood Cliffs, N.J.: Prentice-Hall, 1963.

Fuller, Loie. *Fifteen Years of My Life*. Boston: Small, 1913.

Fülöp-Miller, René, and Gregor, Josef. *The Russian Theatre*. Philadelphia: Lippincott, 1930.

Gassner, John. *Masters of the Drama*. New York: Random House, 1954.

Gauguin, Paul. *Noa Noa*. New York: Noonday Press, 1957; Oxford: Bruno Cassirer, 1961.

Gautier, Théophile. *The Complete Works*. Translated by C. de Sumichrast. London: Atheneum Press, 1900.

Goethe, Johann Wolfgang von. *Samtliche Werke*. Berlin: In Verlag Ullstein, n.d.

Goldoni, Carlo. *Memoirs of Carlo Goldoni: Written by Himself*. Translated by John Black. Edited by William A. Drake. New York: Alfred A. Knopf, 1926.

Gombrich, E. H. *The Story of Art*. New York: Phaidon Publishers, 1951.

Goncourt, Edmond and Jules de. *Journals*. Edited and translated by Lewis Galantière. Garden City, N.Y.: Doubleday, 1937.

Gorelik, Mordecai. *New Theatres for Old*. New York: Samuel French, 1940.

Gregor, Josef. *Weltgeschichte des Theaters*. Zurich: Phaidon Verlag, 1933.

Grimm, Baron Friedrich Melchior von. *Correspondance littéraire*. Paris: Garnier, 1871–82.

Grohmann, Will. *Wassily Kandinsky: Life and Work*. Translated by Norbert Guterman. New York: Harry N. Abrams; London: Thames and Hudson, 1958.

Gropius, Walter, ed. *The Theater of the Bauhaus*. Translated by Arthur S. Wensinger. Contributors: Oskar Schlemmer, László Moholy-Nagy, Farkas Molnár. Middletown, Conn.: Wesleyan University Press, 1961.

Grosz, George. *A Little Yes and a Big No*. Translated by Lola Sachs Dorin. New York: Dial Press, 1946.

Haskell, Arnold. *Diaghileff*. London: Victor Gollancz, 1935.

Hauser, Arnold. *The Social History of Art*. Translated by Author and Stanley Godman. 2 vols. New York: Alfred A. Knopf, 1951.

Haydn, Hiram. *The Counter-Renaissance*. New York: Scribner, 1950.

Heine, Heinrich. *Sämtliche Werke*. Hamburg: Hoffmann und Campe, 1873.

Heller, Erich. *The Disinherited Mind*. New York: Farrar, Straus, 1957.

Hemleben, Johannes. Rudolf Steiner. In *Selbstzeugnissen und Bilderdokumenten*. Frankfurt: Rowohlt, 1963.

Herder, Johann Gottfried von. *Outlines of a Philosophy of the History of Man*. Translated by T. Churchill. London: Luke Hansard, 1803.

Herford, C. H.; Simpson, P.; and Simpson, E., eds. *Ben Jonson: Works*. Vol. VII (Masques). Oxford: Clarendon Press, 1941.

Hoffmann, E. T. A. *Gesammelte Schriften*. Berlin: G. Reimer, 1844.

Hofmannsthal, Hugo von. *Die prosaischen Schriften*. Berlin: S. Fischer, 1920.

———. *Her Extraordinary Immediacy*. Translated by David Berger. In *Die Zeit,* 1906.

Hogarth, William. *The Analysis of Beauty*. Edited by Joseph Burke. Oxford: Clarendon Press, 1955.

Horst, Louis. *Pre-Classic Dance Forms*. San Francisco: Impulse Publications, 1961.

Huizinga, Johan. *The Waning of the Middle Ages*. Garden City, N.Y.: Anchor Press/Doubleday, 1954.

———. *Homo Ludens: A Study of the Play Element in Culture*. Boston: Beacon Press, 1955.

Hultén, K. G. Pontus. *The Machine as Seen at the End of the Mechanical Age*. New York: The Museum of Modern Art, 1968.

Humphrey, Doris. *The Art of Making Dances*. New York: Holt, Rinehart and Winston, 1959.

Hunt, Horton M. *The Natural History of Love*. New York: Alfred A. Knopf, 1959.

Hutchinson, Ann. *Labanotation*. New York: New Directions, 1954.

Ionesco, Eugène. *Four Plays*. Translated by Donald M. Allen. New York: Grove Press, 1960.

———. The Tragedy of Language. Translated by Jack Undank. *The Tulane Drama Review*. Vol. 4, No. 3, 1960.

———. Notes on My Theatre. Translated by Leonard C. Pronko. *The Tulane Drama Review*. Vol. 7, No. 3, 1963.

Jacobsen, Josephine, and Mueller, William R. *Ionesco and Genet: Playwrights of Silence*. New York: Hill and Wang, 1968.

Jones, Robert Edmond. *The Dramatic Imagination*. New York: Theatre Arts, 1967.

Jonson, Ben. *The Works of Ben Jonson*. London: Printed by William Stansby, 1616.

Jouffroy, Alain. *Une Révolution du regard: Conversation avec Marcel Duchamp*. Paris, 1964.

Jung, Kurt M. *Die Kultur aus der wir leben: Eine Kulturgeschichte des Abendlandes*. Safari-Verlag, 1953.

Kerouac, Jack. Meditation in the Woods. *Chicago Review*. Vol. 12, No. 2, 1958.

Kinkeldey, Otto. *A Jewish Dancing Master of the Renaissance*. New York: Reprinted from the A. S. Freidus Memorial Volume, 1929.

Kirby, Michael. The New Theatre. *The Tulane Drama Review*. Vol. 10, No. 2, 1965.

Kirstein, Lincoln. *Dance*. New York: G. P. Putnam's Sons, 1935; A Dance Horizons Re-publication, 1969.

Kisselgoff, Anna. The Changing Avant-Garde in Dance. The New York *Times*. Dec. 24, 1978.

Klee, Paul. *Tagebücher von Paul Klee, 1898–1918*. Edited and introduced by Felix Klee. Cologne: Verlag M. Dumont Schauberg, 1968.

Kleist, Heinrich von. *Sämtliche Werke*. Stuttgart: Phaidon Verlag, n.d.

Knight, Arthur. Dancing in Films. *Dance Index*. Vol. VI, No. 8, 1947.

Kokoschka, Oskar. *Schriften 1907–1955*. Edited by Maria Wingler. A. Langen–G. Müller, 1956.

‡ BIBLIOGRAPHY ‡

Kracauer, Siegfried. *Theorie des Films: Die Errettung der äusseren Wirklichkeit.* Frankfurt: Suhrkamp Verlag, 1964.

Laban, Rudolf. *Die Welt des Tänzers: Fünf Gedankenreigen.* Stuttgart: W. Seifert, 1922.

Lacroix, Paul, ed. *Ballets et mascarades de cour de Henri III à Louis XIV.* Vol. IV. Geneva: Slatkine Reprints, 1968.

Langer, Susanne. *Feeling and Form.* New York: Scribner, 1953.

Lauze, F. de. *Apologie de la Danse: A Treatise of Instruction in Dancing and Deportment, 1623.* Translated by Joan Wildeblood. London: Frederick Muller, 1952.

Lawler, Lillian B. *The Dance in Ancient Greece.* Middletown, Conn.: Wesleyan University Press, 1965.

Lea, K. M. *Italian Popular Comedy: A Study in the Commedia dell'Arte.* 2 vols. Oxford: Clarendon Press, 1933.

Lebel, Robert. *Marcel Duchamp.* Paris: Trianon Press, 1959. Translated by George Heard Hamilton. London: Trianon Press, 1959.

Ledermann, Minna. Strawinsky in the Theatre: A Symposium. *Dance Index.* Vol. VI, Nos. 10–12, 1947.

Leonardo da Vinci. *The Literary Works of Leonardo da Vinci.* Edited by Jean Paul Richter. London and New York: Oxford University Press, 1939.

Lessing, Gotthold Ephraim. *The Hamburg Dramaturgy.* Translated by E. C. Beasley and Helen Zimmern. London: Bohn, 1879.

Levey, Michael. *A History of Western Art.* New York–Washington: Frederick A. Praeger, 1968.

Levinson, André. *Meister des Balletts.* Potsdam: Müller & Co. Verlag, 1925.

Lieberman, William S. Picasso and the Ballet. *Dance Index.* Vol. V, No. 11, 1946.

Lloyd, Margaret. *The Borzoi Book of Modern Dance.* New York: Alfred A. Knopf, 1949.

Lynham, Deryck. *The Chevalier Noverre: Father of Modern Ballet.* London: Sylvan Press, 1950.

Macgowan, Kenneth, and Melnitz, William. *The Living Stage: A History of the World Theater.* Englewood Cliffs, N.J.: Prentice-Hall, 1955.

McGowan, Margaret. *L'art du ballet de cour en France, 1581–1643.* Paris: Éditions du Centre National de la Recherche Scientifique, 1963.

Machiavelli, Niccolò. *Mandragola.* Translated by Stark Young. New York: Macaulay, 1927.

Maletic, Vera. The Process Is the Purpose. Interview with Ann Halprin in *Dance Scope.* Vol. 4, No. 1, 1967–68.

Mallarmé, Stéphane. *Oeuvres complètes.* Paris: Gallimard, 1945.

Malraux, André. *The Voices of Silence.* Translated by Stuart Gilbert. New York: Doubleday, 1953; London: Secker & Warburg, 1954.

Martin, John. *The Modern Dance.* New York: A. S. Barnes, 1933; Brooklyn: Dance Horizons, 1965.

———. *Introduction to the Dance.* New York: W. W. Norton, 1939; Brooklyn; Dance Horizons, 1965.

Massine, Léonide. *My Life in Ballet.* Edited by Phyllis Hartnoll and Robert Rubens. London: Macmillan, 1968; New York: St. Martin's Press, 1969.

Matthews, Brander. *Molière: His Life and His Works.* New York: Scribner, 1897.

Mersenne, Marin. *Harmonie Universelle.* Vol. II. Facsimile edition of original, published in Paris, 1636. Paris: Éditions du Centre National de la Recherche Scientifique, 1963.

Meyerhold, Vsevolod. On the Theatre. *The Tulane Drama Review.* Vol. 4, No. 4, 1960.

Michel, Artur. The Ballet d'Action Before Noverre. *Dance Index.* Vol. VI, No. 3, 1947.

Michelangelo, Buonarroti. *Rime e Lettere.* Florence: G. Barberal, 1858.

Molière, Jean-Baptiste. *Plays.* Introduction by Waldo Frank. New York: Random House/Modern Library, n.d.

Motherwell, Robert, ed. *The Dada Painters and Poets: An Anthology.* New York: Wittenborn, Schultz, 1951.

Mozart, Wolfgang Amadeus. *Briefe und Aufzeichnungen.* Kassel: Bärenreiter Verlag, 1962.

Nettl, Paul. *The Story of Dance Music.* New York: Philosophical Library, 1947.

———. Birth of the Waltz. *Dance Index.* Vol. V, No. 9, 1946.

Nicoll, Allardyce. *The Development of the Theatre.* New York: Harcourt, Brace, 1958.

———. *World Drama: From Aeschylus to Anouilh.* London: Harrap, 1949.

Nietzsche, Friedrich Wilhelm. *Gesammelte Werke.* Munich: Musarion Verlag, 1929.

———. *Thus Spake Zarathustra.* Edited by Manuel Komroff. New York: Tudor, 1934.

Noverre, Jean Georges. *Letters on Dancing and Ballet.* Translated by Cyril Beaumont. London: Beaumont, 1951; Brooklyn: Dance Horizons, 1970.

Paz, Octavio. *Marcel Duchamp: or the Castle of Purity.* Translated by Donald Gardner. London: Golliard Press; New York: Grossman Publishers, 1970.

‡ BIBLIOGRAPHY ‡

Penrose, Roland. *Picasso: His Life and Work*. London: Victor Gollancz, 1958.

Pepys, Samuel. *Diary and Correspondence of Samuel Pepys*. New York: Dodd, 1884.

Petrarca, Francesco. *Rime, Trionfi e poesie latina*. Milan: R. Ricciardi, 1951.

Plato. *Symposium*. Translated by Benjamin Jewett. In *Great Books of the Western World*. Vol. VII. Chicago and London: Encyclopaedia Britannica, 1952.

Plumb, J. H. The Anarchy of Art. *Horizon*. Vol. IX, No. 3, 1967.

Pops, Martin Leonard, ed. Dance. A collection of essays. *Salmagundi: a Quarterly of the Humanities and Sciences*. Saratoga Springs, N.Y.: Skidmore College, 1976.

Priddin, Deirdre. *The Art of the Dance in French Literature*. London: Adam and Charles Black, 1952.

Pronko, Leonard Cabell. *Avant-Garde: The Experimental Theater in France*. Berkeley and Los Angeles: University of California Press, 1964.

Pushkin, Alexander. *The Poems, Prose and Plays*. Translated by Babette Deutsch. New York: Random House/Modern Library, 1936.

Quennell, Peter. *Hogarth's Progress*. New York: Viking Press; London: Collins, 1955.

Read, Herbert. *Art and Alienation*. New York: Horizon Press, 1967.

Reik, Theodor. *Arthur Schnitzler als Psycholog*. Minden: J. C. C. Bruns, 1913.

Rilke, Rainer Maria. *Gesammelte Werke*. Leipzig: Insel Verlag, 1930.

Robb, Nesca A. *Neoplatonism of the Italian Renaissance*. London: Allen & Unwin, 1935.

Rosenberg, Harold. *The Anxious Object: Art Today and Its Audience*. New York: Horizon Press, 1964.

Rousseau, Jean-Jacques. *Politics and the Arts: Letter to M. d'Alembert on the Theatre*. Translated by Allan Bloom. Glencoe, Ill.: The Free Press of Glencoe, 1960.

———. *The Social Contract.* Translated by Willmoore Kendall. New York: Henry Regnery Company, 1954.

Rubin, William S. *Dadaism, Surrealism, and Their Heritage*. New York: The Museum of Modern Art, 1967.

Sachs, Curt. *World History of the Dance*. Translated by Bessie Schönberg. New York: W. W. Norton, 1937.

———. *The Commonwealth of Art*. New York: W. W. Norton, 1946.

St. Denis, Ruth. *An Unfinished Life*. New York: Harper, 1939.

Saintsbury, George. *A Short History of French Literature.* Oxford: Clarendon Press, 1964.

Schmalenbach, Werner. *Kurt Schwitters.* Cologne: Verlag M. Dumont Schauberg, 1968.

Schnitzler, Arthur. *Die Gesammelten Werke.* Frankfurt: S. Fischer Verlag, 1962.

Shattuck, Roger. *The Banquet Years.* New York: Harcourt, Brace, 1958; London: Faber and Faber, 1959.

Shawn, Ted. *Every Little Movement.* Lee, Mass.: Shawn, 1954.

Sontag, Susan. *Against Interpretation and Other Essays.* New York: Farrar, Straus, 1966.

————. *On Photography.* New York: Farrar, Straus, Giroux, 1977.

Sorell, Walter. *The Dancer's Image: Points and Counterpoints.* New York and London: Columbia University Press, 1971.

————. *Facets of Comedy.* New York: Grosset & Dunlap/The University Library, 1972.

————. *The Dance Through the Ages.* New York: Grosset & Dunlap; London: Thames and Hudson, 1967; Munich: Droemer-Knaur; Zürich: Ex Libris, 1969.

————. Guglielmo Ebreo, A Jewish Dancing Master. *The Menorah Journal.* Vol. XLII, Nos. 1 & 2, Summer 1954.

Spengler, Oswald. *The Decline of the West.* Translated by Charles Francis Atkinson. New York: Alfred A. Knopf, 1926.

Steiner, George. *The Death of Tragedy.* New York: Alfred A. Knopf, 1961.

Stendhal. *Oeuvres complètes de Stendhal.* Paris: Champion, 1923.

Stites, Raymond S. *The Arts and Man.* New York: McGraw-Hill, 1940.

Strindberg, August. *Skrifter.* Stockholm: Bonnier, 1945.

Suzuki, D. T. *Zen Buddhism: Selected Writings.* Edited by William Barrett. Garden City, N.Y.: Anchor Press/Doubleday, 1956.

Symonds, John Addington. *Renaissance in Italy.* 2 vols. New York: Random House/Modern Library, 1935.

Tabourot, Jehan. *Orchesography.* Translated by Cyril W. Beaumont. London: Beaumont, 1925; Brooklyn: Dance Horizons, 1965.

Taper, Bernard. *Balanchine: A Biography.* New York: Harper & Row, 1963; London: Collins, 1964.

Tawney, R. H. *Religion and the Rise of Capitalism.* New York: Harcourt, Brace, 1926.

Taylor, H. O. *Thought and Expression in the Sixteenth Century.* 2 vols. New York: Macmillan, 1920.

Terry, Walter. *The Dance in America.* New York: Harper & Row, 1956.

‡ BIBLIOGRAPHY ‡

Treasure, G. R. R. *Seventeenth Century France*. New York: Barnes and Noble, 1966.

Trevelyan, G. M. *History of England*. Garden City, N.Y.: Doubleday, 1952.

Tuchman, Barbara W. *A Distant Mirror: The Calamitous 14th Century*. New York: Alfred A. Knopf, 1978.

Valéry, Paul. *Oeuvres*. Selected and edited by Jean Hytier. Paris: Gallimard, 1957–60.

———. Dance and the Soul. Translated by Dorothy Bussy. In *Selected Writings*. New York: New Directions, 1950.

Vasari, Giorgio. *Lives of the Most Eminent Painters, Sculptors and Architects*. Edited by William Gaunt. New York: E. P. Dutton, 1963.

Wagner, Richard. *Nachgelassene Schriften und Dichtungen*. Leipzig: Breitkopf and Härtel, 1895.

Wells, H. G. *The Outline of History*. Garden City, N.Y.: Doubleday, 1925.

Wigman, Mary. *The Language of Dance*. Translated by Walter Sorell. Middletown, Conn.: Wesleyan University Press, 1966.

Wilde, Oscar. *The Writings of Oscar Wilde*. London: Keller, 1907.

Winckelmann, Johann Joachim. *History of Ancient Art*. New York: Frederick Ungar, 1968.

Wittkower, Rudolf. *Gian Lorenzo Bernini: The Sculptor of the Roman Baroque*. New York: Phaidon Publishers, 1955.

Yates, Frances A. *The French Academies of the Seventeenth Century*. London: The Warburg Institute, University of London, 1947.

Young, Stark. *The Theatre*. New York: Hill and Wang, 1954.

Zorn, John W. *The Essential Delsarte*. Metuchen, N.J.: The Scarecrow Press, 1968.

INDEX

Appia, Adolphe, 307, 326, 351, 360
Après-midi d'un Faune, L', 363–64, 365, 396
Arabic literature, 177–78
Arbeau, Thoinot (Jehan Tabourot), 86, 87, 130
Architecture, 67ff., 112ff., 177, 378–81. *See also* specific architects, places, styles
Aretino, Pietro, 53, 56
Arianna, L', 93
Arias, 95
Ariodante, 100n
Ariosto, Lodovico, 58
Aristophanes, 115
Aristotle (Aristoteleanism), 6, 30, 110, 115, 187, 226
Aristoxenus, 90
Armory Show (New York), 371, 373, 386
Arp, Jean, 374, 375, 377n, 412n
Arrow Against Profane and Promiscuous Dancing Drawn Out of the Quiver of the Scriptures, An, 122
Ars amatoria, 244
Ars Nova, 25
Artaud, Antonin, 423, 424
Art Nouveau, 298, 307, 312, 316, 348ff.
"Art of This Century" gallery, 413, 415
Art poétique, L', 144–45
Art pour l'art, l', movement, 256, 266, 271, 275, 283, 285, 299, 316
Art romantique L', 266
Ascension, The, 116
Ashcan School, 371
Ashton, Frederick, 381
Asia. *See* Orient
Association of American Painters and Sculptors, 371
Astaire, Fred, 401, 402
Astruc, Gabriel, 354
As You Like It, 77
Atellan farces, 58, 59
Athens, 321
Attitude (dance pose), 236
Auber, Daniel, 244
Auden, W. H., 382, 416
Audiences, 124–28
Augustine, St., 18
Ausdruckstanz, 338, 370. *See also* Expressionism
Austria(ns), 104, 119, 183, 204, 205–6, 230, 255, 262, 263, 334. *See also* Vienna
Automobiles, 297
Avril, Jane, 303, 324

Baal Shem-Tov, 123
Babylonians, 177
Baccelli, Giovanna, 172
Bacchanale, 249
Bach, Johann Sebastian, 96, 112n, 166, 262, 392
Backman, E. Louis, 19
Bacon, Francis, 52, 107–8, 109, 190, 211
Bacon, Roger, 6
Baïf, Jean Antoine de, 81, 131–32, 325
Baker, Josephine, 420
Bakst, Léon, 115, 353, 363
Bal, Le, 358
Balanchine, George, 21, 83, 189, 205, 226, 283n, 354n, 356, 393–95, 401, 402, 426, 433
Bald Soprano, The, 361n, 410
Bales, William, 407
Balinese, 423
Ball, Hugo, 64, 374, 375, 377n
Ballad operas, 167–69
Ballarino, Il, 132
Ballerinas, 173–76, 232, 240ff., 278, 287, 354n. *See also* Romantic Age; specific women
Ballet: derivation of term, 43. *See also* Ballerinas; Male dancers; specific choreographers, dancers, periods, places, types of ballet
Ballet à entrée, 82–83, 84, 86, 94–95, 130, 146
Ballet Comique (Balet Comique de la Royne), 74–81, 84, 88, 97, 124, 125, 132, 288
Ballet d'action, 101, 170, 176, 187, 192ff., 263, 264
Ballet de cour (court dance), 6, 36ff., 74–82, 94–95, 124, 125, 130, 148, 164, 171. *See also* specific productions
Ballet de la Nuit, viii
Ballet des Polonais, 75
Ballet Folklorico de México, 397
Ballet-mascarade, 82
Ballet-mélodramatique, 82, 84, 87, 130
Ballet of the Nuns, 220, 221, 240, 270
Ballet of the 20th Century, 429–30
Balletomanes, 211–16, 225, 233, 235, 245, 246, 282, 287
Ballet Rambert, 381
Ballets Russes (Russian Ballet), viii, 115, 327, 329, 351, 361–70, 388, 394
Ballo delle Ingrate, Il, 94
Ballo del Fiore, 132
Ballo lombardo, 39
Ballroom (social) dancing, 281, 339